Prayers for Comfort

David Adam
Rupert Bristow
Nick Fawcett
Susan Sayers
Ray Simpson

Prayers compiled from:

1,000 Prayers for Public Worship — David Adam
Prayers for Inclusion and Diversity — Rupert Bristow
2,000 Prayers for Public Worship — Nick Fawcett
Selected Prayers for Public Worship — Nick Fawcett
More Short Prayers for Public Worship — Nick Fawcett
Prayers for All Seasons — Nick Fawcett
Prayers for All Seasons 2 — Nick Fawcett
1,500 Prayers for Public Worship — Susan Sayers
His Complete Celtic Prayers — Ray Simpson

PRAYERS FOR COMFORT

Copyright © 2013 David Adam, Rupert Bristow, Nick Fawcett, Susan Sayers, and Ray Simpson
Original edition published in English under the title PRAYERS FOR COMFORT by Kevin Mayhew Ltd, Buxhall, England.
This edition copyright © Fortress Press 2019

All rights reserved. Except for brief quotations in critical articles or reviews, no part of this book may be reproduced in any manner without prior written permission from the publisher. Email copyright@augsburgfortress.org or write to Permissions, Fortress Press, PO Box 1209, Minneapolis, MN 55440-1209.

Cover image: Cover photo by wingmar from iStock
Cover design: Tory Herman

Print ISBN: 978-1-5064-5943-1

About the Authors

DAVID ADAM was the Vicar of Lindisfarne, off the Northumbrian coast, for thirteen years until he retired in March 2003. His work involved ministering to thousands of pilgrims and other visitors. He is the author of many inspiring books on spirituality and prayer, and his Celtic writings have rekindled an enthusiastic interest in our Christian heritage.

RUPERT BRISTOW was Director of Education for Canterbury Diocese and a governor of Canterbury Christ Church University from 1995 until his retirement in 2008 and is active as a Reader in Trinity Benefice, Folkestone. He has worked in education—in schools, universities, and administration—at home and overseas. He has also been a specialist adviser to a House of Commons select committee, edited and written for various educational publications, and chaired Kent SACRE (Standing Advisory Council for Religious Education). He is an Honorary Fellow of Canterbury Christ Church University.

NICK FAWCETT was brought up in Southend-on-Sea, Essex, and trained for the Baptist ministry at Bristol and Oxford, before serving churches in Lancashire and Cheltenham. He subsequently spent three years as a chaplain with the Christian movement Toc H, before focusing on writing and editing, which he continues with today, despite wrestling with cancer. He lives with his wife, Deborah, and two children—Samuel and Kate—in Wellington, Somerset, worshipping at the local Anglican church. An enthusiastic walker, he delights in the beauty of the Somerset and Devon countryside around his home, his numerous books owing much to the inspiration he unfailingly finds there.

SUSAN SAYERS is the author of many popular resource books for the church. Through the conferences and workshops she is invited to lead, she has been privileged to share in the worship of many different traditions and cultures. A teacher by profession, she was ordained a priest in the Anglican Church and, before her retirement, her work was divided between the parish of Westcliff-on-Sea, the local women's prison, writing, training days, and retreats.

RAY SIMPSON is a Celtic new monastic for tomorrow's world, a lecturer, consultant, liturgist, and author of some 30 books. He is the founding guardian of the international Community of Aidan and Hilda and the pioneer of its e-studies programs. He is an ordained member of the Christian church and lives on the Holy Island of Lindisfarne. His website is www.raysimpson.org.

1   We remember today all who walk in darkness
    and in the shadow of fear or death.
    We ask your blessing upon the fearful,
    the anxious, and the troubled.
    We pray for all who are in the darkness
    of doubt or despair.
    We bring before you
    friends and loved ones who are ill
    or who are finding it hard to cope with life.

    David Adam

2   We rejoice in your abiding presence
    and pray for all who feel lonely or anxious at this time.
    We remember all who are fearful of the future
    and those who are terminally ill.
    We pray for those who await a doctor's diagnosis
    or who are preparing to go into the hospital.
    We ask your blessing upon all who suffer
    and upon those who care for them.   *David Adam*

3   We give thanks for the new hope and courage
    that is ours through Christ's resurrection.
    We pray for all who are discouraged
    or without hope.
    We remember those who are seriously ill
    and any who are facing death.
    We pray for those who are tending to the ill
    and any who are anxious about loved ones.   *David Adam*

4   Lord, may your Church be an accepting and loving Church.
    May it help to free those who are paralyzed
    by fear and doubt.
    May it reach out to those who do not know of your love
    and bring them to you.   *David Adam*

5   We pray for all who are fearful for their future,
those who are awaiting a doctor's diagnosis
or an operation,
for all who are terminally ill.
Lord, bless all who work in caring for others
and relieving their anxiety.　　　　　　*David Adam*

6   Lord of life, we remember all who are dispirited,
the distressed, the depressed, and the despairing,
all who have lost hope or joy in their lives.
We pray for all who fear the future,
all who have lost sight of you and your love.
We remember also all who are struggling
with poverty or hunger,
the homeless and the refugee.　　　　　　*David Adam*

7   As you appeared to the disciples in the house,
come enter our homes;
come enter into our fear and darkness;
come enter into our enclosed lives and our fear to venture.
Come with the glorious freedom you offer
to the children of God.　　　　　　*David Adam*

8   God of love and peace, we remember before you
all who are weighed down with anxiety or fear.
We pray for those who are depressed
and those who feel they can no longer cope with life.
We ask your blessing upon all who are ill
and all who suffer in any way.
May they come to know your love and your peace.
　　　　　　　　　　　　　　　　　　David Adam

9   Lord God,
when the days are dark and we are weary,
when the stress and the storms increase
and we are in danger of being overwhelmed,
hear us and help us.
May we know you are always with us
and ready to help us.　　　　　　*David Adam*

10 Lord, we remember all disturbed and distressed people,
all who have suffered from traumatic events
or who are troubled in spirit.
We pray for all who are exhausted or depressed
at this time,
for all who can find no rest. *David Adam*

11 Lord, we ask your blessing
upon all who are discouraged or despondent
at this time,
upon all who feel that life is not worthwhile.
May they know of your love and your presence.
David Adam

12 God, we remember all who feel lost
and whose life seems to have no purpose.
We remember all who feel they have failed in life
and all who despair at this time.
May they know your love and your saving power.
David Adam

13 Lord, to turn away from you
is to enter into the darkness
and to fall.
To turn to you
is to rise and come to the light.
To abide with you
is to live in love and peace.
Lord, as we come to you,
give purpose to our days. *David Adam*

14 We pray today for all who are anxious and overworked,
all who are world-weary or deeply troubled.
We remember especially
any who feel the lack of love or attention;
those who feel neglected or unwanted.
We ask your blessing upon all who are ill
and those who have been taken into care. *David Adam*

15 We seek your blessing
    upon all who are oppressed or depressed,
    upon all whose lives are filled with sorrow or pain.
    We remember those who are battling
    with a long-term illness
    and those who feel they are losing mobility or agility.
    We remember in your presence
    all who are struggling at this time. *David Adam*

16 Father, we pray for all who have lost their way in life.
    We remember those who have lost faith
    in themselves, in others, or in their God.
    We pray for all who are finding life desperate
    and are disillusioned or fearful.
    We ask you to comfort and bless
    all who are struggling
    with illness or problems that they cannot solve
    and those who feel unable to find help or hope.
    David Adam

17 We give thanks for our peace of mind
    and we pray for all who are disturbed or distressed.
    We remember those who have had a traumatic experience
    and those who have suffered from betrayal or violence.
    We pray for all who are not at peace
    with themselves or with others. *David Adam*

18 We pray for all who are struggling with life,
    those who are burdened with guilt or anger,
    all who have memories that disturb them. *David Adam*

19 Lord, we bring before you all whose lives are fragmented;
    people who are broken in body, mind, or spirit.
    We remember all who feel shattered and exhausted,
    all who long for your healing touch.
    We pray for all who seek hope and peace,
    that they may come to you and rest in your presence.
    David Adam

20   You are our hope and strength, O Lord.
     We come to you for refreshment and renewal.
     When we are weak, may we trust in your strength.
     When we are fearful, may we turn to you and your light.
     We pray for all who are struggling at this time.
     We remember before you the troubled in mind
     and the distressed in spirit.   *David Adam*

21   We give thanks for places of relaxation and refreshment.
     We pray for all who help us
     to enjoy life and to live in peace.
     We remember in your presence all who are overworked
     or heavily burdened.
     We remember all who are deeply in debt
     or who feel that they cannot cope with life.
     We ask your blessing upon all who are finding life hard
     or who are lonely.   *David Adam*

22   Lord Jesus, your hands are full of power.
     You heal and you bring comfort to people.
     When we are troubled,
     let us learn to put our hands in yours
     and to trust in you.   *David Adam*

23   We give thanks for the renewing powers of our bodies
     and for all who share in the healing and care of others.
     We pray for all who feel their lives are empty
     or meaningless,
     all who feel they have wasted their lives
     or never fully lived.   *David Adam*

24   We bring before you the troubles and the sadness
     of our world.
     We pray for all who have lost their vision,
     who are blind to goodness
     and unaware of your presence or your love.
     We remember especially
     all who feel that life is without purpose and meaningless.
                                                  David Adam

25 Lord, we remember all who are struggling
    with doubt, depression, and despair,
    all who are having difficulty in their daily lives.
    We pray for all who are ill at home or in the hospital,
    especially those who have no one
    to care for them or visit them.   *David Adam*

26 Lord God, in your love you have called us to seek you.
    When we turn to you
    we find you are waiting for us and come to us.
    You meet our hunger and emptiness
    with the richness of your presence.
    This day, dear Lord, renew and refresh us
    for all that we are called to do.   *David Adam*

27 We ask you to bless
    all who are not at peace with themselves,
    all who are disturbed in mind or spirit.
    We ask that all who are ill at this time
    may know your love and your presence.   *David Adam*

28 Lord God, you are light:
    in you is no darkness at all.
    We think of all who are struggling with life:
    homes where there is tension or lack of peace;
    people who are ill and afraid of the future;
    all who are lonely and facing a time of crisis.
    May all know your presence and your peace. *David Adam*

29 Lord of light and love,
    bless all whose lives are darkened
    by illness or tragedy.
    We remember all who feel afraid
    and those who regret work undone
    or doing what they should not have done.
    We pray for all who are terminally ill
    and all who can no longer look after themselves.

                                                David Adam

30 We remember all who walk in darkness
    and who are heavily burdened.
    We pray for all who have lost hope and who despair.
    We ask your blessing
    upon all who are chronically ill
    and those who can no longer cope on their own.
    We pray for all who are approaching death and
    their loved ones who are caring for them. *David Adam*

31 Lord, we pray for your blessing
    upon the world-weary, the worried and worn,
    all who feel overwhelmed and unable to cope.
    We remember all who are ill at home or in the hospital
    and those who care for them.
    We pray especially for any involved in accidents
    or whose illness finds no cure. *David Adam*

32 Lord, stand by us when the last great storm
    seeks to overwhelm us
    and we feel we are sinking beneath the waves.
    Help us to know that in you we will not perish
    but have everlasting life. *David Adam*

33 We remember all who feel weary with life,
    drained of energy, and no longer able to cope.
    We pray for all who struggle against great odds.
    We ask your blessing upon all who feel alone
    and that no one cares for them. *David Adam*

34 Lord, we remember before you
    the troubled in mind,
    all who have painful memories,
    the depressed and the despairing,
    the mentally disturbed.
    Lord, keep our minds strong
    in the knowledge and love of God,
    and help us to proclaim your presence and love.

    David Adam

35 We remember before you
    all who feel confused or troubled at this time.
    We pray for all who are distressed
    and those who are not able to cope
    with what is happening around them.
    May they know your presence and your power.
    We ask your blessing upon all who are ill
    at home or in the hospital,
    especially those who are fearful or lonely. *David Adam*

36 May we not lose sight of things eternal
    among all that happens in our lives.
    We ask your blessing upon all who find life dull,
    all who are depressed or have lost hope.
    We pray for all who struggle with illness
    or difficult circumstances. *David Adam*

37 Lord God, we ask your blessing
    upon all who feel confused about life
    and all who have lost their way.
    We pray especially for all who are caught up
    in the darkness of despair
    and those involved in drugs or vice.
    We pray for those who live a lie
    and cannot face the truth.
    Lord, bless all who are suffering
    from broken relationships
    and who are troubled in heart. *David Adam*

38 Come, Lord, to all whose hope is gone,
    the lost, the despairing, and the deeply depressed.
    We remember the overworked, the world-weary,
    the exhausted, and the worn out.
    We ask your blessing
    upon those who feel wrung out and dry,
    all who feel numb,
    and those whose senses are deadened.
    We pray for all suffering from deep stress or trauma
    and their loved ones caring for them. *David Adam*

39   As we rejoice in your power,
     we remember all whose powers are waning,
     the elderly and the infirm, and all who are disabled.
     We ask your blessing upon all who are ill
     or who have been injured in accidents.
     May they find courage and hope in you
     and in your abiding love.   *David Adam*

40   We ask your blessing
     upon all who are finding life difficult
     through illness or oppression.
     We pray for all who feel their abilities
     are being wasted or thwarted
     through illness or circumstance.
     May we know
     that in whatever circumstance we find ourselves
     God still loves us and calls us to love him.   *David Adam*

41   We remember in your presence
     all whose hands are idle.
     We pray for those who are unemployed
     and redundant,
     those who are disabled,
     and all with waning or failing powers.
     We remember all who are tempted to misuse
     the power that God has given them.
     Lord, we are always in your presence:
     may we live to your praise and glory.
     We are in the hands of God.
     Hallelujah   *David Adam*

42   We pray for all who are terminally ill,
     for all who are in a hospice or in care.
     We pray also for their loved ones in this time of anxiety.
     We remember those who have been bereaved,
     especially all who are left on their own
     and feel lonely or unable to cope.
     Lord, bless all whose powers are failing
     with your love and strength.   *David Adam*

43 Mighty God, when the last great storm overwhelms us
    help us to know you are there
    as the Lord and Giver of life;
    to know we are not alone
    and you will not let us perish.   *David Adam*

44 We remember all who are in the valley
    of the shadow of death,
    all who have passed beyond it
    to light and life eternal.
    We pray for our loved ones departed from us.
    May we all come to rejoice
    in the fullness of your kingdom.   *David Adam*

45 Blessed are you, Lord our God,
    for you created the world out of chaos
    and when chaos seeks to overwhelm us
    you offer us your presence and your peace.
    You are ever with us in the storms of life
    and we know you as our Savior.
    Blessed are you, Father, Son, and Holy Spirit.   *David Adam*

46 Father, all-powerful,
    we remember the needs of the weary,
    the powerless, the ill.
    We ask your blessing on all who feel
    that they cannot cope with life
    or who are drained of their resources.
    We pray especially for those who are terminally ill.
                                                       David Adam

47 Blessed are you, Lord God our Father.
    You have revealed your hidden glory
    in the face of our Lord Jesus Christ;
    in Christ you have given us the hope of life eternal.
                                                       David Adam

48 God of light and hope, we pray
for all who are in darkness and despair;
for those who doubt your presence and your love;
for all in the wilderness, and who find it difficult to pray;
for those who have lost trust in themselves or faith in you.
God, you are with each and every one,
and continue to be their protector and strength.
We pray for the day when they will rejoice in your presence
and in your abiding love. *David Adam*

49 Lord,
as we enter into the stillness, calm our hearts and
our minds.
Let all the storms within us cease, and enfold us in your peace.
We come in weakness to you for strength;
we come in our sinfulness for your forgiveness;
we come wearied by life for your refreshing grace;
we come out of our darkness to your love and light.
Lord, renew, refresh,
restore us by your presence and your power. *David Adam*

50 Lord God,
you uphold the faith that sustains us,
even in the darkest moments.
May others feel that same love,
even if it has been revealed to them in different ways.
Give to all those of faith a special place in your heart,
shown in the compassion of your Son,
as he demonstrated your way. *Rupert Bristow*

51 Father God,
in the midst of joy or sadness,
may we call on the strength of your presence,
to share that happiness or despair.
And may those of different faiths,
and those in search of truth,

     see in our response
     a glimpse of what can be
     and a shared moment of unity,
     with us and with you,
     universal God. *Rupert Bristow*

52   God of peace and calm,
     watch over us in times of struggle,
     when everything seems against us,
     when we feel we are letting ourselves down
     and not doing justice to you.
     Take our cares on your broad shoulders
     and bring us the focus
     to do your will
     and cast our worries aside. *Rupert Bristow*

53   O God who cares,
     take our worries and shake them,
     so that we see ourselves as we really are.
     Take our lives and shake them,
     so that we see who you truly are.
     May we remain on the one true path
     and not be distracted by worries or temptations,
     or by the fear of doing wrong,
     when we are seeking to do the right thing.
     May our risks be your risks, Lord,
     so that together we can get things right. *Rupert Bristow*

54   Teaching Lord,
     enable us to pray without guilt;
     teach us to share without resentment.
     Enable us to challenge without fear;
     teach us to love without lusting.
     Enable us to give without receiving;
     teach us to live without worrying.
     Enable us to thank without condition;
     teach us to follow you without questioning,
     enabling Lord. *Rupert Bristow*

55   Heavenly Father,
we pray for the grace you have freely shown
to remove our fears and worries
about the things we cannot change,
about the concerns that you have lifted from us,
about the issues that do not really matter.
But where we face real difficulty,
big decisions, and tough times,
help us to discern the right path,
knowing you are with us all the way.   *Rupert Bristow*

56   Gracious Lord,
create in us, we pray,
a way to deal with worry
that helps us to face the big issues
without being dragged down by selfish concerns.
Give us the faith in hope to see us through
and the hope of faith to bring us home.   *Rupert Bristow*

57   God of strength and weakness,
you showed your vulnerability
through your Son's mission to earth,
his acceptance of suffering,
his openness to the needs of others.
May his example to the rich and able,
and his reaching out to the meek and the lame,
give heart to all,
challenging the strong and uplifting the weak.
    Rupert Bristow

58   God of triumph and tragedy,
may we all see a glass half full,
in counting our blessings
and knowing our gifts.
May we seek to make the most of those gifts
and take our social needs in our stride.
May our impairments make us stronger
and our disabilities spur us to overcome them,
by perseverance, by determination,
and by your grace.   *Rupert Bristow*

59   Enabling Lord,
        send us out in the power of your Spirit
        to live, to work, to play, and to love
        without self-consciousness or fear.
        Let our frailties draw on your strength
        and our strength inspire others.
        Let us be a community of enablers,
        gracious Lord.   *Rupert Bristow*

60   God of hope,
        bring to us all your Son's inclusive words,
        in inviting all to join him
        in a kingdom free of prejudice.
        Bring to us his inclusive heart,
        in bringing your word to Jew and Gentile,
        rich and poor, able-bodied and disabled.
        May we all learn from those in need
        and give in return our time as much as our resources.
        Rupert Bristow

61   Lord of all time,
        lift up hearts and spirits
        when misfortune strikes.
        Bring wholeness in place of emptiness
        when despair takes over.
        Bring healing to ailments
        when faith is evident.
        May disabilities be transformed
        into strength of spirit,
        which overcomes all and inspires many.   *Rupert Bristow*

62   Loving Lord,
        you know the pain of death,
        through the comfort of your Son
        and his tears at the death of others.
        Bring us your insight and compassion
        when we see the effects of death
        in ourselves and in others.
        Strengthen us to give comfort,
        knowing that you are there to hold our hands
        and strengthen our hearts.   *Rupert Bristow*

63 God of consolation,
be with us in our darkest moments,
when all seems lost and we feel alone.
Banish despair from our hearts
and bring hope in its place,
as we rest in your arms.
May we recognize our vulnerability
as we reach out to you,
and you hold us tight. *Rupert Bristow*

64 Lord of love,
show your love to the troubled and fragile.
Strengthen them in their tribulations,
mighty Counsellor, true friend.
Let the healing begin
as the causes reveal themselves.
Let the transformation last
through the constancy of prayer.
Surprise us, Lord, by the hope of help
and the promise of what's to come. *Rupert Bristow*

65 God of tough love,
create in us, we pray,
a living well of prayerful power,
begun, continued, and ended in you.
May every day bring new possibilities
to replace lost options.
May positive relationships
banish the memories of broken ones.
Let love return on the flood tide
to renew and refresh. *Rupert Bristow*

66 Heavenly Father,
who sees all things, knows all things,
calm the rough seas of our hearts
and quell the turmoil in our minds.
Let calm reign;
let peace rule;
and may we know the certainty
of your sure hope. *Rupert Bristow*

67   Father of all,
let the great hopes of youth
be followed by the sure foundations of faith.
And when troubles come,
and everything seems shaky,
let us recall those hopes, those sure foundations,
confident that, whatever life throws at us,
despair is no match for the love you show,
and the love we receive,
through Jesus Christ. *Rupert Bristow*

68   Source of light and hope,
give us the strength to cope, in mind and spirit,
with all that life throws at us.
In between the joy and the success,
help us to handle suffering and failure.
May we recognize that we learn more about ourselves
when things go wrong.
Let us respond well and without hesitation
to the suffering of others as well as our own. *Rupert Bristow*

69   God of compassion,
create in us, we pray, the capacity to cope,
in illness, in pain, in heartbreak.
Set our spirits free to lift us up
when our body seems to let us down.
Let faith flower in adversity. *Rupert Bristow*

70   Lord Jesus Christ,
you have promised that those who hunger and thirst
after righteousness will be filled,
but we pray today for those who simply hunger for food
and thirst for water.
In our fractured world of rich and poor,
haves and have-nots,
create a yearning for change and a passion for justice,
and may that begin in us,
our willingness to share and identify with others
marking us out as your people,
to the glory of your name. *Nick Fawcett*

71 Living God,
    respond to the cry of the poor
    and the entreaties of the needy,
    and grant that the time will come
    when people everywhere
    receive a fair reward for their labors,
    sufficient for all their needs;
    a time when this world's resources will be distributed justly,
    all having enough and none too much. *Nick Fawcett*

72 Lord of all,
    hear the cry of the oppressed and exploited,
    the hungry and homeless,
    the sick and suffering,
    and help us to hear it too
    and to respond in your name. *Nick Fawcett*

73 God of grace,
    in the darkness of hatred, evil, sorrow, and suffering,
    may your light shine,
    this and every day. *Nick Fawcett*

74 Lord Jesus Christ,
    as you touched those with leprosy,
    restored sight to the blind,
    brought peace to the disturbed,
    and enabled the lame to walk,
    come now to all who are sick in body, mind, and spirit,
    bringing again your healing touch and renewing grace.
    Nick Fawcett

75 Living God,
    when limitations or disabilities make life hard,
    teach us that you love and value us,
    not for what we do,
    but for who we are,
    and may that knowledge teach us to appreciate
    and respect the worth of everyone we meet. *Nick Fawcett*

76 Eternal God,
  we pray for those faced by the prospect of death,
  whether wrestling with terminal illness
  or coming to terms with failing health and advancing years.
  In all the fear and sorrow they may feel,
  give the assurance that not even death itself
  can separate them from your love
  and that you hold in store for them
  things more wonderful than they have yet begun to imagine,
  through Jesus Christ our Lord. *Nick Fawcett*

77 Lord Jesus Christ,
  as you reached out to the sick and suffering
  throughout your earthly ministry,
  bringing wholeness and healing to so many,
  reach out now through all who minister to body,
  mind, and spirit,
  and through them grant your renewing, restoring touch.
   Nick Fawcett

78 Lord Jesus Christ,
  friend of the friendless,
  hope of the hopeless, and joy of the joyless,
  reach out into the hurt and pain of our world,
  the injustice, hunger, and hatred,
  and may the seeds of your kingdom take root and grow.
  In all this world's sorrow and suffering,
  bring a harvest of justice and peace,
  love and celebration,
  for your name's sake. *Nick Fawcett*

79 Sovereign God,
  strength of the weak,
  hope of the despairing,
  comfort of the sorrowful,
  restorer of the broken,
  send us out renewed by your grace
  and help us to do all in our power
  to bring your transforming touch to others,
  through the healing power of our Lord Jesus Christ.
   Nick Fawcett

80 Lord Jesus Christ,
may all those who feel isolated and unloved
find in you a friend they can depend on and,
through realizing how much you value them,
may they discover a sense of worth
that leads to and informs their relationships with others.

Nick Fawcett

81 Light of the world,
shine wherever there is darkness today.
Where there is pain and sorrow,
may the brilliance of your love bring joy.
Where there is sickness and suffering,
may your healing touch bring sunshine after the storm.
Where there is greed and corruption,
may your radiance scatter the shadows.
Where there is hatred and bitterness,
may your brightness dispel the clouds.
Lord Jesus Christ,
light of the world,
shine again upon us we pray,
and illuminate the darkness of this world
through your life-giving grace.
In your name, we ask it.

Nick Fawcett

82 Sovereign God,
you turned the darkest of nights into the brightest of days
through the resurrection of your Son,
our Savior, Jesus Christ.
Come now into the darkness of our world:
into the nighttime of suffering and sickness,
doubt and despair;
into the shadows of hurt and heartbreak,
injustice and evil;
into the bleakness of violence and hatred,
fear and death.
May your new day dawn
and the light of Christ blaze to your glory
as we share his resurrection life,
and rejoice in the victory he has won.
In his name we pray.

Nick Fawcett

83   Sovereign God,
if sorrow,
suffering,
turmoil, or trauma
should cause us to lose hold of you,
tighten your hold on us,
and, in your strength,
see us safely through. *Nick Fawcett*

84   Lord of all,
when life seems dark,
help us to put our trust in you.
Inspire us with the knowledge that,
where all seems hopeless,
you are sometimes most powerfully at work—
challenging, deepening, and strengthening faith,
equipping us for new avenues of service
and opening the way to a richer experience of your love.
In that assurance, lead us forward,
through Jesus Christ our Lord. *Nick Fawcett*

85   Gracious God,
when tears are our food day and night,
and when our heart is breaking within us,
assure us of your love, reach
out with your comfort,
and help us to know that joy will come again. *Nick Fawcett*

86   Living God,
no matter how helpless or hopeless we may feel,
teach us that with you by our side,
all things are always less dreadful than they seem.
Nick Fawcett

87   Loving God,
when life is hard and days are dark,
enfold us in your arms and surround us with your loving care,
holding us close for all eternity. *Nick Fawcett*

88 Living God,
   in the unpredictability of this life,
   faced with the apparent fickleness of fate,
   teach us to trust completely in the sure
   and certain hope you have given in Christ,
   for his name's sake.   *Nick Fawcett*

89 Living God,
   when life fails to measure up to our expectations,
   remind us of the hope we have in Christ,
   through which we can expect fulfilment beyond measure,
   by his grace.   *Nick Fawcett*

90 Living God,
   like everyone else there is much we fear,
   your love not granting us immunity
   from the trials and tribulations of this troubled world.
   Give us strength to meet whatever we may face,
   confident that nothing can finally come between us
   and your love in Jesus Christ our Lord.   *Nick Fawcett*

91 Eternal God,
   teach us that though we may let go of you, you
   will always hold fast to us;
   that though we feel you are distant,
   you are always near.
   In that assurance,
   may we live each day,
   through Jesus Christ our Lord.   *Nick Fawcett*

92 Mighty God,
   teach us that, whatever we fear,
   your love is able to see us through it,
   for it is stronger than evil,
   stronger than death itself,
   enduring for all eternity.
   To you be the praise and glory.   *Nick Fawcett*

93   Lord Jesus Christ,
       as you stilled the storm, so calm the turmoil within us.
       Put our minds at rest and our spirits at peace,
       secure in the knowledge of your never-failing love.
                                                              Nick Fawcett

94   Lord Jesus Christ,
       reach out into our broken lives,
       and bring joy where there is sorrow,
       healing where there is hurt,
       hope where there is despair,
       and peace where there is turmoil.
       In your name we pray.   *Nick Fawcett*

95   Gracious God,
       teach us to use the dark moments we have been through to
       your glory,
       comforting others with the comfort we have found in you
       and staying close to them in their need
       as you have so faithfully stayed close to us.
       In Jesus' name we pray.   *Nick Fawcett*

96   Lord Jesus Christ,
       when there has been no one else to bear the pain or share
       the hurt,
       no one to lend an ear or offer a shoulder to lean on,
       you have been there, faithful and true,
       ready to lift us up and tend our wounds,
       to listen to our cry and hold us close.
       Loving Lord,
       teach us to be there for others in turn.   *Nick Fawcett*

97   Living God,
       teach us that, though we cannot always see it,
       you are always with us,
       even in the darkest moments of life,

sharing in our anguish carrying in yourself the agony of creation,
and working for that day when all suffering shall be ended
and evil be no more.
In that assurance, give us strength to face each day,
whatever it might bring. *Nick Fawcett*

98 Lord Jesus Christ,
we look to you for wisdom and discernment,
strength and support,
guidance and inspiration.
Reveal to us, as we worship you,
more of your sovereign purpose and gracious will,
and help us to anticipate your kingdom
through working for it now,
trusting in your love despite all that fights against it,
confident that, in the fullness of time,
you will come again to reign here on earth,
as you do in heaven.
Equip us, then, to stand firm,
and, in a world of turmoil and strife,
to keep faith that, though all else may fail,
you will not. *Nick Fawcett*

99 Sovereign God,
refresh our faith as we worship you;
rekindle our trust in your eternal purpose,
our confidence that nothing can separate us from your love.
Though we struggle to get our heads around the mechanics of resurrection
or the nature of the kingdom of heaven,
teach us to focus on what we know and understand—
our daily experience of your love,
the blessings you give us here and now,
the light, joy, and peace you have put into our hearts.
Remind us that these are but a taste of things to come;
that whatever we have received,
you hold yet greater things in store,
through Jesus Christ our Lord. *Nick Fawcett*

100 Living God,
    teach us to trust in your future
    and to keep faith in the final dawning of your kingdom,
    but save us from dwelling on such things,
    indulging in futile speculation,
    or being taken in by the conjectures of others.
    Teach us, rather, to live faithfully for you,
    serving and honoring you through following the way
    of Christ
    despite everything that deflects us from it.
    Help us to consecrate the present to you,
    and to leave all else in your hands,
    through Jesus Christ our Lord.   *Nick Fawcett*

101 Almighty God,
    we find it hard sometimes not to despair of our world.
    When we look at its pain and suffering,
    sorrow and despair,
    hatred and division,
    evil and injustice,
    we fear for the future,
    and struggle to make sense of it all.
    Yet we remember today that you too feel sorrow,
    more than we can ever begin to imagine.
    Unlike us, though, you never give up—
    your love willing to give everything,
    even your only Son,
    to redeem, restore, and renew.
    Inspire us through that knowledge,
    and so may we continue to strive for the coming of
    your kingdom,
    until that day when all things are reconciled to you in Christ
    and we are one with you and him,
    now and for evermore.   *Nick Fawcett*

102 Gracious God,
    there are times when we find ourselves
    in the wilderness of doubt and despair.
    We look at our lives,
    at the world,

even at you,
and we are overwhelmed by a sense of hopelessness,
by questions as to why you do not act to establish your kingdom
or respond to us in our time of need.
Help us at such moments, when all seems dark,
to put our faith in you,
trusting that your light will finally shine again.
Inspire us with the knowledge that, time and again,
it has been in the wilderness experiences of people's lives
that you have been supremely at work—
challenging,
deepening,
and strengthening their faith,
equipping them for new avenues of service,
and opening the way to a richer experience of your love.
In that assurance,
lead us forward,
through Jesus Christ our Lord.   *Nick Fawcett*

103 Loving God,
we thank you for all those times when you have come to our aid,
just when we have begun to lose hope.
We face problems and difficulties to which we see no solution,
only for you to give us guidance when we need it most.
We feel hopelessly alone,
only to discover you by our side.
We wrestle with sorrow and despair,
only for your light to break into the darkness,
bringing joy and hope through the knowledge of your love.
Teach us, through such experiences,
to remember that, however bleak a moment may seem,
you will never abandon or forsake us,
and in that confidence may we live each day,
through Jesus Christ our Lord.   *Nick Fawcett*

104 Father God,
    so often in life we find that after joy comes sorrow,
    after laughter, tears,
    after pleasure, pain.
    Deep down we know that we cannot have one without
    the other.
    But sometimes when life is dark we find that hard to accept,
    even wishing we experienced no joy at all
    if it would save us pain afterwards.
    Yet you were present equally, Father,
    in the joy of Jesus' birth
    and the sorrow of his death.
    Teach us, then, to live with both the good
    and the bad,
    the times of celebration
    and the times of despair,
    realizing that, though we may not see it,
    you are present in each of them,
    working to bringing new beginnings,
    new hope,
    whether in this life or the life to come.
    In the name of Christ, we praise you. *Nick Fawcett*

105 Gracious God,
    as the years pass,
    so our energy and enthusiasm for life can pass with them.
    Though some of our goals are realized,
    many are not and probably never will be,
    and the idealism of our youth is all too easily replaced
    by a world-weary cynicism,
    such that, instead of eagerly anticipating the future,
    we are content simply to get by,
    drifting from one day to the next.
    Yet, in Christ, you have given a hope that never fades
    and a purpose that endures forever,
    opening up a life of infinite possibilities
    and constant new beginnings.

Open our eyes to that wonderful truth,
and so, whatever hopes may be dashed or goals thwarted,
may we continue always to travel in faith,
looking forward to that day when your kingdom shall come
and your will be done,
in the name of Christ. *Nick Fawcett*

106 Gracious God,
we thank you that you are always with us,
in the bad times as well as the good,
the difficult as well as the easy,
the sad as well as the happy.
We thank you that
though we have sometimes been unsure of the way ahead,
you have always been there to guide us;
though we have felt discouraged,
you have offered us fresh inspiration;
though we have been in despair,
you have given us hope.
Through all the changing circumstances of life,
we have found from personal experience
that your steadfast love never ceases
and that your mercies are new every morning.
May the knowledge of all you have done
give us confidence in the days ahead,
so that whatever problems we face,
whatever disappointments we experience,
whatever sorrows may befall us,
we will still find reason to look forward,
reason to believe in the future,
and reason to hope.
Lord of all hopefulness,
hear our prayer,
in the name of Christ. *Nick Fawcett*

107 Living God,
we praise you for the promise
that nothing can ever overcome your light.
We thank you that even when life seems dark and hopeless,
when we search but cannot glimpse your presence,

and call yet cannot hear your voice,
still you are with us,
the fire of your love inexorably burning off the clouds
until the sun breaks through once again,
bathing us in its light.
May that knowledge sustain us through the bleakest moments,
bringing the assurance that good will triumph over evil,
hope replaces despair,
joy comes after sorrow,
and life triumphs over death—
even the darkest night turned to day.
All this we ask through Jesus Christ our Lord.   *Nick Fawcett*

108   Lord,
it is hard sometimes not to lose faith in your purpose.
When hopes are dashed,
when dreams are shattered,
when one disappointment piles up on another,
it's difficult not to lose heart completely,
not to retreat into a shell of despair.
We want to believe we can change,
but there seems little evidence to support it.
We want to believe the world can be different,
but experience appears to prove otherwise.
Our heart tells us one thing,
our head says another,
and the latter finally wins the day.
Yet you have promised that nothing in heaven or on earth
will finally overcome your purpose,
and throughout history you have shown that to be true,
constantly overturning human expectations,
returning hope like a phoenix from the ashes.
Speak to us now through the faith and vision of those who
have gone before,
so that, however dark the world may seem,
we too may dare to hope in turn,
through Jesus Christ our Lord.   *Nick Fawcett*

109   Loving God,
so many things in life have promised much but
delivered little.
We have set ourselves targets but failed to hit them.
We have achieved goals
only to find they did not yield the satisfaction we expected.
We have been let down by others
and, worse still, we have let ourselves down
on more occasions than we care to remember.
So often, hope ends in disappointment,
exposed as wistful naivety, misguided ambition, or
sheer foolishness.
Teach us, before all else, to trust in you,
confident that your love will never fail or disappoint us.
Teach us to base our lives on your living word that promises
so much
yet delivers even more than we can ever ask or imagine.

Nick Fawcett

110   Loving God,
we thank you that in the turmoil of life you are always
with us—
your love reaching out,
your hand supporting us, and your grace giving us strength.
Help us truly to believe that,
not just in our minds but also in our hearts;
to put our trust wholly in you,
confident that you will never fail us.
Help us to let go of the fears and anxieties that weigh
us down,
that destroy our confidence and undermine our happiness,
that alienate us from others and prevent us living life to
the full.
Help us to receive the freedom you offer,
which comes from knowing that you hold all things in
your hands
and that nothing can finally separate us from your love.
In the name of Christ we ask it.   *Nick Fawcett*

111   Gracious God,
        we come as we are,
        in all our weakness,
        with all our faults,
        seeking your renewing, restoring touch.
        Reach out in love,
        receive us by your grace,
        and work in us through your Spirit,
        to your glory.   *Nick Fawcett*

112   Gracious God,
        we draw near to you
        trusting not in any goodness of our own,
        but in your grace,
        your love,
        your unfailing, overflowing mercy.
        Open our heart to all you would say
        and our life to all you would do
        by your grace and to your glory.
        Living God,
        meet with us here in the quietness,
        speak to us now,
        as we make space away from the press of the world,
        hear and answer us as we bring our all before you—
        body, mind, and spirit—
        and so may we walk with you always,
        every moment of every day.   *Nick Fawcett*

113   Loving God,
        as we draw near to you now,
        teach us that you are with us always,
        and help us to sense your presence.
        Remind us again of all you have done,
        so that we may trust more fully in all you will yet do,
        through Jesus Christ our Lord.   *Nick Fawcett*

114 Merciful God,
   unworthy though we are,
   we come to you seeking your redeeming,
   renewing, and restoring touch.
   Meet with us in your word and through your Spirit,
   so that we may rejoice afresh in your love
   and show it in our dealings with others,
   to the glory of your name. *Nick Fawcett*

115 Sovereign God,
   we bring you our fractured,
   feeble faith.
   Strengthen and nurture it,
   so that we may know you more fully,
   love you more deeply, and serve you more truly.
   Nick Fawcett

116 Living God,
   our faith is so very weak yet your love for us is so strong;
   our allegiance is often false yet your promises are always true;
   our commitment is poor yet your blessings are rich
   beyond words.
   Accept our worship and help us to honor you
   as freely as you bless us,
   every moment of every day. *Nick Fawcett*

117 Lord,
   we come to you hesitantly,
   overwhelmed by your greatness,
   yet you welcome us with arms outstretched.
   We come guiltily,
   crushed by a sense of failure,
   yet you pick us up and wash us clean.
   We come uncertainly,
   our faith weak and wavering,
   yet you are always close,
   eager to bless us and lead us forward
   into new experiences of your love.

So we come—
joyfully,
gratefully,
reverently—
hungry to worship you,
and once more you are here,
waiting to surprise us with the wonder of your grace.
Receive our praise,
in Jesus' name.
Nick Fawcett

118 Gracious God,
always watching,
always loving,
always caring,
always ready to forgive and forget:
pardon and renew us once more,
in the name of Christ.
Nick Fawcett

119 Living God,
though we have let you down in so many ways,
teach us that you do not judge as we do,
but that you are truly willing to forgive and forget.
Teach us to let go of past mistakes
and to accept the new life you so freely offer,
and so may we live each day as your gift,
nurtured by the love of Christ
and renewed through your Holy Spirit,
to your praise and glory.
Nick Fawcett

120 Loving God,
we remember today all who mourn,
their hearts broken by tragedy,
tears a constant companion,
laughter and happiness seeming a distant memory.
Reach out into their pain,
Heartache, and sadness,
and give them the knowledge that you understand their pain
and share their sorrow.

May your arms enfold them,
your love bring comfort,
and your light scatter the shadows,
so that they may know joy once more
and celebrate life in all its fullness. *Nick Fawcett*

121 God of all comfort,
we bring you this world of so much pain:
our own and that of those around us.
We bring you our hurts, troubles, anxieties, and fears,
placing them into your hands,
and we pray for those countless others facing sorrow
or suffering:
hopes dashed,
dreams broken,
let down by those they counted dear;
betrayed,
abused,
wrestling with depression or illness,
mourning loved ones.
Hold on to us and to all who walk through the valley
of tears.
Reach out and grant the knowledge that you are with us,
even there,
sharing our pain and moved by our sorrow.
Minister the consolation that you alone can offer,
and give the assurance that those who mourn will be
comforted
and those who weep will laugh.
Lord,
in your mercy,
hear our prayer,
in Christ's name. *Nick Fawcett*

122 Loving God,
we pray for all who are bearing heavy burdens—
those facing difficulties and problems to which they can see
no solutions,
wrestling with inner fears and phobias,
racked by anxiety for themselves or loved ones,

troubled about money, health, work, or relationships—
all who crave rest for their souls but cannot find it.
We pray for them and for ourselves,
acknowledging that sometimes we too feel crushed under a weight of care.
Speak to all in your still small voice,
and grant the peace and quiet confidence that only you can bring;
and so may burdens be lifted and souls refreshed.
Lord,
in your mercy,
hear our prayer,
in the name of Christ.

Nick Fawcett

123 Loving God,
we talk so glibly of peace
but find it so hard to pursue it.
We speak of breaking down barriers and living in harmony,
but when it comes to being peacemakers,
we so often fall short.
Forgive the many things within us that make for conflict—
our pride, greed, envy, and intolerance,
our nursing of petty grievances and unwillingness to forgive,
our preoccupation with self and lack of time for others—
so much that pulls apart rather than draws together.
Make us instruments of your peace.
Teach us to heal wounds rather than create them,
to unite rather than divide,
to reconcile rather than separate.
Put a new spirit within us—
a spirit of love and openness,
acceptance and understanding,
healing and reconciliation.
May the peace we so often pray for
begin here and now with us,
in the name of Christ.

Nick Fawcett

124   Gracious God,
      we look at the world sometimes,
      and we despair.
      We see its greed, corruption, hatred, and violence,
      and we can't help asking,
      "How will it ever change?"
      We want to believe,
      and occasionally our hopes are rekindled by moves
      toward peace,
      yet it is hard to keep faith when, time after time,
      such initiatives come to nothing.
      Gracious God,
      help us to recognize that our way of looking at the world
      is not the same as your way,
      and that where we see no prospect of change,
      you are able to transform situations beyond recognition.
      Teach us never to lose sight of all that you are able to do
      and all that you are already doing.
      Inspire us, therefore, to pray for
      and, in our own small way,
      work toward peace and reconciliation,
      through Jesus Christ our Lord.   *Nick Fawcett*

125   Lord of all,
      we long to see peace in our world,
      but the disturbing truth is that faith itself
      seems to contribute toward division.
      We look at history,
      and across the centuries we see a sorry catalogue
      of atrocities in the name of religion.
      We look at the Church,
      and even today, despite all the efforts to build unity,
      there is still suspicion between various factions,
      to the point sometimes of outright hostility.
      We know this shouldn't be,
      and yet we know also that peace doesn't come easily,
      for it can never be achieved
      simply through covering over the causes of our division.

Help us, then, to work for peace in whatever ways we can,
but give us the faith and the courage we need
to accept the consequences that may result from our efforts,
until one day, at last, your will is done,
your kingdom comes,
and all things are made new,
through Jesus Christ our Lord. *Nick Fawcett*

126 Living God,
there is so much suffering in this world of ours,
so much pain, sorrow, and evil.
It is hard sometimes to reconcile all this with it being your world too,
created by you and precious in your sight.
We search desperately for answers,
clinging first to this and then to that,
and underneath there are times when our faith begins
to crumble.
Teach us that, though we cannot always see it,
you are there,
sharing in our anguish,
carrying in yourself the agony of creation
as it groans under the weight of imperfection.
Teach us that you will not rest until that day when all suffering is ended,
when evil is no more,
and your kingdom is established,
and in that assurance give us strength to face each day,
whatever it might bring. *Nick Fawcett*

127 Lord,
you know our faith isn't perfect.
There is much that we don't understand,
much that we question,
and much that is not all it ought to be.
Despite our love for you,
we find it difficult to trust as we know we should,
the things we don't believe triumphing over the things we do.
Yet, for all its weakness,
you know that our faith is real,

and you know that we long to serve you better.
Take, then, what we are and what we offer,
and, through your grace, provide what we lack
until the faith we profess with our lips may be echoed in our lives,
and our faith be made complete.   *Nick Fawcett*

128   Loving God,
sometimes we cannot help but ask "Why?"
"Why me?"
"Why this?"
"Why anything?"
There is so much we do not understand,
so much that apparently contradicts our faith,
leaving us groping for answers,
and all too easily we feel guilty about having such questions,
afraid that somehow we are letting the side down through doing so.
Yet in our hearts we know there is no point pretending,
for we can never deceive you.
So help us rather honestly to admit that
there are things we cannot make sense of,
and to trust that though we may never understand,
you do.   *Nick Fawcett*

129   Loving God,
we do believe.
We believe that in Jesus
you have shown the way, the truth, and the life.
Yet alongside faith there is also doubt.
We do not have all the answers,
and sometimes we seem only to have questions.
Yet we believe that those questions, honestly asked,
can lead us to a deeper understanding of who you are
and what you have done.
So today we offer you not just our faith
but also our doubt,
praying that you will use both to lead us closer to you.
                                                    Nick Fawcett

130 Living God, hear our prayer for caregivers, those who devote so much of their lives to looking after loved ones—parents, partners, children, friends—often at immense personal cost. Strengthen them, that they may find the reserves to continue. Minister to them, so that they may minister in turn. In all they do, may they be sustained by the knowledge that they too are loved, they too are cared for—by you. *Nick Fawcett*

131 Reach out, Lord, to those who walk the streets—young people who've run away from home, vagrants sleeping rough, the destitute and dispossessed. Remind them that though they may not have a roof over their head, they have a place in your heart, each of them being important to you. Bless the work of churches, charities, hostels, and agencies—all who strive to provide food and shelter, and who offer the prospect of new beginnings, opportunities for the future. Teach us where and how we can best respond to others, and also to you. *Nick Fawcett*

132 Savior Christ, reach out to the lonely, those who look out in vain for a knock at the door, a friendly face, a moment of company. However isolated they may be, teach them that you are by their side. *Nick Fawcett*

133 Lord Jesus Christ, despised and rejected during your ministry, reach out to the marginalized—those pushed to the edge of society, their identity denied, rights ignored, and dignity destroyed. Overcome the barriers of fear, suspicion, and prejudice that divide us, estranging person from person, community from community, and, whatever our differences, help us to recognize the true worth of all—to see beyond what keeps us apart to the common humanity that binds us together. *Nick Fawcett*

134 Healing God, bring closer the day when our divisions will be overcome, our differences put aside, and our fear and mistrust ended—a time when we will live in peace together, and you will be all in all. *Nick Fawcett*

135 Lord of all, grant not just peace but reconciliation in our world, an end to all that divides and destroys, so that those previously estranged may come together, shoulder to shoulder, heart to heart. *Nick Fawcett*

136 Lord Jesus Christ, in a world of conflict where so many are at loggerheads, tussling for power and prestige, bring an end to division. Put an end to our posturing, our endless conflict and confrontation, and show us the way to peace. *Nick Fawcett*

137 Gracious God, in a divided world, where chasms of fear, hatred, envy, and injustice come between so many, help us to build bridges—to do what we can, where we can, to construct links, create dialogue, and promote partnership, bringing together those previously kept apart. Where barriers estrange and rifts alienate, help us to be peacemakers. *Nick Fawcett*

138 Lord of all, we think of the millions in this world for whom water is a luxury. We think of dehydrated children, dying of thirst, of communities whose supplies are polluted and diseased, of lands parched, pasture turned to dust.
And we're ashamed, for, like so many, we're swift to bemoan ourselves and slow to count our blessings. Teach us to understand how lucky we are and to think, for a change, of others instead of ourselves. *Nick Fawcett*

139 Forgive us, Lord, for in a world of need, of hunger, injustice, and oppression, we turn our back on others, concerned solely with our own welfare. Remind us that in ignoring them, we ignore you too. *Nick Fawcett*

140 Loving God, we know that if evils are to be tackled, that challenge needs the will of politicians, governments, and leaders, and we pray that they'll do their part. We know the world needs fairer trade and relief of debt coupled with generous, genuine aid, and we pray these will be achieved. But save us from using all this to pass the buck, as though

the ills of this world are not also down to us. As well
as calling for change, help us to change in turn,
ready to play our part before we ask others to play
theirs. *Nick Fawcett*

141 Lord of the nations, we speak of making poverty history,
and we've done that, but not in the way intended. We've
made it part of our world, an accepted norm, a fact of life
. . . and death . . . for countless millions, and though it's not
all our doing, much of it being down to forces beyond our
control, we're all still complicit in the crime, none of us able
to absolve ourselves fully of responsibility. Forgive the evil
of our world, and our share within it, and give us all a
common resolve to tackle poverty and truly
consign it to history. *Nick Fawcett*

142 Merciful God, we've made progress, but not much, each of
us still being part of a wasteful culture, a society built on
disposability that consumes resources with little thought of
tomorrow and still less for others. Give us a greater sense of
responsibility to future generations and to you; an
appreciation of the countless blessings we have received and
the duty we have to use them wisely, so that others may
enjoy them in turn. *Nick Fawcett*

143 Lord of all, in a world where so many cannot fight their
corner; where the rich prosper and the poor are crushed, the
strong thrive and the weak go to the wall; where naked self-
interest leads to friendships being broken, people estranged,
societies divided, and nations driven to conflict; teach us
your way of love and humility, of putting the interests of
others before our own. If we would serve you,
teach us to serve all. *Nick Fawcett*

144 Gracious God, we need to grieve when we lose loved ones,
for the sorrow is real, the pain hard to bear; but we also
need to rejoice, for with you death is not the end but a new
beginning. The shell is empty but has nurtured life; the
casket is bare but its treasure is safe in your hands; the

person we knew we will know again, for they are truly at home, secure in your everlasting arms, alive with all your people, for evermore. May that truth comfort and strengthen those who mourn, giving them the assurance that nothing finally can separate us from
your love in Christ. *Nick Fawcett*

145 Everlasting God, remind us that even in the darkest days of life and the bleak chill of death, you are there, bringing new beginnings. For your life-giving power, beyond containment, receive our praise. *Nick Fawcett*

146 Caring God, thank you for the assurance that in times of sorrow you will be there to comfort—ready to mend our broken hearts and bring us joy once more. *Nick Fawcett*

147 Lord Jesus Christ, thank you for your promise of comfort. Reach out to all who mourn and turn their sorrow to joy, their tears to laughter, and their despair to hope.
Nick Fawcett

148 God of all comfort, when we despair, life bringing hurt and sorrow, give us strength to continue, until light dawns, hope returns, and tears are wiped away. *Nick Fawcett*

149 Redeemer God, reach out to those who feel trapped, imprisoned by circumstances, held captive by past mistakes, present worries, or future prospects. Give to them and to all the liberty that you alone can give, your truth
that sets us free. *Nick Fawcett*

150 Living God, we feel trapped sometimes, imprisoned in our own small world. Reach out to all who feel separated from others and from you; come and set them free. *Nick Fawcett*

151 Gracious God,
reach out to our broken and bleeding world,
and bind up its wounds.
Reach out to those who are sorrowful and hurting,
and bring comfort deep within.

Reach out to all who walk through the valley of tears
and bring the assurance that those who mourn will one
day laugh—
that, by your grace,
tears will give way to laughter,
and despair to delight. *Nick Fawcett*

152 Gracious God,
we bring to you our broken world,
racked by injustice and exploitation,
suffering and sorrow,
hatred and division—
so few signs of hope in our world,
so much that invites despair.
We pray for those who work for change;
all who strive to bring help and healing,
hope and wholeness.
We lift them all to you, Lord. *Nick Fawcett*

153 Lord, we pray for those who have stopped believing things
can change:
all who have lost faith in themselves,
in others,
in life,
or in you.
Gracious God,
bring healing and renewal;
finish your new creation among us.
May your will be done and your kingdom come,
through Jesus Christ our Lord. *Nick Fawcett*

154 Loving God,
hear our prayer for the have-nots of this world:
those who have no homes,
living as refugees or rough on our streets;
those who have no food,
their crops having failed,
their economies burdened by debt,
or their labors not fairly rewarded;

those who have no fresh water,
daily facing the threat of disease and the nightmare of drought;
those who have insufficient resources to help themselves,
condemned to a life of poverty with no prospect of respite;
those who have no access to education, a health service,
or a welfare system;
no one to turn to for help or support.
Loving God,
stir the hearts of all to work for a fairer world
and a more just society.
Challenge all who have plenty to respond to those who
have little,
so that all may share in the riches of your creation
and be able to celebrate your gift of life.
In Christ's name we ask it. *Nick Fawcett*

155 Loving God,
we bring before you the sick and suffering of our world.
We pray for those afflicted in body:
racked by physical pain,
wrestling with disease,
enduring painful surgery,
or coming to terms with terminal illness.
We pray for those disturbed or troubled in mind:
those whose confidence has been crushed,
those no longer able to cope with the pressures of daily life,
those oppressed by false terrors of the imagination,
and those facing the dark despair of depression.
We pray for those afflicted in spirit:
all who feel their lives to be empty,
or whose beliefs are threatened,
or who have lost their faith,
or who have become caught up in superstition, black magic,
or the occult.
Living God,
reach out through all who work to bring wholeness and
healing.
Support and strengthen them in their work.

Grant them wisdom and guidance,
strength and support,
and the ability to minister something of your care and compassion
for all.
In the name of Christ we ask it. *Nick Fawcett*

156 Loving God, thank you that we can be at peace, secure in the knowledge that, though we sleep, you do not.
Nick Fawcett

157 Lord Jesus Christ, thank you for the peace you promise, not removed from this world, but found amid the hurly-burly of life, the stresses and strains of the daily routine. Open our hearts to that special gift beyond understanding, and may it touch each moment of every day. *Nick Fawcett*

158 Gracious God, thank you for your peace that passes understanding—for the knowledge of your love and assurance of your presence that brings rest to our souls.
Nick Fawcett

159 Lord, we will lie down in peace and take our rest, for you are with us, forever by our side. *Nick Fawcett*

160 Almighty God, teach us never to underestimate your strength, even when it looks like weakness; never to lose sight of the power of love, the might of truth, or the force of good, however much hatred, falsehood, or evil may conspire against them. Remind us that nothing in heaven or earth, the present or the future, will finally be able to frustrate your purpose, for you are able to turn sorrow to joy, darkness to light, and death to life—
your love being stronger than all. *Nick Fawcett*

161 Sovereign God, thank you that we can place ourselves in your care, knowing that the same hands that fashioned the universe and brought this world into being will encircle us each day, powerful beyond measure yet gentle beyond words
Nick Fawcett

162 Thank you, Lord, that when we need support, you are there, a shoulder to lean on in time of trouble, a constant source of strength. *Nick Fawcett*

163 God of all, instead of clinging to money and possessions, as though these are the only support we need, may we hold firmly to you, for you alone can keep us from falling. *Nick Fawcett*

164 Loving God, despite the impression we may give to others, we feel weighed down sometimes by heavy burdens, the pressure building until we feel unable to take the strain any longer. Though we can't cope, teach us that you can, your strength being sufficient for all our needs. Help us to entrust ourselves into your gracious arms, knowing you will support us, whatever life might bring. *Nick Fawcett*

165 Living God, thank you that though we are weak, you are strong, always there when we need you, to protect, defend, and support. *Nick Fawcett*

166 Gracious God, we all carry baggage through life, staggering under a burden of guilt, a weight of remorse, a crushing load of fear. Yet we have no need, for you are ready to carry what we can never shoulder alone. Teach us in turn to let go and walk unencumbered, trusting that you hold everything, even us, in the palm of your hand. *Nick Fawcett*

167 Save us, Lord, from sheepish discipleship, from a feeble and fearful faith. Remind us that you turn expectations upside down, making the strong weak and the weak strong. *Nick Fawcett*

168 Mighty God, thank you that, in a daunting world, you are always there beside us, equipping us for the journey of life. Thank you for the knowledge that though we are weak, you are strong. *Nick Fawcett*

169 We're scared, Lord, afraid to confront our fears, but we can't hide away forever. Teach us to face our demons, knowing you are stronger than all. *Nick Fawcett*

170 Sovereign God, thank you for when we wrestle with heavy loads, weighed down by problems that sap our strength and burdens that crush the spirit, you unfailingly come to our aid, helping to shoulder what we can no longer manage to bear alone. Thank you for being there when we need you most, a constant help in times of trouble. *Nick Fawcett*

171 Mighty God, when we grow weary, drained by the demands and duties of the daily routine, renew our strength and rekindle our zest for life. *Nick Fawcett*

172 Almighty God, we're not in control, no more able to dictate our destiny than to create life or defy death, such a feat being beyond our reach. We can shape things, to a point, exerting influence for better or worse, but more often than not we're the one being shaped, swept along by the latest current of opinion or tide of events. Teach us where true power really lies: not in our hands, but in yours. *Nick Fawcett*

173 Lord Jesus Christ, for being there for us, whenever we need you, a shoulder to lean on, a friend in need, thank you. *Nick Fawcett*

174 Gracious God, even when it's hard, everything seeming to count against it, teach us to keep faith, knowing that, however much we falter and however hard we fall, you will lift us up and set us back on our way. *Nick Fawcett*

175 Eternal God, thank you that in a world of change, you are our rock; that in a world of uncertainty, you are solid ground beneath our feet; that in a world of danger, you are our refuge. Thank you that, wherever life's journey takes us, you are always there, our strength and salvation in time of need. *Nick Fawcett*

176   Mighty God, thank you that in the storms of life, when we sometimes feel helpless and alone, unsure what the future may hold, you are always there to guide, protect, and save. Teach us to put our trust in you, come wind, come weather, assured that you will see us through this life to our journey's end. *Nick Fawcett*

177   Loving God, when life brings troubles— stretching our resources, sapping our strength, and testing us to the limit—give us a bulldog spirit, a faith that will not give in but perseveres to the end. *Nick Fawcett*

178   Living God, sometimes we feel knocked about by forces beyond our control, battered this way and that by circumstances until, finally, we can take the punishment no longer. Yet you promise strength to the weary and support to the faint; to see us through however fierce the testing. In the chaos and confusion of life we put our trust in you. *Nick Fawcett*

179   Gracious God, help us to glimpse your light even when life is at its darkest. Though the night of sorrow, fear, pain, or doubt closes in, cold and forbidding, may a glimmer of your love shine through—a glimpse of your presence sufficient to sustain faith, nourish hope, and impart peace. *Nick Fawcett*

180   Loving God, remind us, in the storms of life, when the clouds hang heavy and the world seems dark, that your light continues to shine though all seems in turmoil. Teach us, however distant you may seem, still to trust you, assured that your love will break through and its radiance enfold us once more. *Nick Fawcett*

181   Lord Jesus Christ, thank you that when we reach out, seeking your help in time of need, you are always there, ready to help, to heal, and to hold. *Nick Fawcett*

182 Redeemer God, sometimes life brings us down to earth with a bump—dreams shattered, plans frustrated, happiness destroyed. Help us at such times, instead of feeling sorry for ourselves and cursing our luck, to pick ourselves up and start again, knowing that there is no gain without pain, no joy without sorrow, no laughter without tears. However often we may fall, renew our trust, in life and in you.
Nick Fawcett

183 Though danger threatens, Lord, and trouble is near, teach us that we have nothing to fear, for whatever may harm the body, it cannot touch the soul. *Nick Fawcett*

184 Merciful God, repeatedly, in time of trouble, you have stretched out your hand and provided for our needs. For the constancy of your care, thank you. *Nick Fawcett*

185 Father God, though faith cannot insulate us from the blows of life or protect us from being hurt, thank you for being there to comfort, ready to mend our broken hearts and wipe away the tears. Thank you that, in sickness or in health, joy or sorrow, your arms continue to enfold us, eternity itself held in your embrace. Teach us to trust in you and to find peace in your outstretched arms.
Nick Fawcett

186 Lord of all, reach out to those behind the statistics: the mother whose partner has walked out on her and the children, the worker whose factory has closed down, the trader whose business has folded, the victim of the industrial accident, the manager made redundant, the casual laborer whose services are no longer required. However hopeless they may feel, however disheartened, disillusioned, or despondent, assure them of their worth as individuals, and help us as a society to do the same.
Nick Fawcett

187 Loving God,
you have promised that those who mourn shall be comforted.
So we pray now for each of us here today,
bringing before you the sorrow we all feel at this moment.
Lord, in your mercy, hear our prayer.
We pray especially for A's family,
in their shock and grief,
their pain and loneliness,
the turmoil of emotions that death inevitably brings
to those left behind.
Lord, in your mercy, hear our prayer.
We pray for all those who counted A as a friend,
those in this church,
those who worked with A,
who lived near to him/her,
who shared his/her hobbies and interests—
all those whose lives were, in different ways,
touched by A's presence.
Lord, in your mercy, hear our prayer.
Loving God,
we bring before you now our sense of emptiness,
separation, and sorrow.
Give us your support as we struggle
to come to terms with our loss.
Give strength to face the days ahead.
Give courage when life seems dark.
Give hope when the future seems without purpose.
Lord, in your mercy,
hear our prayer.
Help us to know that your love for A and for us
continues beyond death,
that you are with us in this moment and always,
and may that knowledge bring comfort and hope
today and in the days ahead.
Lord, in your mercy,
hear our prayer,
in the name of Christ.   *Nick Fawcett*

188 Loving God,
   you tell us to look forward to a day
   when your kingdom shall come
   and your will be done;
   a new age when there will be no more suffering,
   sorrow, or death;
   a place where there will be no more mourning and weeping,
   every tear wiped away from our eyes.
   Help us to find comfort in your love.
   We thank you for that promise,
   and we look forward to that time,
   but we pray also for your help now,
   for today our grief is all too painful,
   and the fact of death an all too stark reality.
   Help us to find comfort in your love.
   So we ask you to reach out to us
   and to all whose lives have been enriched
   by A's presence—
   family,
   friends,
   neighbors,
   colleagues—
   each so much the poorer for A's passing.
   Help us to find comfort in your love.
   Loving God,
   reach out now into the darkness of this moment,
   the blackness of our sorrow,
   and grant your light which nothing can overcome,
   your peace that defies understanding,
   and your hope which will never be extinguished.
   Help us to find comfort in your love,
   through Jesus Christ our Lord.   *Nick Fawcett*

189 Lord Jesus Christ,
   you spoke,
   and you brought hope, comfort, and renewal;
   you touched,
   and you brought love, peace, healing, and wholeness.

Come now,
and speak again,
bringing your word of life to all who suffer or are hurting.
Reach out afresh,
bringing your touch of love to all whose hearts are aching
and who cry out for help.
Where there is despair and turmoil,
may your voice renew.
Where there is pain and sickness,
may your hand restore.
Lord Jesus Christ,
you came once,
you shall come again,
but we ask you,
come now,
and minister your grace,
for your name's sake.
Nick Fawcett

190   Transforming God,
ever at work among the poor,
the humble,
the weak,
the lowly,
teach us to live not by our values
but by yours.
When we feel feeble and powerless,
incapable of meeting the challenges before us;
when we feel our resources are too small
and the demands put upon us too great;
when we feel we can achieve little
and so set limits on what you can do through us,
teach us to live not by our values
but by yours.
When we look around us and see no sign of your kingdom,
when so much evil seems to triumph over so little good,
when the problems of our world seem many
and the answers to them few,
when hope seems futile and despair more than justified,
when truth and love appear overwhelmed

by falsehood and hatred,
teach us to live not by our values
but by yours.
Transforming God,
help us to recognize that you can use
what seems small in our eyes beyond all our imagining,
that from the smallest of beginnings
you can bring the greatest of results.
Teach us that you can use others,
that you can use us,
that you can use anyone.
Teach us to live not by our values
but by yours,
to the glory of your name.

Nick Fawcett

191 Living God,
we pray for all those who are weighed down
by the stresses and strains of daily life—
those who long for peace of mind,
who crave rest for their souls,
but cannot find it.
Lord, in your mercy,
hear our prayer.
We pray for those oppressed by worry,
unable to throw off their anxieties,
held captive by a multitude of secret fears.
Lord, in your mercy,
hear our prayer.
We pray for those who cannot let go,
those who find it impossible to relax or unwind,
always fretting over this or that.
Lord, in your mercy, hear our prayer.
We pray for those who lose themselves in busyness,
masking their true feelings
and running from their emptiness,
hoping that keeping active might bring them happiness.
Lord, in your mercy,
hear our prayer.

We pray for those who have lost time for you,
allowing the pressures and demands of each day
to shut you out,
putting any thought of you off until tomorrow.
Lord, in your mercy,
hear our prayer.
We pray for those who have no time for you,
no interest in anything other than their daily routine,
no awareness of their spiritual needs.
Lord, in your mercy,
hear our prayer.
Living God,
speak to each one in your still small voice,
and grant them your peace which passes understanding,
that quiet confidence which only you can bring,
and so may their burdens be lifted
and their souls refreshed.
Lord, in your mercy,
hear our prayer,
through Jesus Christ our Lord. *Nick Fawcett*

192   Lord of all,
we pray for all who are searching for peace in their lives—
those burdened with anxiety,
either about themselves or their loved ones,
facing difficulties and problems
to which they can see no solutions.
God of peace,
reach out and still the storm.
We pray for those wrestling with inner fears and phobias,
torn apart by emotional and psychological pressures.
God of peace,
reach out and still the storm.
We pray for those living among change and upheaval,
especially all who are threatened by violence and warfare.
God of peace,
reach out and still the storm.
To all of those in chaos and turmoil,
all who are restless and troubled,
grant your calm,

your tranquility,
your quietness,
and your peace which passes understanding.
God of peace,
reach out and still the storm,
in the name of Christ.   *Nick Fawcett*

193   Loving God,
you have promised your special blessing to those who mourn,
your comfort to those overwhelmed by grief,
your joy to those enduring sorrow.
So now we pray for those facing sadness,
those burdened by misery,
those weighed down by despair,
those who have lost loved ones
and who are striving to come to terms
with the emptiness and heartbreak they feel.
Lord, in your mercy,
hear our prayer.
We pray for those among our families and friends
who are facing such times,
all those in this church and in our world.
Lord, in your mercy,
hear our prayer.
Loving God,
grant to those who grieve your special blessing.
May they know that your hand is upon them,
your arms encircling them,
and your heart reaching out to them.
Lord, in your mercy,
hear our prayer.
May all who mourn discover the comfort you have promised,
and find strength to face tomorrow,
until that time comes when light shall dawn again,
and hope be born anew.
Lord, in your mercy,
hear our prayer,
through Christ our Lord.   *Nick Fawcett*

194 Loving God,
you have promised that those who mourn shall be comforted.
So now we pray for all those facing sorrow at this time.
Lord, in your mercy,
hear our prayer.
We pray for those whose hopes have been dashed—
their plans laid to waste,
their dreams destroyed.
Rekindle their faith in the future.
Lord, in your mercy,
hear our prayer.
We pray for those who have been let down—
wounded by loved ones,
betrayed by those in whom they put their trust.
Save them from succumbing to bitterness or cynicism.
Lord, in your mercy,
hear our prayer.
We pray for those wrestling with depression—
those for whom life seems empty
and the future dark.
Show them a light at the end of the tunnel.
Lord, in your mercy,
hear our prayer.
We pray for those who are unwell—
afflicted by chronic disease,
suffering from terminal illness.
Support them through all that they face.
Lord, in your mercy,
hear our prayer.
We pray for those who grieve—
those who mourn loved ones,
those coming to terms with personal tragedy.
Cradle them in your everlasting arms.
Lord, in your mercy,
hear our prayer.
Loving God,
hold on to all who walk through the valley of tears.
Reach out to them,
and grant them the knowledge that you are with them,
sharing their pain and moved by their sorrow.

Minister the consolation that you alone can offer,
and give them the assurance
that those who mourn shall be comforted;
those who weep will laugh.
Lord, in your mercy,
hear our prayer.
Through Jesus Christ our Lord. *Nick Fawcett*

195 Walk with us, Lord,
through the times of suffering and pain,
alerting us to one another's needs
and providing for us in whatever ways are best for us.
Help us to trust you through the dark times;
breathe new life and hope
into us when we despair. *Susan Sayers*

196 Loving God, give comfort and healing to all
who are in any kind of need, sorrow, or pain.
May they sense your reassuring presence
and know that you are there with them,
wherever their journey takes them. *Susan Sayers*

197 We pray for the disillusioned and depressed
and all who have lost their way in life;
we pray for those corrupted by evil,
trained in hatred, and twisted by bitterness.
We pray for the transforming of these lives. *Susan Sayers*

198 Healing God, we bring to you
those whose lives are darkened by pain,
fear, or weariness.
Come to our aid;
help us to bear what must be carried,
and take from us all resentment and bitterness,
replacing it with the abundance of peace. *Susan Sayers*

199 Loving God, search for the lost,
bring back those who have strayed,
bind up the injured, and strengthen the weak;
help us all to share in this work of loving care. *Susan Sayers*

200   Heavenly Father, may all whose bodies,
Souls, or minds are aching
know the comforting and strengthening power
of your companionship, and the healing work of your love.
May we be more ready
to support and befriend one another
through the difficult times,
in the name and love of the God we worship.   *Susan Sayers*

201   God of compassion, take
our hearts of stone and
give us feeling hearts, so
that we as the Church may
be more responsive
to the needs and sorrows around us.   *Susan Sayers*

202   Heavenly Father, we pray for those
whose pain screams silently and incessantly;
for those who have no one to confide in,
no one to listen.
We pray for your love to enfold them,
your peace to calm them,
and your healing to transform them.   *Susan Sayers*

203   Lord God, we pray that our households
and neighborhoods,
our places of work and leisure,
may be arenas of praise and thankfulness,
not only in the comfort zones
but particularly through the disturbed
and difficult times.   *Susan Sayers*

204   We pray for all who spend their lives
feeling dissatisfied;
for those who are unhappy, lonely, or overworked.
We ask you to lift their spirits
and give them peace and joy.   *Susan Sayers*

205   As we grow increasingly aware
      of our spiritual hunger,
      we give thanks for the wonder of God's feeding,
      throughout our days.   *Susan Sayers*

206   God of glory,
      with your special affection
      for the discarded and marginalized,
      the weak and the vulnerable,
      we pray for all those who find life
      an exhausting struggle
      or who long for some respite from pain or depression.
      Support them in their troubles,
      bring healing and reassurance,
      and touch them with the gentleness of your peace.
                                                     Susan Sayers

207   We pray for all who are marginalized,
      Scorned, or rejected;
      for those isolated through illness or imprisonment;
      for those who feel that no one understands.
      Surround them all with such love
      that they may know they are precious to you.   *Susan Sayers*

208   We pray that none may be considered expendable,
      or beyond our cherishing;
      we pray for all who have lost heart,
      through pain, suffering, or sin,
      that God's redeeming power may work its wonders
      in the very darkest situations.   *Susan Sayers*

209   God of wholeness,
      we remember those who are aching today
      in body, mind, or spirit;
      knowing that nothing is unredeemable,
      we ask that you will bring good
      even out of these barren places.   *Susan Sayers*

210   We pray for those disturbed by mental illness,
and for all who are rejected and despised.
We pray for all in desolate situations at the moment,
and ask for your comfort and healing. *Susan Sayers*

211   We pray for those who have lost hope
of being rescued, noticed, or valued;
for the complacent who cannot see their poverty,
for the prejudiced who mistake blindness for sight.
Susan Sayers

212   We call to mind all whose capacity to trust
has been damaged;
for those who are victims of injustice or corruption;
for the very young and the very old,
the frail, the vulnerable, and the bereaved. *Susan Sayers*

213   Heavenly Father, as we recall the needs
of those who are sad or lonely,
lost, or afraid of what they have become,
we pray for the knowledge of your love
to wrap warmly around them,
and your living presence
to bring them to a place of safety and hope. *Susan Sayers*

214   We long for those who feel neglected
or rejected by society
to know God's love and acceptance of them.
We long for all those in pain and distress
to be comforted and relieved. *Susan Sayers*

215   Surround with comfort and reassurance
those who feel spiritually dried up
or emotionally drained;
heal and mend broken bodies and broken hearts,
and provide clear pools of water for those
who are walking the valley of misery and depression.
Susan Sayers

216 God of wholeness,
   speak into the despair and loneliness
   of all who struggle with life and its troubles;
   reassure, affirm, and encourage them,
   and alert us to ways we can help. *Susan Sayers*

217 We remember the vulnerable and the ignored,
   the outcasts and the oppressed,
   and pray that we may open our hearts
   to loving involvement. *Susan Sayers*

218 We bring to mind those caught up
   in the frenetic pressures of life,
   and those who are stressed to the breaking point.
   We pray for insight and courage to change things.
   Susan Sayers

219 As we acknowledge the beauty
   of loving even our enemies,
   we thank you for the extraordinary love
   you show us in Jesus. *Susan Sayers*

220 When the layers of resentment
   have turned into rock,
   dissolve them with the rain of your loving mercy.
   Susan Sayers

221 When the luggage we carry from the past
   interferes with our capacity to cope with the present,
   heal the damage from our memories
   and transform our experiences for good. *Susan Sayers*

222 We pray for all imprisoned by guilt, resentment,
   bitterness, and self-pity,
   that they may come to know the relief of being forgiven.
   We pray for all innocent victims,
   we pray that their scars may be completely healed.
   Susan Sayers

223   We pray that those whose bodies or spirits
are heavy with suffering
may be given courage and hope,
ease from the pain, and healing to wholeness.
That we may know how best to help them.   *Susan Sayers*

224   Father, we pray for a greater awareness
of what damages souls and encourages evil,
and for widespread commitment
to addressing the dangers.
We pray for all who earn their living
through selling what destroys lives.   *Susan Sayers*

225   We pray for those who are wrestling with problems
that seem too big to cope with;
for those who have recently received news
that has stunned or appalled them,
and are still in a state of shock.   *Susan Sayers*

226   We pray for those we have upset or angered,
and those who have upset or angered us;
we pray for those who worry us,
and those we love but seldom manage to see.   *Susan Sayers*

227   Father, as we remember those
who have asked for our prayers,
take their needs and provide for them,
take their wounds and heal them,
take their suffering and comfort them.   *Susan Sayers*

228   Lord, you suffer with those who suffer
and weep with those who weep;
we, too, stand alongside them now
in whatever pain, distress, or sorrow is engulfing them,
longing for them to be comforted.   *Susan Sayers*

229   We think of those who are in prison,
       locked in cells or depression or dysfunctional bodies;
       we think of those in hospital wards and accident centers,
       those unable to reach medical help
       and those on long waiting lists for operations;
       as we think of them all, we pray for them all.   *Susan Sayers*

230   Whenever people are enveloped by pain
       or desolate grief or total exhaustion,
       bring refreshment and peace, tranquility and hope.
       Wherever the grip of the past
       prevents free movement into the future,
       bring release and healing.   *Susan Sayers*

231   We pray for all victims of abuse and tyranny,
       or all who suffer long-term effects
       of torture, war, or disease;
       we pray for the grace to forgive,
       and for healing of body, mind, and spirit.   *Susan Sayers*

232   Encourage the hesitant, curb the overpowering,
       heal the sick, refresh the exhausted,
       soften the hardened hearts,
       open the eyes of the complacent,
       and comfort all who are sad.   *Susan Sayers*

233   We pray for those whose lives
       are full of disappointment, disillusion, and discontent;
       for all who struggle with great perseverance
       in difficult circumstances.
       We pray for your strength, encouragement, and direction.
       Susan Sayers

234   Father, we stand alongside all who are hurting
       in body, mind, or spirit;
       all who need courage, support, or practical help.
       Make us willing to become
       part of your answer to our prayers for them.   *Susan Sayers*

235 We thank you for the patient endurance
of so many who suffer so much;
for them all we pray your wholeness
and refreshing,
your upholding and healing. *Susan Sayers*

236 Bring reassurance and practical help
to those who are close to despair;
support those in long-term suffering
and use us as instruments of your healing love. *Susan Sayers*

237 To those who are losing heart
give your heavenly encouragement and patience;
to the young and vulnerable
give heavenly protection;
to the ill and the damaged
give heavenly healing and inner peace,
as you touch our lives with yours. *Susan Sayers*

238 Lord God, there are some who are going through
very distressing, painful, and worrying times.
We stand alongside them now,
and ask for them your comfort, reassurance,
healing, and peace of mind. *Susan Sayers*

239 We pray that all those whose lives
are fettered by the past,
by rejection, guilt, pain, or anxiety,
may be set free and encouraged to live to the full.
Susan Sayers

240 Lord, we pray for peace of mind and spirit
in all those who are distressed or enveloped in pain.
May they know the reality of your inner healing,
and may even the worst situations
become places of growth and new life. *Susan Sayers*

241   We pray for all who are too exhausted
or overwhelmed by circumstances and pressures
to be able to pray;
surround all those who are troubled
and heavily laden
with the revitalizing assurance of your presence,
your understanding, and your love. *Susan Sayers*

242   We pray for all who suffer through others' sin;
all victims of abuse or oppression or apathy;
all whose adult lives are distorted and misshapen
by early damaging experiences
that need your healing. *Susan Sayers*

243   We bring all for whom illness or injury
has caused disruption, uncertainty,
and the prospect of long-term change;
all who find their lives are spinning
out of their control;
give them working knowledge
of your total loving and unchanging presence,
so that in all the changes and troubles of life
they may be assured of your everlasting protection.
Susan Sayers

244   We stand alongside all those who are suffering,
whether in body, mind, or spirit,
and long for your healing and comfort,
your strength for perseverance,
and your patience in the dark times;
we long for your living Spirit
to envelop and sustain them. *Susan Sayers*

245   Holy God, breathe your life into those who suffer;
breathe comfort and wholeness,
forgiveness and new confidence,
breathe peace of mind
and the knowledge of your love. *Susan Sayers*

246   Lord God, we pray for those who cannot think,
for the pain or anguish that engulfs them;
for all whose lives are troubled and insecure;
for those who have little energy left to rejoice.
Bring healing,
and the resources to cope with suffering,
and give us the grace
to carry one another's burdens in love. *Susan Sayers*

247   We bring to you, Lord,
those whom life has damaged,
and all who find it difficult to trust in you;
we bring you those who need refreshment and hope,
comfort, healing, and inner serenity. *Susan Sayers*

248   Holy God, may all that encourages people
in goodness, honesty, and compassion
be blessed and grow;
may all that encourages self-seeking and cruelty,
prejudice, and deceit wither and be exposed
as the unsatisfying garbage it is.
May we learn from one another's cultures
and respect one another's differences. *Susan Sayers*

249   Living God, you can use
and transform all our experiences.
We lay before you now
those who are traveling through a time
of pain or anguish, tragedy or conflict,
which is hard to bear.
We stand alongside them in their suffering,
and offer it to your transforming, healing love. *Susan Sayers*

250   Lord of life,
we pray for all who feel out of their depth,
all who are drowning in their pain,
sorrow, or guilt.
Set them free, O God, and save them,
support them to a place of safety
and fix their feet on the solid rock of your love. *Susan Sayers*

251   We pray for those who are full of tears
and cannot imagine being happy again;
we pray for the hardened and callous,
whose inner hurts have never yet been healed.
We pray for wholeness and comfort and new life.
Susan Sayers

252   We pray for those whose lives feel empty or cheated,
or filled with pain, or worry, or guilt.
For all whose hopes and dreams are in tatters;
all who are in any way imprisoned.
Susan Sayers

253   We pray for all who are oppressed,
downtrodden, or despised;
we pray for those who will not eat today
and all who live in the degrading circumstances
of poverty and powerlessness;
we pray for a heart to put injustices right
and strive for a fair sharing of resources.
Susan Sayers

254   God of mercy and compassion,
we bring to you all those who, through illness,
accident, age, abuse, or human weakness,
are suffering as we gather here.
Gather them up in your love
and give your healing, your strength and courage,
your hope and wholeness.
We make ourselves available
as channels of your love.
Susan Sayers

255   Lord, wherever bodies, minds, or spirits
are wracked with pain,
or too weak or exhausted to pray,
we ask the bathing love of your presence,
and the practical caring of hands working in your name.
Wherever there are doubts and the battle is strong,
we ask your empowering and clear guidance.
Susan Sayers

256 Father, we pray for all who cry out for rest and relief,
all who are carrying terrible burdens
that weigh them down,
all whose poverty denies them the chance of healing,
all whose wealth denies them
the chance of knowing their need of you. *Susan Sayers*

257 Lord, wherever the human spirit
is ground down by oppression,
and wherever our silence allows injustice
and corruption to flourish,
we ask for deeper compassion and commitment;
we ask for our kingdoms to become your kingdoms,
and the desires of your heart to be ours. *Susan Sayers*

258 O Holy Fire,
O Holy Grace,
O Overflowing Silent One:
by your birth
enable us;
by your overcoming of spirits arm us;
by your integrity
make us true;
by your fortitude in trials establish us;
by your self-giving in death change us;
by your mission to unquiet spirits
raise us. *Ray Simpson*

259 Christ of the scars,
into your hands we place the broken, the wounded,
the hungry, and the homeless.
Christ of the scars,
into your hands we place
those who have been betrayed or bereaved;
those who have suffered loss of family or friends,
jobs or homes.

Christ of the scars,
into your hands we place neighbors defamed,
lovers spurned, spouses deserted.
Christ of the scars,
into your hands we place victims of war and crime.

Ray Simpson

260 Lead us from death to life,
from falsehood to truth.
Lead us from despair to hope,
from fear to trust.
Lead us from hate to love, from war to peace.
Deep peace of the Son of peace,
fill our hearts, our workplace, our world.
Echoes the Universal Prayer for Peace   *Ray Simpson*

261 As the sun sets in the west,
may we settle down with you, O God.
Into your hands we place our failings and irritations.
In your presence we give thanks for the blessings of this day.
We will lie down at one with you,
that we may rise up ready to do your will.   *Ray Simpson*

262 We lie down this night with God,
and God will lie down with us;
we lie down this night with Christ,
and Christ will lie down with us;
we lie down this night with the Spirit,
and the Spirit will lie down with us;
God and Christ and the Spirit,
lying down with us.   *Ray Simpson*

263 The almighty and merciful Three circle us,
that awake we may watch with Christ,
and asleep we may rest in peace.   *Ray Simpson*

264 We place our souls and bodies
under your guarding this night, O God,
O Father of help to frail pilgrims,
Protector of heaven and Earth.
We place our souls and bodies
under your guiding this night, O Christ,
O Son of the tears and the woundings,
may your cross this night be our shield.
We place our souls and bodies
under your glowing this night, O Spirit,
O gentle Companion and Soul Friend,
our hearts' eternal warmth. *Ray Simpson*

265 You are our Savior and Lord;
in our stumbling be our shield;
in our tiredness be our rest;
in our darkness be our light. *Ray Simpson*

266 The peace of the Spirit be ours this night,
the peace of the Son be ours this night,
the peace of the Father be ours this night,
the peace of all peace be ours this night,
each morning and evening of our lives. *Ray Simpson*

267 Guide us, our great Mentor,
through the ups and downs of life.
Strengthen us to leave behind what hinders our calling,
and to keep moving toward ever-greater reality.
   Ray Simpson

268 O Being of truth,
O Being of sight,
O Being of wisdom,
give us judgment in our choices.
O Being of life,
O Being of peace,
O Being of time,
be with us now.

We quieten our souls under the stillness of sky.
Peace be upon our breath.
Peace be upon our eyes.
Peace be upon our hearts. *Ray Simpson*

269 Great Spirit, help us to relax into your plan for us.
Unfold it for us as the acorn unfolds into the oak. *Ray Simpson*

270 Ever-shielding Father,
ever-loving Son,
life-giving Holy Spirit,
ever Three in One:
rain grace on us and heal us
and we shall lie down in peace.
Rain grace on us and heal us
and we shall lie down in peace. *Ray Simpson*

271 God, fill your people with your Spirit
and give us skill, ability, and understanding
of every kind of artistic work. *Ray Simpson*

272 Glorious Three,
shine upon our tired and drooping hearts.
Complete the work to which you have called us.
Pour lovingly and generously upon us hour by hour. *Ray Simpson*

273 Zeal of God, fill our being.
Truth of God, light our way.
Peace of God, redeem our past.
Love of God, come in to stay. *Ray Simpson*

274 In the place of fear,
God's strength to uphold us.
In the place of emptiness,
God's wisdom to guide us.
In the place of confusion,
God's eye for our seeing.

In the place of discord,
God's ear for our hearing.
In the place of froth,
God's word for our speaking,
to save us from false agendas
that harm our bodies or souls. *Ray Simpson*

275 Where times are dark,
where wrong parades as right,
where faith grows dim,
Christ, Light of the World,
meet us in our place of darkness.
Journey with us
and bring us to your new dawning. *Ray Simpson*

276 Lord, do not lead us into a time of fearful trial.
But in whatever trials we have to face,
help us to remain true to you,
our King who saves us. *Ray Simpson*

277 Sweet Jesus, I lay before you now
things that are needlessly bitter—
relationships, circumstances.
May your sweetness turn
food into pleasure,
tragedy into triumph,
and ugliness into beauty. *Ray Simpson*

278 Take us under your protection,
O beloved angel of God,
just as the Lord of grace so ordained.
Accompany us at all times
and protect us from worry and danger. *Ray Simpson*

279 O God, all-powerful, you are our strength.
O Lord of the world, our lives are yours.
Whatever be your will, may it be done. *Ray Simpson*

280   We ask for the Light of light,
the vision of the Trinity,
and the grace of patience
in the face of injustice.   *Ray Simpson*

281   *In Times of Trial or Terror*
When people are in danger on the streets,
send big angels to stand between them,
angels from heaven or angels from Earth.
May terror flee.
May calm and confidence return.   *Ray Simpson*

282   *After a disaster or act of terror*
In our devastation,
reach down to us, O God.
In our grief,
reach down to us, O God.
In our anger,
reach down to us, O God.
In our confusion,
reach down to us, O God.   *Ray Simpson*

283   God who weeps over the city,
may we know the abandoned places,
may we sense the destructive patterns,
may we feel the suffering groups,
may we confess the ravages and rage,
may we embrace the hopes and despairs.   *Ray Simpson*

284   Grant us
acceptance of pain without bitterness,
grieving for loss without blame,
forgiveness for frailty without remorse,
renewal of trust without fear.   *Ray Simpson*

285   Sadness and sin behind us be,
farewell to marriage, but friends let us be.
Bless our children in their hurts;
bless us as parents despite our warts.   *Ray Simpson*

286   God of Community,
        bring to birth a community of justice.
        We pray for the powerful
        who impose their will on the weak;
        may they come to know your defenseless love.
        We pray for those who seek revenge through acts of terror;
        may they come to know your defenseless love.
        We pray for those who have lost limbs or loved ones;
        may they come to know your defenseless love.   *Ray Simpson*

287   Great-hearted God,
        who reaches out to all,
        inspire our every nerve and sinew
        to reach out to others with your love.
        May we accept each person as yours.
        May we include each person in our hearts.
        May we find a way
        to walk with those who stumble,
        to watch with those who suffer,
        and to work with those who avoid us.   *Ray Simpson*

288   Into your loss,
        come,
        O Being of Gift,
        O Being of Peace,
        O Being of Life eternal.
        Into your threat,
        come,
        O Being of Strength,
        O Being of Peace,
        O Being of Life eternal.
        Into your despair, come,
        O Being of Hope,
        O Being of Peace,
        O Being of Life eternal.
        Into your devastation, come,
        O Being of Love,
        O Being of Peace,
        O Being of Life eternal.   *Ray Simpson*

289 Bruised?
   The blessing of acceptance be yours.
   Bitter?
   The blessing of forgiveness be yours.
   Angry?
   The blessing of gentleness be yours.
   Suicidal?
   The blessing of trust be yours.
   Broken?
   The blessing of immortality be yours. *Ray Simpson*

290 The blessing of acceptance be yours.
   The blessing of forgiveness be yours.
   The blessing of gentleness be yours.
   The blessing of resilience be yours.
   The blessing of eternal life be yours. *Ray Simpson*

291 O God of Life, darken not to me your light.
   O God of Life, close not to me your joy.
   O God of Life, shut not to me your door.
   O God of Life, crown me with your gladness. *Ray Simpson*

292 Christ of the scars of love, into your hands we place
   those who have been scarred by life:
   those who have been betrayed,
   those who have suffered loss of limb or esteem.
   Christ of the scars of love,
   into your hands we place unwanted babies,
   neighbors defamed, lovers spurned.
   Christ of the scars of love,
   into your hands we place
   those who are victims of violence,
   unethical practice, or false accusation. *Ray Simpson*

293 Healing power of Christ,
   penetrate the brittle shell
   of the ones for whom we pray.
   Where they are no longer present to others,
   attract them to your gaze.

Where they are down and out,
grasp hold of them and raise them up.
Where they are fettered,
set them free to leap and praise. *Ray Simpson*

294 On those who harbor fear,
come, Holy Spirit.
On those whose day is drab,
come, Holy Spirit.
On those whose lives are parched,
come, Holy Spirit. *Ray Simpson*

295 We are appealing to you,
since you are the King of Heaven.
We are praying to you,
since you are the King of Good.
Lift each wasting,
each weariness, and each sickness.
Lift each soreness and each discomfort.
We are eagerly praying to you.
Lift each stiffness
as you separate earth from ocean. *Ray Simpson*

296 Life-giver, Pain-bearer,
we offer you our tears for those broken by abuse
and our anguish for those who rebel against you.
We offer you the pain we endure
from those who are hostile
and our burdens for the needy and poor.
May our sufferings contribute to the suffering
that your universal body needs to complete
in order to transform every last person and place on Earth.
Ray Simpson

297 Dear Father, Mother, Source of my being,
the precious robe with which you birthed me
is torn into shreds.
Love has been scattered.
Yet I long for you, and you long to gather together
the fragments of my life.

You know who I am.
Snatch me from the maze.
Restore me to my right mind.
Heal my wounds.
Return me to fellowship with the human family
and make me one with you. *Ray Simpson*

298 Boundless Nourisher,
help me to retreat in order to advance;
to move out of train tracks and
re-orientate my life with you.
Help me to relax and listen,
to observe and receive;
perhaps to walk in the steps of saints,
or to read and reflect and renew my mind.
Above all, may I stop running away,
and learn to wonder as I wander with you. *Ray Simpson*

299 I will come apart with you, Lord,
that you may still my heart.
I will come apart with you, Lord,
that you may stock my mind.
I will come apart with you, Lord,
that you may steel my will.
I will retreat with you, Lord,
that together we may advance. *Ray Simpson*

300 Lead me, Lord, into a place of prayer,
to live simply, silently, and alone with you,
so that I may die to myself quicker
and Christ may grow in me faster;
so that you may give more of him
to the world that hungers for him.
Echoes words of Catherine Doherty *Ray Simpson*

www.ingramcontent.com/pod-product-compliance
Lightning Source LLC
Chambersburg PA
CBHW071221070526
44584CB00019B/3105

THE CUBAN REVOLUTION AS SOCIALIST HUMAN DEVELOPMENT

Studies in Critical Social Sciences Book Series

Haymarket Books is proud to be working with Brill Academic Publishers (www.brill.nl) to republish the *Studies in Critical Social Sciences* book series in paperback editions. This peer-reviewed book series offers insights into our current reality by exploring the content and consequences of power relationships under capitalism, and by considering the spaces of opposition and resistance to these changes that have been defining our new age. Our full catalog of *SCSS* volumes can be viewed at www.haymarketbooks.org/category/scss-series.

Series Editor
David Fasenfest, Wayne State University

Editorial Board
Chris Chase-Dunn, University of California—Riverside
G. William Domhoff, University of California—Santa Cruz
Colette Fagan, Manchester University
Martha Gimenez, University of Colorado, Boulder
Heidi Gottfried, Wayne State University
Karin Gottschall, University of Bremen
Bob Jessop, Lancaster University
Rhonda Levine, Colgate University
Jacqueline O'Reilly, University of Brighton
Mary Romero, Arizona State University
Chizuko Ueno, University of Tokyo

The Cuban Revolution as Socialist Human Development

Henry Veltmeyer
and Mark Rushton

Haymarket Books
Chicago, IL

First published in 2012 by Brill Academic Publishers, The Netherlands.
© 2012 Koninklijke Brill NV, Leiden, The Netherlands

Published in paperback in 2013 by
Haymarket Books
P.O. Box 180165
Chicago, IL 60618
773-583-7884
www.haymarketbooks.org

ISBN: 978-1-60846-244-5

Trade distribution:
In the U.S. through Consortium Book Sales, www.cbsd.com
In the UK, Turnaround Publisher Services, www.turnaround-psl.com
In Australia, Palgrave Macmillan, www.palgravemacmillan.com.au
In all other countries by Publishers Group Worldwide, www.pgw.com

Cover design by Ragina Johnson.

This book was published with the generous support of Lannan Foundation and the Wallace Global Fund.

10 9 8 7 6 5 4 3 2 1

Library of Congress Cataloging-in-Publication Data is available.

CONTENTS

Acknowledgments ix
Acronyms xi
List of Tables and Figures xiii

1 Introduction 1

PART I

THE HUMAN DEVELOPMENT PROBLEMATIC

2 Human Development, Capitalism and Socialism in Theory 13
   Human Development: Foundations of an Idea for
      Progressive Change 14
   Bringing in the State: From Socialism to Welfare
      Capitalism 24
   Development as Freedom: Human Development in
      Theory 29
   Cuba's Formulation of the Human Development Concept 32
   Capitalism, the Market and the Nation-State 33
   Human Development and Public Agency 42
   Conclusion 43

3 Human Development in Practice: Reform(ing Capitalism)
   Versus (Socialist) Revolution 45
   Dynamics of Capitalist Development 46
   A Policy Framework for 'Sustainable Human
      Development' 47
   Policy Dynamics of Decentralisation and Popular
      Participation 52
   Cuba, Structural Adjustment and Globalization 57
   Dynamics of Socialist Transition and Development 59
   The Socialist Transition in Cuba 62
   Conclusion 64

4 Socialism, Human Development and the Cuban Revolution 67
   Development Under the Washington Consensus 69
   Beyond the Washington Consensus 69

Socialist Human Development in Practice 72
From the Capitalist Market to a Socialist State, 1959–1960 75
Orthodox Central Planning, 1961–1963 80
The Great Debate, 1963–1964 88
Che Guevara and Human Socialist Development, 1964–1969 92
Return to Orthodoxy in Human Development, 1970–1985 99
The Rectification Campaign, 1986–1990 106
Conclusion 114

PART II

DIMENSIONS OF SOCIALIST HUMAN DEVELOPMENT

5 Socialism as Revolutionary Consciousness: Dynamics
of a Revolution 119
Conceptual and Ethical Foundations of Socialist
Humanism 120
Marx on Capitalism and Human Development 121
The Human Development Debate 123
Socialist Human Development as Freedom 125
Marx and Che on Capitalism, Communism and Human
Development 134
Socialist Human Development as Equality and Social
Justice 139
Shaping of a Revolutionary Consciousness 141
Education for Human Development 143
Conclusion 150

6 Human Development as Social Welfare 151
Development Dimensions of Human Welfare 152
Policy Dynamics of Human Welfare 157
Education, Human Development and the Revolution 158
Egalitarianism in the Form of Income Distribution 159
Inside the Revolution: Health Matters 162
Conclusion 168

7 Socialist Humanism and the Equality Predicament 171
Equality in Theory and Practice 173
Cuba before 1959 176
Policy Dynamics of Poverty Alleviation: January
1959–September 1960 184
Policy Measures for Equality 1960–1985 187

Consolidating the Transition 189
Human Development and Work 192
Human Development at Work: Egalitarianism as a
    Socialist Work Ethic 194
Gender Matters: Equality at Issue 196
Revolution and the Racial Divide 200
The Urban-Rural Divide.. 204
Conclusion 205

8 Socialist Human Development
   as Freedom.. 209
   Development as Freedom 210
   Freedom as Emancipation 214
   People's Power in the Cuban Socialist State 217
   Institutional Dynamics of National Politics 220
   Beyond Elections: Debating Democracy and
      Democracy in Cuba.. 221
   The CDR: Security versus Freedom 225
   Civil Society, the State and Democratic Politics....................... 227
   Democracy as Freedom.. 230
   El Barrio and the Dynamics of Participation and Local
      Development 232
   Conclusion 233

9 In Solidarity: A Fundamental Principle of Socialist
   Humanism 237
   Democracy as Social Solidarity... 238
   Solidarity within the Revolution 242
   International Solidarity: Human Development as the
      Export of Human Capital 243
   La Patria Es Humanidad: Internationalism as a Reservoir
      of Socialist Values 247
   Conclusion 251

PART III

A SOCIALIST ISLAND IN A SEA OF CAPITALISM

10 Human Development in an Era of Globalization 255
    Cuba in the Vortex of a Crisis: The Revolution
       Under Siege 256
    Grappling with Inequality 262

Public Action Dynamics of Human Development
in a Crisis.. 266
Freedom and Democracy in a Crisis.. 270
Social Participation and Local Development in an
Era of Neoliberal Globalization... 273
Conclusion... 275

11 Continuity and Change: The Revolution in the New
Millennium... 277
Holding the Line on Socialism... 278
Advances, Virtues and Vices... 281
Challenges of the 'Post-Special Period'....................................... 285
Economic Reforms and Human Development Matters............. 295
Income-Based Social Welfare... 297
The Scope of Raul's Economic Reforms..................................... 299
Contradictions and Problems, Options and Solutions 310
Culture as a Pillar of the Revolution: Critics Within
and Without 313
Fidel Castro on Revolutionary Morality and Education............ 314
Socialist Consciousness and the Battle of Ideas......................... 317
Conclusion... 320

12 Conclusion 321
Human Development Dynamics of Capitalism
and Socialism 322
Revolution as Human Development 323
Human Development as Revolutionary Consciousness............ 325
Human Development as Social Welfare...................................... 325
Human Development as Equality.. 327
Human Development as Freedom... 328
Human Development as Solidarity... 330
Socialism in an Era of Neoliberal Globalization........................ 331
Socialism and Revolution in the New Millennium 332

Bibliography.. 333
Index 365

ACKNOWLEDGMENTS

The authors would like to acknowledge the financial support of the Social Sciences and Humanities Research Council (SSHRC), which financed the field research for the book. This financial support was provided for a project designed and headed by Joseph Tharamangalam, Adjunct Professor of International Development Studies at Saint Mary's University. Henry Veltmeyer served as co-applicant and chief co-investigator on the project, and Mark Rushton conducted most of the field research in Cuba. The authors would particularly like to acknowledge the support and intellectual contributions of Joseph Tharamangalam in conceiving of the project, which was to compare Cuba and Kerala as cases of successful human development that raised serious questions about the connection between economic growth and social development. We would also like to acknowledge the support of Raúl Delgado Wise, Director of the Doctoral Development Studies Program at the Universidad Autónoma de Zacatecas in providing a research base for the publication project and full access to the magnificent facilities and resources of the program.

The authors would also like to acknowledge the emotional and personal support of their respective life partners, Annette Wright and Veronica Cordero Trejo.

Henry Veltmeyer and Mark Rushton,
Zacatecas
January 2011

ACRONYMS

ANAP	Asociación Nacional de Agricultores Pequeños
CDR	Comité para la Defensa de la Revolución
CEPAL	Comisión Económica para América Latina
CIEM	Centro de Investigaciónes sobre la Economía Mundial
CSO	Civil Society Organisations
CTC	Central de Trabajadores de Cuba
ECLAC	Economic Commission for Latin America and the Caribbean
FMC	Federación de Mujeres Cubanas
IFIs	International Financial Institutions
IIE	Instituto de Investigación Económica
INRA	Instituto Nacional de Reforma Agraria
JUCEPLAN	Junta Central de Planificación
NGO	Non-Governmental Organizations
ONE	National Statistics Office (Oficina Nacional de Estadísticas)
OPP	Organismos de Poder Popular
PCC	Partido Comunista de Cuba
PNUD	Programa de Nacionas Unidas en Desarrollo
PRSP	Poverty Reduction Strategy Paper
PWC	Post-Washington Consensus
SDPE	System of Economic Direction and Planning
SHD	Sustainable Human Development
UJC	Unión de Jóvenes Comunistas
UNCTAD	United Nations Commission on Trade and Development
UNDP	United Nations Development Programme
UNESCO	United Nations Economic, Social and Cultural Organisation

LIST OF TABLES AND FIGURES

Tables

1. Popular Participation and Decentralization in Latin America 53
2. Cuba. Economically Active Population (EAP), by Predominant Relations of Production, 1953 and 1970 63
3. Cuba: Global Social Product (GSP) Growth (1963–1974) 95
4. Economic Growth in Cuba, 1970–1981 95
5. Fiscal Expenditures, % of the National Budget 154
6. Conditions of Human Development (2009) 154
7. Income Distribution, 1995 263
8. Cuba–estimated Real Wages (pesos) 300

Figures

1. Health in Cuba 164
2. Cuban Government Health Spending 167
3. Cuba Real Monthly Wages, 1989–2009 298
4. Cuba GDP Per Capita, 1989–2009 (1989=100.0) 299

CHAPTER ONE

INTRODUCTION

Since the collapse of the Soviet Union and the Eastern Bloc in the early 1990s and the strengthening of the United States' economic blockade, many 'experts' have predicted the imminent or inevitable collapse of the Cuban Revolution. However, defying the conventional wisdom of so many specialists not only has the Cuban Revolution and the socialist regime managed to survive one threat to its existence after another—and the 1990s saw the most serious threat to date—but it successfully tacked to the turbulent winds of change that toppled one socialist regime after another and that brought diverse capitalist regimes to the brink of financial disaster in a global (dis)order of neoliberal globalization. Not only has the Cuban Revolution and the socialist regime survived but its notable and widely acknowledged achievements at the level of social or human development, particularly as regards health, education and international solidarity, continues to baffle analysts and Cuba watchers across the world. On this issue, the begrudging comments of James Wolfensohn, President of the World Bank, acknowledging that 'Cuba has done a great job on education and health' and that 'it does not embarrass me to admit it', are telling. Indeed, he added, 'they [Cubans] should be congratulated on what they've done' (quoted by Lobe 2001).

Yet, as noted by Saney (2003) in his brief but well-informed reconstruction in 'Cuba: A Revolution in Motion', notwithstanding substantive achievements at the level of human development, 'the island continues to be ignored by both development theorists and the technocrats in charge of implementing and administering programs that are supposedly designed to lead to the improved wellbeing of the world's people'. For example, he notes, a 1997 World Bank Discussion Paper, 'Poverty Reduction and Human Development in the Caribbean', contains not a single mention of Cuba. Neither does Eigman (2002) in *Globalization and the Developing Countries* or Gray (2002) in *Latin America: Its Future in the Global Economy* give Cuba even a solitary comment. In *Society, State and Market* (Martinussen,

2004: 230), a widely used text on international development, Cuba warrants one parenthetical remark. In a *New Internationalist* issue on the topic 'The Liberation of Latin America' (May 2003), focused on the region's burgeoning challenges to neoliberalism, Cuba is not discussed at all (May, 2003). And in *The Myth of Development* Oswaldo de Rivero (2001: 183) dismisses Cuba as marginal in today's world.

In opposition to this widely held view this book argues that the Cuban Revolution is far from marginal in today's world and warrants a closer look as a model of socialist human development. A re-reading of the Cuban Revolution from this angle allows us to confront several unresolved issues in the theory of socialist humanism and the notion of *human development* popularized by the United Nations Development Programme (UNDP) as a way of saving capitalism from its internal contradictions. The notion of human development is predicated on capitalism, even though no mention is ever made of it. The concern of the economists at the UNDP and other agencies of international cooperation for development is to give a human face to a capitalist development process that is anything but human—to determine the best policy mix and institutional reforms needed to sustain the process.

It is argued that two features of this model, namely the construction of a socialist ethic (revolutionary consciousness) and popular participation in public policy formulation (people power), were critical factors in Cuba's successful navigation of the turbulent sea of global capitalist development and the survival of the Revolution in the face of unprecedented economic and political challenges. Precise forms and particular conditions of socialist human development, it is argued, explain the survival of the Cuban socialism against all odds, and warrant taking another close look at the history of the Cuban Revolution.

Not only does the recent and current trajectory of the Cuban Revolution challenge the conventional wisdom of bourgeois social science as well as the UNDP's approach to human development, but it highlights the debate surrounding the conditions and instrumentalities needed to achieve human development (e.g. capitalism, a strong and interventionist state versus the free market, privatization and neoliberal prescriptions, production versus distribution). Our brief analysis of the conceptual and ethical foundations of the Cuban Revolution also throws some light on the problem of socialist development—how best to proceed in a project to rebuild socialism in the twenty-first century.

The Cuban Revolution not only offers a different conception of development but it raises questions about the system requirements of this development. The UNDP model of 'sustainable human development' is predicated on the institutionality of the capitalist system, but a review of the Cuban Revolution from a human development perspective suggests that socialism provides a possibly more appropriate institutional and systemic framework for human development. In addition, the Cuban Revolution demonstrates the limitations that external geopolitical and economic conditions and internal material constraints impose on the socioeconomic transformation paths available to countries of the global south.

A review of the history of the Cuban Revolution, and a deconstruction of this history in terms of the notion of *human development*, also point towards the possibilities open to those countries interested in pursuing an alternative development path.

The notion of *human development* was constructed and has been advanced in recent years as a means of saving capitalism from itself—to provide a human face to an otherwise destructive and socially exclusive process of capitalist development. The basic assumption of those who advanced this idea of 'human development' (Amartya Sen, among others) is that it is a desirable and possible condition of an advanced but substantively reformed form of capitalism, the result of balancing the agency of the *market*, the basic motor of economic growth which is regulated in the public interest, with the *state*, the agency assigned the primary responsibility for bringing about a society in which everyone has the opportunity to realize their capabilities, and *civil society*, an amalgam of social organizations that share a concern for progressive change.

Another presupposition of 'human development' is that capitalism provides the essential institutional framework for creating the best form of society and human development. The reason for this, it is argued (or more generally, assumed), is that capitalism is uniquely configured around the idea of *freedom*—the freedom of individuals to pursue their opportunities and advance their own interests in the pursuit of life-enhancing goals or what has been termed 'human flourishing' (Deneulin and Shahani, 2009). But socialism, our argument goes, is predicated on a related but significantly different and somewhat quixotic idea, that of *social equality*, pursued if need be at the expense of freedom defined as the pursuit by individuals of their opportunities and interests. The assumption is that *freedom* is more functional and a more realizable condition for human development than *equality*—that equality is a matter of the opportunities available to individuals for realizing their 'capabilities' rather than a social condition for which governments should assume responsibility. On this the UNDP in its 2010 report is to the point: 'For development to enlarge people's opportunities they need equitable access to these opportunities. Otherwise the choices available to many individuals in society (often, entire sectors) are restricted. We must emphasize that equity should be understood as equal access to opportunities, but not equal results because what one does with one's opportunities is in the sphere of individual initiatives' (PNUD, 2010: Synopsis).[1]

The notion of *human development*—of a human or more humane form of society in which the *social*, i.e. as a condition experienced and shared by all, is not in conflict with human nature—can be traced back to the humanist and rationalist philosophy of the eighteenth century 'enlightenment'—to the ideas of *progress, equality and freedom*, which at the time represented ideas in conflict with the real world, an ideal state at odds with the reality lived by almost everyone in society except for the landed gentry, the economically dominant class of rentierist aristocrats, and those that provided for and serviced this class. Whatever the merits of this view—this notion of human development as (economic) progress, (political) freedom and (social) equality is highly contested and can be viewed as eurocentrist[2]—it is possible to trace out the itinerary of this notion of human development in terms of the evolution of these ideas, first, as *ideology* (liberalism-freedom and socialism-equality) and then, in the wake of the second world war, as *theory* viz. a synthesis of these ideas as 'development', understood (at first) as *economic growth*; then as *social welfare* or '(in a

---

[1] Author's translation.
[2] See inter alia Alain Gresh, "Thermopylae to the Twin Towers: The West's Selective Reading of History," *Le Monde Diplomatique*, January 2009. Also Jack Goody (2006) *The Theft of History*. Cambridge University Press; Frank, André Gunder (1998) *Reorient: Global Economy in the Asian Age*. Berkeley: University of California Press; Hobson, John M. (2004) *The Eastern Origins of Western Civilisation*. Cambridge University Press.
[3] Classical or economic liberalism is most often associated with Adam Smith, who conceived of the free play of market forces as the ideal that made the pursuit of individual interest compatible with the greater good of society. Liberalism as a specifically named ideology was associated with a late 18th Century movement towards democracy and self-government. It included ideas of self-determination and the primacy of the individual as the fundamental unit of law, politics and economy. In the 20th

socialist context) as *an equality of condition*; and then as *freedom* (human development).³

In the post World War II context, development was initially conceived of in economic terms as 'progress'—to be precise: economic growth measured in terms of an annual increase in total output (GDP). But in the 1970s, in the changed context of a global capitalist production crisis and the insistent demands of those on the periphery of the capitalist system for revolutionary change, the idea of development was refashioned, and the associated project reconstructed, in a more integrated form encompassing the social dimension. In these terms the idea of development was given a facelift as *equality*, transmuted in development theory as 'growth with equity', and *freedom,* understood in *social liberal* terms, i.e. not as emancipation from oppressive social and institutional structures (a socialist or the Marxist conception) but as a universal right pertaining to each and all individuals. In these terms, and on the foundation of Amartya Sen's conception of *development as freedom* (Sen, 1999), a team of economists associated with the UNDP⁴ constructed the Human Development Index (HDI) as a comparative international measure of human development, and a model of sustainable human development (SHD) as a guide to government policy.

This SHD model was constructed under conditions of an unresolved capitalist production crisis; the fiscal crisis of many welfare-development states; a counterrevolution in development thought and practice;

Century liberalism took various new forms in relation to the development problematic. What is now identified as 'neoliberalism' the theorists and ideologues of the Pelerin Society raised self-interest to a social virtue, making equity as conceived within the framework of the market the dubious equivalent of equality. Around the same time a current of economic thought that we can now identify as social liberalism took form in the context of the Great Depression and the failure of free market capitalism. The defining feature of social liberalism is the belief that capitalism needs to be regulated in the public interest of greater equity and social welfare. These two currents of liberal thought were in contention throughout the early period of development economics but neoliberalism, in the context of a neoconservative counterrevolution to the advance of the welfare-development state eventually emerged victorious in the form of a Washington Consensus on correct macroeconomic policy. However, social liberalism, which in the1970s took form as the Basic Needs paradigm, came back with the idea of human development and a post-Washington Consensus on the need to 'bring the state back in'.

⁴ Lead consultants for the WDR-90 included Amartya Sen, Gustav Ranis, Francis Stewart, Keith Griffin, Meghnad Desai, Azis Khan, Paul Streeten and Mahesh Patel.

⁵ On the Pelerin Society—a neoliberal thought collective—and a complex of Washington-based institutions and policy forums such as the Heritage Foundation see

and a clarion call from the diverse altars of neoconservative (and neoliberal) thought[5] for a 'new world order' in which the forces of 'economic freedom' (the free market, private enterprise) would be released from the regulatory constraints of the welfare-development state. But the economists at the UNDP did not share the neoliberal concept of freedom held by the architects and guardians of this new world order. Even so, like most everyone in the development community at the time, they succumbed to the Washington Consensus on the need to downsize the state and reduce its role in the development process so as to let the market operate freely.

The 1980s saw the implementation of a policy agenda shaped to the perceived requirements of the new world order, which is, first of all, to achieve macroeconomic balance in terms of controlling inflation and balancing international payments and the national accounts; and then, in order to 'get prices right' and activate the accumulation process, to privatize ownership of the means of production, deregulate the product, capital and labour markets, and liberalize the circuits of investment capital and trade in goods (Bulmer-Thomas, 1996).

To all intents and purposes, after several decades of active resistance in the form of organized labour and national liberation movements, capitalist development in the form of neoliberal globalization was back on track in the early 1980s. But by 1989, after only six years of experimentation with neoliberal policies the process of capitalist development and globalization under the Washington Consensus was already in jeopardy, threatened by the emergence of new social movements that threatened to mobilize the mounting forces of resistance against the Washington Consensus and the exceedingly high social cost of adjustment to the new world order. After barely six years of experimentation with these and other neoliberal policies it was evident that they were economically dysfunctional and politically destabilizing, generating, as they did, an ungovernable level of social discontent, protest and resistance. The force of this growing resistance against the inordinate concentration of wealth at one extreme of income distribution and widespread poverty at the other led to a rethinking of the new economic model—a recognition that policymakers had 'gone too far' (in the direction of the free market) and need to 'bring the state back in' in order to establish a more socially inclusive and sustainable form of development (Ocampo, 1998, 2006, 2007).

It was not until the 1990s, with the acknowledgement by policy advisers (Rodrik, 1997; Stiglitz, 1998) and development practitioners that they had 'gone too far' in the direction of the free market, that conditions became available for the implementation of a SHD strategy based on a more pragmatic (socially inclusive, equitable and participatory, and thus sustainable) form of neoliberalism. One condition was the recognition that there was a 'direct correspondence between the advance of globalization, neoliberalism, and the advance of poverty, social inequality, social inequity' (PNUD, 2010: xv).[6] As the UNDP's 2010 Human Development Report on Latin America and the Caribbean concludes:

> The most explosive contradictions...are given because the advance of globalization marches hand in hand with the advance of poverty and social polarization. It is undeniable that the 1980s and 1990s [were] the creation of an abysmal gap between wealth and poverty (ibid.).

The widespread recognition within policy-making and academic circles over the past two decades that a neoliberal form of free market capitalist development is both economically dysfunctional and politically unsustainable, led to diverse attempts to 'move beyond the Washington consensus'—to construct a 'new policy agenda' and an institutional framework conducive to a more sustainable form of 'human development' (Craig and Porter 2006; Sandbrook, Edelman, Heller and Teichman, 2007; Ocampo, 1998, 2006, 2007).

With this new policy agenda, under conditions of a growing disenchantment with neoliberalism, CEPAL launched its neostructuralist program of 'development from within' (ECLAC, 1990; Sunkel, 1993) while the UNDP launched its SHD model, with reference to proactive 'international cooperation', a facilitative policy framework (administrative decentralization, a new social policy), the agency of grassroots or community-based organization, and the support of nongovernmental organizations. Toward the end of the decade and into the new millennium, by diverse accounts, the architects of the PWC could report evidence of some success. In a number of countries the rate of extreme poverty is on the decline, in some cases (Chile, for example; Brazil for another) by as much as 40% since 2000, leading policymakers at a major international policy review in Beijing (IFPI, 2007) to report

---

Mirowski and Plehwe (2009). On this call for a 'new world order' and its transmutation into the idea of 'globalization' see Petras and Veltmeyer (2001).

[6] Author's own translation. This UNDP document is only available in Spanish.

considerable global and regional progress towards achieving the first MDG—to cut the rate of extreme poverty by 50% by 2015.

At the level of ideology and politics the forces of resistance against the neoliberal agenda of 'structural reform' in national policy were blunted or divided, drawn away from the antisystemic social movements and their agenda for revolutionary change, channelled into the system of democratic electoral politics or the new development paradigm of local development and empowering the poor to help themselves,

At the turn into the new millennium, neoliberalism as an economic doctrine and an ideology used to inform policy was in serious decline—and indeed more than a few have written it off as dead or dying, paving the way for a new post-neoliberal era and the formation of a post-neoliberal state.[7] In many countries, especially in South America, the overtly neoliberal regimes of the 1990s—Menem in Argentina, Fujimori in Peru, Cardoso in Brazil, Sixto Durán Ballén and Jamil Mahuad in Ecuador—had given way to more pragmatic neoliberal regimes on the centre-left—neoliberal in macroeconomic policy but committed to a new poverty-targeted social policy as prescribed under the post-Washington Consensus on the need for a more inclusive and sustainable form of human development and a social democratic post-neoliberal state.[8]

After a decade of adjustments to the neoliberal policy agenda, these forces of resistance that did indeed halt or slow down implementation

---

[7] On the proposed or likely form of this 'social democratic developmental state' see Sandbrook, Edelman, Heller and Teichman (2007); also Andrew (2003) and ANC 2007).

[8] Tania Li (2007: 178) argues that 'social democracy is a response to capitalism: no capitalism, no social democracy.' But she also argues that the intervention agents of the state are unable to resolve the contradictions of capitalism or mediate its effects, leading to unresolved tensions or the inability to establish human society, to establish more than a human face (the appearance of freedom and equity) to a fundamentally inequitable society in which some are much more free than others. Sandbrook et al. (2007), however, maintain that capitalism is a necessary structural precondition for an 'equitable social democracy', that social democracy is a particular form of capitalism based on an active civil society and an interventionist state that 'can both manage the delicate trade-offs of class compromises and extend the reach of the public domain without compromising its autonomy' (2007: 91). Such a state, they add, has been severely challenged by neoliberal globalization, but, on the basis of the post-Washington Consensus, social-democratic regimes can 'tame' these challenges, giving countries a competitive advantage because of better infrastructure and a healthier and more productive workforce. In effect, the authors seek to provide a blueprint for an emerging post-neoliberal state. The centre-left regimes that have captured state power in Latin America over the past decade are oriented in this direction.

of the neoliberal agenda, and in some contexts force a change of government, had been demobilized, often under policies pursued by regimes that were overtly anti-neoliberal and oriented towards the political Left. However, with the exception of the Chávez regime in Venezuela—and, of course, Cuba, which had been and still was on a socialist path towards national development—all of these regimes were and are committed towards reforming rather than abandoning the capitalist system, reforms in the direction of social democracy and sustainable human development, i.e. capitalism and structural adjustment with a human face (Esping-Andersen, 2006; Sandbrook, Edelman, Heller, and Teichman, 2007).

This brief theoretically stylized reconstruction of capitalist development in Latin America describes a pattern that can be traced out in most of the region. But it clearly does not implicate Cuba, whose pattern of development in the same historic context has taken a different systemic form.

It was not until the early nineteenth century that the idea began to emerge that human beings could themselves refashion society. It was only with the Industrial Revolution and the emergence of the modern working class that critics of society began to think in terms of a human transformation of social life. And it was with these developments that the idea of socialism from below emerged. But at the start, socialism was largely utopian, elitist and antidemocratic in character. It was only through decades of working class struggle that socialism took the form of a movement devoted to *the self-and national emancipation of the oppressed and exploited*. It was in this sense, rather than in alignment with 'actually existing socialism' in the USSR and the socialist bloc, that the Cuban revolutionaries in the 1960s turned towards socialism as a mobilizing ideology and to Marxist theory.

With reference to this ideological and theoretical turn it is possible to argue—and we do so in this study—that (i) the Cuban Revolution as it was constructed and unfolded over time represents a socialist form of *human development*; (ii) the UNDP model of sustainable human development (and the underlying notion of 'development as freedom') is based on an individualistic social liberal view of humanity and society; and (iii) socialism provides a more effective and sustainable form of human development than capitalism—a thesis that requires us to view the 'human' not as an abstract idea or ideal, a projected goal, but as an effective social condition; and to reconceptualize human development in systemic terms (secure its system requirements) and also to trace out the development path taken by Cuba over the past five decades under changing conditions.

To argue this point this study traces out the development path taken by Cuba since 1959 to date, with an emphasis on the conditions and diverse dimensions of human development; and to assess the achievements and the shortfalls—the pitfalls experienced by the regime and the country on this path towards human socialist development, and its strategic response to these pitfalls.

PART I

THE HUMAN DEVELOPMENT PROBLEMATIC

CHAPTER TWO

HUMAN DEVELOPMENT, CAPITALISM AND SOCIALISM IN THEORY

The argument advanced in this study is that the Cuban Revolution should be understood as *human development*—that it represents a socialist model of human development. This idea is supported by two propositions, one relating to the challenge presented by the collapse of the Soviet model and the disappearance of the 'actually existing' socialist bloc in the Soviet Union and Eastern Europe, the other focused on specific differences between *human development* as conceived by the economists associated with the UNDP (i.e. presupposing the institutionality of the capitalism system) and in its socialist form as represented by Cuba. The first proposition is that certain features of the Cuban Revolution related to the project of creating a more humane form of society, a more human form of development than capitalism, explains the survival of the Cuban Revolution against all odds. In short, it is argued that the survival of Cuba's socialist project can best be understood in terms of the active engagement of Cubans in the revolutionary process of building a socialist society—what we might well term 'people's power'—a fundamental institution of the Cuban Revolution. This aspect of the Cuban Revolution can also be understood in terms of the notion of 'public action' popularized in the context of instituting a socialist form of human development in the Indian state of Kerala (Tharamangalam, 2008).

The second proposition advanced is that the received notion of 'human development' as constructed by the UNDP, and the associated measurement methodology, is entirely but falsely predicated on the culture and institutionality of the capitalist system, and thus unable to grasp the superior socialist form of human development. Capitalism, it is argued, cannot be reformed so as to generate and support human development as a social condition available to all—*human development* as we conceive of it in conditions of freedom, equality and solidarity. This is because the social structure of the capitalist system, whatever its specific form under conditions of private property in the means of social production will necessarily take shape as a class system that precludes human development as a generalized social condition. Thus, we take issue with the UNDP notion and associated model of sustainable human development. It is argued that the system requirements of human development are provided by socialism, not capitalism. In this connection we use the case of Cuba as a pointer towards an alternative genuine (i.e. socialist) form of human development.

To provide the scaffolding with which to construct this argument this chapter reviews various bodies of literature relevant to human development both as regards to capitalism, the dominant institutional or systemic framework implicit in the prevailing discourse on human development, and socialism, the systemic alternative presented by the Cuban Revolution.

Human development has a different meaning in both systemic and institutional contexts. The aim of the literature review is to establish: (i) the itinerary of the HD idea in its historical context; (ii) the strategic and structural dimensions of the development process, with regard to (iii) the dynamics of action and policy associated with the institutions of the state, civil society and the state; (iv) the difference between HD in one systemic context and the other—the policy agenda and institutional framework needed to move forwards, and the system requirements of HD; (vi) the theory and the ideology behind the UNDP's conception of HD; and, with reference to Cuba, (vi) the basic elements of a *SHD strategy*, and the form and conditions of its implementation—to construct the theoretical model, if any, used as a guide for this strategy based on what, with reference to the Kerala model of human development, we choose to term 'public action' and as a framework for critically assessing the achievements and its deficits in Cuba's approach to SHD.

Human Development: Foundations of an Idea for Progressive Change

Human development as an idea evolved under changing conditions in diverse historic contexts, and can be schematized in the form of ten 'moments', which can be reconstructed as follows:

- Its philosophical origins in the eighteenth century Enlightenment (the so-called 'age of reason') and its ideas of *progressive change—liberty equality and fraternity (solidarity)*[1] —and the reformulation of these ideas by Karl Marx in his early writings.
- Construction of two ideologies—*liberalism* and *socialism*—used politically (in the nineteenth century) to mobilize the forces of progressive change in two different directions, that of freedom and equality.
- The construction (in the 1930s and 1940s) of a *welfare state* under conditions of a crisis in the system of global capitalist production and the emergence of a socialist regime in the USSR.
- The declaration (in 1945) of the UN Charter of fundamental human rights, including the inalienable right to happiness and the freedom from want—from the incapacity of each and all to meet their basic physical and spiritual needs.
- The formation of a developmental state, in the post-World War context of the Bretton Woods capitalist-liberal world order (1944–70), with 'development' conceived as a fusion of the ideas of 'progress', 'equality' and 'freedom'.
- The formation (in the 1960s) of a socialist state in Cuba founded on the idea of 'equality' as an essential social condition of human development—the ethical and conceptual foundation of a socialist system.
- Construction (in the 1970s) of a paradigm in which 'development' is conceived as overcoming a deficit in the capacity of society to meet the basic needs of all of its members, and as state-led social reform, a strategy ('growth with equity') designed to spread the wealth—redistribute market-generated incomes at the extremes of wealth and poverty, improve access to productive resources such as land, credit and technology, and improve conditions as well as universalise access to essential government services in the areas of welfare, health and education.
- Construction (in the 1980s) of the 'human development' concept by economists associated with the UNDP and its institutionalization in the form of Sustainable Human Development (HSD).

---

[1] These ideas, as Marx pointed out, were abstracted from the conditions of a class struggle that gave rise to them, reappearing simply or fundamentally as a conflict over competing ideas.

- Implementation (in the 1990s) throughout Latin America, and elsewhere, of a strategy based on a policy of democratic decentralization, participatory development and good governance, and a 'sustainable human development' model constructed on the basis, and within the institutional framework, of capitalism reformed in the direction of social liberalism and the agency of a regulated market and a proactive state;
- A 'strategic public action' response within the Cuban Revolution to a major production crisis in 'the special period' (the early 1990s) and the challenge that it presented to Cuba's socialist human development model.
- Emergence (in the new millennium) of a Latin American movement towards the 'socialism of the 21st century' based on a new culture 'that promotes unity around values such as solidarity [and] humanism…and turns its back on the view that hunger for profit and the laws of the market are the guiding principles of human activity' (Harnecker, 2010).

The Eighteenth Century Enlightenment and the Idea of Progress

The eighteenth century was a crucible of momentous revolutionary change—in the structure of society, in the mode of production and technological capacity, the structure of social and political relations, and in the way in which people understood themselves and the world. It saw the emergence of an intellectual revolution (the Enlightenment), with major centres in France and Scotland. Hitherto, explanation of the nature of the world had been left to the Church, to priests who would interpret the designs of the deity for humankind, and set for humanity rules of behaviour that reflected and gave form to God's will. The theorists of the eighteenth century 'Enlightenment', however, advanced the contrary 'idea' that God did not make 'man' in 'his' own image but to the contrary, that Man made God in the image of the most essential of human qualities and 'capabilities' (to use Sen's term for the 'human potential'), projecting these qualities and capabilities onto a supernatural being and denying for themselves precisely those qualities and capabilities that define and mark the human condition.

What defined and marked the Enlightenment was a rationalist humanist philosophy based on the belief in the power of the human mind, by means of reasoning combined with observation, to understand the world, i.e. to reduce it to laws that explain its inner workings, and to change it viz. the rational principles of freedom and equality that present in ideal form the human essence—what it means to be human. However, together with the idea of fraternity or solidarity, the rallying cries for revolutionary change in France, these ideas, as Marx himself had noted, did not result from the reasoning of eighteenth century humanists, or in a struggle for self-realization of these ideas (the idea of 'progress', or, as Hegel would have it, 'freedom').[2] These ideas simply (or complexly) gave form to aspirations for change in different categories of the oppressed population, an exploited mass of humanity, and their demands for 'progress', to emancipate themselves from the chains of class rule.

Essentially the idea of freedom gave an idealized form to the struggle of serfs to free themselves from the exploitative relations and oppressive weight of serfdom re the customary obligations and rents due to the landowning class; the struggle of intellectuals for the freedom of thought…from the oppressive weight of religious 'authority' and tradition; the political struggle to participate in the construction of laws by which human affairs were governed; and, above all, the struggle of an incipient bourgeoisie of merchants and manufacturers to free their enterprise from the oppressive weight of feudalism, toll payments and taxes used, together with the rents collected from tenant farmers and serfs, to maintain a life of positive privilege for the upper crust of 'society' in the first and second estates—'the haves', as conceived by the moral philosophers of the Enlightenment.

This struggle for emancipation, for freedom and equality, led to the formulation of ideas about an improved form of 'society', transmuted into 'universals', ideas without reality or ideal state of human nature, essential reference points for a far-reaching critique of existing society with conditions that are in conflict with who people really are—that violated what Marx, in his Early Works some decades later, would term the 'human essence'.

However, these ideas—the ideal 'solution' to the human development predicament, as Marx would come to argue—do not emerge until the essential conditions of their realization are at hand. Thus, the *idea of progress*, of a society freed from want, unable to meet the needs of all its members, did not acquire any force, until the technological

---

[2] A contemporary reformulation of the dialectic of the 'idea of freedom'—which, according to Hegel, achieves its consummate form in the modern democratic state—was given by Frances Fukyama in his interpretation of the end of the Cold War and the 'triumph' of Western (capitalist) democracy as the 'end of history' (Fukuyama, 1992).

advances of the industrial revolution and early capitalism made such 'progress' both conceivable and possible. The idea of liberty, for example, did not acquire the force that it would have in 1879 as a rallying cry for revolutionary change until the material and social conditions for its emergence were at hand, namely an emerging bourgeoisie representing new forces of production pushing to expand but fettered by the existing semi-feudal system of property relations. As for the idea of *equality*, conditions for its 'realization' would take another revolution (a socialist transformation of society and the state), the objective (material, structural) and subjective (social and political) conditions of which would take another century or more to materialize—1917 in the case of Russia, 1959 in the case of Cuba.

Liberalism in Theory and Ideology

The idea of freedom was given both an economic and a political form in the 19th century—economic in terms of the freedom of individuals to establish enterprises and engage in economic activity, and political in terms of the 'battle for democracy'—for replacing the institution of monarchy and a ruling class with rule of the common people, engaging men of property and substance, stakeholders in the responsibility of lawmaking and government, the freedom to participate in the process of electing. Democracy or political 'freedom' was won in France and the US as the result of a violent social revolution; in England and Holland democracy was the outcome of a compromise reached between the defenders of the old order and the champions of the new. In 1848 the 'battle of democracy', or the struggle of the bourgeoisie to capture the state apparatus from the landed gentry, spread over Europe, but for the most part the forces of democratic change had not sufficiently matured, and the bourgeoisie was too weak, to establish the parameters of a democratic capitalist state. It would take decades of further struggle to establish democracy and the rule of 'law', and to extend the suffrage, the right to vote, from men of substance and property to other sectors of the population—to the *demos* or 'the people'.

Socialism as Utopia and as Science

The term 'socialism' made its appearance in print in England in 1827. Five years later, the term was used for the first time in a French publication. It is no accident that the socialist idea—and the socialist movement—first appeared in England and France. For socialism to a large extent was a product of two revolutions, one (the industrial) rooted in England and the other (the democratic) in France, the first associated with the origins of capitalist development, the latter with the construction of a modern bourgeois-capitalist state.

The French Revolution of 1789–1799 involved the most massive popular struggles yet seen in history. Rooted in popular hatred of oppressive class rule by a 'society' of oligarchs and landed aristocrats, and the institution of monarchy, the Revolution unfolded via the agency of the masses of poor people uniting under the banner of 'liberty, equality and fraternity'. Beginning as a rebellion against the abuses of the landed nobility and the monarchy, the political institution that represented their vested interests, the Revolution grew into a massive challenge to all forms of oppressive authority in the *ancien regime*, including the priesthood, the higher echelons of which in any case were part of the ruling class, the priests and factory owners. Initially, the battle against the nobility and monarchy unified large sections of society, even the merchants and other elements of an emerging bourgeoisie. But as the Revolution advanced, a new ruling group tried to halt the process in order to maintain their grossly unequal system of property and power. As a result, the popular movement divided into conservative and revolutionary camps, the first seeking an accommodation with and the restoration of legitimate 'authority' (monarchy, churchmen, men of property and substance), the second pushing for radical change in the direction of creating a new society of free individuals in conditions equal for all.

In the conservative camp were those who saw freedom simply in terms of the freedom to own property. In the revolutionary camp were those who represented the Paris poor and who recognized that freedom was impossible without equality; that it was meaningless to talk of liberty if this was confined to the right of some men and women to starve to death while others grew rich off the labour of others. As the radical leader Jacques Roux put it at the height of the French Revolution in 1793: 'Liberty is no more than an empty shell when one class of men is allowed to condemn another to starvation without any measures being taken against them'. And, Roux added, 'equality is also an empty shell when the rich, by exercising their economic monopolies, have the power of life or death over other members of the community' (McNally, 1997).

Out of the French Revolution there emerged the socialist idea that *democracy and freedom require a society of equals—a condition of social equality*. Unlike the English liberals and twentieth century socialists the French radicals recognized that genuine freedom presupposed the liberty of all to participate equally in producing and sharing the wealth of society. They understood that if some had the unequal right to own and monopolize land, wealth or factories, then others might just as unequally be condemned to a life of drudgery, misery and poverty.

But a society of equality arguably requires a state of abundance. As long as economic life remained relatively backward, equality would only mean the common hardship of shared poverty. By the same token, it could be argued—and was by the liberal reformers of capitalist development in the 1970s—that a healthy and thriving popular democracy requires a state of prosperity in which the basic needs of people can be satisfied. Thus, without a certain level of economic development, the revolutionary demand for liberty and equality remained utopian. It was only with the enormous economic development unleashed by capitalism and the industrial revolution that a socialist society based upon equality and abundance became a realistic possibility—at least this was the view of Marx and Engels in opposition to the 'utopian socialists'.

The Industrial Revolution at the beginnings of capitalist development in England conjures up images of dark and dirty textile mills, of ten-year-old children labouring in coal mines, of women and men working 12 and 14-hour days—in short, of suffering and misery. This image was founded on facts in the real world. The industrial revolution that swept Britain, beginning in the last quarter of the eighteenth century, meant a massive dislocation in social life: old communities were destroyed; people were forced off the land, replacing the tyranny of serfdom with the tyranny of factory labour and one tyrant (the landlord) with another (the factory owner or capitalist); industrial diseases multiplied; hunger, poverty and illness spread; and life expectancy actually fell. At the same time, several ingredients of capitalist development held out the prospect of an end to these ills—or at least an improvement in socioeconomic conditions. The new technology and machinery of production that developed, offered the possibility of sharply reducing drudgery and toil and of massively increasing the production of wealth so as to drastically reduce if not eliminate poverty.

Of course, in reality the industrial revolution or industrial capitalism did no such thing. Rather than leading to an improvement in the conditions of labour, capitalism and the new industry were used to increase the fortunes of a few—the bourgeoisie or the new industrial capitalist class. Nonetheless, some writers saw in the industrial revolution an enormous potential for improving the human condition. Even some well-intentioned bankers and factory owners came to believe that the forces of the industrial revolution should be harnessed to serve human ends. Many of these become early advocates of what has become known as 'utopian socialism'.

Britain's best-known utopian socialist was the cotton manufacturer Robert Owen. Like most of the early socialists drawn from the capitalist class, Owen did not call for a mass democratic restructuring of society. For Owen, the working class was a pathetic and pitiful group. Owen's socialism was based on an appeal to the self-interest or morality of wealthy leaders of business and government, to persuade them to improve the wretched conditions of the labouring masses. In this respect, Owen was similar to two early French utopian socialists—Henri Saint-Simon and Charles Fourier. Saint-Simon was a real estate speculator turned banker who rose to great wealth in the decades after the French Revolution. Fascinated by the enormous potential of science and technology, Saint-Simon began to argue the case for a 'socialist' society that would eliminate the disorderly aspects of capitalism—restore 'order' within 'progress' or, as Auguste Comte, his secretary and later founder of Sociology in the tradition of the 'positivist philosophy', would have it, 'progress within order'. Saint-Simon's 'socialism' was decidedly anti-democratic and decidedly non-socialistic in the modern sense of a classless society of free and equal individuals). He did not envisage an expansion of human rights and freedoms, the defining feature and operating principle of liberalism as ideology and the contemporary notion of 'human development' as constructed by Sen and Haq. Instead, he hoped for a planned and modernized industrial society ruled over by an international committee of bankers. In some respects, Saint-Simon anticipated the development of state capitalism. He looked forward to a capitalist system in which industry would be owned and directed by a government made up of scientists, managers and financiers.

The 'socialism' of Charles Fourier, a self-taught eccentric, had more to commend it but suffered from two main defects. First, he dismissed the potential of modern industry for bringing into being a society of abundance and looked nostalgically for a return to preindustrial conditions of life. In this sense, he was a 'conservative', who tended to idealize or romanticize the past, viewing it as stable, bound together by social bonds of mutual obligation and respect, if not idyllic.

Secondly, Fourier looked not to the masses of working people but to enlightened rulers to usher in the socialist utopia. He spent his time drawing up rigid blueprints for the new society and sent copies to rulers like the Czar of Russia and the President of the United States.

Indeed this is the common thread that runs through the outlook of all the early utopian socialists. Each looked to some well-intentioned members of the ruling class to bring about a socialist transformation of society. Each rejected the notion that socialism could only be achieved democratically—through the mass action of working people. For this reason, all their views can be described as variants of 'socialism from above'—a view in which the masses of people are mere playthings of an enlightened elite who will change society in the interests of the masses of people. As the historian of socialism, George Lichtheim, put it: 'French socialism, at the start, was the work of men who had no thought of overturning society, but wished to reform it, by enlightened legislation if possible. This is the link between Robert Owen, Charles Fourier, and Henri de Saint-Simon' (McNally, 1997).

Utopian socialism was conceived of as an enlightened reform of capitalism, i.e. it was not socialism but a reformed capitalist system. In this system the means of production were not socialized but left in private hands. There was, however, a revolutionary doctrine of socialism during this period. Out of the defeat of the popular struggles of the French Revolution, one far-sighted group of rebels centered on Gracchus Babeuf developed a communist perspective. Babeuf and his followers believed that true democracy could only be constructed on the basis of socializing the ownership of wealth. But they could see no way of winning a majority of society to support their communist program. As they saw it, the masses of working people sought little else than protection of their own private property—their plot of land or their workshop. They showed little interest in a socialist transformation of society. For this reason, Babeuf—and his follower, Adolphe Blanqui—could only conceive of a revolution made by a minority, a revolutionary vanguard motivated by (in the words of Che Guevara some hundred and twenty years later) the 'love of humanity' and committed to bringing about a new world of a communist society.

It was Karl Marx, together with his comrade in arms Frederic Engels, who would formulate the idea of socialism as it evolved in the twentieth century—as the abolition of private property in the means of production and as a society of equals, under conditions of human development (society organized as a means of realizing the full potential of each human being, i.e. in conditions of freedom and equality), a society constructed not by an enlightened elite but by mass action—a social revolution constructed not in 'un golpe' through an assault on the state, but in due course via the agency of 'public action', a combination of actions taken by the government and an actively mobilized people.

Socialism as Human Development: Marx in His Early Works

Under capitalist relations of production, Marx argued in the Philosophical and Economics Manuscripts of 1844, the worker is separated from the 'human essence', which is to say, from (i) the product of his own labour, which is appropriated by the capitalist, who stands over him as an alien being to whom he must pay homage; (ii) labour itself, as a process of human development in which under certain conditions (freedom and equality) he is able to actualise and give form to his capacity to produce things of intrinsic and use value to himself and others; (iii) his own nature or 'species-being', which dictates a relation of solidarity with his fellow human beings who share this nature (Marx, 1967).

In the capitalist system the worker works at the behest and under the control of the capitalist, who profits from the labour of others under conditions that impoverish the worker. Capitalist production is designed not to meet the material and spiritual needs of people but for private profit. Labour is the source of society's wealth but it is appropriated by the capitalist and the worker is alienated in the labour process.

The institutional basis of this system is private property in the means of production, which accords the capitalist the right to profit from the labour of others—to dispose of the social product in his own interest rather than meeting the needs of others. In this system, capital, the sum total of society's wealth, is the product of collective labour—of working people—but it appears and takes form as an alien force turned against the creators of this wealth.

Under capitalism workers represent the practical negation (alienation) of the human essence. In philosophical terms, alienated labour represents a fundamental conflict between what is and what ought to be—between the *human* condition in which people are in harmony with their own nature (in conditions of freedom and equality) and the *social* condition (in conditions of alienation and exploitation—the appropriation by capital of the product of labour). This conflict, Marx theorized,³ would generate forces of revolutionary change: an alliance between the 'proletariat', the practical negation of the human essence, and 'philosophy', its theoretical affirmation (representing the idea of freedom). In this revolutionary alliance the workers would 'emancipate themselves' to become 'men' (fully human).

In 1844, Marx came to a different understanding of the dialectic of human development and social revolution (i.e. the idea of freedom in its inevitable advance).⁴ First, his theoretical reflection on a strike of Silesian weavers had led him to the conclusion that in the case of these weavers workers were not just driven by blind material necessity but that their action demonstrated a theoretical awareness of the 'reason' for the class struggle (to resolve the conflict between 'what is' and what 'ought to be'—between the human and the social condition). That is, the proletariat represented the 'identical subject-object' of history—both and at once the practical negation and the theoretical affirmation of the human condition.⁵

Bringing in the State: From Socialism to Welfare Capitalism

Capitalism is an historic succession of social formations and class systems used to expand the forces of production. As such capitalism is predicated on, and requires for its development (capitalist development of the forces of production), four fundamental institutions, each a pillar of capitalist development: (1) *private property* in the means of production, a legal institution used to confirm the rights and prerogatives of private ownership; (2) *the market*, an economic institution used as a mechanism for distributing the social product, allocating to

---

³ In the 'Introduction' to his 'Critique of the [Hegel's] Philophy of Right' (Marx, [1843] 1967).

⁴ The theory of this 'dialectic of the idea' is formulated most assuredly in the philoshophic tradition of German idealism. Kant presented the dialecic of human reason as a mental process—a movement that takes place entirely in thought. Hegel (in the Phenomenology of the Mind) reconstructs the same dialectic but as an historical process. Marx, it has been argued 'stood Hegel on his head' by arguing that the real world is not the manifest form of the 'idea' (of freedom) but the contrary.

⁵ On this understanding of the idealist problematic (the dialectic of the idea of freedom) governing Marx's 'early works' see Veltmeyer (1978). Veltmeyer follows Althusser in identifying an 'epistemological break' between the idealism of Marx's Early Works and the historical materialist conception of society elaborated in *The German Ideology* and the *Communist Manifesto* and that governed his thinking in his mature writings.

each factor of production (capital, labour, land) its appropriate return; (3) *wage labour*, a social institution used as a mechanism of exchange (labour power for a living wage); and *the State*, a fundamental political institution designed to provide legal security to capital, infrastructure for capitalist development, and an executive committee to administer the affairs of the capitalist class as a whole—to secure and advance the economic interests of this class.

Whereas the capitalist mode of production is based on the labour-capital relation, and the political development process on the society-state relation, the capitalist economic development process is predicated on the relation of the state to the market. However, the structure of this relation is conceived of in different ways. There are, in fact, at least eight different conceptions of this relation, including the Marxist theory that we ourselves in this thesis will use as a heuristic device—to analyze the relations and dynamics of state power used to advance the development process.

The Great Depression and the 'New Deal': Saving Capitalism with Socialism

The propensity of capitalism towards crisis, pointed to by Marx (in his theory of the law for average profits to fall), was evidenced in the crash of the system in 1929 and into the 1930s. Conditions in the aftermath of this crash were such that even the most sanguine proponents of the virtues of free market capitalism were forced to admit that a serious remedy was required to forestall the collapse of the system. And the remedy was state intervention in the form of regulatory control over capital, employment-generating public works and government engineered social(ist) reforms—as well as a mixed economy, a combination of capitalism and socialism. Surendra Patel, for many years Director General of UNCTAD's Technology and Development branch, argued that in this effort to save capitalism from collapse under the weight of its internal contradictions the so-called Western (North American and European) 'capitalist democracies' responded effectively to the clarion call for change by Marx and Engels in their *Communist Manifesto* (Patel, 2004).

As Patel saw it, the *Manifesto*'s demands for revolutionary change, including universal education and welfare, became the reforms that constituted what would take form as *welfare capitalism*, or, as it is better known, *the welfare state* based on a mixed economy, and (in the post world war context) a social pact between labour and capital to the effect that the former would share in the productivity gains of capitalist development. Although it was never promulgated, the Constitution of this welfare capitalist state was elaborated by President Roosevelt, in his 1944 message to the Congress of the US on the State of the Union, in the following terms:

The Second Bill of Rights
January 11, 1944

In our day these economic truths have become accepted as self-evident. We have accepted, so to speak, a second Bill of Rights under which a new basis of security and prosperity can be established for all—regardless of station, race, or creed. Among these are:

- The right to a useful and remunerative job in the industries or shops or farms or mines of the nation;
- The right to earn enough to provide adequate food and clothing and recreation;
- The right of every farmer to raise and sell his products at a return which will give him and his family a decent living;
- The right of every businessman, large and small, to trade in an atmosphere of freedom from unfair competition and domination by monopolies at home or abroad;
- The right of every family to a decent home;
- The right to adequate medical care and the opportunity to achieve and enjoy good health;
- The right to adequate protection from the economic fears of old age, sickness, accident, and unemployment;
- The right to a good education.

All of these rights spell security. And after this war is won we must be prepared to move forward, in the implementation of these rights, to new goals of human happiness and wellbeing.
For unless there is security here at home there cannot be lasting peace in the world
—President Roosevelt, January 11, 1944

It is most unlikely that Roosevelt's proposed Second Declaration of Rights or the Welfare State would have come about were it not for the existence and demonstration effect of socialism in the Soviet Union, as well as the struggles for socialist reform and the pressures exerted by organized labour from within the system, and also the pressures for revolutionary change or socialism arising from the movements of national liberation in the economically backward areas of the declining British Empire.

In any case, the end of World War II created a sort of watershed for the idea of a welfare state as an alternative to socialism that preserved capitalism as an economic system and facilitated its 'development'—a renewed process of capital accumulation based on the active intervention of the State within a new world order, and with it the passing of *Pax Britannica* with *Pax Americana*.[6]

Capitalism and Development as Economic Growth: Keeping the Post-Colonial State in Line

The world order established at Bretton Woods, together with the United Nations system of international organizations and agreements, formed the institutional framework for a new phase of capitalist development—two decades of system-wide rapid economic growth described by some historians as the 'golden age of capitalism' (Marglin and Schor, 1990), and by others as *Pax Americana* or the American Empire.

The fundamental agency of this 'development' no matter how understood was the State, assigned by a new generation of liberal (and some radical) economists and social scientists, and policymakers responsibility for 'welfare' and a process of 'nation-building and economic development'—and, in the economically backward areas of societies emerging from colonial rule (in which market institutions and the capitalist class were weak or non-existsent)—the 'function of capital', namely productive investment, entrepreneurship, enterprise management, and marketing.

Reform versus Revolution? From Economic Growth to Social Development

At first, the idea of progressive change was transmuted into the idea of development understood as economic growth—expansion of the forces of production measured as an annual increase in output. A new academic discipline of development economics came into being to provide the requisite tools of policy analysis—a theory of the driving

---

[6] On the dynamics of this process see Petras and Veltmeyer (2001, 2003, 2005, 2010).

force of the development process and its necessary conditions, and of the government interventions that would produce the optimum outcomes.[7] This theory was elaborated in diverse forms and applied to the diverse development plans that the economists and consultants of the World Bank and the IMF presented to policymakers and the state officials in the countries that came under their mandate to provide, with international cooperation, financial and technical assistance to these countries in their development process. In the 1970s, however, under mounting pressure for revolutionary change in the developing countries, this concern for economic growth was combined with a concern for a more equitable distribution of this economic growth, and for creating the conditions needed to stave off the growing pressures for revolutionary change—the alleviation of world poverty, which afflicted (by conservative World Bank estimates) two-fifths of the world's population.

In economic theory this new policy was described as 'growth with equity'—a development goal that combined a capitalist concern for economic growth (productive investment etc.) with a socialist concern for an equitable distribution of the social product and meeting the welfare needs of the entire population. While governments in countries in the global south, such as Brazil, continued to pursue a 'pro-growth' or 'growth first' policy a number of other governments—for example, Sri Lanka, Kerala *and Cuba*—pursuing both a capitalist and a socialist path towards national development, pursued a strategy of combining a policy of *growth with equity*, using the agency of government intervention (state-led development) to do so.

The context for this new development strategy[8] was provided by the growing pressures for revolutionary change and independence, particularly in Latin America but also in Asia and Africa, that provoked a concern among academics and policy makers to stave off these pressures by reforming the system.[9]

---

[7] For a formulation of this theory in its diverse permutations, and a succinct outline and summary of its basic propositions see Hunt (1989).

[8] A very clear and succinct examination of the thinking behind this strategy is perovided by the World Bank in *Meeting the Challenges of Global Development: A Long-Term Strategic Exercise for the World Bank Group* (2007: 39–42).

[9] For a contextualised 'structural' analysis of these developments and their dynamics—from a 'development and globalization as imperialism' perspective—see, in particular Chapter 2 of Veltmeyer and Petras (2010); also Petras and Veltmeyer (2009).

Development as Freedom: Human Development in Theory

In the 1970s mainstream development thinking and practice took a new turn in a concern for alleviating poverty and reducing, if not eradicating poverty in its most extreme form, creating conditions thereby for meeting the basic needs of the entire population. This did not represent a paradigm shift as much as a concern for a less economistic and more integrated form of development—to give it a social dimension.

It was increasingly evident that development understood in economic terms as an expansion of the forces of production and output, and measured in terms of GDP growth, was overly restricted, one-sided and a woefully inadequate way of conceiving of progress in the human condition. With the discovery by economists at the World Bank that up to two fifths of the world's population were deprived of the wherewithal to meet their basic needs, poverty was placed on the development agenda, and development itself was understood and presented in thought and practice as an improvement in human welfare and the quality of life, understood broadly in terms of fundamental human rights and the diverse social conditions attached to these rights.

Conceiving of development in these terms led to diverse strategies for meeting the basic needs of the population and reducing the incidence, as well as alleviating the diverse socioeconomic conditions, of poverty. These included a lack of access to a source or supply of food and nutrition, potable water, housing and shelter; exposure to disease, malnutrition, hunger, and, in some contexts, starvation; exclusion or the lack of secure access to the productive resources and services needed to meet one's basic needs (Streeten, 1981, 1984).

In the 1980s, in the context of a mainstream movement away from development towards globalization and the installation of a new world order, this 'basic needs' paradigm and approach to development was modified and extended to include a concern for 'participation', 'social exclusion' and 'equity' in terms of equalizing the opportunities for individuals to realize their human potential—to bring about an alternative form of development ('another development') that was participatory, more inclusive and equitable, empowering of the poor and women, sustainable in terms of the environment and livelihoods, and 'human' in form and scale.

Within the framework of this alternative mainstream of development thought several economists, including Amartya Sen and Mahbub Ul Haq, were invited by the UNDP to elaborate their conception of development as 'freedom' ('enlarging people's choices' and enhancing capability realization). The result was the *Human Development Report*, published annually since 1990 and serving as an alternative to the World Bank's annual *World Development Report* as a point of reference for measuring advances in development and ranking countries accordingly.

Some would argue that the UNDP's approach to development and its annual report provides not so much an alternative as a supplement to the World Bank's approach and Report. This is because both institutions and reports agree that development is multidimensional, requires an integrated approach and is predicated on capitalism as the underlying system, which is needed to bring about development understood as improvement in the human condition and institutional reform.

In any case, the UNDP's Human Development approach, like that of the World Bank, is 'normative' rather than 'structural'; i.e. it is concerned with the possibilities of bringing about human development within the existing system, identifying specific areas of intervention, rather than with systemic constraints or structural change. The end goal of development so conceived is 'human flourishing' based on an 'equality of opportunity' ('equity' in the discourse of the new paradigm) and the 'expansion of [individual] choice'. To facilitate this 'development' the agency of governments, it is argued, should be oriented towards ensuring an 'equality of opportunity' within the institutional structure of society, and also the expansion of choices available to individuals within this structure. This implies state-led reform (government intervention) to ensure that these opportunities, and the capacity to act on them and realise a person's capabilities, are not biased in favour of some at the expense of others.

The problem, as pointed out by many critics, is that for most societies, and certainly those based on a capitalist mode of production, the social structure is characterised by relations of social class (production, power) rather than individual opportunity (capability, choice); and while such a structure might provide avenues of mobility, such as education and a labour market, for most people the opportunities (for self-realization) are few and the available choices are restricted by the power of some to advance their own interests and position.[10]

---

[10] Only recently have the economists at the UNDP confronted and begun to write about the barriers to human development provided by the dominant relations of production and power.

Under these conditions, the solution is not to empower the poor to act for themselves—invariably the 'solution' advanced by the economists at the UNDP and now even at the World Bank—but to change the structure of the system, and this cannot be achieved by the agency of individuals. That is, it requires not so much reform as an overhaul of the entire system—socialism rather than capitalism—and this means the disempowerment of the rich as well as the empowerment of the poor. This solution, of course, is entirely ignored by the proponents of 'Human Development', trapped in their own mindset and blinded as they are by the dominant ideology.

There are two sides to *development* as conceived by Sen, Haq and other contributors to the UNDP's *Human Development Report*: the formation of capabilities and the use of these capabilities (Haq, 2000). The formation of capabilities gives people the *opportunity* to use them. For instance, skill development, health and education are part of the formation of capabilities and these can be put to use in various types of employment and leisure. Others have described this duality with the terms 'functionings' (being nourished, having friends, etc) and 'capabilities' (the freedom to enjoy functionings) (Alkire and Deneulin, 2009).

The particular means of pursuing human development are very important. Haq (2000) writes about four procedural concerns regarding the pursuit of human flourishing: *equity, sustainability, productivity and empowerment*. People should have equity in opportunities and in the freedom to pursue the ends that they have reason to value. The pursuit of human development should be based on access to and the sustainable use of all forms of capital (human and natural, as well as financial and physical). Goals should be pursued through an efficient use of productive resources. Finally, people must be empowered: they should be the agents of their own development—fulfilment of their potential, realization of their capabilities.

Agency is a central feature of the capability approach as articulated by Sen. The Human Development approach seeks to increase human agency, with people acting as agents of their own development. An agent refers to an actor able to bring about change. Sen in this regard writes that people must be thought of 'as being actively involved—given the opportunity—in shaping their own destiny, and not just as passive recipients of the fruits of cunning development programs' (1999: 53). An expansion of choice inevitably means tradeoffs must be made. People must be able to make their own decisions about what they will pursue, based on what they value. But the concept of agency is not limited to the individual. It also refers to what can be achieved by communities and groups, beyond a simple addition of its members' agency (Alkire and Deneulin, 2009).

Freedom is another essential component of human development, particularly as regards the expansion of choices available to individuals in taking advantage of their opportunities and capabilities (Sen, 1999).

Also fundamental to the Human Development approach is a concern for integrated development—a combination of economic and social development, the economic understood primarily in terms of increasing per capita incomes as a means of improving the physical quality of life, the social as education and health. Although the fundamental agency for development are the poor themselves, empowered to act on their values and opportunities, governments have an important role to play in creating an appropriate institutional and policy framework—to facilitate this development. Inasmuch as human capabilities are partly created or undermined by development policies, markets, the state and other social arrangements and institutionalized practices this normally means reform—ensuring social inclusion and equity in the process.

Cuba's Formulation of the Human Development Concept

> *Human development necessarily entails a concern for culture. Social cohesion, based on culture, in shared values and beliefs, grounds and gives form to individual human development* (PNUD, 1997: 6).

In 1997 the UNDP published its first report on human development in Cuba. The significance of this report, although it is unheralded and to our knowledge not commented upon in the literature, is that it actually includes a subtle but important change in the original concept of human development embodied in the Human Development Reports published to that date. The change is undoubtedly the result of the fact that the report on human development in Cuba was written entirely by Cuban scholars at the Centro de Investigaciones de la Economía Mundial (CIEM). It seems that the worldview of these economists, no doubt steeped in the ideology of the Cuban Revolution and its socialist ethos, filtered and to some extent reshaped the thinking and the values embodied in the UNDP reports. Thus, while the authors of this 1997 report on human development in the Cuba of 1996 took full account of the World Bank's concerns regarding 'poverty and human development' and the need to 'give structural adjustment a human face', and they made clear reference to the 'UNDP perspective' as the enlargement of choice and opportunities for the individual, they also emphasized the importance of 'social cohesion', conceptualized in this study as 'solidarity'. As the Report has it: 'human development is concerned not only for people as individuals but how they interact and cooperate in their communities' (UNDP, 1997: 6). The Report continues: 'Human beings survive in a complex web of social structures... they are *social beings* that value [and need?] participation in the life of their *community*, that sense of belonging which is an important source of wellbeing'. This socially binding spirit of community, the report continues, is grounded in culture, hence human development necessarily entails a concern for culture ('the form in which people decide to live together'), and with its 'cultural basis' ('shared values and beliefs'), a 'sense of social cohesion' is a fundamental pillar of 'human development'. Another such pillar is 'potenciación' (empowerment),[11] a concept presented in the 1995 Human Development Report. In regard to individuals per se but to women as a fundamental agency of change and development ('a critical factor in the reduction of gender inequities'). The point—made by the Cuban authors of the 1997 report—is that capacitation of women (capability formation) is not enough. Empowerment as a concept means that people are in a situation that allows them to 'choose and exercise vital options on the basis of their social consciousness. And unlike the case with other 'development schemes' these options encompass a broad spectrum of issues—political, social and cultural as well as economic'. What this means is 'development of people [*desarrollo de la gente*], *for people* [i.e. not for themselves] and...by the people'.

Capitalism, the Market and the Nation-State

The state as a political system has taken different forms over the years but its origins in the contemporary form as a nation-state were coterminous with capitalism, a system of expanded commodity production that emerged in the early nineteenth century under conditions of 'primitive accumulation' (separation of the direct producer from

---

[11] Nowadays normally translated into Spanish as 'apoderamiento'.

the land and other means of production); a system of mercantilist trade; a process of productive transformation based on an 'Industrial Revolution'; the capitalist development of the forces of production and a corresponding social development—the capital-labour relation, the economic base of the social structure; and what historians have termed the 'battle for democracy' or the democratic revolution.[12] Under these conditions, and on the economic base of the capital-labour relation, the state, as Marx observed, essentially came to represent the interests of the capitalist class, serving essentially as the executive committee of this class to represent its economic interests and advance the process of capital accumulation.

Under these conditions and in this national form the capitalist state assumed or was assigned the following functions, each with a corresponding apparatus and institutional mechanism:

- Protection of the person and property of each and all members of society—to provide legal security to private property in the means of production;
- Lawmaking and legislation—to secure a regime of governance by law;
- Provision of the infrastructure and utilities (water provision, waste management, highways and transportation networks, electrical power, communications) needed to generate a process of capital accumulation and economic development;
- The business of government and administration; and
- Physical and political security, to settle relations of conflict in the distribution of the social product.

In addition to these basic 'functions', the functioning of the state in regard to its assigned 'role' changed over time (as required), particularly in regard to:

- The authoritative allocation of society's productive resources, determining 'who gets what' share of national income (versus the market in its determination of appropriate returns to different factors of production—labour, capital, land);
- The provision of social welfare in the form of universal education and healthcare—a responsibility assumed by the state in the 1930s;

---

[12] As to the origins of capitalism there is a rather contentious but as yet unsettled debate, in which the contributions of Marx and Max Weber are at issue.

- Public works and employment to prime the demand for goods and services, and expand the market—an economic function added to the state under conditions of a global depression;
- Regulation of the capital-labour relation, so as to settle any conflicts in the system of industrial relations—a responsibility assumed by the state in the 1940s under conditions of class struggle;
- The declaration by the United Nations of a charter of universal human rights, including not only a spectrum of political 'rights' (freedom of expression, to organise, etc.) but the inalienable right to 'happiness' and a broad spectrum of social and economic rights, including the right to a decent job or employment, adequate housing and access to education and health services;
- The 'function of capital' (investment, entrepreneurship, enterprise management, marketing), assigned in theory to the capitalist class but assumed by the state in the 1950s and 1960s in the absence or weakness of this class in the economically backward areas of the 'third world';
- The regulation of markets and private economic activity, and the institution of capital controls, in the public interest—a policy attributed to the state by development economists at the time (the 1950s and 1960s) associated with the UN system (UNCTAD, UNCTC, ECLAC);
- Responsibility for economic and social development, including the institution of state enterprises in the strategic sectors of the economy and regulatory control over 'international resource flows'—the operations (foreign direct investment, etc.) of the multinational corporations;
- As and when required, repression of the movements for revolutionary change and radical land reform—a responsibility exercised by the state (in some contexts, particularly in Latin America and the remnants of European colonialism in Asia—Indonesia, Vietnam, etc.) in the 1960s and 1970s under conditions of a class war launched against organised labour (viz. a presumed 'international communism') and a 'dirty war' against diverse forms of 'subversion';
- A policy of structural reforms in the interest of reactivating a process of capital accumulation—under conditions of a new world order (in the 1980s); and
- The new development paradigm and a policy framework designed to empower the poor and create a more socially inclusive and sustainable form of *human* development.

The State and the Market: A Fundamental Relation of Capitalist Development

At issue in the development process vis-à-vis the market-state relation—and also the labour-capital relation and the relation of civil society to the state—are questions of (i) 'agency' (ii) 'structure' and (iii) 'context' (Chalmers. 1995; Evans, 1995; Wade, 2003; Woo-Cumings, 1999; Yun Tae Kim, 1999).

As for 'context' it is matter of periodizing the evolution of capitalism—the unfolding of the capitalist development process. Our own understanding of this 'evolution' is informed, inter alia, by Veltmeyer (2010), both of whom periodize the advanced process of capitalist development in the post-World War II context of the Bretton Woods system, a new world order to regulate and govern international relations; an east-west ideological struggle and a resulting 'cold war'; an independence struggle of national liberation from the yoke of imperialism and colonial rule; a period of system-wide economic growth based on the agency of an interventionist development state as well as an accord between labour and capital on sharing productivity gains.

In this context, the process of capitalist development can be periodized as follows:

- a period of system-wide rapid economic growth (1948–1970) under the aegis and with the agency of the development state;
- a period of transition (1970-83), opening and ending with an outbreak of crisis (from a production crisis in the early 1970s to a fiscal crisis in the north and a debt crisis in the south) and characterised by a process of economic restructuring;
- installation of a new world order (1983–1989) in which the so-called 'forces of freedom' are liberated from the regulatory constraints of the welfare-development state under conditions of the Washington Consensus on the appropriate market-friendly 'structural reform' of national policy; and
- a third cycle[13] of neoliberal reform advanced with a new (post-Washington) consensus on the need to 'bring the state back in' and

---

[13] The neolberal agenda of 'structural' (policy) reform in the 1980s can be seen as a second cycle of neoliberal reforms in relation to the experiments with these policies by the military regimes instituted in the 1970s in Chile, Argentina, Bolivia and Uruguay (Veltmeyer and Petras, 1997).

create a more inclusive form of development based on a 'better balance between the market and the state' (Ocampo, 2007).

Civil Society and the State—Agency and Democracy Matters

The question of 'agency' in the development process revolves around what could be termed the 'state-civil society relation'. As for the 'state' in this relation the key issues surrounding theoretical debate in this area include questions about:

- its political form—whether it is authoritarian or democratic in form (Dominguez and Lowenthal, 1996);
- its social form or class character, viz. the social groups or classes represented by the state or that have captured it as a means of advancing the collective interests of the group or class; and
- the specific dynamics of class power, defined alternatively as the capacity of a group or individuals to make decisions on behalf, and in the interests of, a particular group or class that they belong to or with which they identify; or, in this context of a particular correlation of class forces, to exert one's will against resistance.

There is also a long-standing and shifting debate as to the role assigned respectively to the state and the market, and the weight of each in the development process. Reference to this debate was made above in the summary outline of diverse 'functions' attached to the state in theory and practice under changing conditions of capitalist development. Under conditions of capitalist development available in the 1980s (a conservative counterrevolution, the emergence of conservative regimes committed to neoliberalism), a fiscal crisis, a debt crisis) the State in its government function and administrative apparatus was relegated to a secondary, downsized role vis-à-vis the market as an agency of economic development and an emerging 'civil society'.[14]

The *welfare-development state* (WDS—*my term*) was formed under conditions of a global production crisis,[15] pressures for revolutionary

---

[14] Strictly speaking the market should be viewed as an institution rather than as an agency, i.e. as a means of facilitating the agency of individual members of society in their decisions and actions, their social interactions of economic exchange, based on a calculus of self-interest and available choices.

[15] Theories of this production crisis ranged from Marxist theories of the law for a falling rate of profit (TLFRP) and over-production/under-consumption (Brenner, 2000) to a theory of a 'profit-crunch' that emphasized the working of a *political as*

change (Cuba, etc.) and the 'fiscal crisis' of a state weighed down by the growing cost of welfare and development. This fiscal crisis, together with a failure to close the development gap in the 1970s, created political conditions for a counter-revolution (counter to the 'revolution' in economic thinking wrought by Maynard Keynes) in development theory and practice (Toye, 1997) and calls for a 'new world order' in which the 'forces of freedom' would be freed from the excessive costs, the interference and regulatory constraints of government. The emergence of a debt crisis created the leverage for the World Bank, the International Monetary Fund and other International Financial Institutions (IFIs) to impose a program of 'structural reform' on governments in the region, generating (and justifying) a process of 'globalization'—integration into a global capitalist economy based on the workings of the free market.

Under these conditions the welfare-development state was weakened and dismantled. The State was restructured—forced to retreat from its hitherto predominant economic role (production growth, wealth generation, income distribution). As for economic and social 'development' responsibility in this area was shared with civil society via a policy of administrative decentralization, designed as a means of 'strengthening civil society' and increasing democratic participation (Bardham, 1997; Kaufmann, Kraay and Zoido-Lobatón, 1999; OECD, 1997; UNDP, 1993; World Bank, 1994).

'Civil society' in this context refers to all manner of nongovernmental or social organizations operating in the space between the family and the state. The nongovernmental organizations in this sector (CSOs or NGOs) are associational in form rather than class-based as most social movements and labour- and peasant-organizations, or community-based as are the 'people's organizations' or social movements formed by the indigenous communities in Latin America—particularly in Peru, Guatemala, Ecuador, Bolivia and Mexico.

As such, in the form of an associational-type nongovernmental organization that are 'value-driven rather than profit-oriented or bureaucratically propelled', 'civil society' expanded to fill the vacuum left by a retreating state in a process of 'democratization' (UNDP, 1993:

---

opposed to *economic* dynamic in this crisis (Glynn et al, 1990; Marglin and Schor, 1990) and a theory that capitalism had reached the limits of its capacity to expand global production in the dominant mode of labour regulation (Brenner and Glick, 1991; De Vroey, 1984; Lipietz, 1987; Noel, 1987).

78–90).¹⁶ In Latin America in the early 1980s there were barely several hundred NGOs but in the next decade (1990s) they numbered well into the thousands. The OECD estimated that in the developing countries as a whole in the 1980s the total number of NGOs in the so-called 'third sector' numbered at least 20,000 but the UNDP regards this as a serious underestimate, the actual number being closer to 50,000 and quite possibly higher (UNDP, 2003).

As an expression of 'civil society' and in their 'work with and through people's organizations', these NGOs in the 1990s assumed a critical role in the development process—mediating between the international donors and the local communities and the 'people's organizations', offering them 'financial and other support' (p. 87).¹⁷ The NGOs, the UNDP notes, are 'unlikely ever to play more than a complementary role' in 'eradicating poverty and providing social services' (p. 95), Much more significant is 'their ability to demonstrate participatory models that government might follow—and to keep pressure on governments….encouraging them to focus more on the human development of the world's poorest people'. In this regard, 'many NGOs have placed much of their emphasis on empowerment. The formal purpose of a programme might be improvements in health or literacy…but NGOs have also been concerned with how much each project enhances people's power'. The Report added that 'they have been particularly concerned with how much each project enhances people's power' (p. 87).

In the 1980s, the institutional and policy framework for this mediating role of the NGOs was provided by the Washington Consensus on correct policy—a program of market-friendly 'structural reforms': structural adjustment to the requirements of the 'new world order' of neoliberal globalization (Williamson, 1990). These reforms included

---

¹⁶ The UNDP's 1993 HDR focused on the theme of participatory development—the role of popular participation in the development process, and the importance of democracy and governmental decentralization as the institutional basis of this development. As the UNDP saw it, 'democracy is more than drawing up constitutions, designing new election procedures or holding elections as one-time events'. It is 'a long-term process of reorganizing the institutions of civil society….[to increase] the participation of people] in events and process that shape their lives' (UNDP: 2003: iii). Decentralization of local goverment, in this regard, 'has the potential to improve government decisions with increasing democratic participation' (p. 79).

¹⁷ The authors of the 1993 HDR also pointed out that 'some NGOs are not as non-governmental as they might seem. Although formally independent they might have links to government' (p. 89).

privatization of production, deregulation of markets and private economic activity, liberalization of trade and capital flows, and decentralization. However, by the end of the decade, it was evident that neoliberalism was economically dysfunctional and unsustainable, leading to diverse efforts to re-engineer the reform process (Harvey, 2003; Veltmeyer and Petras, 1997).

It would take a number of years to redesign the structural reform process, but with the contributions of diverse international organizations and financial institutions such as the World Bank, the UNDP and ECLAC, a new Consensus was finally achieved. The fundamental concern behind this new 'post-Washington consensus' was to create a 'better balance between the state and market', a more socially inclusive and sustainable form of people-centred and -led *human* development, and a 'good governance' regime, i.e. based on popular participation in public action (Ocampo, 2006, 2007).

This consensus, embodied in various alternative models constructed at the time—structural adjustment with a human face (Cornia, Jolly and Stewart, 1987); productive transformation with equity (ECLAC, 1990); and sustainable human development (UNDP, 1996, 1997), can be summed up as follows:

- The need for governments to 'stay the course' of 'structural reform'—a 'pro-growth' policy agenda; (ii) a 'new social policy' targeted at the poor—to ensure that 'pro-poor' policies are 'pro-poor' (Lopez, 2004);
- Investment in 'human capital' in the form of education and health (re fiscal expenditures as 'human resource development'); and
- A policy of decentralization, designed so as to (a) create a participatory and equitable form of development initiated 'from within' and 'from below' (Goulet, 1989); (b) ensure greater 'social inclusion' and 'good governance' (Kaufmann, Kraay and Zoido-Lobatón, 1999); and (c) empower the poor to act for themselves, converting them into a 'actor', the 'subject' rather than the 'object' of development, the fundamental agency for bringing about their own development (Veltmeyer, 2007).

Problematizing Civil Society

The notion of *civil society*, formulated and used by the theorists of the eighteenth century to distinguish more clearly between the 'state' and 'society' in their proposals for liberating social change, was resurrected by a new generation of scholars in the 1980s as an agency for self-help, participatory development and democratic politics—to democratize the state-society relation (Veltmeyer, 2007) both in the countries transiting from socialism to capitalism and in the global south. There are, in fact, according to Veltmeyer, three different conceptions of 'civil society', each resulting in a very distinct theoretical—and political—perspective on the dynamics and agency of social change. One, constructed in the tradition of liberal democratic politics, was used in the context of the Soviet Union and Eastern Europe—to identify therewith a possible agency of participatory politics.

A second formulation of the concept hails back to Antonio Gramsci in a critical Marxist conception of the forces of resistance to capitalism. And a third conception of *civil society* was formulated by economists and sociologists associated with the UNDP in a concern to incorporate the 'private sector' (= capitalist corporations and other profit-oriented and -seeking enterprises) into the development process. The problem, according to Diane Mitlin (1998) is that these and such profit-seeking 'capitalist enterprises' were widely viewed at the time as a large part of the problem (the lack of development, the inequality predicament, poverty, etc.). The solution, it was thought, was a strategic alliance of the state and civil society, with 'international cooperation'. Thus, Mitlin argues, the architects of the new development paradigm and policy agenda resorted to the notion of 'civil society' as a means of identifying the broad spectrum of organizations that could be enlisted in the war against global poverty.

In the 1990s, as we noted above, the NGOs were so enlisted, contracted to the purpose of democratizing the state and to mediate between the donor organizations in the development project of assisting the poor in their communities and localities. However, the actual (as opposed to the theoretically defined) role played by the NGOs in practice has been the subject of an extensive and as yet unsettled debate (Veltmeyer, 2007). From the perspective of the World Bank, the UNDP and other international organizations and development associations, the NGOs serve as an important strategic partner in the war on poverty, an important factor in the development process—helping the poor to adjust to the forces of change and to take personal advantage of the opportunities that might be available to them—helping them choose the best pathway out of poverty, empowering them to act in their own interest. On the other hand, the NGOs can also be viewed as 'false saviours of development' (Kamat, 2003).

From a more critical perspective, however, the NGOs function and serve, in effect if not by design or subjective intention, as a handmaiden of neoliberal globalization, as a sort of Trojan horse (Wallace, 2003). From an even more critical perspective the NGOs serve—often unwittingly—as an agent of imperialism, a means of advancing an agenda of demobilizing the social movements, derailing the resistance against neoliberalism (Petras and Veltmeyer, 2010).

Human Development and Public Agency

Based on the precept that HD requires the agency of both the state *and* civil society—that active popular participation and agency is an essential condition of HD—scholars in the liberal democratic tradition assume (and over the years have argued) that the Cuban model or the Revolution has been deficient in this regard; that the Cuban path towards HD by and large has been very much top-down, with decision-making power and public policy highly concentrated in a small group in control of the state, providing few if any channels or institutional forms of popular participation, as the concept of HD would dictate. The hypothesis derived from this 'theory', which attributes extraordinary power of one individual (Fidel Castro) to dictate policy and events, is that the most important policy decisions over the course of the Cuban Revolution have been made by the government, from above, with scant or no popular participation and a weak, if not entirely absent, civil society subordinated to the State.[18] This hypothesis will be put to the test in this study. Indeed, our thesis is that to the contrary the Cuban Revolution was initiated, and has been advanced, on the basis of some 50 years of struggle and what after Amartya Sen we might term 'public action'—a combination of government intervention and popular participation that engages the agency of both the state and civil society. And that it was this feature of the Revolution—the active participation of the people in public decision-making—that

---

[18] Notable examplars of this approach are Oppenheimer (1992) and Quirk (1993). Even Eckstein (1) in her more sociological approach to an understanding of the forces that shaped Cuba in her discussion of diverse policy stances and actions taken emphasizes—arguably overemphasizes—Castro's charisma and his ability therewith to 'impose his will against resistance' and to shape the direction taken by the Revolution. As Eckstein (2003: 3) argued, 'the Cuban revolution is Fidel's revolution'.

allowed Cuba to survive a system-threatening challenge to the Revolution and its socialist system.

Conclusion

The idea of human development, to all intents and purposes (or in regard to the post-World War II development projects of international cooperation, decolonization and nation-building) can be traced back to the ideas of freedom, equality and fraternity (solidarity)—rallying cries for revolutionary change in the eighteenth century and the declared goals of the post-war efforts to bring about improvements in the social condition of people and nations across a global development and ideological divide.

Over time these ideas were acted upon in different ways, giving form to different conditions and diverse forms of social change and development. Development can be viewed in both structural terms (as the result of the normal functioning of the system) and in strategic terms (the result of actions on values and beliefs consciously directed towards a defined goal), but in terms of the latter, we have identified the following major 'moments' in the dialectic of the human development idea:

- The elaboration of two ideologies (liberalism and socialism) to mobilize the forces of progressive change in the directions of freedom and equality
- Construction of the *welfare state* under conditions of a major capitalist crisis and a socialist state under conditions of a 'proletarian revolution' in Russia
- The declaration of the UN Charter of fundamental human rights
- The formation of a development state within the institutional framework of the Bretton Woods system and the fusion of the ideas of 'progress,' 'equality' and 'freedom' as 'development'
- Formation of a socialist state in Cuba based on humanist principles
- Construction of the Basic Needs development paradigm based on a program of state-led social reforms to the operating economic system
- Construction of a model for bringing about a process of 'sustainable human development'
- Implementation of a development strategy based on a Washington Consensus regarding the superiority of free market capitalism, followed by a post-Washington Consensus on the need to 'bring the

state back in' to create conditions for a more socially inclusive and participatory form of development based on the empowerment of the poor, a policy of decentralization and 'good governance'
- A strategic 'public action' response within the Cuban Revolution to a major crisis in the socialist system of production
- Emergence of a movement towards 'the socialism of the 21st century', advanced under the regime of Hugo Chávez in Venezuela, and based on the promotion of a socialist culture of solidarity and humanism.

CHAPTER THREE

HUMAN DEVELOPMENT IN PRACTICE: REFORM(ING CAPITALISM) VERSUS (SOCIALIST) REVOLUTION

This Chapter reviews the major contours of *human development practice* over recent five decades of capitalist and socialist development of the forces and relations of production. This development took both a socialist and a capitalist form. This is to say, both capitalism and socialism developed in several different directions, including human development. In a capitalist form the human development project was advanced in the 1990s as a means of providing a human face to a profoundly divisive and inegalitarian process of capitalist development that had polarized societies across the world society along a class divide between the rich and the poor. In its socialist form the human development project, it is argued, was advanced in the form of the Cuban Revolution.

The context for this human development practice in both capitalist and socialist forms was provided at the end of the Second World War. It included the eclipse of the British Empire and the emergence of *Pax Americana*, the emergence an east-west ideological divide and diverse movements for national liberation in different areas of what would become known as the 'third world' of developing countries in the global south, 'development' as a project of international cooperation (to ensure that these developing countries would follow a capitalist rather than a socialist path towards national development), and the construction of a liberal-capitalist world order (the Bretton Woods System) as the institutional framework for this project.

In the 1980s the capitalist system and the world order designed for it at Bretton Woods was renovated in the form of a 'new world order' (neoliberal globalization) designed to free the 'forces of economic freedom' (the market, private enterprise, capital) from the regulatory constraints of the welfare-development state. The aim was to create conditions for reactivating the capital accumulation and economic growth process. Within the institutional and policy framework of this new world order, the fundamental responsibility for reactivating the economic growth (economic development) was turned over to the 'private sector' and the market, while the state's role in regard to social welfare was curtailed, the responsibility for social development was either transferred to or shared with 'civil society'.

The chapter traces out the contours of capitalist and socialist development that unfolded under these conditions. The UNDP's conception of human development, it is argued, served as the scaffolding for the model that was used to guide policy and the development practice of most countries in Latin America both in the 1990s and the new millennium. In this context, Cuba constituted a lone case of socialist human development.

Dynamics of Capitalist Development

Capitalist development, i.e. the development of society's forces of production on the basis of a capitalist mode of production, is part of a historic process of productive and social transformation, viz. the 'great transformation' of a traditional, pre-capitalist and agrarian society into a modern industrial capitalist system. Although many historians focus on the industrialization or modernization aspects of this development, historians are surprisingly consistent in their basic periodization of this development. Generally the capitalist development process is periodized more or less as follows (Foladori and Delgado Wise, 2011):

- 1500–1800: An initial phase of 'primitive accumulation', in which the necessary preconditions of capitalist development (separation of direct producers from their means of production, the genesis of a capitalist and a working class) are brought together';
- 1800–1870: A phase in the capitalist development of the forces of development based on the formation of industrial capital, in which new production technologies combined with new relations of production to create a system of industrial capitalism based on wage labour and the formation of an industrial proletariat—the 'working class' in Marxist parlance;
- 1870–1914: A period characterized by the globalization of capital and labour (the export of the former and migration of the latter), the fusion of financial and industrial capital in the form of monopoly capital, and what in retrospect might be termed the 'old imperialism' based on an unequal exchange of raw materials/primary commodities for manufactured goods;

- 1914–1944: A period dominated by two world wars, a system-wide crisis in the system of capitalist production, a process of state-led social reform that led to the formation of a capitalist welfare state, and a parallel process of state-led socialist development;
- 1944–1980: A period of capitalist development dominated by the agency and workings of the development state—the so-called 'Golden Age of capitalism' (rapid system-wide economic growth followed by a decade of crisis and efforts to restructure the system;
- 1980–2010: a period of neoliberal globalization, what David Harvey (2005) has termed 'a short history of neoliberalism'.

A Policy Framework for 'Sustainable Human Development'

The policy framework for human development, as conceived and operationalized by the UNDP in its *Human Development Reports*, was constructed in its essentials towards the end of the 1980s when it became evident that the policies of structural adjustment to the requirements of the neoliberal world order, namely integration into a global economy based on the principles of free market capitalism, were not working. The Washington Consensus focused on a combination of stabilisation measures and 'structural reforms' in macroeconomic policy designed in theory to reactivate the capital accumulation (and economic growth) process—placing all countries on the path towards 'general prosperity' (see World Bank, 2005, for programmatic statement of this notion).

The basic policies designed to this end—to restore the economy, were (the) *privatization* (of state enterprises), reverting the nationalisation policies of the previous state-led model; *financial and trade liberalisation*, reverting the protectionist policies of the development state; *deregulation*, reverting the regulative policies of the state-led model of development; and decentralization, designed as a means of bringing decision-making regarding public policy closer to the public, creating conditions for popular participation—engaging civil society in both the political and the development process (Cheema and Rondinelli, 1983; Rondinelli, McCullough and Johnson, 1989).

These Washington-designed and mandated policies, however, did not work *for* development: it served to advance the 'forces of economic freedom' (private enterprise, profit-making, free markets) but not the forces of production (deliver on the promise of economic growth). With the onset of the new world order of neoliberal globalization and financialization in the early 1980s the level of capital formation in Latin America, and the growth rate in GDP per capita, declined precipitously from an annual average rate of 4.6 to 5% in the 1950s and 1960s to an average rate of 3.2% in the 1970s and a decade-long recession (average annual growth down-0.6%) in the 1980s, a weak growth rate of 0.9% in the 1990s in the heyday of neoliberalism, and then a 'recovery' from a crisis to a growth rate of 3.5% from 2002 to 2007 during the primary commodities boom, before collapsing in mid-2008–2009 (OECD, 2010). In addition the 'pro-growth' neoliberal policies implemented throughout the region led to a serious deterioration in the socioeconomic conditions lived by the working classes, and a deepening of the social divide between the rich and the poor.

Recognizing that the neoliberal model was economically dysfunctional, socially divisive and politically unsustainable led the architects of the new world order to redesign an appropriate policy framework under what would come to be known as the 'post-Washington Consensus' (PWC).[1]

The basic principles of this consensus and the fundamental pillars of the SHD model constructed by the UNDP and advanced as a policy framework for national development in Bolivia, were: (1) *productivity-competitiveness* (how to improve the productivity of Bolivia's major economic enterprises and ensure their ability to compete in the world market); (2) social *integration-equity* (how to broaden the social base of national production, improving access to means of production of diverse groups of producers beyond the small stratum of big well-capitalised enterprises privileged by, and benefiting from, neoliberal policies); and (3) state action-governability (how to ensure political order with as little government as possible, i.e. via the strengthening of civil society and participation in public policy).

With reference to these principles, and an emerging consensus on the need for a 'better balance between the state and market' (that 'we

---

[1] The policy dynamics of the post-Washington Consensus (PWC) include: (i) the expectation and promise of economic growth and poverty alleviation; (ii) associated or resulting structural change and social transformation that constitute and open up various pathways out of poverty—labour, migration, farming (World Bank, 2008); (iii) a decentralised form of local governance and development; and (iv) an overarching Comprehensive Development Framework (CDF), and within it a new policy tool—the Poverty Reduction Strategy Paper (PRSP)—introduced at the G8 Summit in 1999.

had gone too far' in dismantling the state), the economists at ECLAC, the UNDP and the World Bank, the major institutions that assumed responsibility for redesigning the model came up with the following 'new policy agenda':

- to pursue (at the macro-level) a 'pro-growth' (and ostensibly 'pro-poor') policy of 'structural reform'—essentially to stay the course with this fundamental pillar of neoliberalism;
- under this policy to deepen the structural reform process, extending it to the labour market ('labour flexibilization') and the modernization of agriculture;
- to replace the universalist social policy of the old model of state-led development with a 'new social policy' targeted at the poor and their communities—to reduce the incidence of indigence and alleviate poverty;
- to 'bring the state back in' regarding development policy and programming in the areas of health and education, to improve thereby the social infrastructure of economic development ('human capital'): a well-educated, healthy and productive workforce;[2] and
- to generate a process of participatory development and conditions of 'good governance' (a 'democratization' of the state-civil society relation) by means of a local development strategy based on a decentralization policy.[3]

This model, in its various permutations ('productive transformation with equity', 'structural adjustment with a human face', 'sustainable human development', was widely albeit unevenly implemented throughout Latin America in the 1990s. An interesting feature of the model was the theoretical and policy convergence between the thinking associated with the World Bank (liberalism, neoliberalism), on the one hand, and ECLAC (structuralism, neostructuralism) on the other.[4] Another apparent feature of this convergence is the incorporation of

---

[2] From a long-term development perspective economists at the World Bank the operational agencies of the UN system argued the need not only for a more socially inclusive approach to development and to build human capital, but also to avoid disrupting those investments in conditions such as nutrition, health and education ('in people') that promote social mobility and allow citizens to move out of poverty.

[3] 'Participation' in this context was viewed theoretically as the 'missing link' between 'productive transformation' and 'equity', and as a such, an essential condition of a more inclusive and broad-based form of development from within and below (Boisier, 1992; Sunkel, 1993).

[4] On this convergence see Sunkel (2003).

several socialist principles and institutions into the new policy framework—in particular, equity in the distribution of the social product, in the determination of 'who gets what'.[5] Within the capitalist framework of this principle, 'equity' is transmuted from a substantive sharing in the conditions of economic growth into a more formal concern for 'equality of opportunity'—equalising opportunities for the poor (World Bank, 2000). The aim here was and is to create a more sustainable and equitable form of human development, as well as a more humane form of capitalism, a more inclusive form of neoliberalism.

Another interesting dimension of this theoretical convergence and the new policy framework is a convergence of sorts between capitalism and socialism, between the policies advocated under the post-Washington Consensus and policies pursued at the outset of the Cuban revolution. Not that the convergence is all one-way. As it happens, under conditions experienced by Cuba in the 'special period' in the 1990s, and the circumstantial need to structurally adjust the Cuban economy to the new capitalist world order, the Cuban government was obliged to introduce in sequence a number of 'capitalist' or 'market friendly' reforms, particularly in regards to foreign investment, tourism, restoration of a private market and certain forms of private enterprise (on this see, inter alia, Saney, 2004).

As for the outcomes of these policies, pursued by most countries in the region within a capitalist institutional framework and by Cuba within a socialist framework, they have been mixed at best, affected and to some extent determined as much by changing conditions in the world economy as by the policies themselves, which, in any case, were rarely implemented consistently.

Throughout the decade of the 1990s, under divergent policy regimes—capitalist in most cases and socialist in the case of Cuba—there was an upsurge of direct foreign investment. As it turned out this investment was more 'productive' for Cuba than it was for most countries in the region in which a large part of capital inflows served to acquire existing enterprises, many of them subject to privatization, rather than inducing a process of productive transformation via technological conversion. Another apparent 'function' of the diverse forms of inflows of private capital—FDI, portfolio investment, loans—in the

---

[5] The socialist principle here is formulated by Raul Castro in a recent speech in the following terms: 'to each according to his work, from each according to his ability'.

region (Cuba excepted because of the controls placed on this capital) was to accumulate capital.

In this connection, Saxe-Fernandez (2002) estimates that over the decade (from 1990 to 1999) regional outflows of capital in the form of repatriated profit, dividends, interest payments, resource rents and royalty charge, exceeded investment inflows and loans by as much as $100 billion—a veritable haemorrhage of financial resources. Under conditions of this capital outflow and (neoliberal) policies of structural adjustment to the requirements of the new world order, Latin America as a whole experienced a relatively low rate of economic growth. Growth for the region as a whole over the 1990s averaged 1.3% a year, little more than the previous decade that was to all accounts 'lost to development'. There were some indications of 'productive transformation' accompanying this growth, but it as also evident that the new social policy under the PWC had failed to produce its desired or intended outcome: greater 'equity'—at least, at the level of changing socioeconomic conditions of production and income. It is entirely possible that the new development strategy and consensus policies (social liberalism, as Ernesto Zedillo, erstwhile president of Mexico, defined it) might have led to a greater 'equality of opportunity' for the urban and rural poor—their stated aim. Perhaps, the development community failed to capacitate the poor in taking advantage of their increased opportunities, which the World Bank (2008) in its most recent *World Development Report*, sees to be predominantly in agriculture and labour (wage paying jobs) and migration.

At the level of experienced socioeconomic conditions, the dominant trend throughout Latin America in the 1990s, including Cuba for different reasons, was increasing inequalities in access to productive resources and assets, and in the distribution of income. The statistics on this are startlingly clear and point to the supposedly 'pro-poor' 'pro-growth' policies mandated by the neoliberal model and pursued under the PWC. The order of the day (the decade, rather) was increasing inequalities, albeit with a modest reduction in the overall level of poverty—from 45.7% to 36.5% over the course of the decade (ECLAC, 2008: 74).[6] The only country that experienced a significant reduction

---

[6] It is evident that the 'poverty line' measurement of poverty, particularly in the methodology of the World Bank ($2 a day, $1 for extreme poverty), has led to a statistical reduction of the incidence of poverty while the alternative, more integrated

in the rate of poverty was Chile, and by most accounts this was the result of a more consistent implementation of the post–Washington Consensus. The optimum outcome under this consensus is increased inequalities (an incentive to growth) but a reduced incidence in the rate of poverty. But the general rule governing developments in the 1990s was 'growth (and productive transformation) without equity', leading the World Bank and its strategic partners in the war on poverty to formulate a new anti-poverty strategy within a new 'comprehensive policy framework'—a policy of requiring aid recipients to produce a 'Poverty Reduction Strategy Paper (PRSP)' that outlines the government's efforts regarding policy reduction (and its commitment to the principles of good governance, etc.).[7]

Policy Dynamics of Decentralisation and Popular Participation

Human development as conceived by the economists at the UNDP is predicated on a human rights approach to development and a social liberal notion of 'development as freedom'. In the 1980s it was theorized that the institutionalization of these ideas required 'popular participation'—the 'missing link' in the development process (to ensure both 'productive transformation' and 'equity')—and a policy of administrative decentralization (Rondinelli, 1983; ECLAC, 1990). Popular participation and a policy of decentralization are widely celebrated today as appropriate and effective institutional responses to the challenges of development and the need for good governance and an empowerment of the poor, freeing them from the constraints that impeded their self-development. In these terms, diverse schemes for administrative decentralization of the state and participatory development were introduced by a large number of Latin American governments in the 1980s and early 1990s—as a euphemism, it might be said, for governmental meanness (Table 1). And they have come to represent central tenets of national strategies for poverty reduction and democratization under the post-Washington Consensus in the 1990s.

'basic needs' measure would not only show a much higher rate of poverty but little to no reduction.
[7] On the PRSP see, inter alia, Dijkstra (2005).

Table 1. Popular Participation and Decentralization in Latin America

Country	Peru	Ecuador	Colombia	Venezuela	Mexico	Bolivia
Date intro	1983 1984	1978 1986	1982	1978	1983	1994
Govt	Belaunde, Garcia	Roldos, Cordero	Del Barco	Herrer, Campins	De la Madrid	Sanchéz de Lozada
Int. Orgs New Orgs	UNDP Dialogue Imanacuy	UNDP Partic. Comm.	UNDP PEZ, TZ, CAPACA	OAS Territorial Assocs.	UN Councils, Neigh. Del.	UNDP OTBs
Objectives	Reg. dev. Decentraliz. Welfare	Dev Training, Urban dev.	Decentraliz Dev. H & E	Soc dev Planning	Dev planning,	Local dev,
Resources	Munic. res. % GNP	2% GNP plans	50% GNP to munic.	Inv. In	Transfer	20% GNP
Location	Municips. CONADE	M.Labour Public Cos.	Municips.	Municips.	Municips.	Municips.

Source: Based on Martinez (1996: 114).

Popular participation and decentralization meant a more inclusive form of development and the opening of new channels of communication between local peoples and their central states. Greater numbers of people, including previously politically invisible and 'hitherto excluded' groups such as women and the poor, were given unheard of access to local structures of power (Stiefel, and Pearce, 1982). International organizations such as the UNDP and the World Bank, and policy-makers under the PWC, backed and continue to support administrative decentralization as a way to improve both the efficiency and the responsiveness of governmental institutions, as well as providing the poor opportunities to pursue one of several pathways out of poverty (Palma Caravajal, 1995; Montano, 1996; Ospina, 1997).

The major testing ground and laboratory for this strategy and associated policies was Bolivia. The World Bank, for example, in the 1990s pushed for legislation in the direction of decentralization and popular participation, using both the carrot and the stick—and the Presidency of Gonzalo de la Sánchez [Goni], a close ally and a committed ideologue of neoliberalism—to implement enabling legislation and 'structural reform'.

In Latin America, popular participation and decentralization programs were not the result of a regional political mood-swing. By and large they were carried out as a part of the structural adjustment process at the behest and with the support of the 'international community' represented in particular by the UNDP and the World Bank (Palma Caravajal, 1995; Martinez, 1996; Caravajal 1995; Stiefel and Pearce, 1982). In the drive to make local government structures and institutions function as an agency of local development and 'good' [i.e. 'democratic governance'] the municipality, a legacy of the centralized Napoleonic state structure shared by many countries in the region, was cast in the role of an agency for local development (the 'productive municipality'). In Latin America this also means the decentralization of increased levels of resources, technical and financial, to the local governmental level (Nickson, 1997; Palma Caravajal, 1995). Newly created and legally empowered local institutions were granted a role in the direction and supervision of the newly available finances.

However, whereas an emphasis on 'democracy' was strong amongst international organizations such as the UNDP, beyond the fulfillment of technical requirements there was little or no concern given to the impact that these reforms had on the population, i.e. whether they made a difference to the empowerment of the 'hitherto excluded' and marginalized communities. In particular, no interest was given to the actual impact on the social relations of power within each country. Indeed, as regards decentralization and popular participation programs, it was simply presumed that their implementation was enough to produce democratic results (Mohan and Stokke, 2000).

Given the increasingly obvious limitations of international policy which relied on restructuring mechanisms such as decentralization and popular participation to create democratic government, a number of analysts and 'development experts' began to ask why such a weak policy was so widely and so uncritically accepted (Stiefel and Wolfe, 1998; James, 1999; Nelson and Wright, 1995). Some analysts (Veltmeyer, 2007) minced no words in arguing that the new development paradigm of local development was designed as a means of turning the rural poor away from the confrontational direct action politics of the social movements.

Others were not nearly so blunt and hard-hitting in suggesting that one of the main reasons why such policy has been able to pass with so little criticism relates to a lack of 'conceptual clarity within the field of development itself'. For example, Wendy James (1999: 13) in this connection warns that there appears 'to be a climate of language which pervades the genre and can make it difficult to see the difference between advocacy and analysis, or even to see clearly what is being advocated'. That is, the implication is that the outcome of reform is ambiguous because the goals and intentions of development experts and government reformers are themselves ambiguous. Words such as 'participation', 'mobilization', 'self-reliant development', 'dialogue', 'empowerment', are interchangeably used by governments and the organizations that support them in these efforts. Some authors (for example, Stiefel and Wolfe, 1998) have suggested that this conceptual confusion serves a purpose in allowing governments and international organizations to limit themselves when convenient to general proclamations and advocacy of participation without having to spell out the practical implications, the political aspects, and thus the power consequences of participation.

Through the practice of policy, the World Bank and governments who support it aim to create a new kind of subject, i.e. individuals who are self-sufficient and responsible for their own self-improvement. Here the idea matches the analysis of 'advanced liberalism' in that the aim is to govern without governing society, that is to say, to govern through the regulated and accountable choices of autonomous agents, citizens, parents, employees, investors. Much like tenants' associations in Britain during the 1980s, it is the people themselves, rather than trained professionals, who are deemed to have the requisite skills and relevant knowledge essential for improving their quality of life. Indeed, as in this case, poverty for the new subject is represented not as a social problem, but as a new possibility for poor individuals to experience *empowerment* through the actualization of their own self-management.

Under the logic of 'new public management', the state only acts to create the organizational conditions for its citizens' self-realization. In this new dispensation, experts no longer act as the direct functionaries of a 'social' state. Instead, they act as competitive providers of information and knowledge—not as an agency of development but only as facilitators of the process. However, in terms of policies for change, appearances really can be deceptive. Much of the literature on development, and the kinds of programs it legitimates, rest on a particular understanding of political participation as leading to the emancipatory empowerment of communities of people in the development process. It is implied that poor marginalized populations are capable by themselves of achieving development.

All they need is some preliminary financial and technical assistance. 'Help them to help themselves'. Needless to say, this is not the way reform works. In practice, development practitioners and legislating governments question the knowledge and ability of people to help themselves. The fact that local populations have developed complex forms of organization and survived the odds and the forces of change ranged against them is ignored.

Because local people are thought by government to lack the capacity and sufficient consciousness to bring about social transformation, they are made to participate in development through institutionally controlled structures for participation. This is widely viewed as 'participatory development', an essential condition of human development as conceived by the UNDP and implemented throughout the region in the 1990s.

Cuba, Structural Adjustment and Globalization

As for Cuba there is evidence of a similar outcome of policies pursued not under the PWC but rather the pressures of neoliberal globalization (Lara, 1999).[8] As the direct outcome of these policies, income inequalities increased throughout the 1990s, to the point of resurrecting the spectre of poverty at one extreme of the income distribution. Several studies (e.g. Espina Prieto, 2004) established a clear trend in this direction in the 1990s, under conditions of economic crisis and liberalising policy reforms, and despite a continuing commitment to established social security and human development programs.[9] In regard to social inequality in the distribution of income, its major source was the creation of a dual economy, one geared to the peso, the other to the dollar—a policy that created a major distortion in the economy as well as an entirely new social divide in which professionals such as doctors and teachers would earn considerably less than service workers in the tourist sector, and many Cubans were forced to reduce material consumption to a bare minimum. Under these conditions, it is estimated that the Gini Index of income inequality, which had dropped from 0.57 in 1958 to 0.28 just four years later, rose to .38 in 2000 (Espina Prieto, 2004; Ranis and Kosack, 2004). However, it should be kept in mind that this international standard for measuring inequality does not have the same import in Cuba, given that it is based entirely on the statistical distribution of income and that healthcare and education in Cuba are free and universal. As a result of the government's inclusive social policies, many of the population's basic needs

---

[8] When the fall of the Soviet Union plunged Cuba into its worst crisis in the early 1990s then-President Fidel Castro bitterly announced that the US dollar would become legal tender alongside the Cuban peso. State foreign exchange shops opened, family businesses were allowed and the country opened up to foreign tourism and investment as Castro tried to stave off a complete collapse of the economy. He said he had no choice if Cuban socialism was to survive, despite the inequality and social problems the measures would create. According to Cuban sociologists, that may have been an understatement.

[9] A study by Nerey and Brismart (1999) identified a quantitative and qualitative weakening of social services provision towards the end of the 1990s. However, for lack of distributional data on this weakening it it is not possible to determine whether it is at all connected to the predicament of rising inequality or a non-income dimension of poverty at the lower end of the income distribution.

are met, and extreme poverty is eluded, even with the access to relatively little earned income.

By all accounts Cuba over the past decade has experienced a dramatic upturn of the economy, a change that is reflected in a persistent trend towards economic recovery and expanded growth. The question is: to what degree is this recovery and economic upturn the result of public policy or changed conditions in the world economy? In this regard, the strong demand in China and Asia for minerals, energy and other natural resources has created conditions for a primary commodities export boom, which, it would appear, to some extent (in regards to nickel in particular) has benefited the Cuban economy. However, except for the export of nickel Cuba is not as well positioned as some countries to participate in this boom and to benefit from the global turnaround in the terms of trade, so we can assume that the economic recovery, to some extent anyway, can be attributed to the dynamics of public policy. In any case, the significant aspect of this recovery is that the government introduced measures (in 2005 and again in May 2008 with shift from Fidel to Raúl Castro in the presidency) designed to ensure a more equitable social distribution of the fruits of economic growth as well as a strengthening of the system of social security.

Again, this is in decided contrast to the economic model in place in the rest of Latin America. Despite robust rates of economic growth, especially in South America, under changed conditions of the international division of labour—with rates of per capita growth averaging from 5.7% in 2005 and not much less since—and a presumed generalised commitment to policies designed to reduce the incidence of poverty, social inequalities throughout the region in this period have increased. Although in a number of cases the rate of poverty has in fact been reduced, at least as defined in terms of official statistics, in no case has there been an improvement in the standard of living for the majority of the working population. Indeed, both in Chile and Argentina, countries that have led the recent economic recovery as well as a commitment to the new social policy under the PWC, conditions in the popular sector of society have deteriorated even in the context of an increase in the rise of the average wage and the participation of labour in national income. Even in Bolivia, which has seen the unprecedented rise to state power of the indigenous social movement as well as windfall profits and additional export-derived resource rents, conditions over the past two and a half years have gotten worse for the poor, not better.

Dynamics of Socialist Transition and Development

Above we outlined a framework for periodizing phases of capitalist development—the capitalist development of the forces of production. Given the worldwide development of the capitalist system—its extension into a world system, as conceptualized and argued by proponents of a 'world systems' perspective on the process of capitalist development—it is also possible to frame the history of socialist development in similar terms, that is, with reference to different phases in the development of capitalism as a world system. At the same time some theorists of socialist development argue that the issue is not the development of socialism with reference to the history of capitalist development as a world system but rather the dynamics of a transition from capitalism to socialism, regarding which various metatheories or models have been constructed (Martínez Heredia, 2001: 40).

According to Marxist theory, the transition from communism to capitalism requires a maturation process of creating conditions for the progression from incipient levels of socialization of property and overcoming social inequalities to the full and comprehensive realization of that socialization and equality. The different stages entail (i) a period of transition from capitalism to socialism; and (ii) a period of transition from socialism to communism. But except for the proposition that the state in the transition from socialism to communism would be stripped or lose its 'political function' (as an instrument of class rule) and would ultimately 'wither away' as the antagonism of a class divided society are resolved, only the first transition has been theorized.

In this theorization the presumption is that the transformation of capitalism into socialism is predicated on the control and use of the state apparatus by a political agency constituting the vanguard of the subaltern classes and committed to socialist principles. The state, in other words (as theorized by Marx and Lenin after him), will take the form of a 'dictatorship of the proletariat', that is, an instrument of class power—the social and political power of the subaltern classes converted into an agency of revolutionary transformation. From its functioning as the executive committee of the capitalist class as a whole the state in the process is converted into the executive committee of the hitherto exploited and oppressed classes.

It is further theorized that in the period of transition different forms of property and commercial relations would continue to coexist under conditions that will vary in different specific national experiences, but that the transition towards socialism will not be left to the anarchy of the market but planned. In theory (from the perspective of some Marxist scholars) there was no reason to suppress the market or the persistence of other than capitalist relations of production, but they should be regulated and subordinated to the instrumentation of collective decision-making and state planning.

As for the political aspect of the transition there is a fundamental tension and difference in theory between the view (the Soviet centralized planning model) that the socialization of production and the socialist transition should be planned, advanced by the centralized power and the authority of the State, and the contrary view (the soviet collective model) that socialism should take the form of workers controlling their workplaces, communitarians their communities. This difference in socialist theory was resolved in Russia and the Soviet Union, by Stalin and his regime under conditions that either called for or allowed a 'strong' centralized state. These conditions were both external (hostile international relations with the leaders of the capitalist democracies) and internal (the resistance against the socialization of production by the mass of peasant farmers). Under these conditions the transition towards socialism in the USSR was commanded by the centralized power and planning mechanisms of the State, establishing what the Soviets termed 'the state of all the people' but what would come to be more generally known as the 'Soviet model' (although strictly speaking the model was based on the centralized state power, not the power of the soviets). The mechanism of state centralized planning was designed to ensure the socialist distributive principle of 'from each according to their abilities, to each according to their needs'.

Another important debate in the socialist transition emerged in the 1960s in the context of a policy designed to eliminate not only all vestiges of capitalism but all forms of private property, that is, the market as a mechanism of economic exchange. Cuba launched a 'revolutionary offensive' in this direction in 1968, eliminating all forms of private property and the market by administrative fiat. However, at virtually the same time, the Communist Party of Yugoslavia began to experiment with the notion of a workers self-management regime, replacing the mechanism of centralized state planning with workers' control over their workplaces and workers' self-management, devolving a measure of decision-making power as to social production to the workers. The theory and practice of workers' self-management was at odds with the prevailing Soviet model of socialist national development, leading to an extended debate as to the nature and possible role of the market under socialism—the socialist market.

A third set of debates at the time (in the 1960s and 1970s) revolved around the nature of socialism under conditions given to countries in the 'third world'—'third world socialism'. Among socialist scholars in the capitalist west, the issue was reduced to a matter of socialist development on the periphery of the world capitalist system, or the contradictory dynamics of socialism and underdevelopment. Under the conditions of peripheral capitalism it was theorized that socialism, as well as capitalism, would take a different form and tracked along different paths—Chinese, Vietnamese, African, Cuban.

As to the specific forms that the transition and socialism would—and indeed did—take on the periphery of the capitalist system there was no end of debate, and different forms of practice that attempted to give form to socialism under different and changing conditions of capitalist underdevelopment in Africa, Asia and Latin America.

As for Cuba, the debate revolved around conflicting ideas as to role and weight of the subjective and objective factors in the process of revolutionary transformation (on this see Chapter 3). Within Cuba there were two basic perspectives on this issue, one represented most clearly by Che Guevara, the other by José Marti. As Guevara saw it the critical factor in the socialist transition was the creation of a 'socialist man and woman' (Valdés Paz, 1994: 36) in the context of the socialist development of the forces of production. For Che as for Marx, the forces of production and their corresponding social relations are *'two different sides of the development of the social individual'*.

With abstracted reference to the 'socialism-underdevelopment' debate Fernando Martínez Heredia (2001: 20, 40) identified three necessary conditions of revolutionary transformation in the transition to socialism: (1) the supremacy of politics over economics and the orientation of the latter towards meeting the needs of the majority; (2) elimination of any existing obstacles to that end, mainly capitalist private property; and, echoing Guevara (3) popular participation, organized with the revolutionary consciousness that socialism needs to be constructed 'from below'. As for the first two conditions they apply to all historical contexts and different forms of socialist transition. However, the third condition, as we will argue in Chapter 4 applies more specifically to Cuba, which is to say, it is a defining characteristic of the Cuban Revolution as it would unfold over time.

The Socialist Transition in Cuba

As for the history of the Cuban Revolution it can be understood in terms of conditions generated by the global process of capitalist development on the periphery of the system, and in terms of conditions that are specific to Cuba, conditions that responded to the 'public actions' used to advance the revolutionary process. With reference to these conditions the Cuban Revolution can be traced back to 1959, i.e. the victory of the 26th of July Movement, and from the class struggle leading up to it. Cuban historians and economists such as Espina Prieto (1994, 2008), Valdés Paz (1994), and Martínez Heredia (2001), and the Cuban Communist Party (Partido Comunista de Cuba, 1981), have identified the following key phases in the history of the Cuban Revolution. Each phase can be understood in terms of conditions that are both external and internal to Cuba, conditions that to some extent necessarily respond to public actions taken in a strategy to advance the Revolution, and conditions that arise from the structure of Cuba's international relations and the changing dynamics of the global economy:

- 1953–1959: a period of class struggle for control of the state (in the form of the 26th of July Movement)
- 1959–1961—a period of revolutionary change ('popular democracy, agrarian transformation and anti-imperialism')
- 1962–1975—a period characterized by the construction of a socialist state—the socialist development of the forces of production and society
- 1976–1989—a period of consolidation and rectification of errors
- 1989–1999—a special period of crisis, adjustment and restructuring
- 2000–2010—a period of recovery, continuity and change.

This periodization coincides with the official understanding of the history of the Revolution proclaimed in the documents of the Communist Party (PCC, 1981)—derived from a rather homogenized interpretation that plays down the national and regional peculiarities of the socialist development process. In the PCC version particular attention is given to 1975 and the different forms taken by the State in the period leading up to and following this watershed year. Essentially, according to the analysis provided in the PCC documents, the issue of political power was resolved early on in each period. In the first phase the dynamics of political power were constructed theoretically—with more than a passing reference to Lenin's reading of Marx's *The Gotha Programas*—as a Party-led 'democratic-revolutionary dictatorship of the popular masses' (workers, peasants, the urban petit bourgeoisie, and other elements of the population opposed to the dominion of imperialism and a 'bourgeois-latifundista oligarchy'. In the second phase the dictates of political power were understood in terms of an alliance of rural workers and other social sectors with interests opposed to the capitalism as a political and economic regime (PPC, 1981: 57).

The transition to the second phase of socialist construction was characterized by the expansion and radicalization of the socialization process—expropriating the property of big capital and converting it to state ownership, and transforming the corresponding relations of production. In the process the state assumed ownership of virtually all of the means of social production, a process advanced initially on the basis of expropriating big capital in both its national and foreign forms, and then, in the 'revolutionary offensive' of 1968, in the virtual elimination of 'private enterprise'. The dynamics of this socialist transformation in the social relations of production are captured in Table 2:

Table 2. Cuba. Economically Active Population (EAP), by Predominant Relations of Production, 1953 and 1970

	1953	1970
State workers	8.8	87.5
Private sector workers	63.3	1.3
Self-employed	24.0	1.2
Other non-state workers	3.9	10.0
Total	100.0	

Source: Comité Estatal de Estadísticas (1987).

The PCC documents, in effect, describe what in other Latin American contexts has been referred to as a 'welfare-development state'—a state that assumed responsibility for the 'welfare function' (to ensure the wellbeing of the population), the 'function of capital' (productive investment, entrepreneurship, management and sales) and the 'development function' (to advance the forces of production, broaden access to productive resources, ensure an equitable distribution of the social product). The difference is in the social form of the state—the class alliance that sustains it and the predominant social relation of production. As for the socialist State in Cuba it was constructed on the basis of several pillars laid down in the early years of the Revolution and cemented in subsequent years. However, the institutional structure of this State allows for various diverse 'models' that can be used to guide policy within an economic system—models, understood (González (2000: 5) as a particular 'set of principles, mode of functioning and mechanisms of action'. In these terms the fundamental difference and shift signaled made by 1975 was not in the system but in the model used to guide and implement policy. The details of this shift are discussed in Chapter 4.

Conclusion

In the post Second World War context, development, whether viewed in structural or strategic terms, unfolded within the institutional framework of two distinct systems—capitalism and socialism The project of international cooperation for development was designed to ensure that the developing and undeveloped countries of the so-called 'third world' would not fall prey to the lure of communism and that they would pursue a capitalist line of national development. Pressures for revolutionary change in the 1950s and 1960s, and the demonstration effect of the Soviet model of socialist development, led to the formation of diverse welfare and economic development regimes, and a broad program of state-led social reforms to the capitalist system The high costs of these programs led to a counterattack against the forces of progressive change and the construction of a new world order in which the 'forces of economic freedom' were released from the regulatory constraints of the welfare-development state.

In the face of this 'counterrevolution' the proponents of progressive reform advanced diverse ideas for bringing about alternative forms of development that are socially inclusive and participatory, human in scale and form, constructed from below rather than from above, people-led and-centred, equitable and empowering of women and the poor, and sustainable in terms of the environment and rural livelihoods. While the Washington Consensus on the need for free market capitalism took form as a new economic model of neoliberal globalization and a program of market-friendly 'structural reforms', proponents of progressive change and government intervention designed and placed on the policy agenda a model to guide policy in the direction of sustainable human development.

Throughout the post-Second World War period and until the 1990s development unfolded in two different systemic contexts, providing developing countries that were formally non-aligned room and opportunities to opt for but also to manoeuvre between a capitalist and a socialist path. In the historic context of US imperialism and an oppressive class rule power, and the specific conjuncture of growing resistance to imperialist exploitation and oppressive class rule, Cuban revolutionaries turned towards socialism to provide the system requirements for their human development project. Throughout the 1960s and subsequent decades Cuba proceeded along this path, tacking to the winds of change.

Changing conditions in the 1980s and 1990s created different contexts for human development in both its capitalist and socialist form. A capitalist form of human development was advanced and promoted by the economists at the UNDP, with variable degrees of success. Human development in this form throughout the 1980s and 1990s and beyond, bound by the institutional and social structures of a capitalist society and economy, had to contend with conditions generated by contradictions inherent in the system. The major contradiction is that under a private property regime, given the power of capital and its relation to the state, the freedom accorded the capitalist class in the pursuit of profit undermines the ability of workers and people in the subjugated popular sector to pursue lives that they have reason to value. The freedom of capital is the unfreedom of labour; the forces of capital accumulation, even when regulated by the state in the public interest, militate against human development, providing opportunities for some to accumulate wealth at the expense of many others, limiting their opportunities for self-advancement and exposing them to forces that prevent many of them from even meeting their basic needs.

A corollary of this conclusion—that capitalism does not satisfy the requirement of human development for freedom and equality; that capitalism at the level of both freedom and equality is inherently inhumane; and that giving capitalist development a human face does not change this fact—is that socialism should provide better system requirements. This is because socialism by definition, in theory if not in practice, is geared to the values of freedom and equality, and commits a governing regime or State to the institutionalization of these values not just as a formal or legal right but as a substantive human condition—under conditions that are equal for all. In this respect Marx formulated the dictum that 'the free development of each is the condition for the free development of all'. We might also hypothesize, and here state as a guiding principle, that 'the free development of all is the condition for the free development of each'. This corollary in subsequent chapters is formulated as a hypothesis and a guiding principle—to give direction to our study into the dynamics of socialist human development in Cuba.

CHAPTER FOUR

SOCIALISM, HUMAN DEVELOPMENT, AND THE CUBAN REVOLUTION

Development is an elusive term that has aroused heated debates and is mired in controversy (Drèze and Sen 1989). In the 1950s and the 1960s development signified economic growth, or the increase of the GDP per capita, but at the end of the 1960s this conventionally accepted equivalence became the target of criticism for a number of reasons, including the following: (i) economic growth does not necessarily bring with it an improvement in human welfare and flourishing (for example, countries with a high GDP per capita may suffer high unemployment and poverty); (ii) GDP per capita may be meaningless if it conceals substantial inequalities in wealth and income distribution; and (iii) human welfare is better measured in terms of access to essential social services such as sanitation, education and healthcare than income, even if national income were distributed relatively equitably.

The pendulum of thinking on development theory in terms of output or 'growth' (production) versus equality or equity (distribution) since the late 1960s has oscillated in an extended but shifting and as yet unsettled debate. In this debate there were essentially two positions. One the one side were the economists who argued that a degree of social inequality is not only a needed incentive to spur economic growth but is an acceptable cost of 'progress'. On the other side were those who argued for social equality as a matter of fundamental social justice and equity, with a focussed concern with issues such as inequality and poverty, In the 1970s, however, there emerged another viewpoint regarding the need for 'growth with equity', argued from the perspective of liberal reform and social reform. From this perspective growth and equality need not be traded-off: the alleviation of the social problems derived from market-led growth, such as social inequality and poverty, cannot be sustained in the long run without the savings and investment needed to promote growth. What is needed is to rely on the private sector and the market to generate growth but for the government to regulate the market and to use the mechanism of progressive taxation to redistribute some of the market-generated income in the public interest of equity. In addition, the government should secure as much *equity* (equal opportunity) as possible in accessing productive resources such as land, education and income-generating assets or employment, as well as *social inclusion* (universality) in the provision of essential social services.

This position was argued by those concerned with 'efficiency', on the one hand, and 'equity' on the other. The basic argument, advanced with different permutations, was that the key to economic growth, its 'driving force', is the rate of savings and productive investment of these savings, but the increase in investment does not guarantee or result in growth unless it is efficiently and equitably distributed.

Although it would take another three decades of debate and various shifts in theory and policy to settle these issues, this meant that (1) access to productive resources such as land, capital, technology and labour needs to be extended and improved. In this connection, initial inequalities in the allocation of or access to productive resources was seen by some as a major impediment to economic growth. In addition, (2) investment in education and health contributes to a healthier labour-force with better skills, thus improving productivity and promoting growth ('human capital' in economic terms). Furthermore, (3) growth is not merely a matter of efficient investment in the application of science and technology to production, but it is also influenced by the role of institutions and economic policy (an appropriate policy and institutional framework, a point argued by advocates of 'institutional economics').

The implication of these ideas is that the State is the fundamental agency of economic and social development. The resources and power of the state is needed in regard to (i) institutional or structural (state-led) reform in regard to an allocation of, or improving access to, productive resources or income-generating assets; (ii) provision of essential services regarding social or human development; and (iii) the redistribution of market-generated income in the interest of equity—redistributing this income in the form of social (and development) programs, and capping wealth generated income at the top (providing a ceiling on investment income) and cushioning those at the bottom (insulating low income earners from the worst of poverty, alleviating the pain).

In the 1970s the search for a more embracing or holistic concept of development (integrating the economic and the social) and a better balance in the use of indicators to measure development led to a new focus and calls for a 'new development paradigm': the satisfaction of basic needs (prescription of the World Bank) and the achievement of full employment (objective of the ILO), which culminated in 1976 with the World Employment Conference on the Basic Needs Strategy. At the turn into the 1980s the Overseas Development Council sponsored the construction of a 'Quality of Life Index' comprised of multiple indicators but broadly focused on poverty and meeting the basic needs of the population.

Development under the Washington Consensus

However, developments in the 1980s conspired to push this new paradigm (the concern for meeting basic needs, ensuring growth with equity, alleviating poverty etc.) off the development agenda, in many cases almost entirely. For one thing, application of structural adjustment policies, combined with the severe economic and fiscal crises, provoked an increase in poverty and increased inequalities in wealth and income distribution—and a concern with the destabilizing effects of the 'inequality predicament'. At the same time, the turn towards a 'new economic model' and the Washington Consensus on the need for a neoliberal policy agenda shifted the concern of mainstream development theorists and policy advisers away from poverty alleviation and equity back towards growth—neoliberal 'pro-growth' (structural reform) policies. As for the *war on poverty* it continued but on a different track—that of a new paradigm in which the responsibility for development shifted away from the state towards civil society...to the agency of the poor, empowered to act for themselves with international cooperation in a strategic partnership with 'civil society'.

Beyond the Washington Consensus

In the 1990s, the growth of social inequalities and the political instability it engendered, led to a rethinking of this agenda—of the role of the state in the need for greater social inclusion and creating a new policy agenda that would strike a better balance between the market and the state. Meanwhile, the concept of development was given a new twist, a reformulation focused on the issue not of equality but of freedom—expanding the choices available to individuals in acting for themselves, empowering them to act / take advantage of their opportunities, and on the need for institutional development and a new policy agenda, to create thereby a level playing field and an equality of opportunity ('equity' as the World Bank understands it).

In the debates in the 1970s and extended into the 1980s, little attention was given to incorporating external economic indicators in the measurement of development, a deficit corrected by Latin American structuralism, which focused its concern on precisely the external factors such the location of a country in the world economy and the relations among countries and regions. In the late 60s and 1970s theorists of 'dependency' had explained underdevelopment in these terms, as a relation of 'dependency' of the countries on the periphery on those at the centre, which used its power to extract a surplus from the producers and workers on the periphery. However, in the 1970s this theory was discredited, and together with the Latin American structuralism (Cepalismo) lost relevance and influence in the new world order of neoliberal globalization, which privileged free market capitalism and Neoclassical theory of economic growth based on productive investment of national savings (and, according to institutionalists, appropriate institutional development).

Currently, for the purpose of 'aid' provision, major international organizations that have constituted themselves as development associations rank countries on the basis of distinct 'development' indicators. The World Bank in its annual *World Development Report* (first published in 1978) in 1996 classified and ranked 133 countries in three major categories based on real per capita GNP in US$: low-income, middle-income (subdivided into lower and upper) and high-income, hence based on the conventional concept of development. The Bank, in the context of, or response to, severe criticisms acknowledged that per capita GNP does not by itself measure welfare or success and in development and in 1988 began to publish a yearbook companion on *Social Indicators of Development*. But so far it has not integrated them with its major indicator. It was left to the UNDP to do so—to construct an index that integrated the economic and the social (a long and healthy life, acquisition of knowledge and a decent standard of living). In 1990 it began to publish an annual *Human Development Report*, a yearbook in which countries across the world are ranked according to their level of HD, measured on the basis of an index composed of three variables: two social (life expectancy at birth and education—adult literacy, school enrolment) and one economic (real GDP at purchasing power parity rates in US dollars). The result was quite a different—sometimes radically so—ranking from that offered by the World Bank in its uni-dimensional focus on GNP or per capita income. Cuba, for example, is ranked in the lowest development category by the World Bank but in the highest by the UNDP, pointing towards a lack of correlation between the economic and the social. Indeed, a recent UNDP study (Gray and Molina, 2010) into human development trends since 1970 finds that 'the income and non-income components of HDI change have a near-zero correlation'.

The concepts and indicators of development used by the World Bank, the UNDP and other development associations are in practice related to diverse goals and approaches chosen to pursue it—and to the underlying system (capitalism) presumed to provide for 'development' or the improvement of social conditions. It is assumed that socialism, except for some principles incorporated into the system (mixed economies), is antithetical to 'development', especially as regards 'freedom' (see our discussion in Chapter 8). This of course is the opposite assumption made by many Marxists or theorists of socialism, namely that capitalism, as the source of the 'problem' (inequality, poverty, unemployment etc.), cannot be part of the 'solution' (development).

Within the institutional and policy framework of the capitalist system, 'development' is predicated on institutional reform—to create conditions of social exclusion, equity (equal opportunity) and good governance or sustainability—and an appropriate policy agenda (pro-poor/pro-growth). With numerous permutations, there were two basic approaches to development in this institutional or systemic context: (i) growth vs. equity; and (ii) growth with equity. The first (i) is to allocate resources to promote economic expansion (normally with a predominant role accorded to the market) on the assumption that there will be a 'trickle-down' effect that will eventually lead to an improvement in the living conditions of all the population including the poor. The second approach assigns priority to public services, employment promotion by the state, reduction or alleviation of poverty (especially in its extreme forms) and income inequality as an incentive to 'growth'. More recently, within the framework of a PWC, there have been diverse arguments and efforts designed to not only create a better 'balance between the state and market' but to combine both approaches in the belief that such a 'mix' is both desirable, needed and possible. In this connection the UNDP (1996: 6) went back to the 1970s debate to argue that there is 'a reinforcing relationship between equity and growth'. But the controversy as to whether or how the two approaches to development within capitalism are compatible, or whether there is an inevitable trade-off between them, lingers.

Dreze and Sen (1989), in launching their concept of HD, argued that this duality in approach is both simplistic and false: that it is possible and necessary to combine them, and to do so—without being explicit in this regard—*within* the operating capitalist system. That is, their premise was that it *is* to bring about development within capitalism; that it does not require socialism but rather institutional reform and a policy agenda designed to equalise opportunities for the hitherto excluded (equity) to realise and act on their entitlements, an expansion of choice and the capacitation of individuals to act on their own behalf: 'empowerment' of the poor, as it would be termed some decade later within the framework of the PWC.

The critical feature of this way of thinking and practice was that it was entirely based in the institutionality of capitalism. At issue throughout these debates was what type and level of reforms were called for, shifting from the market to the state but never beyond it—never any questions about the system itself, no questioning of its fundamental pillars: *private property* in the means of social production; (ii) the *state* as an agency for providing legal security to private property and supreme role of the capital accumulation process—the capital accumulation function; (3) the *market,* allowed to operate as freely as possible within a capitalist institutional and social context; and (4) *wage labour* as the fundamental social relationship of production—source of revenue or earned income. 'Development' in other words should take a capitalist form.

Socialist Human Development in Practice

Although the Cuban revolutionaries in their quest for state power were motivated more by nationalism and anti-imperialism than socialism per se the Cuban Revolution was initiated and advanced on the presumption that (i) capitalism (and imperialism) was the fundamental source of the miserable socioeconomic conditions lived by most of the population (Mesa-Lago 1981); (ii) without social justice there is no democracy, and conversely, without democracy there is no social justice; (iii) freedom and equality only have meaning in the context of the value attached by socialists to solidarity; and (iv) that the solution to these problems (its system requirements) is socialism—understood as the socialization of production and the equitable distribution of the social product under conditions of social equality and solidarity, understood as the union or spirit of fellowship arising from common responsibilities and interests, as between all members of society and peoples across the world in their struggle for independence, freedom and social justice.

In 1958 compared with other Latin American countries at a similar level of development the Cuba had a very low degree of public ownership in the means of production and regulation of capital (Mesa-Lago, 2000: 171). US capital owned pubic utilities such as electricity and telephones and controlled a significant share of banking. The only extensive state ownership was found in education and healthcare but conditions in these areas reflected the class character of a capitalist state.

The market-based economy was highly dependent on the production of a single commodity, sugar, dependence reflected in the social structure of agricultural production. While the rural sector of most societies in Latin America was dominated by social relations of independent or peasant small-scale production, and in social terms by a large number of poor and proletarianized peasants, rural society in Cuba was predominantly constituted by a rural proletariat, viz. an advanced degree of the social conversion of the traditional peasantry into a rural wage-earning working class (Zeitlin, 1970).[1] The weight of the proletariat in the social structure was reflected in the relatively high share of labour (wages) in national income—65% according to Mesa-Lago (2000: 172). While sugar generated close to 30% of GNP and represented 81% of exports, up to 25% of the labour force was employed in the sugarcane fields and sugar mills (Perez-Lopez, 1995), a fact that goes a long way in explaining the relative success of the Cuban revolutionaries in attracting massive support from the rural population.

Notwithstanding the miserable condition of most people in the popular sector of a class divided society government legislation on labour conditions and social security under Batista was among the

---

[1] As Pollitt (1977) points out, pre-revolutionary rural Cuba included people who combined small-scale agricultural production or 'independent farming' with wage labour, what in the contemporary debate on the nature of the 'peasantry' is termed 'semi-proletarianization'.

most advanced in the region—at least according to Mesa-Lago (2000: 172). At the same time trade unions were relatively strong, again reflecting the weight of workers in the sugar industry in the economy and the social structure. But the high degree of unionization in the sector of rural work (relative to other countries where peasant farmers were in the majority), and the relative strength of the union movement, the sugar industry was plagued by a high degree of seasonal unemployment, a structural feature of the industry that union power could not change and that was combined with a conjunctural tendency towards stagnation and chronic unemployment. One effect of this structure and situation was that in the annual slack period, the high rate of rural-urban migration reached almost epic proportions, generating economic and social problems that the government was unable or unwilling to address. A CERP study suggests that both open unemployment and rural out-migration was on the increase in the 1950s, fuelling the problem of deteriorating conditions in the countryside.

Added to these deteriorating economic conditions in the countryside was a high degree of social exclusion from essential government services, in health and education and other areas. These services were concentrated in the urban areas, especially Havana—a situation not unlike in other countries in the region but that in Cuba took a more political form, precisely because of the relatively advanced state of service provision).

According to Mesa-Lago (2000: 173) there is a relative consensus among foreign scholars on how best to periodize the 'Revolution', with the possible exception of Zimbalist and Eckstein (1987). As for Cuban scholars, as we note in Chapter, they generally follow the same periodization but stress the continuity of the process rather than the discontinuities (Rodriguez, 1989). In this context these Cuban scholars mark 1959, 1962, 1975 and 1989–1990 as milestones marking different stages in the revolutionary process.

With an emphasis on major shifts in government economic policy as well as certain discontinuities Mesa-Lago identifies seven stages in the revolutionary process from 1959 to 1995. As he reconstructs it, public policy over the period was characterized by a series of pendulum shifts between central planning and the market, with 'an overwhelming predominance of the former' (p. 174). Intertwined with the shifts in policies affecting economic organization were shifting policies concerning development strategy—policies, we argue (and on this we follow Zimbalist and Eckstein, and a virtual consensus of Cuban scholars, rather than Mesa-Lago who de-emphazises if not entirely ignores the 'equity' dimension of the growth model used to guide government policy), were generally and consistently shaped by an enduring commitment to socialism as a model of human development.

From the Capitalist Market to a Socialist State, 1959–1960

As argued by Mesa-Lago the Revolution lacked an explicit ideology, although Fidel Castro referred to what Mesa-Lago (2000) terms a 'vague doctrine of humanism' and without a doubt the whole revolutionary enterprise was motivated by a fundamental concern for 'national liberation' from colonialism, imperialism and sovereignty, as well as emancipation of the population from oppressive class rule. In addition to 'humanism' some scholars also detected the influence of Latin American structuralism, particularly in regard to economic development strategy and policy (import substitution industrialization) and income distribution and progressive taxation policies, which were implemented in a number of developing countries and states (for example, Costa Rica, Sri Lanka, Kerala) in the same and the following decade under the 'growth with equity' social reform model (Zimbalist, 1985). Of course, scholars such as Mesa-Lago with a clear ideological bent (liberalism and capitalism) downplayed the humanism and social reform dimensions of the Revolution's initial policies, arguing if not attempting to prove that the revolutionaries were anti-humanist 'crypto-Marxists'.[2] In any case, the proof is in the pudding so to speak, and the revolutionaries once in power soon showed a decided predilection towards humanism and social reformism, particularly in terms of improved access to the means of production in land and income distribution, as well as the agency of the state, which liberal ideologues at the time and since equated with 'socialism' but was central to the prevailing economic development theory.

---

[2] On the question of the wide scholarly disagreement in the literature on Cuba's performance Susan Eckstein (1992) argues that ideology rather than 'deficient data' is at issue. Jorge Pérez-López, in his review of the literature ("Thinking about the Cuban Economy in the 1990s") in the same volume implies that differences in assessments are attributable mainly to data deficiencies.

Mesa-Lago and others attribute this policy orientation not so much to 'crypto-Marxism', statist authoritarianism or socialism as to 'ignorance in economic matters' and the 'applicator of guerrilla techniques to the Cuban economy': privileging a 'willingness, consciousness, morale, austerity and loyalty'—and 'the zeal and hard work of the leaders, the audacity of improvisation an support of the people'—over 'material and human resources, technology and knowledge and expertise' (1981, 2000: 175). In either case, one of the first policy moves made by the government was to collectivise ownership in the means of production, particularly land—a policy that gained momentum as the decade unfolded. Of course, this policy of expropriating latifundia (farms exceeding a ceiling of 400 ha) was by no means restricted to Cuba; the 1980s was the heyday of social reformism under the developmental model of 'growth with equity'. But in Cuba the reform was more far-reaching or radical than in other cases and because of the penetration of US capitalism it took on a more radical aspect of nationalization and 'anti-imperialism' (expropriation of land owned by US capitalists).

The first Agrarian Reform law, promulgated in May 1959, was accompanied by the confiscation of the property and assets embezzled by officials of the overthrown Batista regime; the expropriation of rental housing for social distribution (and housing rents were reduced by 50%), state intervention in economic enterprises (factories, warehouses, transportation) abandoned by their owners or in which labour conflicts disrupted production; and the confiscation of property of those who failed to pay taxes or were either convicted of counterrevolutionary crimes or in exile (Mesa-Lago, 2000: 176). As for the land reform, most of the latifundia, particularly the sugarcane plantations and cattle ranches, were indeed taken over and the land redistributed either among peasants who had worked it without ownership or converted it into state-run agricultural enterprises or cooperatives, thereby initiating an agrarian revolution rather than reform.

In the second half of the 1960s the pace of socialization and stratification increased, extended to all US or foreign-owned oil refineries, US-owned sugar mills, banks, businesses and utilities. In March the revolutionary government nationalized the Cuban Telephone Company. The Ministry for the Recovery of Embezzled goods, founded by the Revolution, nationalized 14 sugar mills and in April 1959 announced that it had recovered more than US$400 million for the people. On June 29, in response to US aggression it took over Texaco and on July 1, ESSO and Shell. And in August all US companies in the oil, communications and electricity sectors were nationalized. In October, this nationalization process, a form of socialization in the name and cause of 'national liberation' (arguably a socialist condition of human development), was extended to all domestic and foreign banks and large capitalist enterprises, including 105 sugar mills, 50 textile companies and eight railroad companies. By the end of the first decade all domestic wholesale and foreign trade and banking, and most transportation, industry, construction and retail trade, and more than one-third of agriculture, was under state ownership and control.

As Mesa-Lago noted, this transfer of ownership effectively 'liquidated' capitalism and severely restricted the workings of the non-capitalist market. In this context, several government agencies were created to regulate what remained of private economic activity and to substitute central planning for the market. The central Planning Board (JUCEPLAN) was initially established in March 1960 not as agency for central planning but to coordinate government policies and to guide the private sector through indicative planning, much as in Japan and the emerging Asian NICs. Financing of economic development was also increasingly coordinated and conducted through the state, via the Ministry of Finance and the National Bank, private financing largely restricted to agriculture. The Ministry of Labour, according to Mesa-Lago, who, like most liberals is adverse if not hostile to socialism in any form, played an important role in establishing labour conditions—'the first step', Mesa-Lago adds, 'towards taming trade unions' (2000: 177).

The socialization process provoked the exodus not only of the ruling class of owners but of a wide swath of managers, technicians and professionals of all sorts—in sociological terms the professional-managerial or upper middle class. However, the revolutionary government acted judiciously and swiftly in replacing this class through an extensive and open professional training and educational program, initiating a policy that would take some years to iron out the wrinkles but that ultimately would bear fruit and pay off in the formation of a new cadre of professionals that were solidly committed to the revolutionary project.

As for economic development, the leadership in its strategy associated the island's economic problems with sugar dependence, hence their first development strategy was to lessen this dependence and move to diversify economic production by means of an import substitution strategy, a strategy proposed by ECLA at the time, and a program of agricultural diversification (Ritter, 1974). Another aspect of this strategy, which was initiated in 1960 and ended in 1963, was a move to reduce economic dependency on the US that included a trade agreement with the USSR. This agreement committed the Soviet Union to buy one million tons of sugar annually and to supply oil, machinery and chemicals in return. In the mid 1960s US-owned refineries refused to refine Soviet oil crude, hence they were nationalised and by the end of the year practically all of Cuba's oil was imported from the Soviet Union, beginning what in respect could be seen was a new economic dependency, one that would spell near disaster 25 years later with the collapse of the USSR and with it a predominant trade relationship.

At the level of labour, the hitherto dominant capital-labour relation had been broken, and thus the government, via the Ministry of Labour, began (in 1960) to set wages and regulate labour conditions. From a human development perspective this was an important 'development' since the government by means of a pay-scale mechanism was able to thereby ensure in short order a relatively equitable social distribution of national income, most of which by the end of the 1960s took the form of wages for work. Because of the socialization ('collectivization' as Mesa-Lago has it), employment in the state sector had grown from some 9% to about one half of the labour force (Mesa-Lago, 2000: 178).

In the agricultural sector, endemic seasonal employment was reduced initially not by public action or administrative fiat but by structural change—the aggregate result of the decisions made by thousands of proletarianized peasants and the rural poor to migrate to the cities, especially Havana. In this process the population of Havana in the 1960s increased to twice the average growth of the 1950s. The children of these migrant families were given immediate and equal access to a growing number of schools constructed as a matter of priority, while the migrants themselves were largely absorbed into the rapidly growing labour market for jobs in the armed forces, state security and police, unions and other mass organizations, public works and social services. In addition, thousands of young peasants received scholarships for education programs that delayed their entry into the labour market as well as facilitated a process of social transformation from small-scale peasant farmers and rural workers to an urban working and middle class. A key aspect of this process was a massive literacy campaign conducted by thousands of volunteer teachers that virtually eliminated illiteracy in less than a year as well as dramatically improved the opportunities for self-advancement available to the masses of the rural poor. From a human development perspective this 'development' had a transcendental significance. In other parts of Latin America the same process of productive and social transformation (modernization, urbanization and capitalist development) was well underway but subject to the vicissitudes and painful adjustments of the market, and generally leading to the absorption of rural surplus labour not into work for wages but to the growth of 'work on one's account' in the burgeoning informal sector and the associated 'planet of slums' (Davis 2006). The rural-to-urban migrants in this process were generally excluded from public education, reflected in significantly higher rates of illiteracy than in Cuba.

Notwithstanding the relatively low level of labour remuneration and the scepticism in this regard of economists in the liberal tradition, the vast majority of the proletarianized and semi-proletarianized rural workers were decidedly better off as a result of this new labour regime. For another thing, the government rationed to each family a minimum supply of essentials that reduced the dependence on earned income in meeting the household's basic needs. Except for agriculture, collectivization had virtually eliminated dividends, rents and interest forms of income. For another, the rate of unemployment was reduced and the relatively flat pay-scale differential in the state sector ensured an unprecedented degree of equity or fairness in the social distribution of income.

No longer would a relatively small upper and middle class of well positioned individuals be able to appropriate and dispose of the lion's share of the social product, leaving the bulk of the population to fend for themselves in the interstices, or on the margins, of the system. To the degree that meeting the basic needs of the entire population and improving the standards of living with an appreciable degree of equity are fundamental principles of socialist human development, the Cuban Revolution began to deliver quickly and early on the promise of a more 'human' form of society, albeit under difficult economic conditions and a very sporadic rate of economic growth. Under these conditions aggregate income actually expanded as a result of the extension of free education and healthcare and subsidized housing, as well as the reduction of electricity rates and urban housing rates by as much as 50%. Mesa-Lago (2000) makes passing reference to this 'development' but in his concern for a 'Stalinist' 'command system' of centralized planning he deemphasizes its social and political significance for human development. And the concentration of fiscal expenditures on expanding social services in the rural areas also helped reduce the urban-rural gap in living standards as well as ensure a very high level of support for the Revolution in the rural areas, a political development that most clearly distinguishes the Cuban Revolution from the Russian. In fact, in this connection Ernest Mandel notes, 'the Cuban Revolution is distinguished by the fact that it succeeded in both gaining and maintaining the support of most of the popular masses for the revolutionary project' (1971).

Orthodox Central Planning, 1961–1963

With the US-sponsored Bay of Pigs invasion and the declaration that Cuba was socialist, the year 1961 marked a decisive break with the US at the level of international relations. Having turned away from the market at this level—largely because of the intransigence of the US administration but also to secure the survival of the Revolution—towards the Soviet Union, the government leadership decided to model its economy on the Soviet system of centralized planning. The next few years were dominated by the efforts of the regime to install this model in the production system.

In spite of warnings against an overly broad and too rapid collectivization and socialization by some Marxist planners (e.g. Charles Bettleheim and René Dupont), as Mesa-Lago (2000: 181) pointed out 'that process continued unabated'. In 1961 all private educational institutions and large hospitals were nationalized. In 1962 the government introduced rationing to ensure that the most basic needs of all Cubans would be met, and most remaining private retail trade stores were collectivized into a state network of groceries and shops. While this policy, according to Mesa-Lago, would result in a noticeable decline in the quality and perhaps the quantity of supply it also ensured that the basic needs of the entire population were met as well as relative equity in the distribution of the social product. In the same year (1961) the private agricultural cooperatives that had been established in 1959 were transformed into state farms, reducing the size of the non-capitalist private sector and the scope of the market in agricultural products.

In 1963 a second agrarian reform law expropriated land of farms of more than 67 Hectares, eliminating as a result the mid-sized independent farmer from the production process. In the meantime the state secured control of the private sector in agriculture through INRA, which introduced a system of procurement quotas—the compulsory sale of a part of the agricultural crop to the state at prices set below the market.

This system, of course, was designed to feed into the state distribution system of grocery stores and ration cards—thereby socializing and de-commodifying access to foodstuffs and essentials. The remaining peasant farmers in the private sector were incorporated into the state-controlled National Association of Small Farmers (ANAP). Finally, in 1963 the socialization of private social insurance funds was completed, and all of these funds were integrated into a state social security/healthcare system.

By 1963, as Mesa-Lago (2000: 182) points out, only 30% of agriculture and 25% of retail trade (mostly street vending) remained in the private sector. The socialization and collectivization of production, therefore, was completed with relative speed and notably without the violent conflicts and bloody confrontations that accompanied the process in other socialist countries at a comparable stage of national development—or, for that matter (and entirely ignored by the likes of Mesa-Lago), that characterized the process of agrarian transformation in capitalist countries.

The shift from the capitalist market to centralized state planning was influenced, as Mesa-Lago (2000: 182) notes, by Western Marxist scholars such as Leo Huberman, Paul Sweezy, Paul Baran at *Monthly Review* and others (Ernest Mandel, for example). But he notes that most of the technical advice came from the Soviet Union and Czechoslovakia. Rejecting the alternative of market socialism (theorized in the 1920s and 1930s and in the 1950s and 1960s put into practice by Yugoslavia), the Cuban leadership at the time opted for a highly centralized planning model introduced under Stalin the 1920s and favoured by the Soviet Union ever since. This model was first introduced into Cuba in 1961 with JUCEPLAN, the agency charged with the responsibility of formulating and securing the implementation of an annual and a series of medium-range plans. A network of central ministries and agencies were created to command the recently collectivized and nationalised economic sectors. The National Bank of Cuba became the treasury, the issuer and comptroller of the currency, depository bank and the manager of credit.

In the industrial sector, state enterprises producing the same type of goods were merged into trusts controlled by the corresponding central ministry. In 1958, according to Mesa-Lago, there were about 38,300 industrial firms but by 1961, 18,500 industrial enterprises, accounting for 80% of industrial production, had been combined into several trusts (p. 183). In agriculture, state farms on the Soviet model had been integrated with either INRA or the Ministry of Sugar. By the mid 1960s most foreign-owned agricultural and industrial enterprises had been nationalized, provoking both US governmental ire and the exodus of many professionals, technicians, managers of capitalist enterprises and of course their owners.

Early on in the 1960s, barely a year into the Revolution, several medium-term national development plans based on the Soviet model were drawn up by the Polish development planner Michael Kalecki and the French Marxist economist Charles Bettleheim and the Russian Efinov among others. But the perceived failure of the diversification strategy in 1963, pursued with reference to these plans, raised serious questions about the economic model of centralised planning and generated a major debate about the central planning mechanism and about the form that Cuban socialism should take (see next section). As in every capitalist country then and since, according to Mesa-Lago there was no popular participation in the formulation of these plans or public policy, although Limia (2010) begs to differ and Bettleheim (1964), in his reconstruction of Marxist economic and political theory, social participation is an absolute requirement for socialist development. In any case, popular participation in economic strategy and public policy was not at issue in the 'great debate' on Cuba socialism. Rather, at issue in this debate was the question of the relative importance and weight of material and moral incentives in the economic development process. Economists attuned to orthodox economic thinking and the Soviet model argued the need for material incentives whereas Ernesto [Che] Guevara notably espoused the importance of moral incentives.

In any event, by 1963 the initial plans for economic growth based on an import substitution form of industrialization was widely perceived to have failed, even though hard data on economic growth in this period are not available (Mesa Lago, 1969). Nevertheless, even though 'we lack statistics' Mesa-Lago is able (or chooses) to assert that 'it is clear that economic growth continued in 1961, fuelled by the second largest sugar crop in history…[and t]he output of key industrial products (in 1963)…decreased or was stagnant' (2000: 191). The perceived problems at this early stage in the country's economic performance (bottlenecks, shortages and surpluses, the decline of investment productivity) was attributed by Mesa-Lago to a failure of the central planning model and associated 'inefficiencies in the allocation and use of capital' (p. 191).

The failure of centralized planning and the strategy of industrial diversification Mesa-Lago attributes not only to the ideologically perceived inherent deficiencies of the Soviet model[3] but the overly rapid pace of socialization—'collectivization' as Mesa-Lago incorrectly sees it—which led to the destruction of 'millions of economic micro-relations' formed under the market and vital to decision making in a complex economy and impossible for the state to substitute in a short timeframe (p. 184). One of many examples of this state planning failure was that agricultural products badly needed in the cities were either lost in the ground, forgotten or, after being harvested spoiled because of unavailable transportation. Another example, according to Mesa-Lago—and this ironically, given the revolutionary regime's prioritization of social and human development—was an overemphasis on production, reducing social services spending and sacrificing consumption on the altar of 'investment efficiency' and increased production (p. 185).

A feature of the Soviet development model was rapid industrialization based in part on 'agrarian transformation'—transformation of the peasantry into an industrial proletariat. According to Lenin, the practical theorist of the Russian Revolution, this process was fraught with serious pitfalls and should not be accelerated at the expense of the peasant farmer, who should both participate actively and be brought along willingly into the process. As we have already noted and will further argue, this marks a clear difference between the Soviet model of socialism and the human development model exemplified by the Cuban Revolution.

Rapid industrialization had clearly worked in the Soviet Union—although not as conceived by Lenin but rather as mandated by Stalin in total disregard of Lenin's warnings and precautions, and at an

---

[3] This model, as Mesa-Lago describes it, specifies five procedures: (1) construction of basic economic directives consisting of aggregated guidelines [desirable growth rates, sectoral allocation of investment, the distributional shares of consumption] decided on by the Executive and handed down to the planners; [2] a 'global model' or aggregated projections and overall targets prepared by the planning agency [JUCEPLAN]; [3] preparation of 'control' figures or preliminary disaggregated targets set in consultation with relevant enterprise officials; [4] construction of 'directive figures' or final disaggregated targets; and [5] control adjustments [p. 184].

enormous social cost borne by millions of small-scale agricultural producers and peasant farmers: inducing a rapid process of heavy industrialization by means of transforming a traditional economy of backward poor peasants into a modern industrial economy—at a relatively advanced standards of living, constituting thereby what for decades (until the collapse of socialism between 1989 and 1991) was regarded as a 'second (Eastern) world of development' vis-à-vis the 'first (Western) world of capitalist development' and a 'third world' of developing and underdeveloped countries.

Nevertheless, in Cuba the 'Soviet model'—again, according to Mesa-Lago but also other economists who concluded that the model was not applicable to small island states—was a 'dismal failure' in that it depended on conditions (e.g. an industrial working class, a sizeable/expanding domestic market, opportunity to export manufactured goods to the west) that were simply not available or could not be created by administrative fiat or centralized power (p. 187).

In regard to this issue of socialist development a critical factor is what has been theorized extensively as the 'agrarian question' in a capitalist development context—the penetration of capitalism (or socialism) in the countryside and the resulting transformation of the structure of production relations. In the context of the Russian Revolution this meant what for Lenin would be a slow and protracted process of converting a mass of poor and economically backward 'peasants' into a proletariat with a socialist consciousness—the willing and active participation in a process of socialist reorganization—the socialization of production and consumption.

As Bettleheim (in Guevara, 2006: 166) quotes and reconstructs Lenin's position on this question vis-à-vis the Russian Revolution, the conversion of the small-scale agricultural producer or peasant—to 'transform his psychology and habits is a matter of several generations', an 'extraordinarily protracted' process; the peasant as an independent commodity producer in this process will have to supported and brought along slowly, 'satisfying the peasants' demands', a revolutionary process of consciousness transformation (and active willing engagement) that entails a long struggle, an extended self- and political-educational process.

But the point is—a point not fully appreciated by orthodox Marxist theorists such as Bettleheim who insisted in viewing Cuba through the lens of the Russian experience—Cuba was very unlike Russia in regard to both the *objective and subjective conditions of socialist transformation*

(Guevara, 2006: 101). On this see the argument advanced in Chapter 4. For one thing, Russia at the time of the Revolution was essentially a society of economically backward serfs or peasants wedded to the land and working it as individuals, albeit in the context of widespread communalism and even vestiges of feudalism. Cuba, on the other hand, exhibited the highest degree of rural proletarianization of any country in Latin America. Most of the economically active population in the rural society did not constitute a peasantry of small agricultural producers, but rather worked on the sugar plantations and mills for wages, i.e as a rural proletariat. By the mid 1950s over half the labour force, including in the sugar sector, was unionized and the proportion of the island's labour force in the organized labour movement was one of the largest in the world (O'Connor, 1970). Indeed, this was likely a major factor in the success of the Cuba revolutionaries in attracting the support of both the rural and urban population.

It is assumed in many studies of the Cuban Revolution that its rural base of support was composed predominantly of 'peasants' but in fact much of this peasantry had been proleterianized. In any case, having achieved state power, the Cuban revolutionaries did not have to confront what for the Russian revolutionaries was a major obstacle: the virtual non-existence of a rural proletariat organised and predisposed towards socialism by the weight of the material conditions of their social existence.

Lenin in this situation counselled a slow and laborious process of working supportively with the peasant producer in a dialectical process of political education and the transformation of consciousness—in effect, a 'cultural revolution' (as quoted by Bettleheim in Guevara, 2006: 100). This was advice, that Stalin, as it turned out, totally ignored in a policy of rapid socialization (overly rapid for Lenin) and forced 'transformation'. But conditions in Cuba, however, were radically different, explaining in good part the distinctive feature and singular peculiarity of the Cuban Revolution: 'the fact that it achieved the support of the vast majority of the popular masses for the Revolution' (Mandel, 1971: 311).

What made it difficult to apply the Soviet model of heavy industrialization—another island state, Taiwan, in the same timeframe, albeit more populous and operating with a different system, *was* able to employ this strategy for its national development—was the structure of Cuba's external relations with the Soviet Union and the socialist bloc. The structure of this relation was based on the exchange of sugar for oil and the importation by Cuba of Soviet industrial products and manufactured goods. This exchange relation, according to some (Ritter, for example) was tantamount to a new 'dependency' (essentially replacing one for another), also implied a fatally flawed technological dependence. In the 1970s and in the first half of the 1980s, when the rest of Latin America was caught in a downward development spiral of external debt and virtually zero economic growth, the Soviet model of centralized planning in Cuba did in fact begin to bear fruit, generating the highest economic growth rates in the region as well as in the history of the Revolution to that point. But in the second half of the 1980s this engine of growth, as in the Soviet Union itself, began to sputter and slow to a crawl, a victim, according to Mesa-Lago and other such liberal (capitalist oriented) economists, of over-centralized and bureaucratized planning as well as technological sclerosis.

Via the socialization of both production and consumption, and a relatively flat pay-scale scheme with well-defined lower and upper limits, income inequalities were significantly reduced in this period of 'orthodox' centralized planning and, according to Mesa-Lago (in fact, he provides no hard data on this point) reduced consumption and restricted social services. Private owners of health and educational services lost their high income and market privileges; large and medium-sized farmers, both corporate and individual, were wiped out and, having lost their perquisites of private property, either abandoned the country or had to adjust to straitened circumstances and reduced incomes. Because most means of production had become state-owned (except for 30% in agriculture and 25% in retail trade and small business), practical all incomes were fixed and paid by the government, with a consequent flattening of the income distribution structure.

There are no official data on income distribution prior to and under the Revolution in its early years; only gross speculative estimates and surmises made by Western scholars on the basis of obvious developments such as earned income as the almost exclusive source of income. Two estimates indicate a substantial redistribution in the first four years of the Revolution but with an important difference: one estimate, based on family income in 1958 and 1962 was that about 8% of income was transferred from the wealthiest quintile to the poorest 40% of families (MacEwan, 1981). The other estimate, based on personal income in 1953 and 1962, suggested that 16.5% of income was transferred from the wealthiest quintile but with only a small portion (4.1%) going to the poorest (Brundenius, 1979: 184; Zimbalist and Brundenius, 1989). In either case, there is little doubt that there was dramatic redistribution of income in the first four years of the Revolution—the years perceived by Mesa-Lago as a 'dismal failure' in the regime's economic performance. And this is because if we take into account the even more dramatic improvement in social inclusion of the poor in essential government services and in what in a capitalist context is viewed as the 'social wage'—the income equivalence of the benefits provided by the government.

Social services continued to expand in this early stage—from the second to the fourth year of the Revolution, but according to Mesa-Lago (2000: 193) 'at a much slower pace'. Mesa-Lago deduces this not from any statistics but from the declining share of the social sector in the budget in relation to productive investment. In fact, the level of social service provision is not a mere artefact of this budgetary statistic. Mesa-Lago himself made note of the structural change wrought in the first year of the Revolution in terms of nationalizing and bringing under state ownership the major hospitals and educational establishments, and, as a matter of policy, the extension of related social services into the countryside, and with this a dramatic increase in school enrolment in the popular sector and among the poor. Unfortunately he fails to recognize the implications of these developments: a significant improvement in the lives of ordinary Cubans even without additional budgetary outlays. Instead Mesa-Lago emphasises the presumed deterioration in the quality of healthcare and university education associated with the shortage of medicines and the exodus of close to one half of the university professors and doctors (2000: 194).

Of course, like other capitalist-oriented liberals Mesa-Lago totally discounts the value, and the psychological and political effects, of mass mobilization on the revolutionary consciousness of the poor and the hitherto excluded, the downtrodden, exploited and oppressed. After all, popular participation in public policymaking did not become a theoretical and practical issue for policymakers until well into the 1980s, and then only within the mindset of 'alternative development' theorists and development practitioners. It is in the context of these mass mobilizations and campaigns in the early years of the revolution that Che Guevara spoke and wrote of socialism as a revolutionary 'ethic' or 'consciousness' in the same way that exponents of the new development paradigm would conceive of 'popular participation' as freedom and as such as a necessary condition of human development.

The direct engagement of the masses of the poor in the revolutionary process was also the context for the awakening of 'proletarian humanism' (versus 'bourgeois humanism')—the transformation of 'man' from an object into a 'subject'. For Che this in fact was the 'significance' of 'socialist planning' as well as socialist culture and education (Guevara, 1964).[4]

The Great Debate, 1963–1964

Implementation of the Soviet model of socialist development and planning techniques from 1960 to 1963 raised serious questions and provoked a major debate about alternative forms of socialist development—what form socialism should take in Cuba in consideration of received and alternative theory as well as conditions specific to Cuba. This debate occurred over the course of a year (1963–1964) and could be condensed in the form of around 16 essays, five of which were written by Che Guevara himself.

At issue in this 'great debate' was whether the Soviet model was appropriate for an insular plantation economy. In the context of this debate it was in fact decided to postpone heavy industrialization and return to sugar as the engine of development. Accompanying and to some extent preceding this shift in development strategy was a lively ideological-economic debate between two models of economic organization in particular: one advanced by Che, the other by the Russian economist E.G. Liberman.

Che Guevara advanced what might be seen as an idealistic or subjectivist line of thought along the line of Mao's 'Great Leap Forward' (applied in China in 1958–1960) and contrary to conventional Soviet doctrine. In effect, Che believed that 'subjective conditions' (ideas, values, beliefs, attitudes...) could decisively influence the 'objective conditions' of economic production, i.e., the 'material base' of the social structure. The group of ideologues and theorists surrounding

---

[4] Bettleheim (1964) posits this in theoretical terms as a transformation in 'el comportamiento del hombre' (the formation of a socialist consciousness or what Che would come to term 'socialist ethics' or the 'new man') resulting from a revolutionary change on the organization of production and a corresponding change in the correlation of class forces. In Bettleheim's words: 'la palabra decisive para modificar el comportamiento de los hombres esta constituida por los cambios aportados a la producción y su organiación. La educación tiene esencialmente por mission hacer desaparecer actitudes y comortamientos heredados del pasado...'

and following Che Guevara argued that a successful raising of socialist consciousness could actively shape rather than merely respond to the development of the forces of production. This would allow a country such as Cuba to build socialism directly without waiting for capitalism to create the objective conditions for it.

Two actions were advanced by the Guevarists as means of achieving socialist development. One was the elimination of the market though the full socialization of the means of production, centralized planning and budgetary financing, elimination of mercantile relations among enterprises, the eradication of the market pricing mechanism and money in relations of exchange, and a de-emphasis of material incentives. In the subjective realm, material economic incentives were replaced with consciousness-raising among managers and workers. This would require a revolutionary socialist consciousness and the creation of a 'new man', who, contrary to the *homo economicus* of classical economic theory, would be unselfish, frugal, egalitarian and motivated by patriotism and human solidarity rather than greed, and would give his or her maximum effort to the collective good in exchange for the satisfaction of everyone's basic material and spiritual needs. This 'new man' would be the product of socialist consciousness-raising through education, mass mobilization, unpaid voluntary labour, moral incentives and the extension of state social services. If the two actions were taken at the same time the result would be economic development *and* socialist consciousness.

Confronting Che's strategy was a group of more pragmatic if not orthodox socialist economists led by Carlos Rafael Rodríguez, then director of INRA, and made up mostly of pre-Revolutionary pro-Soviet Communist party members. This group believed in and advocated a form of 'market socialism'—the application of selected market mechanisms and embedding them in a socialist organization of production. The economic model of this system was designed by the Russian economist Liberman and experimented with and put into practice first in Eastern Europe and then, in the early 1960s, in Russia first under Krushchev and then Brezhnev-Kosygin as a means of revising a sluggish economy (Mesa-Lago, 2000: 196). Sticking rather close to conventional Marxist thought and Soviet doctrine, Rodríguez and the group that he led argued that development planners cannot ignore objective conditions and that a socialist country cannot go further than the economic structure allows. The material base of the economy needs to be developed first and this would in turn create the necessary subjective conditions, raising the socialist consciousness needed to advance the forces and the corresponding relations of production (Rodríguez, 2006). The transitional stage of socialism in the progressive development from capitalism to communism cannot be skipped.

In the transition, Rodríguez argued, there will be some traits of the capitalist path and some features of a socialist future—essentially a 'mixed system', a hybrid form of social organization engaging both the market and the state. Also, Rodríguez and his group argued, the socialization of production and consumption should be paced and moderated so as not to exceed its limiting conditions. While in support of centralized planning Rodriguez and his group of planners argued for the need to improve economic efficiency by using selectively market tools and to increase productivity by means of productive investment in new technology and technological conversion. In this model greater autonomy was accorded local enterprises in the hiring, deployment and firing of labour, in investment decisions and in the use of money as a means of economic exchange. This 'pragmatist' group (so defined by Mesa-Lago), together with Marxist consultants such as Dumont and Bettleheim, was against budgetary financing, advocating instead enterprise 'self-financing'. Most importantly, to foster labour productivity the group advocated material rather than moral incentives. They believed that to ignore the laws of supply and demand, and the need for material incentives, would have a negative impact on production and slow down the development of the forces of production.[5] Most importantly, at the level of distribution they believed in 'to all according to their contribution (or work)' and were willing to accept a substantive degree of social inequality as the price of economic efficiency (Mesa-Lago, 1978).

At the end of the debate in 1964 it was the pragmatists who had the upper hand in shaping public policy in Cuba. In practice this meant that both the Liberman and the Che Guevara planning model were used in different sectors of the economy, producing a considerable degree of incoherence in overall development strategy (Mesa-Lago, 2000: 197–198). At the level of financing there was a similar policy mix, with the Liberman model of enterprise 'self-financing' used for about 31% of enterprises and the Guevarist model of centralised finance controlled by the central bank used for the rest (p. 199).

---

[5] On this issue see in particular Che's essays on the 'law of value'.

However, of greater significance regarding *human development and socialism* are the policies formulated and public actions taken in regard to labour and employment, and distribution and social services. As regards the former, a new law of 'labour justice', enforced since 1965, removed the right to strike and introduced sanctions for the violation of labour discipline, empowering enterprise managers to impose them. These actions could be, and indeed have been, seen by liberal human rights advocates as a diminution of fundamental human right.

On the other hand, advocates of this policy and these actions argue that the right to strike makes no sense outside the context of a labour-capital relation, and that this and other 'political' rights should be understood and placed in a broader context of fundamental respect for economic human rights such as the right to fulfilling work, decent housing, education, healthcare, access to food and the necessities of life, and the fundamental responsibility of the state to ensure these rights. In this connection, every citizen was guaranteed freedom from want and access to health and educational faculties, as well as housing and employment. As for the right to work and meaningful employment, all Cubans who wanted and were able to work were encouraged to do so. Workers who were redundant to the social need for their particular work would be retrained or relocated as needed or as jobs were available, and received a full salary until they could be retrained or transferred.

As for income distribution, an arguable litmus test of socialism at the level of the individual, the Guevarists inside and outside the government supported a steady move toward 'distribution according to need' by gradually removing the monetary wage and extreme wage differentials, and expanding the 'social wage'—social services provided without cost and guaranteed by the state. There were, as Mesa-Lago (2000: 204) noted, 'strong egalitarian overtones' in this approach as well as a belief that a change in human values would help achieve the transformation of the 'old economic man' into a 'new man'. Nonmaterial incentives would be gradually replaced by moral incentives as this new socialist culture took root.

Conversely, Che's opponents both inside and outside the government—and there were many of them—believed that in the transitional period distribution should be according to one's contribution or work rather than need. They endorsed material incentives. They were cautious about the further extension of free social services and endorsed moderate user-fees or charges to cut down on social-service waste and excessive costs. However, a full system of material incentives, such as bonuses for extra effort or performance and collective profit sharing, was not implemented—in part because of the indecisive conclusion to the policy debate.

Both sides in this debate, as it turned out, supported work quotas and pay scales for wages (the Guevarists less enthusiastically), the implementation of which contributed to a further reduction in social inequality. In this regard, in 1965 the wage differential ratio between the highest and lowest groups of paid workers in the wage scale was 4.3 to 1 (Zimbalist and Brundenius, 1989), although Mesa-Lago extends it to 10 to 1 by differentiating between the pay of a cabinet minister and an 'agricultural peon' at the two extremes of the salary/wage scale. In any case, even without available clear estimates of income distribution at this stage of development (1964–1965), there is reason to believe that further advances were made at the level of social equality, an important dimension of human development in a socialist context.

Che Guevara and Human Socialist Development, 1964–1969

For three years Fidel Castro abstained from participating in the wide-ranging and relatively open ideological and policy debate regarding the best or most appropriate organizational form of social development. But in the summer of 1966, after Che Guevara had resigned as Minister of Industry and left Cuba for Bolivia (to lead the revolution on South America), and Rafael Rodríguez had resigned from his post as Director of INRA, Fidel as Head of State announced the new directions in economic organization that the revolutionary leadership, *in broad consultation with all sectors*,[6] proposed to take the country. At the time there was considerable talk about serious differences between Fidel and Che in their conception of socialist development and the direction it should take in Cuba. However, what Fidel announced was

---

[6] Mesa-Lago generally downplays or ignores this consultative or participatory process, viwing policy-making as entirely top-down in the authority of Fidel, and his capacity to impose his will. Limia (2009), however, emphasises the diverse institutional channels and effective opportunities for popular participation in public decision-making and policy-formulation both then (in the 1960s) and since.

essentially along the lines of what Che Guevara had been pushing, albeit in a more radical and even more idealistic form.

Guevarism in Practice

The socialization process resumed at this point (1966–1968), with a concentration on two major remaining pockets of private ownership: agriculture and services. By the end of 1968 only 20% of agriculture and 2% of transportation services remained in the private sector. In 1967, again after broad consultation with the affected groups, the government took four steps to further reduce the private sector in agriculture: (1) workers on state farms were dispossessed of their family plots used theoretically for their own consumption but in practice for barter or sale on the black market; (2) private land tenure was limited to the lifetime of the farmer and could not be inherited; (3) ANAP, the National Association of Small Farmers, agreed not to sell agricultural surpluses from private farms on the market but to turn over all production to the government on the basis of *acopio* prices; and (4) private farmers were encouraged to join collective work brigades and mutual aid groups, effectively socialising their labour-power and equipment.

The remaining 25% of retail trade left in private hands plus the little left in industry and transportation was collectivized in one single (most 'foul', according to Mesa-Lago) stroke in March 1968 under the banner of a 'revolutionary offensive'. More than 58,000 small businesses, including retail food outlets, consumer service shops, restaurants and bars, repair and handicraft stores, and street vendor stalls, were put out of operation in what in retrospect has to be seen as a mistaken belief that the market is capitalism, effectively confusing or equating the private sector with capitalism. The ostensible or officially stated reason for this offensive, however, was not prevent capitalist development or class formation but to eradicate corruption and illicit purchases that small business operators made from private farmers, purchases that boosted the black market.

Although the government did not restore this vital component of the private sector until the twenty-first century, in the context of a belated response to the economic crisis and a required adjustment to the new world order, it was evident that the state was in no position to gather, aggregate and use the information to maintain the production of goods and services in this sector. Fidel Castro admitted as much, acknowledging that the newly appointed managers, most of whom, according to Mesa-Lago were inexperienced housewives and members of the diverse neighbourhood Committees for the Defence of the Revolution (CDR), had neither the entrepreneurship, knowledge nor the skills to set up or manage these enterprises. As a result, the Revolution was deprived of an enterprising class of small business owners who could have substantially contributed to he Revolution's supply of useful and much needed goods and services as well as to the quality of life, an essential condition of human development.

According to Mesa-Lago the emphasis of the government on capital accumulation (expansion of national savings and their productive investment) at the expense of social consumption—a structural failure of the model used by the government to guide policy over the years—reached a climax at this stage of Cuba's national development. An increase in national savings, and the cut in consumption, was engineered by a drastic curtailment of the private sector and the market, expanding the scope of the ration card, the reduction of imports deemed to be unnecessary and the exporting of products previously assigned for internal consumption (Mesa-Lago, 2000: 211). In addition, and perhaps contrary to the goal of increasing economic efficiency as well as the national savings rate, material incentives were reduced, replaced with exhortations to work harder, save more and accept a measure of deprivation with revolutionary spirit if not fervour. Although, Mesa-Lago admits, it is impossible to determine the share of the national budget allocated to financing production (apparently the state budget was discontinued at this phase—for some ten years) the investment share going to the productive sphere apparently was increased from 78.7 to 86.8% from 1965 to 1970, the highest rate ever reached under the Revolution (CEE, *AEC*, 1984a).

But it appears—and on this point a number of economists, both foreign and Cuban, were in agreement with Mesa-Lago (2000: 212)—that this level of investment of the national savings was achieved at such a cost (exceedingly low consumption) that it did not achieve its desired and stated aim: far from it. Apparently, the allocation and use of capital by the managers of the economy was extraordinarily inefficient, leading to relatively disappointing rates of economic growth. With the induced involution of the domestic market, and the lack of domestic supply and purchasing power capacity, the export sector was in no position to assume the role as the engine of economic growth. The economic growth figures for the 1960s in Table 3 tell the tale: a pattern of sporadic ups and down, with no steady rate. The pattern of uneven growth undoubtedly reflects the shifts in policy that Mesa-Lago (2000) pointed to and reviewed in this chapter.

Data provided by Leogrande and Thomas (see Table 4) point to a similar pattern of very uneven growth in the second decade of the Revolution, with major spikes in 1970, 1972–1973, 1978 and 1981, and a major downturn in 1979–1980 and then—no matter how measured—a spectacular growth spurt in 1981.

Fidel Castro announced the shift in the government's macroeconomic and development policy (i.e. the economic organization model)

Table 3. Cuba: Global Social Product (GSP)[7] Growth (1963–1974)

Year	GSP (current prices)	Rate of change (percent)
1963	6013.2	−1.1
1964	6454.5	7.3
1965	6770.9	4.9
1966	6709.3	−0.9
1967	7211.6	7.5
1968	7330.9	1.7
1969	7236.1	−1.3
1970	8356.0	15.5
1971	8966.5	7.3
1972	10417.91	16.2
1973	11921.8	14.4
1974	13149.0	10.3

Source: Leogrande & Thomas (2002).

Table 4. Economic Growth in Cuba, 1970–1981

	1970	'71	'72	'73	'74	'75	'76	'77	'78	'79	'80	'81
GSP	15.5	7.3	16.2	14.4	10.3	7.0	2.8	2.2	11.4	3.2	3.6	25.9
GDP						4.9	8.2	7.3	1.1	−4.1		19.6

Source: Leogrande and Thomas (2002: 328–329).

---

[7] Until 1989 Cuba reported economic growth as changes in the 'global social product' (GSP) rather than in Geoss Domestic Product (GDP) figures, the standard normally used for international comparisons. In the GSP income is reported in current, rather than constant, pesos. Table 4 allows us to compare the two accounting methodologies re growth.

at the annual Congress of the Federation of Cuban Workers (CTC) in 1966. In a declaration of fundamental principle in support of the revolutionary process the unions confirmed that the task of workers was to increase output and productivity. As Mesa-Lago (2000: 217) sees it the unions in this context had been transformed into and were nothing more than 'transmission belts of Cuba's Communist Party directives'. However, it is evident that Mesa-Lago on this point either adopts an ideological stance or has no understanding of the role played by unions or the trade union movement under socialism or in a process of revolutionary transformation—in the change wrought in this role from that of a capitalist system in which the capital-labour relation is the base and at the centre of the economy. Mesa-Lago (2000: 217) makes a pointed statement about the union movement in Cuba having 'withered away' by 1970 and the consequent democratic deficit. Indeed. A trade union movement as such, i.e. as it exists and works in a capitalist economy, might indeed be expected to 'wither away' in a socialist context in the same way that the state as such, i.e. as an instrument of class rule, was theorized by both Adam Smith and Karl Marx to 'wither away' in the future. On the other hand, it could be argued that the premise of an identity of interest between labour (the unions) and the state (the administration) is illusory and to the degree that there is a discrepancy, or even a contradiction in principle, between them the question of 'true democracy' (socialist democracy) arises. On this issue see Chapter 8 (Human Development as Freedom).

By 1970, a decade into the Revolution, 86.3% of the labour force (excluding the military and the security forces) was employed by the state. The 13.7% of non-state employment was mostly independent farmers (11%) and a small number of self- or privately-employed (CEE, *Encuesta*, 1981; Mesa-Lago, 2000, 382, Table III.24). But in addition to the paid labour force, the Revolution mobilized a significant pool of volunteer labour, particularly in regard to meeting the government's annual sugar harvest. However, again according to Mesa-Lago (2000: 217) the value of this volunteer labour was more symbolic than real. In actual fact, the deployment of this volunteer labour was riddled with inefficiency. Volunteer labour was often used when there was no need for it. And in other cases volunteers spent hours waiting to be transported to the sugarcane fields only to remain idle once there for lack of needed tools. Also the cost of mobilizing, feeding and providing the volunteers with seeds and tools was often higher than the meagre addition to total production. A document released by the CTC in the mid 1970s after the announcement that the sugar harvest target would not be met acknowledges the problem, pointing towards a policy revision regarding voluntary labour. The document first of all criticized the practice of union leaders exhorting workers to volunteer additional labour after the daily work schedule and on weekends and vacations. Secondly, the document exhorted managers and unions to raise production in the future by means of better organization of paid labour and full use of productivity increases rather than relatively or very inefficient volunteer labour. A few months later Fidel Castro officially acknowledged that despite the enthusiasm and ideological support shown by volunteers for the revolutionary effort poor organization and use of voluntary labour was a waste of time and effort.

At the level of industrial production there were also problems. By 1970 enforcement of work quotas had weakened and the level of production achieved in 1965 had eroded, in part it turned out because of the lack of correspondence—even an inverse relationship, according to Mesa Lago (with reference to an official report)—between industrial productivity and the wage share of value added (2000: 217). Apparently, this report cited by Mesa-Lago criticized the suppression of production bonuses and other material incentives, and the futility of replacing them with moral incentives and political education, in effect challenging the Guevarist approach to expanding economic production. According to another report released by the PCC production targets had also been undermined because of bureaucratization and labour absenteeism. The socialist system, the report acknowledged, had failed to replace the checks and incentives of the market system: wages had ceased to be an incentive because there was more money in circulation than goods to spend it on, and unemployment was no longer a concern and thus useful as a means of maintaining labour discipline. By September 1970 absenteeism apparently reached 20% of the labour force because workers were able to stay home and still be able to buy with the money they had earned the scarce rationed goods available. In response to this problem a law against 'loafing', enacted in 1971, established an obligation to work for all able bodied men from ages 17 through 60, severely sanctioned unjustified absenteeism, reduced the possibility of working outside the state sector and double dipping for extra wages, and labelled as vagrants or malingerers the wage workers temporarily employed in what remained of the private sector. A mass campaign to detect violators of the law got 100,000 men to join the labour force, half of them in agriculture (Mesa-Lago, 1971, 1981, 1982, 2000: 218).

Over the course of this period there was a major push towards further equalization of social conditions, primarily by means of work organization. Workers were asked to waive overtime pay, extra pay for arduous work and work bonuses, as well as in-kind awards (trips, refrigerators, motorcycles...) granted to sugar workers as incentives to increase production. Family plots used by state farmers to supplement household consumption were eliminated and extra pressure was placed on private farmers to sell their produce to the state at low *acopio* prices—already, in 1970, 60% below their 1965 prices, leading farmers to resort to the black-market instead or cut production when this market was suppressed (Mesa-Lago, 2000: 219). Also, at a most general level wage differentials were to be rescued by raising the floor and lowering the ceiling on wage levels. Eventually every worker would receive the same wage, be he a cane cutter or engineer. Free social services would also be expanded and even food and clothing would be free, further reducing the need of money. Housing rent was set at 6% of monthly income and families with a monthly income of less than 25 pesos at the time were exempted from paying rent. The rationing of food and other essentials in this period was also significantly expanded by the government, effectively eliminating hunger and poverty. Also, health and social security coverage has expanded to cover virtually the entire population; it was universal in healthcare and reached almost 89% of the labour force on pensions (Mesa-Lago, 2000: 225).

The revolutionary government invested heavily scarce financial resources in social welfare, particularly in regard to health, education, access to nutritious food and employment. The government was clearly intent on the provisioning of social welfare but also a fully functioning socialist system in which conditions were equal for all. No data for wage scales at this stage are available but the extreme differential between the highest and lowest wage among economic sectors was reduced from 3.6 to 1 in 1966 to 2.6 to 1 in 1971 (Mesa-Lago, 2000: 225). By the few accounts available this flattening in pay scale had the effect of further reducing the income gap between the wealthiest and the poorest households, and drawing both towards an enlarged middle layer. The problem, however, was one that Marx in his scorn for utopian socialism had recognized: insufficient development of the forces of production, leading to a sharing of poverty rather than wealth.

Not that Cubans at the time were poor in any absolute sense—in terms of an inability to meet their basic material and spiritual needs. As we argue in Chapter 4 in comparison with other countries in the region where wealth and income based on social production was class divided to the point of poverty and misery for close to or well over half of the population, in Cuba at the time (prior to the Special Period) there was virtually no poverty, defined as an inability to meet basic needs.[8] At the same time given the level of development of the forces of production there was a general situation of low income and material consumption based on the relatively equal distribution of the scarce goods available but also, according to Mesa-Lago (2000: 219–224), a stagnant economy, a decline in productivity and the quality of goods as well as a sizeable reduction in the level of public investment in social services.

Return to Orthodoxy in Human Development, 1970–1985

By several accounts the government in 1970 faced an economic debacle and had few options in dealing with it. A radical return to the market was out of the question given the ideological commitment to socialism. The option of further radicalizing the revolutionary economy in the direction taken from 1966 to 1970 was blocked by the apparent chaos of the Guevarist-Castro experiment, which some compared to the disaster of the Great Proletarian Cultural Revolution in China just as they had compared the industrialization drive of the early 1960s to Mao's 'great leap forward'. The one available—and according to Mesa-Lago the 'only logical'—option was to turn towards the Soviet model of 'timid economic reform' advocated by the 'pragmatists' in the 1964–1966 debate and introduced in the Soviet Union itself in 1965. The new phase of socialist development engineered on the basis of this economic model, characterized by 'pragmatism and politico-administrative institutionalization' would last some fifteen years—until 1985

---

[8] Espina Prieto reviews the shifts in Cuban scholarship on this issue in the context of the Special Period, which effectively restored 'poverty' as an agenda item and a policy issue, after an earlier generation of scholars worked from the presumption that the revolution in effect had effectively resolved the issue. We reconstruct Espina Prieto's review and analysis of this literature in Chapter 10 in the context of the Special Period.

when the engine of steady economic growth began to falter, precipitating a short period of anti-market 'rectification' reform (1986–1989).

In several speeches in the 1970s Fidel Castro as Head of State and government spokesman criticized the preceding stage of the Revolution as 'utopian' and explained the mistakes made in the following terms. Lacking the economists and other scientists and theorists able to make a significant contribution to the construction of socialism, and showing contempt for the positive experiences of the more advanced socialist countries, Cuba had sought its own way in an attempt to invent a new form of socialism. But, he noted, here the leadership's approach was overly idealistic. Ignoring serious difficulties it proceeded on the assumption (or in the hope) that sufficient will and intent could overcome the absence of objective conditions, a major mistake as it turned out. The leadership, he admitted, was guilty of idealism in believing that the attitude of a conscious vanguard minority applied to society as a whole.

At the same it was becoming clear that it is easier to change the structure of the economy by advancing the forces of production and creating the material basis for socialist development than to change social consciousness, which in any case, as Marx had argued, tends to follow rather than precedes the development of the forces of production (Bettleheim, 1964). Thus it is a mistake to believe that Cuba could abandon capitalism and catapult itself directly into socialism, with everyone having a socialist consciousness at the outset and conforming to its moral ethics. It was evident that Cuba first had to construct the foundations of socialism and then move carefully and deliberately, resisting the temptation to jump by leaps and bounds when realistically it could barely walk. The forces of production first had to be expanded on the basis of conditions at hand, both objective and subjective. This was the task and this would be the action taken by the leadership on behalf of the Revolution. If it tries to go further than circumstances permitted the Revolution would only be set back (for citations and reference to Fidel Castro sources on this see Mesa-Lago, 1978, 1981).

Despite some efforts to decentralize decision-making and introduce some timid market mechanisms in the 1970s (in agriculture, services and housing construction), the socialization of both production and distribution (consumption) was slowly advanced, with a resulting increase in national output and a relatively equitable sharing of the output, and with it a tangible improvement in social conditions for all

Cubans. Advances in health and education were particularly notable, as reflected in available statistics (Eckstein, 1994). In the agricultural sector the aim was to gradually eliminate any vestiges of the private sector and the market by purchasing the land when owners died or retired, or voluntarily through political education, so that the remaining private farms would be absorbed into state farms or the cooperative sector.

As a result of this policy between 1967 and 1983 the number of private farms declined by 58% while the number of cooperatives increased from 44 to 1,472 and the number of cooperative farmers increased from a few hundred to 82,611 (Mesa-Lago, 2000: 229). By 1986 80.8% of the land in production was organized in the form of state farms; another 10.2% was worked by cooperatives and 6.5% was in the private sector; while another 2.5% was in family plots on state farms, which were eliminated in 1967 but reinstated in the 1970s on the assumption that they were intended for self-consumption and cultivated by brigades for state deliveries rather than individually.

Notwithstanding the push toward further collectivization in 1980 and the early years of the decade some liberalization and measures to decentralize decision-making regarding production were introduced. The most important such measure in the agricultural sector was the introduction in 1989 of free peasant markets in which small private farmers could sell their agricultural surplus (after meeting the state *acopio* obligations) at prices set freely by the market, albeit with certain restrictions and under rules such as the prohibition of 'middlemen' or sales outside the production zone. The aim was to encourage farmers to increase their output and improve the quality of supply, as well as eliminate the black-market and rationing (Mesa-Lago, 2000: 229–230). In 1978 the government also legalized and encouraged self-employment in the service sector—for example, hairdressers, tailors, gardeners, taxi-drivers and photographers; artisans and tradesmen such as electricians, carpenters and mechanics; and professional services such as engineers, architects, lawyers, physicians and dentists. Under a new system of free labour hiring, state enterprises could contract with artisans and the self-employed for goods and services, providing them with inputs in exchange for 30% of their profits. In cities like Havana small manufacturers began to sell their products and wares on the free market.

The policy moves by the government in the direction of the free market were made experimentally in the expectation that the self-employed, in exchange for their freedom of enterprise, should contribute to the public good from which they have benefited, as well as well as an underlying concern for class formation or capitalist development. The contribution would be in the form of a tax on self-employed labour and the production of goods and services in short supply.

In 1982, Fidel Castro, reflecting the concern of the regime for possible class formation, launched an attack on those 'self-employed were becoming 'rich' by gouging the consumer'—'prostitution of the self-employment concept', 'repulsive violation' of the rules and an example of 'corruption' not to mention 'capitalist greed'. Citing examples of such corruption and market abuse (selling handmade manufactures at ten times the official price on the Havana 'free' market) Fidel accused the small businessmen of being 'robbers' and 'becoming a new bourgeoisie with capitalist attitudes', a 'spoiled lumpen proletariat which was corrupting the masses' (quoted by Mesa-Lago, 2000: 230–231).

As in the case of the farmers' free markets, which were opened and closed and then reopened, the government's clampdown on self-employment and micro-entrepreneurs was seen by Mesa-Lago and other Cuba-watchers and analysts as damaging to production incentives as well as the 'entrepreneurial [and capitalist] spirit', and in contradiction to the government's goal of improving the supply and quality of goods to the population—a 'development' predicated on the free market.

Finally, in the first half of the 1980s, in the middle of a boom in national production (while other countries in the region were in a state of economic crisis), the government relaxed existing restrictions on private housing construction, a policy that, combined with expanding self-employment, led to a housing market boom between 1980 and 1985—the strongest dwelling construction boom in the history of the Revolution, according to Mesa-Lago. It was also a period of robust economic growth that came to an abrupt end in the middle of the decade, precipitating a 'rectification' campaign.

In the light of the production failures of the previous period of national development in the 1960s central planning was reinstated as a means of allocating resources to different factors of production and in distributing the social product. The first and second 5-year plans (1976–1980, 1981–1985) and a 20-year development plan (1980–2000), were elaborated, and the study of economics, accounting and management systems and techniques revived (Mesa-Lago, 2000: 231).

The new economic model, named the System of Economic Direction and Planning (SDPE), was introduced in 1976, at the tail end of a strong economic recovery, and scheduled to be fully in force by 1980. The SDPE, according to Mesa-Lago was a moderate version of the economic reform introduced in the Soviet Union in 1965 with poor results and it had features of the model experimented with by the 'pragmatists' in 1964–1966:

- Decentralization of state enterprises (breaking them down into smaller units and expanding their number from some 300 to 3,000 between 1968 and 1979)
- Transfer of many decisions from the central planners to enterprise managers
- Give a greater role of 'scarcity prices' in allocations
- Replacement of budget financing with enterprise self-financing
- Use of profit as an indicator of managerial performance, together with indicators such as output, cost, quality and productivity as a measure of managerial performance; and
- Reinforcement of work quotas and a broader wage scale and the restoration of material incentives. However, Mesa-Lago notes, by 1980 very few of these planning elements were in place or fully operational.[9]

At this point in the history of the Revolution, and this phase of Cuba's national development (1971–1985), the emphasis on egalitarianism—a hallmark of the Revolution (together with national liberation from the jaws of US imperialism) from its inception and well into the 1960s—came under criticism from all sides. The resulting expansion of wage differences, the reintroduction or strengthening of material incentives, the use of the market and prices as a partial substitute for rationing and the halt to or curtailment of some free social services, all led to some or a greater degree of social stratification and inequality

---

[9] Mesa-Lago (232–233) enumerates at length a list of the SDPE's failures in the implementation of the first five-year plan. Although this list does not include it, it is evident that the fundamental failure not just of the SDPE but of a command economy based on the mechanism of central planning is: the failure to 'get prices right'. In this connection, Mesa-Lago (2000: 235) recalls that the prices of most consumer goods in Cuba were frozen in the early 1960s and remained largely unchanged for some two decades. As a result, by 1980 the gap between world prices and domestic prices in Cuba had expanded dramatically, seriously distorting them to the point that they were utterly useless to planners as points of reference.

(see Chapter 10 for an analysis of these dynamics and their implications for human development).

The pursuit of wage equality and the communist principle of distribution according to need were criticized at this point of time as idealistic errors, aberrations or petit bourgeois sentiments that did not take into account the workers' productive effort. Wage differentials in his context were defended as an incentive for those with labour skills, heavy responsibilities and tough or dangerous jobs, even a greater social or economic contribution. In 1973, the CTC, representing unionized labour as well as management, proclaimed a return to the socialist principle of distribution according to work and a return to wage differentials, albeit within a relatively flat range across different occupational categories—4.9 to 1 (Brundenius, 1984; Zimbalist and Brundenius, 1989). The old wage scale was seen as too egalitarian; hence a wage reform in 1981 increased relative wages of highly skilled labour. Other sources of a relative, albeit limited, increase in income distribution and social inequalities derived from this distribution were the incomes of small private farmers, handicraft workers and artisans and small manufacturers and some middlemen in economic exchanges.

There was also a steady increase in the supply of consumer goods during this period, except for the recession of 1979–1980, which was preceded and followed by a steady rate of annual growth in production. This growth led to a higher rate of material consumption, although the prices were stratified and segmented; generally prices of rationed goods were considerably lower than those that entered the market, with a corresponding social stratification of consumption; those in the lower income brackets could not afford goods priced in the market. For example, a TV or refrigerator at the time might cost from four to five months of average wages.

According to Mesa-Lago (2000: 245), citing data constructed by the Institute of Domestic Demand, less than one third of all goods by the end of the decade were rationed, although this calculation is by value rather than need *and* the most important foodstuffs and basic necessities, beverages, etc. were highly subsidized or rationed at a very affordable or low price. But what the introduction of the market meant was the institution of two categories or classes of consumers: (i) most workers in the lowest three income categories (over 60% of the population), who were entirely or almost entirely reliant on rationed goods and whose capacity to consume in terms of the range and quality of goods was very limited; and (ii) a stratum of the population in the highest two income categories with a substantially higher level of material consumption and capacity to choose among a broader range and higher quality goods. This stratification of consumers was further accentuated by the cuts in state subsidies, the suppression of gratuities like free meals in workers' cafeterias and free telephone calls, and a significant increase in the prices of many non-essential but desired consumer goods in 1981. The government raised the lowest wages but not enough to compensate for the loss of purchasing power of the lowest income groups or to significantly expand the domestic market.

While there was some diminution of social equality in income distribution in this period at the level of essential social services regarding human development (health, education and social security) there was a substantial improvement. In both cases the change in social condition reflected a change in public policy, the former in a concern to increase labour productivity (excessive egalitarianism seen as a drag on economic growth), the latter in a renewed commitment to improve the quality of life for all Cubans, the litmus test of socialist development. To advance human development at this level (health, education, social security, welfare), and to improve the quality of labour (a healthier, more highly qualified and skilled labour force) the government substantially increased the share of the national budget allocated to health, education, social security and welfare (see Chapter 6 for an analysis of these policy and social dynamics, and the resulting social conditions). Investment in social services jumped from 14% in 1970 to 23% in 1975 (CEE, AEC, 1984a, 1985a) and then slowed down to 18% in 1985, at the time the highest level by far of such investment in all Latin America.

Social expenditures per capita, which had already increased by 35% in the previous period, climbed by another 60% between 1971 and 1975, slowing down somewhat thereafter—to 42% from 1976–1979 and 32% from 1980 to 1985 (Mesa-Lago, 2000: 249). The statistics summarized and analyzed in Chapter 6, and used by the UNDP to rank Cuba in the High Human Development category, provide eloquent testimony to the tangible improvements in the quality of life in Cuba wrought by these policies. The major dimensions of improvement in the social conditions of life and development were social security and welfare, education and health, with decent housing well behind and, and by a number of accounts, then and now in a deficit situation vis-à-vis social needs and entitlements (in Cuba decent housing is a right, not a commodity).

The reason that this as yet unresolved housing deficit situation is so important is not just because decent and affordable housing is a fundamental human right (at least in Cuba), and as such a condition of human development, but because of the connection between housing and health. In the development literature, lack of decent housing is often used as a proxy variable for lack of access to clean water and lack of adequate waste treatment/disposal, both of which have a negative effect on health. In the case of Cuba this might not be the case but even so there are studies and some evidence[10] to suggest that inadequate housing (in the case of Cuba, two to three generations of family members often forced to share available shelter and housing) is a major source of individual and family stress—and such stress is not good for health, either directly or though its impact on family and community dynamics.

The Rectification Campaign, 1986–1990

The first half of the decades of the 1980s saw Cuba's engine of economic growth working with relative efficiency and equity. The economy was growing at a greater speed than ever—at a rate that would not be seen until 2005, twenty years on and well into a sustained recovery from its 'special period'. But in 1986 the government launched a 'rectification process' (RP), which, for the rest of the decade, set Cuba against a emerging trend in the socialist camp and elsewhere towards market-oriented reform in the new world order of neoliberal globalization. Theoretically the RP was designed to find a middle ground between the 'idealistic errors' of the Guevarist model used to guide policy from 1966 to 1970 and the 'economistic mistakes' of the SDPE 'pragmatists' from 1976 to 1985—seen as eroding the socialist foundations of the Revolution by mechanically copying from other socialist countries a model not suitable to Cuba. In practice, many of the RP policies reverted to the Guevarist model: a recentralization of decision-making (decentralization seen as weakening the power of the state, a feature of neoliberalism); reduction of material incentives and expansion of moral persuasion; reintroduction of voluntary labour and massive labour mobilization in agriculture and in the form of construction

---

[10] Communication from Sam Lanfranco, a specialist in the field (July 20, 2010).

brigades to help close the gap between availability and the social need for housing, probably the greatest deficit in the achievements of the Revolution at the level of human or social development (apart from what some (Otero and O'Brian, 2002) see as the 'democratic deficit'— the absence of democracy.

The reasons for the RP were and remain the subject of debate. Cubans themselves point to diverse domestic factors such as widespread corruption, crime and waste under the SDPE; a declining revolutionary spirit (a problem of intergenerational retention) and, in particular, the growing inequalities (Rodríguez, 1990a). Some foreign scholars supported or justified the RP with reference to external factors such as the growing balance of trade deficit in addition to domestic problems (Zimbalist and Eckstein, 1987; Zimbalist and Brundenius, 1989). Mesa-Lago (1990) emphasized ideological-political factors such as the resistance of Fidel Castro himself to delegate power (decentralization) and the concern that a material incentives regime would weaken the capacity of the Revolution to defend itself from imperialism.

A major flaw from an orthodox economics perspective (Mesa-Lago for instance) was 'that it did not produce an integrated economic-organization model to substitute for the SDPE', which, Mesa-Lago (2000: 265) adds, is 'fundamental for a socialist command economy, especially one that eschewed markets'. What the RP *did* produce was: (i) a deepening and extension of the socialization process, virtually eliminating the private sector; (ii) a recentralization of decision-making and the virtual disappearance of the SDPE macroplan; (iii) a reemphasis on enterprise self-financing; (iv) an expanding budgetary deficit and—from an orthodox economic perspective—further 'price distortions' (Mesa-Lago, 2000: 265); (v) promotion of non-traditional exports (biotechnology, etc.) and foreign tourism combined domestically with a strategy of domestic food security and self-reliance; (vi) tighter control of he labour market combined with labour mobilization and the use of labour brigades; and (vii) increasing egalitarianism via rationing, the reduction of material incentives and the expansion of moral incentives (Mesa-Lago, 2000).

The RP restricted the remaining vestiges of private property and the market by abolishing the peasant markets and accelerating the process of integration of small private farms into cooperatives; eliminating the activities of small private manufacturers, truck owners and street vendors; reducing the scope of self-employment; and placing further restrictions on the private construction, selling, the rental and the inheritance of housing.

In the spring of 1986 Fidel Castro launched a new and stronger attack against both peasant markets and private farmers, equating their 'private enterprise' with the worst of capitalism. The farmers were allegedly making exorbitant profits by selling their product on the markets (he gave examples of unlikely incomes up to $5,000 and even $250,000 a year). They resisted integration into cooperatives—CPAs (more likely) and in the flaunting of their evidently higher incomes constituting an obstacle to cooperativism. He also stated that some private farmers delivered barely 10% of their output to the state while only a dozen or so out of a total 98,000 paid taxes, thus taking from but giving nothing to the country. In addition, the unsatisfied demand for agricultural products led to a very lucrative black market, allowing these farmers enormous profits without having to bear the 'social costs' paid by their counterparts in the cooperative and state sectors. To stop these and other abuses the markets for small-scale private agricultural production were abolished and Fidel publicly opposed the reconstitution of the private sector and the reintroduction of free markets until 1993, when radically changed circumstances, indeed the worst economic crisis in the history of the Revolution, forced the government's hands, obliging it to restore the market, albeit in regulated form. By 1989 only 3.3% of land under agricultural production was in the hands of private farmers; 78% was used by state farms. Cooperatives accounted for 18.7% (CCE, *AEC*, 1989a).

The new policies vis-à-vis the private farmers, however, even if or when the government succeeded in curbing the abuses of private enterprise, had a negative effect on overall agricultural production in that the private farmers had produced a disproportionate share of total production. According to Mesa-Lago (2000: 267), even though private farmers only accounted for an estimated 10% of total agricultural production (vs. 3.3% of land use), the subsequent shortfall in agricultural production was a direct result of the stifling of private enterprise and a reduction in the weight of material incentives. 'It would have been more sensible,' Mesa-Lago argues, 'to control the true legal violations by the farmers and enforce the law (on *acopio* and taxes) instead of eliminating the incentive of the free markets and pushing the integration of farmers (into CPAs or cooperatives)'.

As it was production and delivery under *acopio* did not increase while the black market boomed. In addition, Mesa-Lago argued, the

CPAs on which the government pinned their hopes and staked their plans for increased agricultural production were generally inefficient and many of them were unprofitable for the following reasons: many thousands had retired, leading to a significant decline in the number of cooperative producers (from 69,896 in 1985 to 63,000 in 1990) and creating and a significant deficit in the pension fund; many co-op members had no or poor managerial skills; labour effort and productivity in the cooperative sector was low, many workers allegedly working half the normal time and with no material incentive to work harder and produce more; and there were 'excessive expenditures' on housing and (economically) 'unjustified payments' to coop members (2000: 267).

Non-agricultural entrepreneurs in the private sector—small manufacturers, transport operators, street vendors and other self-employed workers—also came under attack by the government. The government reported (Castro, according to Mesa-Lago) that many micro entrepreneurs sold their output to state enterprises with cooperatives acting as their sales agents. Some 'entrepreneurs set up their own shops, obtained raw materials (often from state enterprises or coops), began to use machinery and hired workers to expand production. About 10,000 private truck owners transported agricultural products from private farms, merchandise from the manufacturers, and people, earning 50,000 to 100,000 pesos annually in an economy where the average wage was barely 3,000 pesos. The government acknowledged that these activities flourished because the state did not produce these goods. It also acknowledged that many teachers, professionals and public servants were forced or led by circumstance (hard times, difficulties in making ends meet) to work privately as well as publicly for additional income. Many teachers, for example, in this connection gave private lessons to enable children from higher-income families to better prepare for university entry exams and so, according to Mesa-Lago, fostering an element of privilege and inequality (although professional jobs were not necessarily and often were not the highest paid, offering as they do instead greater opportunities for self-realization and selfless social contribution). Finally, the government in the person and office of Fidel Castro, noted the opportunities for self-enrichment (rather than social contribution) provided by the private market in house construction, which allowed many an 'entrepreneur' to become rich by building houses on lots and with materials for which they did not pay market prices and selling them on the free market; indeed some individuals caught up in this 'entrepreneurial spirit' simply bought an then resold houses for a profit, without in effect making any social contribution at all.

The government promised that the gap left by the reduction of the private sector and the elimination of the market would be filled by the state through the expansion of procurement (*acopio*), marketing agencies, the parallel market and state enterprise, as well as the reintroduction of housing mini-brigades and new construction contingents (Mesa-Lago, 2000: 268). However, as Mesa-Lago (2000: 269–288) notes and analyses in some detail, none of these mechanisms worked because of the fundamental inefficiency of state enterprise as opposed to private enterprise, even with the use of material incentives.

Rectification and Human Development: Consolidating the Achievements of the Revolution

The overall goal of RP was to put the Revolution back on track regarding Che Guevara's dream and vision of socialism as human development—generating a 'new man and woman' imbued with a revolutionary spirit and a socialist consciousness about the need for, and a possibility of, creating 'another world' of freedom, equality and the welfare of all. The means and policy instruments for advancing the Revolution in these terms included the strengthening of a socialist consciousness at the workplace through increased workers' participation in economic functions and public policy, a greater concern for increasing productivity and output (tightening quotas, etc.), fighting corruption and improving labour discipline and restoring the moral impulse to social contribution (vs. personal advancement) and unpaid voluntary work.

In regard to workers' participation in the making of public policy (and 'continuous planning')—a key objective of the rectification campaign—the CTC Congress held in 1989 complained about the inadequacy of mechanisms for workers' participation in planning and that work managers (and perhaps policymakers) tended to treat production assemblies, as well as neighbourhood assemblies and community councils, as mere formalities, discounting the input of workers in the policymaking process. Also questioned was the ability of workers to participate in decisions related not to the economy as a whole but to the system of labour remuneration, conditions of work and job security, as well as the hiring and firing, and redeployment of workers according to management criteria of enterprise efficiency, which, some workers argued, should be balanced against workers' rights and collective decision-making power.

As for labour mobilization—another mechanism of rectification—the policy was implemented primarily in agriculture (sugar production) and construction (housing). The construction brigades eliminated under the SDPE because of their presumed inefficiency, were reinstated in 1987 as a keystone for solving the serious and growing housing and construction deficit. Fidel publicly argued in this connection that the previous inefficiency problem was eluded or solved in the new approach because (i) brigade members were surplus workers released from enterprises; (ii) the remaining workers kept production up at the enterprise and fulfilled the output quotas without asking for overtime—a matter of moral commitment; and (iii) the state reimbursed the enterprise for wages paid to brigade members, and provided them with proper supplies (which the state had failed to do in the earlier period). However, whereas Fidel in 1988 praised the brigade workers for creating a new revolutionary labour spirit and working miracles in 1989, just a year later, he reversed that judgement, noting that the brigades were generally disorganised and very inefficient. As a solution to this problem he proposed instead the agency of 'construction contingents' formed not with surplus enterprise workers, many of whom were not professional construction workers, but with workers who were carefully selected, well paid, fed and housed in return for producing 'labour miracles'.

The government at first argued that these 'construction contingents' were indeed productive and efficient (0.70 cost per peso produced vs. 2.40 per peso by the brigades). However, the Cuban Institute of Economic research (IIE) fond that the production of one peso in value implied as much as 11 pesos in hidden costs (Mesa-Lago, 277). However, Fidel discredited all criticisms as made by 'worms', who looked only at the 'negative side' of things. When the new Secretary of the CTC in 1990 complained that contingent workers earned more than the Ministry of Construction, Fidel replied that 'Ministers do not have to break stones or drive bulldozers'—a 'socialist' perspective that would no doubt appear 'irrational' to the extreme from a capitalist or orthodox (even heterodox) 'economics' perspective (Mesa-Lago, 2000: 277).

Echoing his speeches of the Revolution's 1966–1970 idealistic phase Fidel in 1986, at the beginnings of the Rectification Program, noted that it was a mistake to think that socialism could be constructed on the basis of material incentives. While material incentives were central to capitalist development, he argued—echoing Che: '[s]ocialism must be built with awareness and moral incentives'. With material incentives, he added, wages were paid disproportionately to the work done, with payments set according to six different work quotas rather than one, and that wage differentials were excessive—with a 10 to 1 ratio. Also, he argued, bonuses were too easy to get: often, as new technology was introduced without an upward adjustment in the work quota, everyone received a bonus, which might be viewed as price (of labour) distortion within a socialist context. And, Fidel continued, there are many such examples of the distorting effects of material incentives, which, in any case, could not match moral incentives in their ethical dimension—consciousness of one's social contribution to the welfare of society as a whole rather than self-advancement, the object and definition of economic freedom under capitalism.

Under the RP, Fidel (and the collective leadership to which he gave voice) for practical reasons accepted the socialist distribution formula ('to each according to his or her work') but application of this formula was closely monitored to prevent violations of the law and abuses. In any case, the RP had a solid egalitarian foundation in its emphasis on moral incentives, criticism of extreme wage differentials, denunciation of the high private sector earnings, and concern for market-generated distortions in the egalitarian distribution of incomes. The inception of an economic downturn in 1986 also forced or led to a policy of expanded rationing, which worked as a tool for procuring egalitarianism. Also the government's new wage policy was used to advance egalitarianism. In 1987 the lowest rate on the wage scale was increased from 75 pesos/per month to 100; from 82/93 to 107, and 95/107 to 118 (Zimbalist and Brundenius, 1989). As a result, the ratio of highest to lowest wages (the fundamental source of income in Cuba) was reduced from 5.5 to 1 in 1981 to 4.5 to 1 in 1987, and in real terms this ratio was maintained or even reduced, in subsequent years as Cuba entered the 'special period' of war (and crisis) in peacetime.

Initially the RP aimed to expand social services for human development, but the crisis tempered this policy. The share of social service in the state budget, one indicator of the government's priorities, increased from 41.8% in 1985 to a record 45% in 1988—a level unheard of even in the most advanced capitalist welfare state. Investments in social services rose from 17.7% of total investment in 1985 to 21.5% in 1988. Social expenditures per capita were also programmed to grow (by 13% from 1986 to 1990) notwithstanding their already high share of fiscal resources and declining fiscal revenues in the context of lower rates of economic growth (0.2 or −0.8% per capita from 1986–1989 according to CCE, AEC, 1989a).

As for social security, entitlement conditions were relaxed for pensions: the retirement age in 1987 was reduced while pensions were increased—benefiting some 690,000 pensioners (Mesa-Lago, 1993c). In this context, social security costs (including healthcare) surpassed 9% of GSP in 1990, the highest ever, and total security expenditures exceeded the one bullion peso mark in 1986 and kept growing, even into the crisis of the 'special period'. The number of pensioners surpassed one million in 1990, 64% more than in 1979. Significantly, the number of physicians per 100,000 inhabitants increased from 22.5 to 36.4 between 1985 and 1990, mainly because of the rapidly growing number of physicians (a matter of socialist policy) and the family doctor program, which provided primary healthcare for the entire population on the basis of one fully staffed clinic per 60–700 inhabitants.

In terms of other indicators of human welfare and 'development' the availability and quality of consumer goods and the level of material consumption undoubtedly shrank in the downturn of the second half of the 1980s, albeit under conditions of increased egalitarianism, an important indicator of 'human development' in a socialist context.

As for social indicators related to education, a critical factor and condition of human development in both a capitalist and socialist context, UNESCO reported a 6% illiteracy rate in 1990 among those 15 years and older. Enrolment in secondary and higher education kept increasing in this phase, reaching 88% and 23% of the respective age groups.

Infant mortality continued its impressive falling trend between 1985 and 1990: from 16.5 to 10.7 per 1,000, exceeding the target rate of 15 by 29%. ECLAC reported an increase in life expectancy from 74.3 years between 1981 and 1985 to 75.2 in 1986–1990.

There are no data on social security coverage for this stage but pension expenditures increased by 44%. As for housing it appears that the brigades in 1986–1990 built only 18,315 housing units as opposed to the annual target of 100,000. Total housing construction over the period appear to have fallen, aggravating a serious housing deficit, the one most notable shortfall in the Revolution's remarkable achievements at the level of social development, and a matter of concern in that housing generally affects health, a major condition of human development. Other shortfalls in the Revolution's achievements, or deficits in regard to the physical quality of life, would include transportation services and access to food as regards not so much nutrition and caloric intake as quality and range of choice. Although difficult to measure for the lack of hard evidence on the physical quality of daily life before the onset of the production crisis in 1991–1993 indications are, based on anecdotal evidence and recollections by those who lived through this period, that the level of material consumption at the time was severely constrained—austere at best. This might not been as a major factor in the determining the level of human development in terms of education and health, where the achievements of the Revolution are indisputable and well documented, but material consumption is nevertheless an important condition of the physical quality of life.

The *Human Development Report* includes a measure of per capita income, and ranking relative to other countries in the region, which can be used as a crude indicator of the level of material consumption. However, given the virtual absence of the market a determination of the goods available through the ration card (*la libreta*) provides a better measure of the consumption of material goods in terms of quantity and range if not quality, even though there is little question that the state was and is unable to provide anywhere near the quality of goods available on the market in most countries. As for the quantity and type of goods available with the 'libreta' the rationed goods were—as they are still today—highly subsidized by the state, reducing the value of per capita income as a measure of physical consumption. Most essentials in goods and services at the time required very little disposable income or were free, so the issue of per capita as a measure of the physical quality of life or material consumption boils down to an accounting issue: how the total production of goods and services is officially calculated. On this issue there been much debate and some controversy but it appears that the UNDP finally came to accept the accounting methodology and framework used in Cuba.[11]

Conclusion

The revolutionary process from 1959 to 1989, as has been noted by diverse scholars, unfolded in a pendulum swing mode in a search for

---

[11] Mesa-Lago (2005) nevertheless views this as a problem.

balance between economic growth and equitable social development. However, within these twists and turns, and experimentation with different policies and strategic adjustments, the revolutionary regime did not waver in its fundamental commitment to what we choose to term 'socialist human development'. The policy dynamics of this development will be explored in its critical dimensions (socialist consciousness, human welfare, equality and social justice, freedom and democracy, social solidarity) in the following chapters.

PART II

DIMENSIONS OF SOCIALIST HUMAN DEVELOPMENT

CHAPTER FIVE

SOCIALISM AS REVOLUTIONARY CONSCIOUSNESS: DYNAMICS OF A REVOLUTION

Revolution is a sense of the historic moment; it is changing everything that should be changed; it is *complete equality and freedom*; it is being treated and treating others like human beings; it is *emancipating ourselves through ourselves*, and through out own efforts; it is defying powerful dominating forces inside and outside of the social and national sphere; it is defending values that are believed in at the cost of any sacrifice: modesty, selflessness, altruism, solidarity and heroism; it is fighting with audacity, intelligence and realism; it is to never violate fundamental ethical principles; it is the profound conviction that there is no force in the world capable of crushing the strength of truth and ideas. ...

Revolution is unity, it is independence, it is fighting for our dreams for justice for Cuba and for the world, which is the foundation of our patriotism, our socialism and our internationalism

—Fidel, May Day Address, May 1, 2000.

The connection between socialism and human development was at issue in an extended 20th century debate on 'western marxism'[1] and, although thereafter[2] disappeared from the agenda of scholarly research and debate, it has been a matter of concern of some anti-capitalist movements and revolutionary regimes on the capitalist periphery, most notably (in the current conjuncture) in Venezuela. As for this concern in the case of Cuba see Silverman (1973), especially the chapters by Che Guevara. The concern for human development—to create a

---

[1] On this debate (From Lukács and Gramsci to Socialist-Feminism) see Gottlieb (1989).
[2] The disappearance of this debate coincided with the interventions of Luis Althusser in the 1960s debate on Marxist thought and the weakening of the Frankfort School of Critical Theory in the wake of the 1960s protest movements against capitalism and the Vietnam war. Some elements of a continuing debate can be traced out in the publications of *Insurgent Sociologist* (now *Critical Sociology*), but the humanist strain in Marxist thought was subsequently superseded by structuralism, until this form of Marxist analysis and theory came under attack in the 1980s turn towards poststructuralism, postmodernism and postdevelopment. On this itinerary of Marxist thought see Veltmeyer (2010a).

new more humane society and a more human form of development—has also been the subject matter of theoretical discourse and debate (see the 1960s debate on Marxist thought) that can be traced back to Marx's early writings in the mid-1840s.

In this chapter we will trace out the general contours of this debate, with particular reference to the thinking and writings of Marx and the debate on the nature of socialist development in the 1960s precipitated by the reflections of Ernesto [Che] Guevara on the Cuban Revolution. It is argued (Part I) that the basic elements of this thinking by Marx and Che, together with the thinking and writings of José Marti on the struggle for national independence, constitute the conceptual and ethical foundations of socialist human development in Cuba. Part II of the chapter focuses on the process of construction of a revolutionary or socialist consciousness in Cuba. The argument is that this revolutionary consciousness is a critical dimension of socialist human development in the Cuban context.

Conceptual and Ethical Foundations of Socialist Humanism

The idea of human development as the development of a society organized as to allow for the flourishing of human nature, and to achieve 'complete equality and freedom', is grounded in the eighteenth century philosophy of rationalist humanism, and the social and political movements for transformative change arising out of the recognition that society at the time was anything but human in form, i.e. the condition of most people was in conflict rather than in accord with human nature.

The notion of human nature in this context was embodied in the principles of freedom and equality, i.e. in ideas that at the time existed only in ideal or ideological form as values, requiring collective action in the direction of a new society based on freedom, equality and solidarity, the social conditions of which were given to a privileged or powerful few but denied to most. The ideological and political form of this idea of human development was socialism, which in the nineteenth century was embodied in the emergence of a broad movement for revolutionary change in the social and institutional structure of actually existing society. The hallmark and rallying cries for radical change or the revolutionary transformation of society were the belief in the need for *freedom, equality and fraternity or solidarity*.

Behind these ideals and the associated struggle for revolutionary change was the concern and growing demand for a new social order, a classless and communal form of society in which 'the free development of each is the condition for the free development of all'. Karl Marx was one of the most consequential theorists of this struggle, a major progenitor of the associated idea of human development.

Marx on Capitalism and Human Development

The nature of capitalism, Marx once observed, comes to the surface in a crisis. At that point it is possible to see things that were hidden—that the whole system is based on and revolves around profit making, and that workers exist for capital rather than the reverse in which social labour serves 'to satisfy the worker's own need for development' (realization of their human potential).

Marx conceived of human development as an alternative to capitalism, a socialist system in which the forces of production are developed to serve human needs rather than private profit, and that engage different relations of production under which workers are neither exploited nor alienated from their human nature as social beings.

However, historical circumstances dictated that this system would be first formed in Russia where the forces of production had not yet matured, developed by capitalism, to the point of securing the material basis for this social or human development. As a result, pressured by the capitalist west, and confronting resistance to the socialization of production from a majority of poor peasants concerned to preserve their existing relation to production, the leadership in the Russian Revolution turned to the state as a means of both advancing rapidly the forces of production and catching up to the capitalist west. In the process there was little concern for ensuring human development—to reclaim Marx's vision or bring about socialism as he had envisioned it, as a means of ensuring full development of the human potential. 'The rest', as has been said and written, 'is history', a history oriented towards the development of the forces of production rather than the full development of all human potential.

'What is the aim of the Communists?' asked Marx's colleague Friedrich Engels in his early draft of the *Communist Manifesto*. 'To organize society in such a way that everyone can develop and use all his capabilities and powers in complete freedom and without thereby infringing the basic conditions of this society' (in Lebowitz, 2006: 13). In Marx's final version that new society appears as an 'association in which the free development of each is the condition for the free development of all'.

This idea of society as the development of the human potential, and of socialism as the means and goal of this development, runs throughout Marx's work. What indeed is wealth, he asked, 'other than the universality of individual needs, capacities, pleasures, productive forces... the absolute working out of his [the individual's] creative possibilities?' (Lebowitz, 2007: 13). However, the realization of the human potential, as Lebowitz notes, 'does not drop from the sky'. It requires the development of society in which individuals do not look at each other as separate, merely as means of advancing and enriching himself. When we relate to each other as human beings, rather than as self-seeking owners and as means of serving our personal ends, we produce for each other and contribute to society as a whole precisely because to do so is personally fulfilling, a means of confirming the membership of each and all in the 'human community' bound together by fraternal ties or bonds of 'brotherly love'—or, as in Che Guevara's conception of revolutionary (socialist) consciousness, the 'love of humanity'.

Capitalist Relations of Production

The story told by economists who celebrate capitalism is that competition and markets ensure that capitalists will satisfy the needs of people—not because of their humanity and benevolence but as Adam Smith put it, 'from a regard to their own interest'. Capitalism as a system 'is so organised as to allow, if not compel, each individual to pursue their self-interest'. The basis of this system is the existence of two classes of individuals: the owners of the means of production, which tend to be converted into 'capital' (ways of generating wealth), and the working class, the producers of this wealth, who, dispossessed from the means of production are obliged to exchange their capacity to labour for a living wage. The key to this system is 'freedom': the free exchange of labour power against capital—the unfettered capacity of the owners of the means of production to hire labour and dispose of their capital (and the social product), and the 'freedom' of the workers who are 'free' in the sense that they can sell their labour power to whoever they choose but who are unfree in that they cannot choose to sell or not their capacity to labour. Their survival or subsistence depends on it, and to secure this subsistence like those on the other side of their relation to capitalist production they cannot be, or are not, concerned with realizing their human potential or the betterment of society as a whole.

The 'system' provides capitalists with the freedom and the capacity to exploit labour as the source of private profit while compelling workers to exchange their labour power for a living wage. This exchange, the economic and social basis of the capitalist system, has the appearance of freedom, a fair and free exchange, but the reality is that the workers are subject to the 'dull compulsion of economic forces' that, as Marx theorized as far back as 1844, alienate them from the 'human essence'— from the product of their labour, which stands over them as an alien force in the person of the capitalist or his agent; from themselves, i.e. their human nature as a social being, and from their 'species being'— the human essence of freedom and equality (Marx, 1967). Under these conditions, Marx argued, rather than being a means of realizing the human potential work becomes the source of alienation. And rather than enriching themselves by the fulfilment of their human capabilities, the harder they work the poorer the workers; workers, in fact, labour only to enrich the capitalist, impoverishing themselves in the process.[3]

The Human Development Debate

Since the human development concept's reinvention in the 1980s and its incorporation into the development discourse of the UNDP the discussion and relatively little debate about 'human development' has been entirely premised, albeit rather unfocused, on the system of capitalist development and the politics of liberal democracy. What is ironic about this intellectual turn is that to that point, and indeed in the decade preceding the UNDP's construction of human development, philosophical humanism was the standpoint and fundamental source of criticism by 'western Marxists' of capitalism; i.e. the ability of the system to expand the forces of production and generate 'economic growth'

---

[3] For Marx the labour process is the essence of human development, the means by which he fulfils his human nature. But this is only when labour or work is not given in its alienated form as it is under capitalism.

was acknowledged but this 'development' was unbalanced against the fundamental inhumanness of capitalism—its conversion of human beings into 'factors of production' and its alienation of the human essence in terms of freedom and equality.

This humanist critique of capitalism, founded on the philosophical humanism of Marx's Early Works, in the late 1960s and 1970s was at the centre of a virulent debate among Marxists as to the nature of Marxism and the best way to understand capitalism. However, there is no evidence that the founders of the notion of human development in the 1980s made any reference at all to this debate in effectively turning Marx upside down to argue, in effect, that rather than alienating people from themselves and their human nature capitalism could not only be humanized but constitutes the systemic foundation of human development.

Presupposing the institutionality of capitalism in their conception of human development there was no question in the minds of the concept's originators that the capitalist system was the foundation and indeed only framework for achieving human development. Thus, any questions—and questioning—at that point and since has focused not on the system itself but on its institutional structure—what changes can be made in a progressive direction (to create better conditions for human development) and what might be the best policy agenda to advance human development (see, for e.g. Griffin, 1989; Griffin and Knight, 1989).

Oddly enough, in regard to socialism there has been little questioning by its advocates and supporters about the system itself. Periodic debates over the economic viability of socialism and ways of advancing it have focused mainly on technical issues of technological development and information, incentives and resource allocation related to the expansion of society's forces of production—how to create the material basis for meeting the basic needs of the population under conditions of a premature transition towards socialism; i.e. where capitalism had been insufficiently developed to provide conditions for its emergence. In Marxist theory it was the role of capitalism to advance the forces of production to the point of capacitating society to meet the material needs of the entire population—creating thereby a precondition for postcapitalist or socialist development. In this concern, as with the economists of capitalist development there was comparatively little concern for the human conditions of socialism—and a relative neglect of the fundamental socialist human development concerns of the founders of scientific socialism, particularly Marx, who was fundamentally concerned in all of his writings with the human development dimensions of both capitalism and socialism. It turns out that this concern, and a socialist debate on HD, was focused on Cuba and effectively revived by the reflections of Che Guevara on the Cuban Revolution (on this see the essays, especially those by Guevara in Silverman, 1973).

In the 1960s this socialist debate on HD (the great debate of 1963-64) was sharply focused on Che's reflections on 'the new man and woman' in the new society in the making, and recently revived in Venezuela after several decades of neglect, was a reaction to the concerns of 'western Marxism' at the time (in the 1960s and 1970s) about the inhuman and inhumane dimension of capitalism, particularly as regards labour under capitalism (epitomized by Braverman, 1974). However rather than focusing on the same issue—how socialism provides better conditions for a non-alienating form of development—the focus of social theory in the 1970s was on production issues—on the superiority of socialism over capitalism in meeting the material needs of the population or technical issues related to how best to advance the forces of production under socialism. It was not until recently, in the context of Venezuela's Bolivarian Revolution, that a humanist conception of socialist development, founded on Marx's reflections on the nature of capitalism and his theory of alienated labour, was resurrected (see Lebowitch, 2007). From this perspective socialism is fundamentally about freedom and equality as conditions of human development, conditions that are antithetical to capitalism and that can best be advanced by socialism.

Socialist Human Development as Freedom

In the late 1960s and early 1970s, in the context of an extended debate among Marxists on Marxist philosophy (structuralism, humanism, historicism), there was a widespread preconception that Marx's vision of socialism and communism was infected by an anti-ecological and anti-humanist bias inherent in a scientific (materialist and structuralist) conception of capitalist and socialist development, and belief in the idea of 'progress' based on a progressive advance in dominating 'nature' (using it to extract resources for development). With reference to this conception it was widely held that Marx's scientific theory of capitalist development and his vision of the future was not a particularly useful guide to understanding the requirements and dynamics of socialist development. However, for many 'western Marxists' Marxism was rooted in the rational humanism of his early writings. It was understood that Marx relied on science for his analysis of capitalism but that he abandoned science in regard to the construction of socialism–the view that the future could be structurally determined and thus understood in scientific terms. The construction of socialism required class-conscious action, the agency of the working class informed by a scientific theory of capitalism, but without any blueprint or guiding principles.

Another common misperception is that Marx and Engels, eschewing all 'speculation about ... socialist utopias', thought very little about the system to follow capitalism, and that their entire body of writing on socialism or communism is represented by the *Critique of the Gotha Program*, a few pages long, and not much else (Auerbach and Skott, 1993: 195). But in reality, the nature of the system of post-capitalist economic and political relationships in an alternative future of a classless society is a recurring thematic in Marx's major and many of his minor works. And notwithstanding the scattered nature of these discussions it is not difficult to glean from them a coherent vision based on a clear set of organizing principles. First, a close reading of Marx's discussion of communism or socialism, and associated (non-market) production and communal forms of property relations, reveals that his vision of the future was informed by human developmental concerns—specifically by the idea that under conditions of revolutionary transformation socialist development would be based on, if not directed by, a (socialist) consciousness of the need for and possibility of human development.

In other words, Marx, like Che Guevara had assumed in the context of the Cuban Revolution, socialist development would be progressive not in terms of advancing society's forces of production (capitalism would lay the foundations for this development) but in terms of the corresponding relations of production and human development concerns: that socialism was fundamentally more humane form of development relative to capitalism; that capitalism was fundamentally inhumane in terms of freedom and equality and that this problematic of emancipation could only be resolved by socialism; capitalism could not be saved by giving it a human face.

Although Marx does not provide a detailed blueprint of post-capitalist society, his vision comprises a coherent set of principles that can inform the struggle against the alienation of 'Man', exploitation and oppression in favour of a system that promotes sustainable human development. Indeed, this is how Che Guevara understood Marx (see his essays in Silverman, 1973b). And it is a fundamental impulse behind the Cuban Revolution as it has unfolded.

Freedom as a Fundamental Organizing Principle

A fundamental organizing principle of SHD is the need for freedom—of socialism as 'complete freedom' (Fidel) and 'the search for a fully democratic society' (Harnecker). But the concept of freedom in this principle is fundamentally different from the concept formulated by Amartya Sen, and articulated in the UNDP's conception of HD. This conception of freedom is predicated on the expansion of choice for each individual in accessing the market in a system of commodity production. That is, individuals are viewed in their relationship to the means of consumption rather than production. And in this connection the focus is on the individual's 'opportunities'—their freedom of choice—viewed in the abstract—as a formal right and he responsibility of governments to level the playing field and ensure 'equity' (an equality of opportunity), to empower the individual to act on this opportunity and to capacitate. However, the fact is that most individuals are generally unaware of the forces operating on them, limiting their opportunities—forces beyond their control and often beyond their understanding. Typically, both analysts and development practitioners, focused as they are on the individual *qua* individual rather than in their relation to others as a social being, leads them to view 'freedom' purely as an abstract right, as an ideal rather than a practical or realizable idea. Marx's conception of freedom, and that of Che and the Cuban revolutionaries, is altogether different.

For Marx the *first* and most basic feature of communism is to overcome the separation of the producers from the necessary social conditions of production that is endemic to capitalism as a system of commodity production. This new 'social union' entails a decommodification of labour power plus a new set of communal or social property rights in regard to the social product. In this regard, communist or 'associated' production is planned and carried out by the producers and communities themselves, without the class-based mediations of wage-labour, the market and the state. Marx makes this point repeatedly and illustrates it with reference to and in terms of the primary means and end of associated production: *free human development*.

Marx specifies capitalism as the 'decomposition of the original union existing between the labouring man and his means of labour', and communism as 'a new and fundamental revolution in the mode of production' that 'restore[s] the original union in a new historical form' (1976: 39). That is, communism is the 'historical reversal' of 'the separation of labour and the worker from the conditions of labour, which confront him as independent forces' (1971: 271–272). Under capitalism's wage system, 'the means of production employ the workers'; under communism, 'the workers, as subjects, employ the means of production ... in order to produce wealth for themselves' (Marx, 1968: 580).

This new union of the producers and the conditions of production 'will', as Engels phrases it, 'emancipate human labour power from its position as a commodity' (1939: 221). Naturally, such an emancipation, in which the labourers undertake production as 'united workers' (see below), 'is only possible where the workers are the owners of their means of production' (Marx, 1971: 525). This worker ownership does not entail the individual rights to possession and alienability characterizing capitalist property, however. Rather, workers' communal property codifies and enforces the new union of the collective producers and their communities with the conditions of production. Accordingly, Marx describes communism as 'replacing capitalist production with cooperative production, and capitalist property with a higher form of the archaic type of property, i.e. communist property' (Marx and Engels, 1989: 362).[4]

A *second* aspect of Marx's conception of freedom is class struggle: emancipation not from oppressive structures that restrict the freedom

---

[4] As stated in *The German Ideology*, 'the appropriation by the proletarians' is such that 'a mass of instruments of production must be made subject to each individual, and property to all ... With the appropriation of the total productive forces by the united individuals, private property comes to an end' (Marx and Engels, 1976, p. 97). Marx's vision thus involves a 'reconversion of capital into the property of producers, although no longer as the private property of the individual producers, but rather as the property of associated producers, as outright social property' (Marx, 1967, III, p. 437). Communist property is collective precisely insofar as 'the material conditions of production are the cooperative property of the workers' as a whole, not of particular individuals or sub-groups of individuals' (Marx, 1966: 11).

of thought and action of each individual qua individual (a liberal conception of freedom) but emancipation from the freedom of proprietors and capitalists, owners of the means of production under conditions of private property, which endows property owners with the legal right and the power to dispose of the social product—to extract surplus value from social labour and profit from it at the expense of the direct but unassociated producers.

In these terms Marx theorized freedom as an emancipatory struggle. Marx theorized the dynamics of this struggle in several ways, first on the basis of socialist humanism, and then, in his later political writings, historical materialism. At first, in 1843 he theorized the revolutionary struggle—for emancipation—in terms of the combination of two forces—'philosophy' which would provide the social revolution with its active element (theoretical awareness of the proletariat as the practical negation of their human essence), and the proletariat would constitute the passive element, the material basis, of an emancipatory process: overcoming the negation of the human essence. In 1844, however, made aware of the revolutionary character of the working class,[5] Marx formulated the theory that would guide his thinking and practice ever since—of proletarian self-determination, in which the working class is no longer regarded as merely the passive element or material basis of the revolution, acting out of necessity but without theoretical awareness of itself as an agent of revolutionary change, but also its active agency—the 'identical subject-object' of history in Lukacs' rather philosophical formulation of this principle.

As we will see, despite the vanguardist conception of leadership, the leaders and ideologues of the Cuban Revolution, including in particular Fidel Castro and Che Guevara, saw the Revolution in similar terms—as the intended consequence of the class-conscious action of the proletariat, a consciousness forged in the heat of the struggle itself.

A third aspect of the struggle for emancipation relates to conditions under which the means of production are not only privatized but

---

[5] In 1943, a strike of textile workers (weavers) in Silesia led to an important breakthrough in Marx's thinking—recognition that the working class represented not only the material force of 'necessity' but the 'active force of thought', acting not out of blind necessity, as the practical negation of the human essence, but with class consciousness, awareness of itself as not only the practical negation of the human essence but its theoretical affirmation—in terms defined by Georg Lukacs the 'identical subject-object' of history.

denationalized, i.e. fall under foreign ownership. Marx himself did not theorize this condition of unfreedom or the associated struggle for national liberation—this aspect of freedom. Thus the Cuban revolutionaries turned not to Marx but to José Marti in conceiving of the Revolution as national liberation, freedom from the oppression of foreign ownership. In Fidel's words: 'Revolution is ...*emancipating ourselves*...it is defying powerful dominating forces inside and outside of the social and national sphere...it is independence, it is fighting for our dreams for justice for Cuba and for the world...the foundation of our patriotism, our socialism and our internationalism' (Fidel, Speech, May 1, 2000).

Development as the Free Development of Individuals as Social Beings

The socialization of production, a fundamental principle of socialist development, should not be mistaken for a complete absence of individual property rights. Although communal property 'does not reestablish private property for the producer', it nonetheless 'gives him individual property based on the acquisitions of the capitalist era: i.e. on cooperation and the possession in common of the land and of the means of production' (Marx, 1967, I: 763). In this regard, Marx posits that 'the alien property of the capitalist ... can only be abolished by converting his property into the property ... of the associated, social individual' (Marx and Engels, 1994: 109). He even suggests that communism will 'make individual property a truth by transforming the means of production ... now chiefly the means of enslaving and exploiting labour, into mere instruments of free and associated labour' (1985: 75).

Regarding the overriding imperative of socialism as Marx and Engels conceived of it—*the free development of individual human beings as social individuals*—they insisted that in 'the community of revolutionary proletarians ... it is *as individuals that people participate*', precisely because 'it is the association of individuals ... which puts the conditions of the free development and movement of individuals under their [own] control—conditions which were previously left to chance and had acquired an independent existence over against the separate individuals' (1976: 89). Stated differently, 'the all-round realization of the individual will only cease to be conceived as an ideal... when the impact of the world which stimulates the real development of the abilities of the individual is *under the control of the individuals themselves*...' (p. 309).

In class or class-divided societies, 'personal freedom ... exist[s] only for the individuals who *developed* under the conditions of the ruling class'. But under the 'real community' of communism (socialism), '*individuals obtain their freedom in and through their association* [with others]' (p. 87). Instead of opportunities for individual development being obtained mainly at the expense of others, as in the competitive markets of class societies, the future 'community' will provide 'each individual [with] the means of cultivating his gifts in all directions; hence *personal freedom becomes possible only within the community*' (p. 86). In short, communal property is individual insofar as it affirms each person's claim, as a member of society, for access to the productive resources, conditions and results of production as a conduit to her or his development as an individual '[for] whom the different social functions he performs are but so many modes of giving free scope to his own natural and acquired powers' (Marx, 1967, I: 488). Only in this way can 'the old bourgeois society, with its classes and class antagonisms', be replaced with 'an association in which *the free development of each is a condition for the free development of all*' (Marx and Engels, 1968: 53).

The most basic way in which socialism a la Marx promotes individual human development is by protecting the individual's right to a fair share in the total product for her or his private consumption. The *Manifesto* is unambiguous on this point: 'Communism deprives no man of the power to appropriate the products of society; all that it does is to deprive him of the power to subjugate the labour of others by means of such appropriation' (Marx and Engels, 1968: 49). In this sense, 'social ownership extends to the land and the other means of production' (Engels, 1939: 144). An equivalent description of the 'community of free individuals' is given in *Capital*, Vol. I: 'The total product of our community is a social product'.

This raises the question as to how the distribution of individual workers' consumption claims will be determined. In *Capital*, Marx envisions in general terms that 'the mode of this distribution will vary with the productive organization of the community, and the degree of historical development attained by the producers'. He then suggests that one possibility would be for 'the share of each individual producer in the means of subsistence' to be 'determined by his labour-time', i.e. his contribution to production (1967, I: 78). In the *Critique of the Gotha Programme*, this conception of labour time as the determinant of individual consumption rights is less ambiguous, at least for 'the first phase of communist society as it is when it has just emerged after prolonged birth pangs from capitalist society' (Marx, 1966: 10). Here Marx projects that the individual producer receives back from society—after deductions have been made for a state managed common fund—precisely what is given by him or her to society: a quantum of labour. Individual producers or workers in effect receive a certificate that they have furnished such and such an amount of labour (after deducting their labour for the common fund), and with this certificate they can draw from the social stock of means of consumption as much as commensurate with their contribution and insofar as the individual labour-time standard codifies the ethic of equal exchange regardless of the connotations for individual development. In this context, Marx notes, the distribution of a share in the social product is still infected by 'the narrow horizon of bourgeois right'. But he then goes on to suggest that 'in a higher phase' (communist society), labour-based individual consumption claims would be 'fully left behind' allowing society to inscribe on its banners: *from each according to his ability, to each according to his needs!* (1966: 10). It is in this higher phase that a communist (or socialist) 'mode of distribution...allows all members of society to develop, maintain and exert their capacities in all possible directions' (Engels, 1939: 221). Here 'the individual consumption of the labourer' becomes that which 'the full development of the individuality requires' (Marx, 1967, III: 876).

But even in the early phase in the transition, 'the means of individual development assured by communal property' are not limited to individuals' private consumption claims. *Human development* will also benefit from the expanded social services (education, health services, utilities, and old-age pensions) financed by deductions from the total product prior to its distribution among individuals. Hence, 'what the producer is deprived of in his capacity as a private individual benefits him directly or indirectly in his capacity as a member of society' (Marx, 1966: 8). Such social consumption will, in Marx's view, be 'considerably increased in comparison with present-day society and it increases in proportion as the new society develops' (p. 7). For example, Marx envisions an expansion of 'technical schools (theoretical and practical) in combination with the elementary school' (1966: 20). He projects that 'when the working class comes into power, as inevitably it must, technical instruction, both theoretical and practical, will take its proper place in the working class schools' (1967, I: 488). Marx even suggests that the younger members of socialist society will experience 'an early combination of productive labour with education'—presuming, of course, 'a strict regulation of the working time according to the different age groups and other safety measures for the protection of children' (1966: 22). The basic idea is that 'the fact of the collective working group being composed of individuals of both sexes and ages, must necessarily, under suitable conditions, become a source of *humane development*' (1967, I: 490). Another, related function of theoretical and practical education will be to 'convert science from an instrument of class rule into a popular force', thereby 'convert[ing] the men of science themselves from panderers to class prejudice...state parasites and allies of capital into free agents of thought' (Marx and Engels, 1985: 162).

Along with expanded social consumption, a 'shortening of the working day' under socialism will facilitate human development by giving individuals more free time in which to enjoy the 'material and social advantages...of social development' (Marx, 1967, III: 819–820). Free time is 'time...for the free development, intellectual and social, of the individual' (1967, I: 530). As such, 'free time, disposable time, is wealth itself, partly for the enjoyment of the product, partly for free activity which—unlike labour—is not dominated by the pressure of an extraneous purpose which must be fulfilled, and the fulfillment of which is regarded as a natural necessity or a social duty' (Marx, 1971: 257). In other words, in Marx's view, expanded free time—an assumed or essential socialist condition of work—embodies an ethic of human self-realization.

It is important to recognize the connection between human development and the development of the productive forces in Marx's vision—a connection that is unsurprising insofar as Marx always treated 'the human being himself' as 'the main force of production' (1973: 190). However, socialism can represent a real combination and union of all the producers with the conditions of production only if it ensures each individual's right to participate freely and to the fullest of her or his ability in the cooperative utilization and development of these conditions. The socialized character of production means that 'individuals must appropriate the existing totality of productive forces not only to achieve self-activity, but also to safeguard their very existence' (Marx and Engels, 1976: 96).

To be an effective vehicle of human development, this appropriation must not reduce individuals to interchangeable cogs in a giant collective production machine operating outside their control in the alienated pursuit of 'production for the sake of production'—or for the sake of profit for the owner. Rather, it must enhance 'the development of human productive forces' capable of grasping and controlling social production at the human level in line with 'the development of the richness of human nature as an end in itself' (Marx, 1968: 117–118).

Although socialist distribution has 'a universal character corresponding to...the productive forces', it also promotes 'the development of the individual capacities corresponding to the material instruments of production'. Because these instruments 'have been developed to a totality and only exist within a universal intercourse', their effective appropriation requires 'the development of a totality of capacities in the individuals themselves' (Marx and Engels, 1976: 96). In short, 'the genuine and free development of individuals' under socialism is enabled by and contributes to 'the universal character of the activity of individuals on the basis of the existing productive forces' (p. 465).

In this context Marx and Engels did not—as many today—treat planned resource allocation as the most fundamental factor distinguishing socialism or communism from capitalism. A more basic characteristic of socialism is its de-alienation of the conditions of production vis-à-vis the producers, and the enabling effect this new union would have on free human development. Stated differently, they treated the socialist system or the planning mechanism (in contradistinction to the use of the 'market mechanism') in the allocation or distribution of shares in the social product as instruments of the human developmental impulses unleashed by the new communality of the producers and their conditions of existence.

The decommodification of production is, as discussed above, the flip-side of the de-alienation of production conditions; the planning of production is just the allocative form of this reduced stunting of human capabilities by their material and social conditions of existence. As Marx wrote: commodity exchange is only 'the bond natural to individuals within specific limited relations of production'. The 'alien and independent character' in which this bond exists vis-à-vis individuals proves only that 'the latter are still engaged in the creation of the conditions of their social life, and that they have not yet begun, on the basis of these conditions, to live it' (1973: 162).

Marx and Che on Capitalism, Communism and Human Development

Marx argued that 'if we did not find concealed in society *as it is* the material conditions of production and the corresponding relations of exchange prerequisite for a classless society, then all attempts to explode it would be quixotic' (1973: 159). He referred to 'development of the productive forces of social labour' as capitalism's 'historical task and justification ... the way in which it unconsciously creates the material requirements of a higher mode of production' (1967, III: 259). In short, the 'original unity between the worker and the conditions of production ... can be reestablished only on the material foundation which capital creates' (1971: 422–423).

The problem, of course, is the historic fact that in Cuba, as in prerevolutionary Russia, capitalism had not yet developed to the point of fulfilling its historic mission—to create the material requirements of a higher mode of production. What then is to be done? And how? But first: what are these requirements? Do they entail the development of production and consumption to the point where scarcity—and thus the need for economics as the management of scarcity—disappears? That is, if scarcity and poverty persist is socialism premature and unworkable (and thus presumably non-viable)? Not necessarily. For one thing, capitalism never has and nowhere creates the conditions of general affluence—or the ability to meet the material needs of the entire and different classes of the population. Marx is clear on this point. Even when capitalism develops the forces of production to make the meeting of everyone's basic needs technically possible, the dynamics of capitalist development creates new needs and demands that must be met, and, more importantly, it both requires and tends to generate the conditions of mass impoverishment and immiseration, even, as is evident today, with the most advanced form of capitalism.

Marx's position on this point is that by developing the productive forces, it creates the possibility of a system 'in which coercion and monopolization of social development (including its material and intellectual advantages) by one part of society at the expense of another are eliminated', partly by means of a 'greater reduction of time devoted to material labour in general' (Marx, 1967, III: 819). In short, insofar as it develops human productive capabilities, capitalism negates not scarcity as such (in the sense of satisfying all possible material needs), but rather the scarcity rationale for class inequalities in human developmental opportunities. In Marx's words, '[a]lthough at first the development of the capacities of the human species takes place at the cost of the majority of human individuals and even classes, in the end it breaks through this contradiction and coincides with the development of the individual' (1968: 118).

Capitalism, as Marx (1973: 158) sees it, potentiates a restricted form of human development insofar as it makes production an increasingly social process, 'a system of general social metabolism, of universal relations, of all-round needs and universal capacities'. However, only with the socialization of production, which capitalism itself unconsciously promotes in the same way that it promotes the unification of different forms of labour, can one foresee 'free individuality, based on the universal development of individuals and on their subordination of their communal, social productivity as their social wealth' (p. 158). For Marx, capitalism's development of 'the universality of intercourse, hence the world market' connotes 'the possibility of the universal development of the individual' (p. 542). Thus it is, as Che Guevara emphasized in the debate on how best to promote economic and social development in Cuba, that in praising capitalism Marx had in mind not the growth of production and consumption as such, for their own sake, but their implication for human development—'the universality of individual needs, capacities, pleasures, productive forces etc. created through universal exchange' under capitalism (p. 488).

It is with reference to this idea that Che Guevara, closely following Marx's humanism, formulated what would become his motto—'The ultimate and most important revolutionary aspiration: to see man liberated from alienation'.

Freedom as Revolutionary Struggle / Socialism as a Cultural Revolution

A socialist production system is not simply inherited from capitalism, needing only to be signed into law by a newly elected socialist government. It requires 'long struggles, through a series of historic processes, transforming circumstances and men' (Marx and Engels, 1985: 76). Among these transformed circumstances, Guevara declared—going back to Marx on this point—will be 'not only a change of distribution but a new organization of production, or rather the delivery (setting free) of the social forms of production…of their present class character…' (p. 157).

This 'long struggle' scenario for post-revolutionary society is a far cry from the interpretation put forth by Marx's critics who have Marx endorsing capitalism as the material basis of socialist development and the state as the fundamental instrument and agency of social transformation. But in fact, Marx's view of the social transformation process corresponds more closely to the view that the construction of socialism requires public action and what we might term 'social democracy'—a combination of actions from above and below, building a new society from within, community by community, neighborhood by neighborhood, workplace by workplace.

In Marx's view, the struggle for 'the conditions of free and associated labour...will be again and again relented and impeded by the resistance of vested interests and class egotisms' (1985: 157)—a situation (and political condition) that led Lenin, in the context of the Russian Revolution, and Che Guevara in the context of revolutionary Cuba, to argue the need for leadership and a revolutionary vanguard party, to assume the responsibility of leadership, and the state as the fundamental repository of political power to steer the socialist ship of state. This is precisely why socialism's human developmental conditions, according to Che Guevara will be generated in large part by the revolutionary struggle itself. Both the taking of political power by the subordinate classes and the subsequent transformation of society's material and social conditions.

Marx and Engels had argued this point in more theoretical terms. In their words, communist or socialist 'appropriation...can only be effected through a union, which by the character of the proletariat itself can again only be a universal one, and through a revolution, in which, on the one hand, the power of the earlier mode of production and intercourse and social organization is overthrown, and, on the other hand, there develops the universal character and the energy of the proletariat, which are required to accomplish the appropriation, and the proletariat moreover rids itself of everything that still clings to it from its previous position in society' (1976: 97).

As noted earlier, Marx had argued that 'the emancipation of the working classes must be conquered by the working classes themselves'. The reason for this is clearly understood by Che Guevara—and, according to him, by the other revolutionaries—in the following terms: the struggle for human development ultimately requires 'the abolition of all class rule', and the working class is the only group capable of undertaking such a project. However, the advancement of the revolutionary process sits on the horns of a dilemma: the proletariat as the 'identical subject-object of history', an agent of revolutionary change, is not constituted automatically. As Marx stated as a matter of principle: people make history but not under conditions of their own choosing. They are, in effect, both the authors and the product of their circumstances, and to change people one needs to change these circumstances. On the other hand, changing these circumstances (creating a 'new society') requires people to be other than what they are. It requires, as Che understood it, 'a new man and new woman', which in turn could only be formed in the context of the revolutionary process of creating a new society. In other words, as Marx had argued and Che emphasized, people become other than what they are—transformed—in the process of struggle, a struggle with diverse dimensions, including a *cultural revolution*, the genesis of a revolutionary socialist consciousness that everyone is a social being, part of a larger whole, and needs to act in solidarity with others—motivated by a 'love of humanity'.

As Che interpreted Marx, the revolutionary process is itself the fundamental crucible of change, creating as it does the necessary conditions of revolutionary transformation: a revolutionary or socialist consciousness of the need for change, and the creation of a class of new individuals committed and schooled in struggle to bringing it about. As Che saw it this meant constant struggle and 'education'…'self-education', and militant action in the service of one's fellow human beings.

Marx and Che on Revolutionary Consciousness and Political Practice

A consistent theme in Marx's political writings was the need for revolutionary practice, the simultaneous changing of people's circumstances and of themselves. By struggling against capital to satisfy their collective needs workers produce themselves in such a way as to prepare them for a new society; they come to recognize the nature of the system and to realize that they *cannot* limit themselves to guerrilla wars against the existing system; that they need to act collectively in order to change the system, changing both society and themselves in the process. And that, Marx recognized, is the point at which capitalism can no longer be sustained. The *objective* conditions of revolutionary transformation are created by a development of the forces of production to the point at which they can no longer be expanded on the basis of existing relations. However, a process of revolutionary transformation also has *subjective* conditions: a class that is conscious of the need to change society and its power to bring about change—itself as the agency of revolutionary change.

However—and this for both Marx and Che was the paradox of social change—a 'revolutionary consciousness' and the creation of a 'new society' required 'a new man and woman' while the creation of this 'new man and woman' required a 'new society'—a 'chicken and egg' dilemma.

As for agency, according to Che, revolutionary change—the transformation of society requires both a population mobilized and armed with a revolutionary consciousness and a revolutionary government… a government able to mobilize the people on behalf of the policies that meet the needs of the people and lead to the realization of human development. Here the essential matter is the capacity or the degree to which the government is able to free the population from a culture of possessive individualism and consumerism and the ideological dominion of capital.

Only with this emancipatory praxis can the government hope to facilitate human development—prioritise human development, i.e. the development of human needs and capacities via the development of the forces of production. The second step is by means of 'public action', a combination of social and political power vested in the Organs of Popular Power (OPP) within the state apparatus, using this power to bring about the revolutionary transformation of society and the people that make it up (the new man and woman). This means the transformation of a society in which the owners of the means of production are in a position and able to enrich themselves by exploiting the labour of others, and in the process appropriating the lion's share of the social product. It means the creation of a new society in which all individuals can fully realize their human potential—a society advanced by a revolutionary government with the active mobilized support of 'the people' under the conditions (of freedom and equality) that define human development.

According to Che, who here closely follows Marx, the necessary conditions of human development and revolutionary change is a cultural revolution—the creation of a new man and woman freed from a concern for self-interest. Under this circumstance the agency of change includes *education, self-education, liberated labour* and above all, *participation in the struggle for revolutionary change* (Guevara, 2006).

Socialist Human Development as Equality and Social Justice

The conceptual foundation of philosophical (as well as ideological and political) *liberalism* is the idea of freedom—freedom of the individual qua individual from the undue constraints of society, in one or more of its organs, on the freedom of the individual to act and think. From a conservative perspective this freedom finds its acceptable and legitimate limits in what is good for society as a whole. However, from a liberal individualist perspective, the freedom to think and act can and should be restricted only to the point at which the freedom of one individual interferes with the freedom of another or others, regardless of what might be conceived of by some as 'the good of society as a whole'. Within these limits, there are degrees of freedom ranging from close to absolute and universal, i.e. given to all members of society, to an oppressive state of unfreedom in which individuals are incapacitated from making any decision-making power related to the social conditions that affect them or the forces that operate on them.

In liberal economic and democratic theory the optimal or most favourable conditions for individual freedom are found in a system of capitalist democracy that combines the capacity of each and all individuals (within legally defined limits) to participate freely and fully in the institution of democratic elections, and the equal opportunity of each and all individuals to act in their own interest for self-improvement in the market, a market that might be 'free' or regulated in the public interest.

In the institutional context of capitalist democracy the idea of freedom as progress or development (defined improvements plus needed change) is understood and operationalized as the 'expansion of choice' vis-à-vis the market or consumption. As for social equality it is transmuted into a formal or legal right of each individual to take advantage of his or her opportunities, which is to say (as conceived by the World Bank and other international 'development' associations), as an 'equality of opportunity' (or 'equity'). That is, social equality is not conceived of as a substantive social condition but rather as a formal right that relates, as Max Weber might have written, to an 'abstract individual, theoretically conceived' just for the sake of analysis.

In a socialist conception of human development equality is viewed and operationalized very differently: as an equality of condition rather than opportunity, an equality that the state is obliged to protect and advance in the interest of fundamental human rights and as a matter of social justice.[6] In this socialist conception, the existence and reality of

---

[6] The documents of the 1959 Revolution compiled by Bell Lara (2006) are replete with formulations and declarations by Fidel and others along these lines of concern with correcting deeply rooted social injustices, particularly in relation to race and class.

the condition of social inequality reflects the working of structural factors and forces generated by the class structure of the capitalist system. The main structural source of social inequality is the institution of private property, a point emphasized in the documents of the 1959 Revolution compiled by Bell Lara et al. (2006), without any theoretical or ideological reference, only to the long and heroic struggles of the peasants, blacks and workers against oppression and exploitation.

In this practical rather than theoretical conception of socialism capitalism appears, and is constructed, as the embodiment of social injustice, the appropriation by the few of the means of production and what the vast majority in society have laboured to produce. Social equality thus requires the abolition of private property and demands a alternative system for organizing production: the socialization (and renationalization) of production—to liberate the country from the oppression of class rule and foreign ownership.

Shaping of a Revolutionary Consciousness

A review of the thinking behind the Cuban Revolution makes evident the realization by the leaders of the Revolution that the creation of a new society based on social justice and solidarity requires above all a 'cultural revolution'—a profound transformative change in the values and concerns that motivate people in their everyday lives and in their individual and collective actions as social beings. Sociologist Joe Tharmangalam (2008: 12), with reference to a development strategy pursued for over five decades in Kerala, describes this problematic in the following terms: 'a transformation in human consciousness and a paradigm change in social values and ideals, in people's conception of and commitment to social and distributive justice, human rights, and in people's aspirations for themselves and their children'.

Che Guevara was very insistent on this point—on the need for a Cultural Revolution as a condition of socialist human development. At issue, as he saw it, was the need to forge a revolutionary consciousness based on a socialist ethic of human development—a new society in which the socialist ideals of freedom and equality are both reinstitutionalized and realized. For Che this meant making a fundamental breaking from a capitalist culture of possessive individualism, a social and cultural transformation wrought by means of 'education, self-education and mass organization'—the mobilization of the masses in support of the Revolution.

Initially, the group that formed around Fidel Castro in the project of an armed struggle for state power in Cuba had placed their hopes in the possibility, if not likelihood, of a spontaneous popular uprising that would accompany the intrepid action of the rebels against tyranny. In others words, they were convinced that the subjective as well as objective conditions for revolution were present in the Cuban people, and that all that was needed was a push (Guevara, 1967: 509). But it did not take long for the rebels in the Sierra Maestra to realize that the masses were not necessarily with them subjectively, confronting them with the problem of developing in them a revolutionary consciousness (Medin, 1990).

In the account given by Medin of subsequent developments, the revolutionary struggle for power ended up bringing about a change not just in the consciousness of the masses but also in an understanding by the rebels that revolutionary consciousness would have to be developed gradually, particularly as regards the peasantry, a fundamental social base of the struggle. Gone was the expectation of a spontaneous uprising. What emerged in its place was the recognition of the need to develop a revolutionary consciousness and that the struggle itself would create the conditions for this transformation in consciousness. And Che was clear that this transformation cut both ways, changing the consciousness of both the peasantry and the rebels themselves. Some time later, Che wrote that '[t]hose long-suffering, loyal inhabitants of the Sierra Maestra...never suspected the role they played as forgers of our revolutionary ideology' (1982: 173). On the one hand, '[w]e convinced them that once they were armed, organized and had lost their fear of the enemy, victory was certain'. On the other, 'the peasantry...imposed agrarian reform on the revolution'.

Theorizing about this situation *a posteriori* and projecting it as a revolutionary thesis Castro and Guevara both remarked that revolutionary consciousness did not have to be inherent in the masses—indeed this was not likely; that a few dedicated people could constitute themselves as a vanguard to initiate revolutionary action, and serve as a catalyst of change. But the fundamental task of committed revolutionaries was to forge a revolutionary consciousness.

Upon achieving power the revolutionaries realized that the process of creating a revolutionary consciousness had only just begun—that the revolutionary struggle, an essential condition for *shaping revolutionary consciousness on a national level*, would continue. What this meant, particularly for Che, with Fidel the chief theorist and ideologue of the Revolution, was education and a process of mass mobilization designed to actively engage the population in the revolutionary process of creating a new society based on a fundamentally different ethic and ethos. Engagement in the struggle, Che argued, was itself an important form and condition of 'self-education'—a growing consciousness of the need for a new society that capable of meeting the material and spiritual needs of all members of society. And indeed, the revolutionary struggle for power in Cuba had brought about some of the objective and subjective conditions of such a development, the potential for revolutionary transformation. However, once power was achieved the problem of realizing this potential emerged—a problem, according to Che of self-education and figuring out how to engage the struggle in this changed context.

Education for Human Development

In Kerala, another exemplar of socialist human development, access to education and the institution of a public education system accessible to all, particularly the hitherto excluded lower castes, was a major demand of the social reform movements that brought a socialist human development regime to power (Tharamangalam, 2008). But in Cuba education, both self-education in the process of collective struggle (as in the mass literacy campaign of 1961) and the institutions of formal system set up by the revolutionary regime, was linked intrinsically to the Revolution's goal of transforming Cubans into the 'new man and woman', mobilizing and empowering them to actively participate in the revolutionary process of creating a new society, and transforming themselves in the process. At the beginning the public system of education had little to do with any policy or plan for economic development. It had to do with creating conditions that would allow Cubans from all walks of life to realize their full human potential and to transform themselves in the process. On this see Che Guevara's discussion of the dynamics of creating 'the new man and woman'. Following Fidel Castro's promise to turn the nation into a gigantic school, education was declared to be every one's right (Malhotra 395).

In addition to organizing one of the best and free public school systems anywhere Cuba captured the world's attention, just two years into the Revolution, for its innovative and revolutionary nine-month literacy campaign which mobilized 100,000 secondary students and other volunteers to impart the skills of reading and writing to 707,000 adults in all parts of the country. A notable aspect of this mass participation, which was especially important in healthcare, was the pivotal role of 'women's agency'. Not surprisingly, today women make up nearly half of all physicians as well as directors of hospitals and polyclinics (Mehrotra, 402).

In the 1950s, and even in the 1960s, the situation was quite different regarding the active participation of women in different areas of social life and public decision-making, empowering them to act collectively in the collective interest. The same applies to the masses of urban and rural poor who, prior to the Revolution, suffered from an exceedingly high level of social exclusion, unable to actively participate in decision making related to critical conditions of their lives and livelihoods. The Revolution, via participation in the process of revolutionary transformation at the level of these mass campaigns had a powerful liberating effects on the masses.

The literacy campaigns may be regarded as one of the many pivotal and symbolic 'moments' in the historical path travelled by Cubans in their cultural revolution. As Che Guevara conceived it, the makeover or revolutionary reconstruction of consciousness—from capitalist to socialist values, required and entailed an enriched educational process—a process of formal education, in addition to a process of 'self-education', for which the revolutionary process itself was the school.

From the outset, *education*, both in the form of schooling as a state-funded socially inclusive (universal) development program and *self-education*, via active participation in the process of revolutionary change, was conceived by the architects of the Cuban Revolution as the fundamental strategy for creating and maintaining a revolutionary consciousness based on a socialist ethic of human development.

One of the agencies set up by the government to implement this strategy was the EAC [Escuela al Campo] ('School in the Countryside'). The EAC was specifically and purposely created as a space to secure revolutionary values during a time in life when youth are 'searching for their individual identity as a person'. The Cuban Ministry of Education terms the EAC 'an incubator for revolutionary commitment', serving to instill revolutionary citizenship values of hard work, sacrifice, patriotism, equality, anti-imperialism, responsibility, collectivism and solidarity with the proletariat, thus creating a revolutionary consciousness to socialize new generations of Cubans into socialist values of human development, converting a value into an organizational principle and a cultural tradition of revolutionary change. *Conciencia,* for Che Guevara, was more than denoted in the English translation of 'consciousness' or 'awareness'. It entailed a 'commitment to action' forged in a process of political education and active participation in revolutionary struggle (Guevara, 1957). Fidel Castro defined *conciencia* as 'an attitude of struggle, dignity, principles and revolutionary morale'.

Theorizing a posteriori both Fidel and Che remarked in the 1960s that *conciencia* was not or did not need to be inherent in the masses but, rather, that 'the vanguard, the guerrilla band [in the context of the struggle for power, was] the driving force behind mobilization, [the] generator of revolutionary consciousness' (Guevara 1965). Cuban youth, the projected vanguard, in the context of the 1959, as a result of active participation in the struggle emerged as a force for recreating the revolutionary values, fervour and commitment of that time. Active participation in the revolutionary struggle was itself a major vehicle for this development, for the creation of a revolutionary consciousness.

Other vehicles included schooling initiatives such as the EACA and mass mobilizations such as the 1961 Literacy Campaign, which mobilized over tens of thousands of urban youth to remove themselves to some of the most remote regions of the island to teach reading and writing and to impart a new understanding of Cuban history and its future, alternative values of socialist human development.

The idea of the EAC was conceived based on previous successes in using mass mobilization in the countryside to raise consciousness. The leadership in the revolutionary government knew that a revolutionary consciousness 'could not be developed merely by means of propaganda or indoctrination but must arise fundamentally from revolutionary praxis' (Medin, 1990: 6)—from an active participation in militant armed struggle or other such mass action and mobilizations. In the 1950s, the Rebel Army in the Sierra Maestra gained the support of *campesinos* by teaching them literacy skills. The 1961 Literacy Campaign followed *Conciencia*, as Fidel and Che conceived of it, resulted not only in a profound attachment to new socialist ideals and the values embedded in the Revolution but also an ideological commitment to the Revolution on both cognitive and political levels. As noted by the Cuban intellectual José Antonio Portuondo: 'The young literacy teachers discovered their country, and in a year of direct experience, of immediate contact with the oppressed of country and city, they earned their degrees as revolutionaries and were ready to effect a radical transformation in the unjust social order' (1980:17). The New Latin American Left at the time was familiar with this process of transformation as 'conscientization' (Freire, 1970) or 'politicization'. Cubans called it 'conciencia'.

By 1966, the EAC became a major focus of Cuban educational policy (Blum, 2008). As noted by Blum in his review of the EAC experiment its aims were clearly defined. 'It was to produce a new kind of citizen, imbued with the love of…country, ready for [revolutionary change and committed]…to increasing the wealth of the community, realizing the value of labour and prizing it…'. More specifically, as Blum notes, the EAC was aimed at reducing or overcoming the disparity between town and country, to establish close links between school and life, to educate the rising generation for work by actually working and, in line with a common objective, to demand the highest possible standards while respecting the personality of the pupils (Araujo, 1976: 12).

The revolutionary government placed a high value on relating study and work in a humanizing process of productive labour. In a formulation that owes much to Marx (see discussion above), the Cuban conception of education emphasized the holistic development of a new socialist citizen, who Che Guevara termed the *Hombre Nuevo* (New Man and Woman), to be achieved by formal and self-education programs that involved students in a process of productive labour, and workers in lifelong study and reflection. Although the integration of study and work schedules was later abandoned as practical productive labour continues to form an important part of the school curriculum. Thus teachers are expected to plan their lessons ahead of time to accommodate a designated month of agricultural service. Indeed it is deemed to be their revolutionary duty to encourage and recruit as many students as possible for this 'voluntary' service.

Denise Blum (2008), an American anthropologist, has made a close on site study of the actual dynamics of the education system vis-à-vis the inculcation of socialist ideals and revolutionary values of the new society. As a participant-observer, the author relates observations, interviews and surveys from her experience in a Cuban Escuela al Campo ('School to the Countryside', or EAC) camp located on a collective farm outside Havana. The Pioneers, the youth section of the official Cuban Communist Party, organize the EAC program nationwide. The program's rugged, military lifestyle experience is required for city-based junior high school students in Cuba, an essential rite of passage in the politicization and socialist consciousness-raising efforts of the Revolutionary Government. Blum in this connection argues that beneath the revolutionary symbols and activities of the EAC, a new and latent socialist consciousness has evolved for some time, one that reflects neither an absolute nor an erosion of socialist ideals.

As Blum constructs it the construction of a socialist consciousness was a matter of education and the school curriculum itself in many ways prepares students for the EAC. For example, she notes that in mathematics textbooks word problems use the agricultural context for learning arithmetic. In the civic education textbook set in the curriculum 'El amor al trabajo' (the love for work) is a prominent theme; young people are portrayed as heroes in different types of work, including daily life—defending *la patria* (the homeland), in construction, sports, education and culture. One photo shows a teenager aiming an AK–47 and others depict young people actively engaged in productive work. Under the pictures are statements such as '[t]he defense of the socialist patria is the greatest honour and the supreme duty of every citizen'; 'Work in socialist society is a right, a duty and a motive of honour for every citizen'; and 'Voluntary work, the cornerstone of our society' (Blum, 2008: 208).

This use of education as an instrument of consciousness-raising or conscientization was a key tactic in the Revolution's human development strategy. As early as July 1960, the FAR and the Dirección Nacional de las Militias (National Directorate of the Militias) began to train civic instructors who were to 'give revolutionary talks in their respective militias, unions [and] work centres' so as to 'create true revolutionary consciousness in the men and women who form their endless ranks' [*Verde Olivo*, July 1960]. The same approach was taken in preparations for the 1961 literacy campaign. In this campaign, the materials to be used were carefully designed so as to adjust the context to the standpoint and realities lived and understood by the illiterate masses of peasants and the urban poor, many of whom were recent migrants from the countryside. In the preparation of these materials, according to a UNESCO Report on the subject (Medin, p. 8), teachers studied tape-recorded conversation guides to ascertain 'not only the idiom of the illiterate but also his social and economic viewpoint'. As for the actual content of the curriculum it was designed, as theorized and projected by the Brazilian educator Paulo Freire, so as to lead students to understand the realities of their social existence, to conscientize them and empower them to act. In this context, illiterates were taught not only how to read and write—a language, but the language of revolution.

The 'Special Period' (officially from 1990 to 2004) was marked by a new notion of the ideal citizen with a socialist consciousness—the *Hombre Novísimo*, literally an 'Even Newer Socialist Man' (viz Che's 'new man and woman'). During the revolutionary period from 1959 through the 1970s, the ideal Cuban citizen was a person with the humility and stamina of the *campesino* combined with the education, ideology and commitment of a revolutionary. During the Special Period, the Communist Party, shorn of any role in the public process of democratic elections but, as a vanguard organization, assigned primary responsibility for maintaining ideological commitment to the Revolution, began to idealize a new kind of Cuban citizen—the *hombre novísimo* (even newer man), who was 'urban' and 'educated' with a campesino morality and soul, and profoundly Cuban in his or her identity. This 'hombre novisimo' was still a communist in his modesty and loyalty, and a revolutionary in his or her love of humanity, but less aligned with a political party and more inspired by the philosophy of Jose Martí. The *hombre novísimo* had an even stronger sense of national patriotism and unity with Latin American and worldwide struggles against imperial domination.

The problem with this notion of the *hombre novísimo* was how to rescue Cubans from the growing threat of a capitalist 'pseudo-culture' of alienating consumerism and possessive individualism, and to defend the Revolution from the forces of neoliberal globalization. Again the EAC was pressed into service as a mechanism of acculturation, a means of combating the disease of capitalism (the virus of consumerism) and 'resurrecting the authentic soul of Cuba' (Blum, 2008).

To establish the way in which the EAC served to create conditions for the formation of the 'hombre novísimo' Blum studied the self-reported views of parents and the youth involved in the EAC. What she found was a 'dialogic and hybrid quality' present in the way parents and youth think about and rationalize the EAC experience. As she constructs this finding—somewhat problematically, it has to be said—parents and youth see the EAC program as 'both meaningful and important and meaningless and unimportant'. For example, the parents, according to Blum, harbour anger and resentment that the state does not provide the necessary resources for them to participate in the program while spinning 'empty promises' that 'hard work will bring material abundance for all'. The problematic aspect of this formulation is that it is most unlikely that 'the state' in any of its personifications would possibly argue that 'hard work will bring about material abundance for all'. The author presents no evidence in this regard. It would be highly contradictory to fight and counter a capitalist culture of consumerism with a promise of 'abundance for all'.

Blum is more convincing in her account of the way that the EAC in its 'structure' serves to reinforce a socialist culture of substantive equality, that is, an equality not so much of opportunity, which in many contexts is reduced to an abstract right without reality, but more of equality as a widely shared social condition. The problem here is a disjunction between the experience created by the EAC, which is one of sharing, and the conditions in Cuban society created by policy responses to the economic crisis. The structure of the EAC equalizes and inverts relations of inequality and social hierarchy, and it creates many shared experiences. Also, the collective work experience of the EAC tends to blur social distinctions. The provision of community service in the countryside also helps break down barriers between intellectual and manual forms of labour, between the countryside and city, between the *campesino* or peasant farmer and the urban professional, between the working and middle classes.

Most important in terms of rebuilding a socialist ethic and a revolutionary consciousness in conditions of economic crisis the EAC experience, in Blum's findings, foster an atmosphere of 'empathy, love (of humanity), humbleness and service to and with the *campesinos*'. Blum also found that the EAC experience encouraged students to think independently (from parents) and to take on leadership roles, including participation in self-government, became brigade leaders, and barrack inspectors. In many instances, emulation, a socialist type of competition, existed in most camp activities. Emulation involved not only recognition of exemplary workers but recognition that one only become exemplary when one helps others to succeed. The intense emotional and physical engagement and investment in a rural, rugged area is conducive and perhaps fundamental to building or nurturing a socialist and revolutionary consciousness, and passionate civic commitments, under conditions of the Special Period.

As Blum constructs it, the EAC is an intimate social space that produces networks of friendship and solidarity. As students participate in the ritualized act of daily agricultural labour and barracks-cleaning routines, they actually ignore the constant exhortations about their low productivity, apathy, nonparticipation, sexualized behaviour and partying. These are the personalized moments when they 'inject' the authoritative, officialized sphere with elements of the imaginative, unpredictable behaviour, which becomes the new, 'normal' life in Cuban socialism during the Special Period.

Conclusion

The demand for more equitable and sustainable forms of human development is a critical factor in a growing worldwide rebellion against the institutions and agents of global capitalism—the transnational corporations, the IMF, World Bank, WTO, etc. But this movement needs a vision that conceives of these institutions and their policies as part of an exploitative system: capitalism. And it needs a framework for the debate, reconciliation, and realization of alternative pathways and strategies for negating the power of capital over the conditions of human development. That framework is socialism. Towards these ends, it could be argued that Marx's vision and political project remains 'the most thoroughgoing and self-consistent project of social emancipation and hence…worth studying as such' (Chattopadhyay, 1986: 91).

Another project that warrants a closer look and further study in this regard is the way in which the Cuban Revolution exemplifies this vision, advancing and acting on it in the form of a cultural revolution that created the ethical and conceptual foundation of a socialist form of human development.

CHAPTER SIX

HUMAN DEVELOPMENT AS SOCIAL WELFARE

> The quest for sustainable development is above all the search for development itself, understood not just as economic growth but as the transformation of economic and social structures in order to improve the quality of life of the population and achieve the progressive formation of new values.
> —Fidel Castro, 1992[1]

From a UNDP perspective, human welfare is primarily a matter of education, health and income, as reflected in the HDI, a composite of three social welfare variables (a long and healthy life, acquisition of knowledge and a decent standard of living). From a socialist or human rights perspective, however, human welfare is also a matter of housing and security as well as education, health and income. This conception of human welfare, a fundamental feature of socialist systems, was institutionalized in the United Nations Charter of Human Rights signed by the assembly of fifty nations at the United Nations Conference in 1945.[2] The universal declaration promulgated by the UN enshrined 29 universal 'human rights' including the right to life, liberty and security of person, but also freedom of thought, education and work (free choice of employment, just and favourable conditions of work), 'a standard of living adequate for the health and wellbeing of himself and of his family, including food, clothing, housing and medical care and necessary social services'.

Most of the countries that participated in the UN ratified the UN Charter as a matter of principle and government responsibility—to

---

[1] Fidel Castro, Speech at the Land Summit in Brazil, *Granma*, June 28, 1992, p.3.

[2] The preamble of the UN Charter in 1945, which began with 'We the People...', was a first step in a move to establish the concept of a 'family of nations', an equitable world order and a system of multilateral conflict resolution. The charter was conceived as a people's charter, expressing the 'common aims' of humankind. One of its main objectives was to apply multilateral negotiation mechanisms for the promotion of economic and social advancement of all peoples. To this end, topics such as decolonization, disarmament, economic and social progress, world trade, debt and the environment, industry and labour, science and technology, finance and foreign exchange, gender and development, and more recently peace-keeping, were placed on the agenda of diverse organizations within the UN system.

ensure that human rights are respected and that the basic needs of the population are met as a social condition of human development. The US Congress, as it turned out never actually ratified the UN Charter, precisely because it defined jobs, healthcare and housing, as well as basic education, as human rights rather than as commodities, thus holding the government responsible and accountable for ensuring access to them rather than leaving it to the market and the life-chances of each individual.

Even though economic and social policy at the inception of Cuba's revolutionary government was not guided by an explicit socialist ideology the UN Charter of Human Rights was a major reference point in the government's view of revolutionary change and human development—to ensure the welfare of the entire population. The centrality of human welfare provision in the project of the Cuban Revolution is reflected in not only in the complex of policy measures adopted in the early years but also in the Constitution, the first article of which declares that each member of society is guaranteed the right to political freedom, social justice, individual and *collective* wellbeing, as well as—significantly—solidarity.

Development Dimensions of Human Welfare

In September 2000, the Heads of State of 189 United Nation-member countries agreed to measure progress towards eliminating extreme poverty by 2015. They established eight goals—known as MDG for Millennium Development Goals—with 18 targets. Four years later, Cuba submitted a report on its commitment and developments in this regard. Some goals had already been met: universal primary education; gender parity and empowerment; and a further reduction in the child mortality rate.

A study published the year after (December 2005) by the *Medicc Review* in suggested that Cuba was well on track regarding the UN targets and deadline on the remaining goals. Based on statistics and reports by UNDP, WHO, FAO and related regional organizations the study placed Cuba at the top of all Latin American countries in providing the greatest *opportunities for human development*, particularly as regards the elimination of unnecessary and avoidable inequalities considered to be unjust. In the words of this report:

'The combination of free and universal healthcare and education, public participation, and the willingness by the government to implement policies to maximize equity, has had positive effects on health outcomes'. For example, maternal mortality rate had fallen from 57 per 100,000 births to 38.5 over the last decade. Almost all Cubans (95.2%) had access to potable water and plumbing (94.2%). Other indicators were: under-five mortality rate: 7.7 per 1000, which was better than the average of the 'most developed' or 'advanced' countries and the best performance of all 'developing' countries (89–161); 99% of births attended by professional staff; 5.5% of low-birth weight babies. Also Cuba has one of the fastest aging populations (15.4% are over 60 years old) but instead of cutting back on old age benefits, as happened in so many capitalist 'democracies', they were increased. In 2005, the minimum pension was raised by another 50%.

Other comparisons between socialist Cuba and capitalist US and the UK showed remarkable human rights advantages that socialism provides its people in contrast to capitalist societies. Note, for example, the following comparisons in regard to budget expenses, which can be taken as a reflection on a government's priority concerns.[3]

The US and the UK governments have many times and consistently accused Cuba of being a systematic abuser of 'human rights', and continue to do so. Yet the US and the UK spend so much more money on war, defense and policing in settling their security concerns than on human welfare. In Cuba it is the opposite. See, for example, the following comparisons of social conditions for 2004–2005.

In Cuba, there are no gender or race-based exclusions or appreciable disparities in rights, wages and other forms of remuneration for work and economic activity, or access to vital public services. But in the US and the UK gender or race-based social inequalities regarding income and other welfare measures are extensive and profound. For example, Weisbrot and other social scientists in regard to the US note that poverty rates among people of 'color', mostly Blacks and Latinos, in the US have climbed as high as 40% and that up to 90% of all black youth will be on food stamps at some point during their childhood years. The appalling conditions of this income poverty include the fact that one out of every three black adults will be incarcerated at some point over their lifetime (*The Economist*, 2010).

---

[3] The following facts and figures are taken from each government's budgets and relevant ministries, from WHO, UN Millennium Development Goals, CIA Factbook, Cuban Economic Studies Centre, Cuban Armed Forces Review 1997, January 2002 NACLA, Cuba's Granma, and the US magazine *Medicc Review*.

Table 5. Fiscal Expenditures, % of the National Budget

	Cuba	
	1994	2005
Budget expenses	$14.5bn	$25.7bn
Education	9.2%	19.4%
Health	7.4%	12.5%
Social security	10.5%	13.6%
Housing/municipal	2.5%	5.5%
Defence/police	4.7%	7%

Table 6. Conditions of Human Development (2009)

	Cuba	US	UK
Life expectancy	78.5	79.1.	79.3
Infant mortality	5	8	6
Doctors per capita	1-160	1-280	–
Literacy	100%	97%	99%
Unemployment	1.9%	5%	4.7%
Poverty[4]	0	12%	17%

Source: UNDP Human Development Report 2009; *State of the World's Mothers 2010*—Save the Children, May 2010; World Health Organization *Core Health Indicators*; Cuba's Office of National Statistics (ONE).

An explanation of these and other conditions is not hard to find. It is found in the social and economic structure of income inequality generated by three decades of neoliberal policies designed to free capital from government restrictions and to deregulate private economic activity. In this connection, As of 2006, the United States had one of the highest levels of income inequality, as measured through the Gini index, among high income countries, being one of only few developed countries where income inequality has increased since 1980. Between 1980 and 2008, the mean after-tax income for the top 1% tripled, as compared to an increase of 69% for the top quintile overall, 20% for the middle 40% of households, 17% for the second quintile and 6% for the

---

[4] This is according to Ridenour (2007). However, it must be noted that according to some Cuban economists (see the discussion on this in Chapter 7), given the erosion in the coverage of the rationcard and the low purchasing power capacity of the Peso an estimated 20% of Cubans in the 1990s could be regarded as income poor.

bottom quintile. The main causes of this trend have been attributed to the diminishing political clout of labour unions, and less government redistribution as well as decreased expenditure on social services, but without a doubt the main cause can be found in the hold on the levers of public policy by the dominant ruling class, particularly the privileged Wall Street financiers, the big bankers and the directors of the country's major transnational corporations.

In regard to this trend towards greater social inequality it is commonplace among social scientists to point towards the disappearance of the middle class and the increased polarization of society between a small class of multi-billionaires and super-rich, and an upper/upper middle class stratum of very well-off (mostly functionaries and dominant class service providers), and a very large class of impoverished workers and people, mostly black or Latinos, struggling to survive. Even Alan Greenspan, a leading architect of the model of free market capitalism that has dominated government policy over the past three decades has been constrained to admit that the steady growth in income-based social inequalities in recent years is a 'very disturbing trend' (Greenspan, 1998). Significantly this trend by all accounts has dramatically accelerated since then.

In Latin America generally we can detect a similar trend tending to the extreme of poverty at one social pole and highly concentrated wealth at the other (ECLAC, 2010). This trend towards increasing inequality was halted, and to some extent in reverse, during the era of the welfare-development state (from the 1950s to the 1970s) but the pattern of growing social inequalities resurfaced in the 1980s under conditions generated by the neoliberal reforms of the Washington Consensus on the need for market-friendly and –led policy agenda.

But in Cuba, despite the slowdown in the rate of economic growth in the second half of the 1980s, and an economic downturn of crisis proportions in the early 1990s, access to essential government services for human welfare was not appreciably affected. In the conditions of the Special Period some economic and social conditions of human welfare did deteriorate. The crisis provoked a 35% fall in GDP and, according to Mesa-Lago, a severe deterioration in a number of social indicators: university enrollment dropped 58%, maternal mortality jumped 123%, mortality at age 65 and above increased 15%, and the incidence of contagious diseases and child malnourishment rose dramatically (Mesa-Lago, 20005). The only exception was infant mortality, which continued to decline.

However, notwithstanding this deterioration in the social conditions of human welfare, throughout the Special Period not one school and not one clinic closed down—in stark contrast to the experience elsewhere in Latin America. And at issue was not only the public provision of social welfare but the workers in these establishments. As noted by *Trabajadores*, a newspaper published by the Cuban Confederation of Workers (CTC), regarding Raúl Castro's economic reforms, 'Cuba will never resort to the easy and inhumane formulas of neoliberalism, based on massive dismissals'.[5] In effect, despite the seeds of social inequality and poverty sown by the market reforms and policy adjustments of the 1990, the basic fabric of human welfare, and Cuba's fundamental achievements at the level of human development, remained intact. On this see Chapters 10 and 11.

As for poverty, discussed more fully in Chapter 6, the issue is how it is defined and measured. At the level and in terms of income there is no doubt that the crisis and reforms of the 1990s resurrected the spectre of 'poverty'. On this see Espina Prieto and her colleagues, who, under these conditions and in the conjuncture and in the wake of the Special period, classifies up to 20% of the Cuban population as income-poor. However, when poverty is defined as a multidimensional condition or in basic needs terms rather than on the basis of income alone, it is still possible for some to argue that in Cuba there is no 'real' poverty (hence the figure of '0' above). Arguments in this connection are sustained by reference to the fact that education, healthcare and basic welfare are provisioned universally without social exclusions. And illiteracy, another major social condition of poverty, is virtually non-existent in Cuba. At the same time an estimated 33% of Latin Americans still live in poverty no matter how defined (by some definitions the poverty rate is much higher), 42 million people (9%) are illiterate, and at least 1 in 10 is unemployed (and because so many people do not bother to search for non-existing jobs and work for themselves or each other, the real unofficial unemployment rate is much higher.

But in Cuba it could be argued that no one is indigent, goes homeless or in a state of malnutrition or hunger, or threatened by starvation,

---

[5] The context for this comment was the admission by Raúl Castro himself that Cuba might have up to a million excess jobs in the public sector, which employs close to 95% of Cuban workers. But in terms of the commitment to decent remunerated work as a fundamental right the government prefers the policy of what Arch Ritter, a Canadian economist with a specialist interest in Cuba, terms 'ridiculously high' underemployment over outright dismissal and consequent unemployment.

as is the case for many millions in other parts of Latin America—even (by some accounts) in the US and UK. Cuba also has the lowest infant mortality rate of all Latin American and developing countries. All children are vaccinated against 13 diseases free of charge, and Cuba produces 12 of these vaccines. Save the Children (2010) ranks Cuba as first among 77 developing countries in its human welfare index regarding the health of mothers and women in general. Save the Children's 2010 Report notes that while worldwide there are 57 countries with critical health workforce shortages, meaning that they have fewer than 23 doctors, nurses and midwives per 10,000 people, in Cuba (as noted above) there are 160 doctors per capita, even with the export of 'human capital' (thousands of doctors, physicians and surgeons—and teachers—in the service of international solidarity).

These and other human development achievements are not matters of economic growth—contingent on the rate of economic growth. Expenditures and investments on or related to human welfare are matters of constitutional principle and fundamental human rights. The Cuban Constitution, for example, states 'that no child be left without schooling, food and clothing; that no young person be left without opportunity to study; that no one be left without access to studies, culture and sports'. In terms of this fundamental commitment, a matter of choice and principle, within a few years of the 1959 Revolution, 100,000 voluntary education brigadistas taught 707,000 to read and write, eliminating illiteracy in the process. In pre-revolutionary times under Batista, there was 23% illiteracy and 44% of primary school-aged children did not attend school. Only 17% of secondary school-aged children attended school. But by 1961, the revolutionary government had secured for each child a classroom. The 10,000 unemployed teachers under Batista, one-quarter the entire number, were all teaching with a pay raise. Already by 1961 the education budget had been tripled and 10,000 new classrooms had been constructed. Subsequently, in the following years, the government allocated a significant share of its fiscal resources to education, both in infrastructure, human resource development or teaching training, and expanding educational opportunities to all Cubans.

Policy Dynamics of Human Welfare

To the degree that we can write of a Cuban model of socialist human development it is based on the following: (i) the elimination, or drastic reduction, of private property in the means of social production, eliminating thereby the structural source of inevitable class-based social inequalities; (ii) social ownership in the form of the state, providing a fundamental institutional mechanism for advancing the public over private interests and ensuring a commitment to the wellbeing of all citizens; (iii) policy-making focused on converting the principles of equality, social justice and solidarity into social conditions shared by the population as a whole, without social exclusions; (iv) the state as the authoritative leading force in the planning process and the key actor in the design and implementation of social policies; (iv) a unified and centralized system of social policy-making to ensure the universality and egalitarian extension of basic social services, a fundamental socialist condition of human development; (vi) the centrality of distribution as an instrument of social justice; (vii) an emphasis on income equality (leveling the range of distribution) and social consumption to ensure distributive justice; (viii) free and open access to different forms of employment and education to the highest level, to provide opportunities for capability realization for all categories of the population, leveling thereby existing social inequalities and advancing towards a more egalitarian society; (ix) in the current context of growing inequalities the alleviation of income poverty alleviation via the management of development policies; and (x) maintenance of these policies, and the implementation of socialist principles, as the inalienable responsibility of a state that is responsive to the people and accountable to them (Espina Prieto, 2005: 200).

The fulcrum of Cuban social policy within this policy framework has been, and continues to be, satisfaction of the basic need for food, education, health, culture, sports, and social security. In regard to these needs the policy is universal in terms of inclusion and egalitarian in terms of access to the resources and services provided to meet these needs. However, Espina Prieto (2005) argues that paradoxically this egalitarian distribution approach, contrary to its intent actually reproduces social inequalities because 'it provides a very weak response to the specific needs of social groups suffering unfavourable initial conditions [thus], failing to provide equal access to the appropriation of benefits distributed homogeneously...'

Education, Human Development and the Revolution

In development theory education is assigned a crucial role as an agency for social mobility and human development—for expanding the opportunities available to individuals to enable and capacitate them for improving their lot—and giving them the freedom to choose...to expand their opportunities and improve their social condition, allowing them greater scope for realising the human potential, giving form to their capabilities. This is particularly the case for the UNDP in its conception of human development as freedom The HDI gives equal weighting to education as a variable of human development as per capita income (a proxy measure of social welfare) and health.

Cuba's achievements in these areas of human development can be attributed to policy priorities, which reflect the government's conception of the centrality of education as a condition of human development as well as other dimensions of human welfare such as health. The consistent and steady improvement in the conditions of education and health, captured in the HDI, can be directly correlated with investments and expenditures, which do not track economic growth rates as they normally do in capitalist societies but reflect on the government's priorities and commitment to ensuring and improving conditions of human welfare (on this see OECD, 2010).

Egalitarianism in the Form of Income Distribution

Income is an important factor in the HDI, given equal weight with health and education as a measure of social welfare. But the income variable in this index is per capita income, i.e. income aggregated for the population as a whole and expressed as a statistical average, and thus without any consideration of its social distribution. Given the principle of 'equity' in the theory of HD (arguably as important as 'freedom') this is a major defect.

To correct this defect, it is proposed that the income factor be measured in terms of several variables of distributional inequalities such as the share of the poorest quintile of households in national income or the ratio of the top to bottom quintiles of households.[6] Alternatively, one might use the Gini coefficient, the international standard measure of income distribution; or even the UNDP's supplementary Poverty Index, which includes several non-income variables. A strict poverty line measure of income is not a particularly useful methodology in the Cuban context, given the reduced need for income in meeting basic

---

[6] For a critique and alternative formulation of this measurement problematic regarding the HDI see Hicks (1997).

needs; it only provides a measure of the level of material consumption, which is a limited indicator of poverty. An alternative method based on the calculation of a basket of basic goods and services, both marketed and provided by the state, would be more meaningful.

In addition to a household distribution of income and access to basic services, it is important to measure income distribution and social stratification by social groupings and spatial or territorial location in the economy, as well as social factors such as gender, race and ethnicity, and occupational class.[7] In a capitalist system the capital-labour relation in the distribution of national income (the respective shares of wages and investment income) is a critical issue but not in a socialist system. Because of the way that official statistics are collected it is important and probably most feasible for the purpose of income distribution analysis to group and categorise the population by occupation and gender.

---

[7] In the Cuban system of public sector employment, analysis of the stratification of earned and labour income is normally not based on the concept and the analytical categories of 'social class', which are important tools of analysis in the context of capitalist societies. Rather, analysis is on what sociologists in the functionalist tradition and in other contexts term 'occupational class', with reference to social groupings formed by the structure of work. In Cuba this structure is set as a result of government policy regarding pay scales per occupational group. In the 1983 *Reforma General de Salarios* parameters of a pay-qualification scale were set in a range of 13 groups, allowing for a differentiation between maximum and minimum pay within a range of 4.5 to 1. Given the preponderance of wages and salaries in the distribution of total household income at the time—before the Special Period and the construction of a dual economy, that is—this regulated payscale structure also ensured a relatively flat distribution of total earned income, in the order of 4/1 in the ratio of the top to bottom quintiles of households versus ratios of 18/1 and higher in countries such as Brazil, Peru and Paraguay (UNDP, 1996).

However, there are several unexplained and underresearched discrepancies in the structure of income distribution. For example, according to *Instituto de Trabajo* data, 93% of workers at the time fit within a payscale range of only 2.3 to 1 (Nerey and Brismart, 1997: 11). But, according to a study of income distribution that groups the population into ten income categories by level of income the ratio of top to bottom deciles of income earners is closer to 10 to one (Espina Prieto, 2005). In this study, Category I (income in a range of 0–50 pesos; 40 pesos on average) includes 19.3% of income earners; Category II ((income in a range of 51–100 pesos; average 75) includes another 22.7% of the population; while Categories III-IV (101–200 pesos; on average 150), the group in the middle of the income scale, encompasses 25% of income earners; and, at the top of the income distribution Category V ranges from 201–500 pesos (23.5%) to 1201–2000+ (1.6%). In a statistical analysis of income distribution by the *Oficina Nacional de Estadísticas*, based on five strata of income earners, the distance between the top and the bottom strata is drastically reduced to a ratio of 2.3 (an average income of 40 pesos for the lowest 19.3% of income earners, 75 pesos for the next 22.7% of earners, 150 pesos for the middle strata and 250 pesos for the average household in category V (ONE, 2001).

A number of Cuban researchers have conducted research and analysed the social distribution of income in different historical contexts in terms of both statistical groupings (deciles/quintiles of households or income earners) and diverse social and regional groupings of the population. What they have found for the 'special period' and its aftermath is a pattern, with little regional variation, of a relatively flat distribution of labour income (because the limits of variation are set by government policy and regulation) but increasing disparity in the distribution of total income—a process of 'restratification' induced by or resulting from the economic crisis and government policies implemented in response to this crisis (Espina Prieto, 2004).[8]

By all accounts, the major structural factor and policy variable in this development (increasing disparities in the social distribution of income) was the creation of a dual economy, with a restricted and segmented access to dollars (via an occupation in the tourist sector of the economy or migrant remittances) and a significant reduction in the purchasing power of the peso.[9] It is estimated that the purchasing power of the peso was reduced to the point of poverty defined in terms of the level of access to sufficient income to purchase nutritious food and basic necessities (Espina Prieto, 2004: 209). The fundamental problems here are the inadequate purchasing power of the peso and the reduced capacity of the government-issued ration card to access necessities of life. As a consequence, it is estimated that the level of material consumption in the 1990s was reduced to the point of malnutrition and income poverty for a significant but difficult to determine segment of the population—perhaps as high as 30%, depending on the measure of the income needed to access the basic basket of household goods and necessities of life that are not made available by the government.

---

[8] The restratification process identified by several researchers in the 1990s is by the same accounts the result of a process of 'destratification' and the 'desalarization' of broad occupational segments, the introduction of 'worker incentive programs' as well as a self-employed worker sector, and alternative non-work sources of income (migrant remittances, self-employment, etc.), all leading to a process of concentration and polarisation of incomes (Espina, 1999).

[9] A number of studies have been conducted on the impact of the dual economy on the social distribution of income and on the social divide generated by this distribution. By all accounts this social division did not materialise to the point of class formation—allowing individuals to save and invest, and accumulate capital. Nevertheless, the social inequalities derived from economic dualism was enough as to require policy address, although it was only, in May 2008, after years of this dual economy approach to economic development, that the government began to dismantle the structure of a dual economy.

In any case, this calculation of relative poverty only relates to an income or consumption measure related to material conditions such as malnutrition. Because of the universally available ration card and essential services, and government policy regarding housing costs, income poverty is relative. There is no evidence of the destitution and conditions of absolute or extreme poverty that affect a substantial part of the population in every other country in Latin America, but nevertheless Espina Prieto (2004: 209) for one points to indications, if not clear evidence that 'a significant portion of the Cuban population [in the late 1990s, faced] more scarcity and a lack of fulfilment of [their] basic needs'.

Inside the Revolution: Health Matters

It is often said that if you have health that you have everything. Health is a critical dimension of human development and a major priority of any human development regime. A population's state of health is reflected in the indicators of extreme poverty, the conditions of which are normally measured in terms of health, and improved on the basis of public action made with a commitment to improving the human condition.

Nothing is as indicative of the government's commitment to social welfare and human development as the achievements of the Revolution in regard to improving the health of the population. In 1959, the new revolutionary government inherited a healthcare system that was relatively advanced for the developing world. But the facilities were not shared equally. Primary care for the poor and rural population was virtually non-existent (Diaz-Briquets, 1994; Roemer, 1976). Approximately half of Havana's population were members of *mutualistas*—a system of privately financed healthcare used mostly by the rich, who were able to afford it (Diaz-Briquets, 1994). *Mutualistas* had double the government's health budget and controlled most of the resources. In 1959 there was one university and one medical hospital, along with a dominant private and rudimentary public health sector. Two thirds of the 6,300 physicians and four fifths of the medical beds were located in Havana. Cuba imported 40,000 pharmaceutical products, of which 80% came from the US. Fewer than 1,500 of the physicians worked in the public sector (Roemer, 1976), and many of these physicians and surgeons joined their counterparts in the private sector in an exodus of professionals after the Revolution, requiring the government to invest in a massive rebuilding and medical professional training program.[10]

In 1961 MINSAP, the Ministry of Public Health was created and all major private hospitals were nationalised (Mesa-Lago, 1981). A slow integration of all other health facilities into the public domain started in 1962 and the next year healthcare was state administered and almost exclusively financed by the Cuban government. The first polyclinics were also introduced in 1962. They would be the cornerstone for healthcare over the next decade. Each was staffed by a general practice physician, a nurse, a paediatrician and a social worker. They were charged with the provision of healthcare in workplaces, childcare centres, homes and neighbourhoods. They conducted health screening, vaccination, blood drives, neighbourhood vector control activities, and organised community-based participation (Whiteford and Branch, 2008).[11] The pharmaceutical industry was also nationalised and preventative care as well as diagnostic tests and medication for hospitalised patients were made available without cost to patients. People were financially responsible for their own medication, dental care, hearing aids and wheelchairs but these were made available at subsidised prices and free for those on low-income (Spiegel and Yassi, 2004; Mesa-Lago, 1981). Before the end of the first decade, an extensive medical system was in full swing, providing facilities for research and medical training, and extending healthcare to the entire population.[12]

---

[10] By the mid-1960s, 3,000 physicians had emigrated, mostly to take up residence in Miami and elsewhere in the US. Before the revolution there were 920 citizens for one doctor; beween 1962 and 1964 this ratio worsened to 1,200–1,500 (Mesa-Lago, 1981). Thus, the immediate health impact of the Revolution was negative. But by 1978 Cuba had the lowest ratio in all of Latin America with 675 people per doctor (Mesa-Lago, 1981).

[11] Mass campaigns against polio, malaria and tetanus were launched in 1962 with the agency of the CDRs, which worked in community health outreach and were used to ensure the thorough implementation of the campaign in the target areas. They were also used to monitor pregnant women and give advice on pre-natal care, breastfeeding and registration at birth (Hirschfeld, 2007; Diaz-Briquets, 1994). Before the revolution, a relatively high number of births already took place in hospitals (63%). This increased to 73% in 1965 and 91% in 1970, having important implications on maternal and infant mortality (Mehrotra, 2000).

[12] In the interest of equity, and to correct the urban-rural imbalance, the government prioritised the extension of the medical system into the countryside. By 1963, 122 rural health centres and 42 rural hospitals were established (Hirschfeld, 2007) and,

The successful development of this system has been well documented and studied.[13] It is evidenced, inter alia, by the data presented in Figure 1 on infant mortality rates, an indicator of Human Development used by the UNDP. These figures indicate that at first the infant mortality rates actually increased but from 1970 on, infant mortality rates began to significantly decrease, reaching rates similar to those in OECD countries. For example, the most recent statistics available indicates for Cuba an infant mortality rate identical to Canada at 5.0 per 1,000 births and better than the US rate (7.0), and significantly below the regional average (20.7).

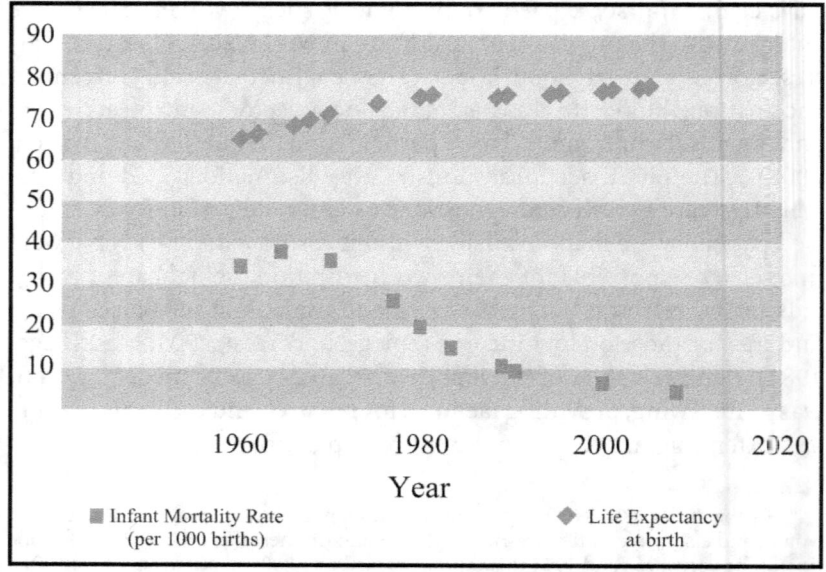

Figure 1. Health in Cuba
Source: Monk, 2010: Tables 4.1 and 4.2

---

to make access to physicans more equitable newly trained physicians were obliged to serve one year in rural areas. This was later extended to two years.

[13] In the early 1970s, the polyclinic model was evaluated. It was found to be 'cumbersome, inequitable, and inefficient' (Whiteford and Branch, 2008, 22). In 1974 the polyclinic's functions were expanded to include care for the elderly and treatment of chronic disease. The health care system was modified to the Community Medicine model in the mid 1970s. This introduced research and teaching activities to the polyclinic, as well as assessments, risk evaluations and extended hours of continuous care. In the 1980s, the system evolved further to the Family Doctor Program. This placed a doctor and nurse in every Cuban community. By the 1990s, the goal of having the pair serve between 120 and 160 families was finally reached.

As for life expectancy, another HDI variable, statistics show a trend of steady improvement as of 1959. The most recent data give Cubans a life expectancy of 77.5 years (81 for women), well above any other developing countries and comparable to conditions found in the most advanced countries in the world now classified by the UNDP as having achieved 'very high human development'—Denmark (78.2), and comparable to the US (79.1), New Zealand (80.1) and Canada (80.6) (UNDP, 2009).

While the economic crisis of the 1990s did not influence life expectancy and infant mortality rates, at least as reflected in the official statistics provided by WHO and the UNDP, it did impact health. There was a deterioration of less commonly used health indicators. For example, average daily caloric consumption dropped by 33% between 1989 and 1993, reaching a low point of 1,800 calories a day.[14] Between 1991 and 1993 there was an outbreak of optic neuropathy, which was associated with reduced nutrient intake. However, swift recognition of the problem resulted in treatment and the distribution of vitamin supplements, and none of the 50,000 affected people died as a result (Perez-Lopez and Diaz-Briquets, 2005). Special measures were also taken to protect children, women and the elderly. Even so, the number of underweight newborns increased, a clear indicator of the impact of the economic downturn on health.

In addition, the Special Period meant a decreased ability to import, which also affected the health of some Cubans indirectly. Water quality deteriorated as a result of the difficulty in procuring products related to the supply of clean water. The shortage of fuel and spare parts also led to a deterioration of garbage collection, impacting general sanitary conditions. Over the counter and prescription medication, particularly for non life-threatening ailments, were in short supply, further affecting the quality of health (Eckstein, 1994). On the other hand, there were some unintended beneficial health outcomes based on the increased use of bicycles as a means of transportation (Perez-Lopez and Diaz-Briquets, 2005). In any case, the reversal of some trends in health indicators was short-lived, and within two years, even before the economy recovered, health indicators had reverted to former levels. The HDRs from 1998 to date provide evidence of this.

---

[14] The low cost rations provided 1,200 calories a day during this period (Diaz-Briquets and Perez-Lopez, 2000).

These notable improvements and achievements in the area of health are the clear outcome of public action taken in this direction over the years, action that flows from a principle enshrined in the Constitution as a human right and government responsibility. The commitment to this principle as a fundamental universal right is reflected in the connection that has been found between public investments on health infrastructural development and fiscal expenditures on healthcare (Monk, 2010). Figure 2, in this regard, indicates a clear and long-term consistent trend towards improvement both in the state of health of Cubans in general and public investments and fiscal expenditures as a share of government revenues. This trend departs from the norm in other Latin American countries and indeed, according to the CECD (2010), capitalist societies generally. In these societies, the CECD concludes, total health expenditures as a share of total fiscal expenditures varies with the rhythm of economic growth: when the economy expands and per capita income increases health expenditures go up; when the economy contracts these expenditures are reduced (OECD, 2010).[15]

Figure 2 evidences a pattern of long-term steady growth in fiscal expenditures on health from 1959 to 2000 and a pattern of accelerated growth since. On a closer look (see Monk, 2010) fiscal expenditures on health nearly doubled between 1959 and 1960. By 1965 the amount was almost triple that of 1960. A substantive increase in resources devoted to health continued until 1990. In 1990–1991 there was a slight decrease in health expenditure but in 1992 and 1993 it increased again. In 1994 there was another slight decrease in health expenditures but then from 1995 on fiscal expenditures on health returned to the trend of annual increases. The health budget mushroomed from 1.2 billion pesos in 1995 to 4.9 billion in 2008 (Ministerio de Salud Pública, 2009).

Health expenditures also increased as a percentage of total expenditures and on a per capita basis (Monk, 2010). From 1975 to 1985 health expenditures fluctuated between 2 and 3% of total expenditures.

---

[15] The pattern identified by the OECD also applies to pre-Revolution Cuba. It seems that between independence and the revolution the mortality trend was highly sensitive to changes in the economy (Diaz-Briquets, 1994). When economic conditions improved, so did mortality rates; similarly, during the 1930s, when there was an economic downturn, mortality rates worsened. Living conditions were directly affected by changes in the value of sugar exports. Although Cuba was an agricultural exporter, it imported much of its food. As a result, when foreign exchange was scarce less food was imported.

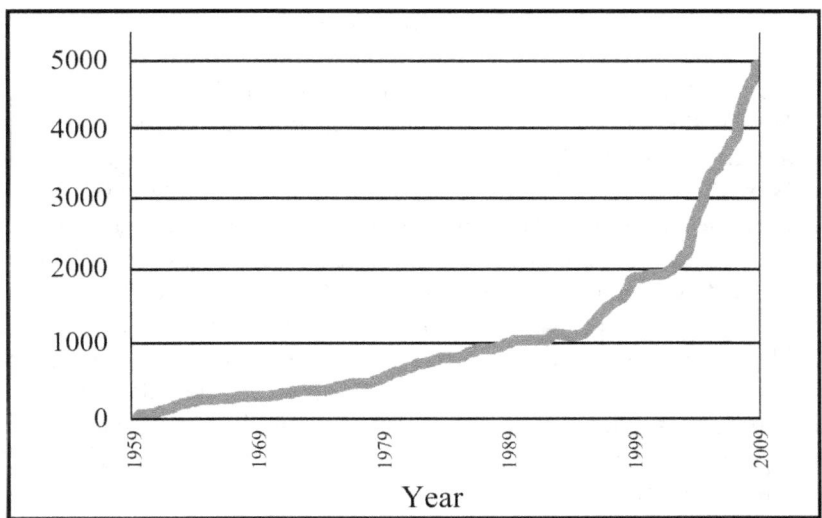

Figure 2. Cuban Government Health Spending
Source: Monk (2005): Table 4.3[16]

In 1986 they increased to just under 4%, and in 1987 and 1988 they were just under 5%. This decreased to 4.2% in 1989. The relative size of health expenditures increased substantially in 1990 to 6.5% of total government expenditures. The share of total expenditure allocated directly to health continued to increase in the 1990s in the midst of an economic downturn of crisis proportions. From 2003 to 2008, in the midst of an economic upturn based on a primary commodities boom, from 10 to 15% of the budget was spent on health (Comité Estatal de Estadísticas, various years); and in 2009 14.2% was, compared to 13.7% in the US, 11.6 and 13.1 in Uruguay and Argentina, 8.0 and 14.5 in Ecuador and Brazil, but as much as 25.6% in Mexico (UNDP. 2009).[17]

---

[16] The *Anuario Estadistico de Salud 2009* presents data on total and per capita health expenditures from 1959 to 2009. There is no indication of whether the currency is held constant for a certain year to account for inflation. However as the figures differ slightly from those reported in the *Anuario Estadistico de Cuba*, it may be assumed that some calculation has been done to make the data comparable.

[17] The figures provided by the UNDP on health ansd education and expenditures suggest that public expenditures on social programs is not necessarily a good indicator of the government's commitment to human welfare and development: fhere are clearly many other factors involved in determining the government's allocation of fiscal revenues, and the figures do not correlate regime type (dogmatic neoliberal, pragmatic neoliberal, populist, etc.).

Conclusion

The most surprising feature of developments in Cuba from 1959 to 1989 was the level of human development in terms of social welfare achieved with relatively low levels of per capita GDP and sluggish rates of economic growth. Throughout the 1960s and 1970s the revolutionary regime struggled to maintain some equilibrium between economic growth and social development. It managed to sustain a steady advance in regard to social development, its policies reflected in a steady improvement in the social conditions of Cubans, but, as evidenced in Table 4, the regime did not manage to find a steady hand on the helm of economic growth. While economic growth fluctuated wildly, the key indicators of human development, particularly in regard to health and education but also employment and housing, point towards a significant improvement in social welfare, not just for certain groups but for the population generally. Normally—rather, in development theory—indicators of economic and social development are closely correlated, the second generally tracking the first. But in Cuba not so. And there can be no doubt as to the agency of this development. Rather than prioritizing economic growth, and assuming that economic growth will inevitably or naturally bring with it an improvement in social conditions (from the workings of the market), the revolutionary regime prioritized social development and used the agency of the state to bring it about. This conclusion has important implications for human development theory, viz. the centrality of public action and the role of the state.

Not that another conclusion could not be drawn from our findings. The superior performance of the Cuban state to the economy might well be interpreted by economists and policymakers working within the orthodox paradigm of economic development that there is an inevitable trade-off between growth and distribution, and that in consideration of the higher rates of economic growth achieved by regimes that prioritized a 'growth first' policy could be justified both theoretically and programmatically.[18] The response to this that we would give

---

[18] This indeed was the Washington Consensus in the 1980s, subsequently modified in the recognition that 'we had gone too far' in the direction of free market capitalism and that the 'state should be brought back in' to promote 'growth with equity' (pro-growth that is pro-poor). However, this did not mean a return to the welfare-development state of the 1950s–1970s; rather it meant investing in health and education as sources of human capital (improving the social infrastructure of economic

on the basis of our findings is that it depends on how development is conceived—as a political project consciously directed towards a desired end? Or as undirected, the result of the normal functioning of the system?—and the priorities of the government: whether these be oriented towards economic growth, the fruits of which are very unevenly distributed; or whether they are designed to advanced the level of human development under conditions 'equal for all'.

Another conclusion that we draw from our findings is that in the context of the economic model that was used to guide economic and social policy all across the developing world, the strategy pursued by the Cuban government could well be described as Beatrice Díaz (1992) did, as designed to produce 'growth with equity'. Of course, Cuba was not the only government at the time to pursue a *growth with equity* strategy. The government of Kerala certainly did (within the framework of a communist party regime) as did governments in nation-states such as Sri Lanka and Costa Rica, in these cases as part of a capitalist economic regime. What this strategy meant was an orientation of the government's fiscal resources and expenditures towards an investment in people and on social infrastructure (human capital formation) as well as productive transformation and economic growth. And it also meant that economic growth must be included in the mix of human development policies; that efforts should be made to ensure an equitable or fair distribution of this growth; and that the government is the agency of these efforts. As for economic growth it is evident that governments have a role to play but our study does not address the broader questions at the centre of the economic development debate about the preferred relationship between the public and private sector, and how to balance the role of the market and the state in this regard.

---

growth) and assuring greater social inclusion in government expenditures and programs in the interest of expanding opportunities for the poor to improve their own situation.

CHAPTER SEVEN

SOCIALIST HUMANISM AND THE EQUALITY PREDICAMENT

> ...free and independent as men were before, they were now...brought into subjection...particularly to one another; and each became in some degree a slave even in becoming the master of other men: if rich, they stood in need of the services of others; if poor, of their assistance; and even a middle condition did not enable them to do without one another. Man must now, therefore, have been perpetually employed in getting others to interest themselves in his lot, and...in promoting his own. Thus he must have been sly and artful in his behaviour to some, and imperious and cruel to others, being under a kind of necessity to ill-use all the persons of whom he stood in need, when he could not frighten them into compliance, and did not judge it his interest to be useful to them. Insatiable ambition, the thirst of raising their respective fortunes... inspired all men to a vile propensity to injure one another, and with a secret jealousy, which is the more dangerous, as it puts on the mask of benevolence, to carry its point with greatest security. In a word, there arose rivalry and competition on the one hand, and conflicting interests on the other together with a secret desire on both of profiting at the expense of others. All these evils were the first effects of property, and the inseparable attendants of growing inequality.
>
> —Jean Jacques Rousseau, *Discourse on Inequality*, II.

In June 2010, ECLAC launched a new roadmap for change and development in the region in which it announced that it is 'time for equality'—for 'closing gaps', 'opening trails', and, most importantly, finally confronting head-on a problem that has always been sidestepped both politically, in development practice and government policy, and systemically (except, as it turns out, by Cuba). The 'problem' presented in ECLAC's Report is that of 'structured inequality', defining a sad reality that, as Rousseau notes in the opening quote, is one of the 'evil effects of property' to which Rousseau refers, is entrenched in colonial policy and imperial power, and reproduced by centuries of capitalist development and several decades of neoliberal policies. With these policies, the authors of the study point out, inequalities have 'multi[plied] in every sphere of society' and structural heterogeneity '...has increased over the past three decades in most of the region's countries'.

The Report's 'discussion' of this problem 'is informed by a bitter experience of inequality'.[1] 'The evidence of the final two decades of the last century in the region', they continue, 'shows it actually going backwards where equality was concerned'—defining the parameters of a problem that can no longer be avoided, eluded by giving deference to the dominant socioeconomic and political interests at play in the capitalist development process.

As for the source of the problem the Report is clear enough. It is located and can be found in the institutionalized practices and 'structures' brought about by the most powerful of these interests, that have been advanced by policies of 'neoliberal globalization' instituted under the Washington Consensus. This theme is echoed in a parallel Report on the state of human development in Latin America published by the UNDP in 2010. In the words of this Report there exists a 'direct correspondence between the advance of globalization, neoliberalism, and the advance of poverty, social inequality, social inequity'. And, the Report continues, '[t]he most explosive contradictions…are given because the advance of [neoliberal] globalization marches hand in hand with the advance of poverty and social polarization. It is undeniable that the 1980s and 1990s [were] the creation of an abysmal gap between wealth and poverty' (PNUD, 2010: xv). This gap, it could be added, constitutes the most formidable obstacle to achieving human development.

---

[1] In the synopsis of their 'understanding' of inequality and how to 'combat' it, the authors of the ECLAC study note the following: 'The acute inequality that has long marked Latin America and the Caribbean has its roots in the colonial era, when broad swathes of the population were denied rights because of their race or social class and subjected to slavery, serfdom and expropriation of resources. Under later republican regimes, privileges continued to be reproduced in other ways, and asymmetries in rights and living conditions were maintained. Lastly, the pattern of development and modernization served to perpetuate socio-economic divides based on race, ethnic origin, gender and social class. The productive structure and the education system helped to ingrain and reproduce inequality and, to a great extent, continue to do so today.

Successive bouts of social struggle have succeeded in extending rights to traditionally excluded sectors. Yet Latin America and the Caribbean remains the most unequal region in the world in terms of income distribution. The reforms of the 1980s and the impact of the debt crisis actually widened income gaps, and it was only in the past decade that this trend was reversed, thanks to more inclusive labour market dynamics and the State's assumption of a more active role in income transfer. The consequences of these levels of inequality on wellbeing have been amply documented, and they continue to prevent the fruits of growth from being transferred to the poorest sectors. Between 1990 and 2002, income distribution remained very rigid in the region'.

Undeniable it might be, but it was not until 2010 that the UNDP made the connection between structured social inequalities and poverty, a connection long made in the scholarly literature critical of capitalist development in its neoliberal form. UNDP Regional Director Heraldo Muñoz, in this same connection notes that 'Inequality is inherently an impediment to progress in the area of human development, and efforts to reduce inequality must be explicitly mainstreamed in the public agenda'. For the UNDP, he adds, 'equality is instrumental in ensuring meaningful liberties; that is to say, in terms of helping all people to share in meaningful life options so that they can make autonomous choices'.

ECLAC, in its 2009 publication of the *Social Panorama of Latin America*, and in a 2010 study on Latin American development, similarly concludes that it is 'time for equality: closing gaps, opening trails', and that the agency for doing so is the state, with 'international cooperation' and 'social participation'.

Equality in Theory and Practice

Human development as deconstructed in this study is founded on three core ideas—freedom, equality and solidarity. However, these ideas implicate diverse and very different understandings, and some debate, as to how to put them into practice—convert an ideal state into reality, giving these ideas institutional form as principles of 'social and economic transformation [and] the progressive development of new values' (to quote Fidel Castro).

In Chapter 2 it was argued (and we expand on this point in Chapter 8) that freedom, an essential condition of human development, i.e. a condition in which all members of society are able to realize their capabilities and fulfil their full human potential, requires a system that allows all members of society, not just a select or privileged few, to actively participate in the making of decisions and taking action on these ideas in regard to conditions that affect (either inhibit or facilitate) their capacity for collective self-determination. In some contexts this means freedom from oppression, *emancipation* from those structures or institutionalized practices that inhibit this capacity, and that unduly restrict their freedom to act. In other contexts it means *equality of opportunity*—the freedom of each individual to act on their opportunities in the realization of their capabilities. Either way (in one context or the other) freedom implies *social equality*, i.e. conditions equal for all, conditions that cut across the 'intersections of social inequalities'—'multiple sources of disadvantage, such as class, gender, caste, race, ethnicity'—militate against human development (Sen, Iyer and Mukherjee (2009).[2]

This much is understood and generally agreed to—at least by social liberals and socialists who share the view of social change as liberating and progressive.

However, while the social liberalism of the economists at the UNDP and responsible for the HDR might well be aligned ideologically, if not theoretically, with socialism at the level of freedom (re the need for emancipation), no such alignment or agreement is possible when it comes to equality. The reason is twofold. First, while liberalism in all of its variants (economic, social, political, neo) is fundamentally individualist, focused on and concerned with the individual as the locus of action, socialists view people not so much as individuals as *social* beings, part of a larger collectivity that gives meaning to their lives and to both development and society. Secondly, socialism is fundamentally concerned with creating a form of society in which conditions are equal for all, i.e. defined by equality as a shared social condition. Liberalism, on the other hand, is concerned with equality not as a

---

[2] The authors point towards an increasing awareness among scholars and practitioners in the field of health and human development about the importance of understanding and to measure the effects of these intersecting inequalities on health and thus human development. Thus this 'intersectionality' is 'a topic for which there is growing interest and evidence'. Even so, 'several questions as yet remain unanswered' and 'gaps [that] partly reflect limitations in the quantitative methods used'. Of course, this 'inequality predicament' entirely eludes the UNDP in its Human Development Reports, even in its most recent Regional Human Development Report, which, like several recent other ECLAC reports (ECLAC, 2010, for example), focuses on the inequality problematic of human development: social inequality and inequity as structural obstacles to achieving human development. In this 2010 Regional Human Development Report clear reference, and some very minimal (non-structural) analysis is made of the structured ('intersecting') inequalities that mark all capitalist societies, and particularly societies in Latin America (excepting Cuba). A brief review of this report suggests that the problem of social inequalities vis-avis human development is not so much methodological (although this is a problem, as the authors of the Report acknowledge) as theoretical (and ideological). Sen, Iyer and Mukherjee (2009) at least include 'class' in its list of intersecting inequalities. But the UNDP continues to avoid any reference to or discussion of class, except in the case of this Report, a section on the importance of an undefined 'middle class' for human development (increases awareness of the opportunities that exist for self-advancement). In its lising of social inequalities ('gender, ethnicity, race'), 'class' is conspicuously absent.

social condition but as a matter of opportunity—equal opportunity for each individual to realise her or his human potential.

The practical or political difference between these two conceptions of equality—equal opportunity or as a widely shared substantive social condition—is that the former implies an institutional structure that is not biased or does not discriminate against any particular individual because of the groups he or she might belong to, or because of their social characteristics; and that in this regard allows for institutional reform—change in the individual's position within the institutional structure. This form of change (institutional reform) can be accommodated to the existing system, which today is generally based on the capitalist mode of production. However, to create conditions 'equal for all' (a substantive social equality) requires more radical change—not institutional or liberal reform but systemic transformation.

The capitalist system is so structured that no institutional reform can resolve what might be termed the 'inequality problematic'—a fundamental inequality in the social relations of production and power, and the conditions that ensue from these relations. Capitalism is based on private property in the means of production and the exploitation—and betimes the oppression—of one class by another. On this basis human development cannot be achieved by simply reforming the system. These reforms, as proposed, for example, by the UNDP in its model of 'sustainable human development', could very well create a more humane form of capitalism—a more *human* (socially exclusive, equitable and participatory) form of development. But a strategy and policy of institutional reform cannot resolve the conflict between the human and the social, creating conditions equal for all. Human development so conceived is incompatible with a class-divided and—dominated system based on exploitation and oppression, conditions that arguably are endemic to capitalism. And these conditions, it could also be argued (and we do), were fundamental to understanding the genesis of the Cuban Revolution and the form that it has taken—socialist human development.

Other reasons to opt for social equality—egalitarian social relations of production and power, and equality as a substantive social condition—include the finding by sociologists that structured inequality undermines society and its institutions, generates and perpetuates poverty, and weakens social cohesion and a communalist or socialist culture of solidarity. We expand on this point in Chapter 8.

Cuba before 1959

In 1959 the socioeconomic situation in Cuba was the not atypical outcome of a class divided society, a capitalist system and what has been described as a neo-colonial model of economic development (Santos, 1960). This model, like all forms of capitalist development, was predicated on private property in the means of production, the concentration of property (in land and economic enterprise) in a small ruling class of big landowners and a class of local and foreign capitalists, and ties of subjugation and dependence on an imperial power.

The persistence of extreme poverty was a central concern not just for Cuba but for other former or neo-colonies, particularly in sub-Saharan Africa. As for Latin America the magnitude and depth of the problem and its resistance to change, generated pressures for revolutionary change as well as reform. In the 1960s, the US opened up another front in the war against global poverty—in addition to international cooperation with the development efforts of the economically backward countries of the 'third world'. The aim was to pacify the fires of revolutionary ferment—to avoid the emergence of another Cuba.

The need for a response to a generalized situation of widespread and extreme poverty led CEPAL, in 1978, to undertake a study on the entire problematic. Titled 'Inter-institutional Project of Critical Poverty in Latin America' it provided a theoretical framework for a series of case studies, including one on Cuba, leading to similar studies on the same theme by other UN organizations and the World Bank, all focused on the problematic of reducing the incidence of extreme poverty and alleviating the pain of poverty.

A study by Rodriguéz and Carrazo (1987), conducted within the framework constructed by CEPAL, provided an evaluation of the process of social development initiated by the Cuban Revolution to eradicate poverty. The problem was conceived of as the inevitable product of a social structure and an economy based on a neo-colonial model, and, not to put too fine a point on it, US imperialism. In these terms the eradication of poverty was deemed to be the most immediate problem for redress by the revolutionary government, and it was evident that this would require structural change, an undoing of the colonial model and an overhaul of the entire system sustaining it, a stance that was based not on socialist ideology but on direct experience and an understanding of the history of Cuba to date.

The Neo-Colonial Model

In the years leading up to the Revolution, American investment in Cuba comprised more than 11% of the total U.S. investment in Latin America and the Caribbean (Ewan, 1981: 13). By 1959, US corporations controlled 40% of sugar production and 75% of arable land. They also owned more than 90% of electric and telephone utilities, 50% of the railways, 90% of mining assets, 100% of the oil refineries and 90% of cattle ranches. US interests dominated the transportation, manufacturing and tourism sectors. As for the US banks they held over one quarter of all bank deposits.

Prior to 1959, American investments were widespread, penetrating diverse sectors of the economy. The bulk of these investments were in agriculture, especially in sugar production. In the development of sugar industry and exports US capital was invested directly and heavily, dominating sugar production on the island. Just 13 US-owned sugar latifundias by 1958 owned 1,173,015 hectares of land, representing 47.2% of the land dedicated to sugar production. These investments were immensely profitable, resulting in an estimated fivefold return on capital invested.

A characteristic of the neocolonial model is monocultural production for export. Another is the dependence on exports to one market— the United States. This dependence was enforced by various so-called 'treaties of commercial reciprocity' (1902, 1934) as well as regulations on sugar quotas and an Agreement signed in the context of GATT in 1957. Under these agreements, 72% of exports and 71% of imports were concentrated in the US. This situation of 'external dependence' was aggravated by a seriously growing trade deficit with the US, which grew $347.2 million from 1949 to 1958.

Monocultural dependence was deeply rooted in the structure of neo-colonial relations with the US. From 1903 to 1925 the economy grew at an annually averaged rate of 6.2%. The centrality of sugar in this growth was reflected in that statistics in the sphere of sugar/sugar products in total production, which rose from 29% in 1905 to 42% in 1925. At the same time the share of sugar in exports grew from 59% to 84%. Its growth at the time was sufficient to absorb the labour released in the process of capitalist development, although a lot of this labour was held in reserve for seasonal peaks in the production cycle. In addition the government imported labour from Spain and the Caribbean to help maintain in reserve an army of surplus labour for the industry. With the saturation of the US sugar market in 1925, the Cuban economy entered a stage of stagnation and then crisis at the onset of the 1929–1933 depressions in the world capitalist system. The vulnerability of the Cuban economy, based on excessive dependence on one crop/the US market was evident in the level of national income generated by the economy. From 1925 to 1933 it fell 59%, creating some of the objective conditions of revolutionary transformation. However, it would take another two decades to create the subjective (ideological and political) conditions.

In the post-World War II period, the production and social crisis of Cuba and other 'economically-backward' areas of the capitalist world could no longer be ignored, leading, in the first instance, to pressures for revolutionary change, and in the second, to international cooperation for development to stave of these pressures. Another impetus behind the 'international development project' was the success of the USSR in its policy of rapid industrialization and socialist development, which in the post war context provided for the countries working to escape their colonial ties a socialist option for pursuing their national development and a reference point in the struggle for national liberation—for the emancipation from the oppressive weight of imperial power.

It was at this point that Harry Truman (1948) launched his Point-4 Program of financial assistance. Of course, for Cuba there was no assistance forthcoming and precious little productive investment by the corporations that dominated production. Annual growth from 1950 to 1958 at an average rate of 3.5% was fuelled not by productive investment in the dominant sugar industry but relatively unproductive investments in other areas of the economy, relying heavily on inflating the economy—expanding the money supply without a corresponding increase in the real economy. Most investments were concentrated in infrastructure, public works and services that sustained the existing structure of production without changing it or increasing labour productivity. As for agriculture as in most places under the prevailing economic development model it was generally neglected or used as a reservoir of surplus labour or resources that could be exploited (extracted at below production cost rates) for the benefit of 'urban development' (i.e. keeping the subsistence costs and price of urban labour as low as possible).

Poverty as the Legacy of Capitalism and Neo-Colonialism

In the 1950s the structure of production in Cuba generated a relatively low level of economic growth, and the fruits of this growth were very unevenly distributed, leading to a situation of extreme poverty for at least a third of the population, and twice that rate in the large pockets of rural society populated by landless or proletarianized rural workers. The World Bank, in this regard, in a 1951 study observed: 'there is a very wide gap between the income of a relatively few high-income receivers at the top and the mass of low-income receivers'. Moreover, as documented and analyzed by Saney (2003), racial discrimination was rampant, with whites inhabiting a different Cuba than blacks. This societal fissure was delineated most starkly in the urban/rural divide, with the wealthy urbanites reveling in a lifestyle and patterns of consumption that sought to replicate the 'American dream'.

The reality was very different in the rural areas. A quarter or so of Cuba's population were landless peasants, dependent on unstable seasonal employment and living a precarious existence. The land was concentrated in the hands of a few large landowners, many of them American corporations. Before the Revolution, Cuba reflected the urban/rural divide patterns prevalent throughout the Third World. In the countryside, as documented by Saney, over 80% of the dwellings—*bohios* as they were termed—were thatched-roofed and mud-floored. Only 10% had any plumbing or electricity (Glazer 1989: 77). In addition, more than one-third of the rural population suffered from infestations of intestinal parasites and other diseases. Malnourishment was the reality. Meat was a dietary rarity, with only 4% of Cuban 'peasants' consuming it as a regular part of their diet; only 1%, according to Saney (2003: 11), had access to fish, fewer than 2% eggs, 3% bread, 11% milk, and almost none ate green vegetables.

This dietary pattern reflected the prevailing poverty. The average pre-1959 peasant income was less than a third of the national average. Moreover, the illiteracy rate was 45%, with 44% having no formal education. Fifty-four percent of rural homes had no toilets and 84% depended on rivers or unmonitored springs and wells for water (Scheer and Zeitlin, 1964: 21). However, as Saney observes, the rural standard of living was not an anomaly within Cuban society. It represented the extreme deprivation experienced by the majority of citizens. The national unemployment rate was 25%. While most urban dwellings had access to electricity, fewer than half had sanitary facilities and more than 50% of these facilities were inadequate. In 1959, most of the 1.4 million Cuban dwellings were in substandard condition (Glazer, 1989: 77) and the illiteracy rate stood at 26% of the population—over 80% in the rural areas.

Social inequality and poverty were matters of uneven capitalist development, i.e. the dispossession of the direct producers from their means of production under conditions of semi-poletarianization, low income and poverty. As for land tenure, the structure of which determined the major conditions of poverty endemic in the rural areas, the large latifundistas, more than half of which were foreign, disposed of 45% of the arable land. Twenty-five thousand of the biggest producers, some 1.25% of all landowners, accounted for 75% of the arable land. Some 8% of farms concentrated 71% of the land while 91.9% accounted for only 29%. In this situation only 21.7% of the arable land was actually in productive use, while only 4% had irrigation and only 12% fertilizers, reflecting the relatively low level of productive investment and capitalist development of the forces of production, In these conditions 64% of direct agricultural producers or farmers did not own the land they worked, and many were obliged to pay rent at 2–9 pesos per hectare. As for income, 66.6% of farms received only 27.3% of farm income while 7.9% of farms concentrated 47.4%.

Under these conditions not only did a significant part of the rural population not have the purchasing power capacity, but by and large they were excluded from access to essential government services which were concentrated in the urban areas and primarily directed towards the middle class. The lack of income, and exclusion from social services, left a large part of the rural population destitute, unable to meet their basic needs, and providing the revolutionaries encamped and active in the countryside with the objective conditions of a revolutionary struggle. The 'subjective' conditions, it turned out, would be created by the revolutionary process itself as well as events in this process such as the coup of March 10th, 1952, and subsequent actions by the Batista class dictatorship that made the need for radical change (particularly regarding the neo-colonial model) evident and activated the forces of social revolution.

As for the 'objective' conditions of this revolution—the situation that many Cubans found themselves in—they are manifest in some of the available statistics. In 1953, 8.4% of the 'economically active population' (EAP) was officially listed as 'unemployed' and thus without income. By 1957 the unemployment rate grew 50%—to 12.5% (although a study by ONE identified up to 16.4% as unemployed and another 17% as 'employed in part' or 'without pay'). In addition, ONE noted that at last 25% of the labour force was un- or under-employed— 600,000 seasonally and 300,000 permanently. And, of course, this did not take into account the very low level of labour force participation by women. As for the women in the labour force, the vast majority were employed in the low-wage service sector, predominantly in the area of domestic service, with an exceedingly low level of labour remuneration. Only 5.8% of women, somewhat less than one half of whom were living an economically active existence in rural society, were employed for wages (as opposed to 'economically active') in agriculture; close to 20% were employed in the industrial sector but again in low-pay ghettoes.

One other possible factor in the determination of the subjective conditions of social revolution was the comparatively high level of proletarianization in rural society (high relative to other countries in the region). Whereas in other countries in the region most of the rural population was tied directly or indirectly to the land and active in agriculture, a comparatively high percentage of the rural population in Cuba worked in industry rather than agriculture, i.e. worked in the sugar mills and the processing of sugar for wages. According to the *Censo de Población y Viviendo de 1953*, there were around 200,000 'peasants' in pre-revolutionary Cuba as opposed to 600,000 agricultural workers, and 100,000 sugarcane workers. And an estimated three-quarters of all peasants were poor and semi-proletarianized. In fact, Zeitlin (1970) saw this as a critical factor in the success of the Cuban revolutionaries in mobilizing support for the revolution.

Thus a large part of the economically active population was dependent on the sale of their labour-power and access to government services in meeting their basic needs. But it was estimated that at the time—in the 1950s, that is (from 1942 to 1958)—the peso had lost over 60% of its value. Added to the fact that many households had only one solid income earner in this situation a large number of Cubans were all too close and in many cases mired in poverty, unable to meet their basic material needs.

The class system that produced and reproduced this poverty was based on a very unequal and inequitable distribution of wealth and income. Data presented and analysed by Brundenius (1981) show that 50% of the population with the lowest average income disposed of

10.8% of the national income. At the same time the richest 5% disposed of 27% of the national income. Calculated differently, the ratio of the top to bottom deciles of income recipients in 1953 was 38.8/0.6 while the comparable ratio by quintiles was 57.9/2.1 (Brundenius, 1981: 47). It is evident and confirmed by later studies that this disparity in the distribution of income was a critical factor in the production of widespread poverty.

The incidence and depth of poverty, an undoubtedly important source of support for the Revolution, is reflected in the pattern of material consumption in the years immediately prior to the Revolution (1957–1958). It is estimated that 69% of the household expenditures of peasants and 43% of households in Havana, the city with the highest concentration of urban population and government services as well as income, was on food; 1.7 and 27.4% on housing; 15.5 and 8.4% on clothing and shoes; and 13.7 and 21.1% on other consumer goods and services. There is no systematic breakdown or social distribution by income class of these expenditures and patterns of consumption, but it is evident that average income allowed for little latitude for consumption beyond immediate material needs. By a standard measure common today, in which any household that requires more than 70% of household income to meet their basic material needs is deemed to be relatively poor, poverty was widespread and endemic in prerevolutionary Cuba. And at least a third of the population, likely two-thirds in the rural areas, were not only income-poor but destitute if not homeless.

Education, Health and Housing as Conditions of Poverty

As for non-income dimensions of poverty the critical factor is access to essential government services in this area—education, healthcare, sanitation and welfare and social security (and in some limited contexts housing: in most, it is a marketed commodity rather than a public service, often using up to a half of household income). Regarding education, the exceedingly high level of social exclusion at the time is evident in the rate of illiteracy, estimated at around 12% in the urban areas and 43% in the rural areas, which, by population, accounted for well over one half of the population (p. 22). What is both disturbing and most revealing vis-à-vis the later priority emphasis placed by the Revolution on the campaign to eradicate illiteracy—a major hallmark and achievement of the Revolution—is the pattern of an increase in the illiteracy rate: 22.1% in 1943, 23.6% in 1953 and a staggering 44% in 1957 (p. 22).

No doubt this exceedingly low score on such an important indicator of human development reflects neo-colonial policy rather than the capitalist nature of the state. In any case, as a result of this policy, neglect or social exclusion in 1958, at the eve of the Revolution, over a million Cubans were illiterate; another 1.5 million were semi-literate; in the population 15 years and older the average years of schooling was only three years; 600,000 children were without any schooling at all; and 10,000 teachers were without jobs (p. 23). Added to this dismal situation were the exceedingly low level of teacher training and the lack of graduates of technical and higher education programs able to respond to the requirements of economic and social development.

The state of health services in the country was such as to place beyond the reach of the poor and most of the working classes basic health services. Even the lowest stratum of the middle class had relatively poor access to health services and was unable to pay for private care and having to suffer the relatively poor state of public health services (except for Havana).

As for the government's budget, only 5.3% was allocated to the health sector, as compared to 7.4% in 1994, just three years into the Special Period and 12.5% today. As for the 'human resources' (trained and educated personnel) available for social development in the area of health there were only 6,250 doctors for a population of some six million. Most doctors (an estimated 65%) were living and working in Havana, leaving most of the population seriously under-serviced or without any access to essential services in the area of health. There was a substantial and serviceable private sector of health services but these services were out of reach for all not in the elite or the solid middle-class sector. In the pharmaceutical sector, the market was almost entirely controlled by foreign firms, with negative consequences for public health services.

Notwithstanding the absence of reliable data the state of health of the Cuban population is reflected in the following statistics: life expectancy: 62.3 (1950 approximately); infant mortality: 40/1000 live births (1958); maternal mortality: 118.2/10,000 (1960) and the incidence of tuberculosis: 15.9/100,000. And, of course, these statistics relate to a statistical averages rather than conditions experienced by actually existing social groups.

As for housing and related services and conditions, according to the *Censo de Población y Vivienda* of 1953 46.6% of all housing at the beginning of the decade was in a state of 'ruin' (74.2% in the rural areas) and only 4.1% had any sanitary installations; only 10.4% of households had access to running water in their housing and only 10% access to electric power. 36% of housing was rented and average rent was equivalent to 20% of the average wage. The housing deficit was estimated to be in the order of 700,000 units.

Policy Dynamics of Poverty Alleviation: January 1959–September 1960

In the context of the legacy of the neo-colonial model, especially the conditions of *inequality*—the uneven distribution of the social product, society's wealth and national income, and at one extreme of this distribution, widespread poverty, understood as a deprivation of 'the material and spiritual needs of…the 'human collectivity" (93: No. 41: 39); and *unfreedom*—a condition of 'dependency' and oppression resulting from foreign ownership, imperialist exploitation of the country's resources and labour, and control of the strategic sectors of the economy—dependence on conditions controlled from the outside and in-country representatives of imperial power and foreign capital.

In terms of these conditions the Revolution aimed and was intended above all to redress the poverty and inequality predicament of capitalist development—to correct the most aberrant social inequalities; and to bring about the emancipation of Cubans from the ties of colonial subjugation. That is, the Revolution was conceived as a project of 'social and economic transformation' required to meet the 'material and spiritual needs of …the human collectivity'. In these terms the Revolution could well be viewed as a human development project requiring a 'radical transformation' of society, not reform of this or that institution—to humanise capitalism—but an overhaul of the entire system.

The project of a social revolution was outlined by Fidel Castro as early as 1953 in his famous 'history will absolve me' speech. In the Speech he outlined a 6-point program of revolutionary change: (1) the land question (redressing the inequitable land tenure system); (2) industrialization (viz. an escape from relations of dependency/revert the colonial model of the economy); (3) housing—to correct this deficit in meeting the population's material needs; (4) unemployment— (5) education and (6) health. The changes need to solve these problems and bring about these improvements in social and economic conditions—in creating a more humane and human society—would require, Fidel emphasized, the conquest of 'public freedoms' and democracy—participation of people in decisions and public decision-making that affect them.

As for the radical changes needed to bring about these improvements in social conditions it was the most 'progressive' classes—the peasants and the workers (in this context resorting to prior theory about revolutionary change)—who would guarantee the profound radical changes needed in the social and economic structure of production.

The initial revolutionary measures were aimed at the redistribution of wealth. In this connection Castro declared: 'The problems concerning land, the problem of industrialization, the problem of housing, the problem of unemployment, the problem of education and the problem of the health of the people; these are the six problems we would take immediate steps to resolve' (quoted in Huberman and Sweezy 1960: 38). Pharmaceutical prices were reduced by 15–20% and electricity rates by 30%. Minimum wages in the agriculture, industry and commerce sectors were raised. Taxes were lowered for the middle and working classes, while increased for the rich (Pérez Jr. 1999: 479).

The new revolutionary government recognized that one of the most pressing needs of Cuban society was resolving the housing problem. This was embodied in the Moncada Program, authored by Fidel Castro, which outlined the primary objectives of the Revolution (Canton Navarro, 2000: 215). Thus, the critical first steps taken were to deal with the housing crisis. These measures included a decree that prevented evictions and, under conditions in which for many workers housing rent consumed more than half of a worker's wages, reduced rents by 30 to 50% (Glazer, 1989: 77; Canton Navarro, 2000: 216). Also in concordance with the Urban Reform Law, a program of government-constructed housing was begun. These houses were leased with lifetime occupancy rights, with rent set at a maximum of 10% of family income (Glazer, 1989: 78). By 1972, 75% of Cuban homes were owner occupied. At the end of the 1990s, more than one million Cuban families had become homeowners (Canton, Navarro, 2000: 215).

These measures were an integral component of other key policy initiatives that encompassed radical agrarian reform, urban reform, the nationalizion of the banks and industries, and an overhaul of the education system (Glazer, 1989: 77). In the immediate aftermath of January 1, 1959, the following measures in the direction of removing the major structural obstacles to integral or human development, were taken:

(1) the Agrarian Reform Law of May 1959; (2) the wealth that was illicitly gained though 'dirty business' and use of the state apparatus was confiscated and (3) measures were taken to ensure an immediate redistribution of income in favour of the working class, redress of the unemployment and improvement in the physical quality of life.

The most far-reaching of these revolutionary measures were embodied in the Agrarian Reform Law. In May 1959, the First Agrarian Reform Law was passed. This was followed by the Agrarian Reform Law of 1963 (Pérez Jr. 1999: 479). Before this Agrarian Reform, 0.6% of Cuba's landowners controlled 35.2% of the land. Half of the land, encompassing 46% of the best-quality and arable land, was held by just 1.5% of landowners. This situation reflected the social reality that the vast majority of small peasant farmers—an estimated 150,000 families—were sharecroppers, tenant farmers and squatters, with an additional 500,000 agricultural workers, representing another 200,000 rural families, confined to seasonal and casual underemployment. They alternated between sugar and coffee plantation work and unemployment (Huberman and Sweezy, 1960: 110–133). The First Agrarian Reform multiplied peasant proprietorship to the extent that over two-thirds of small peasant farmers owed their land to the Revolution (Kay, 1988: 1240).

Under the first agrarian reform, land holdings were limited to a thousand acres. The large sugar companies and the twelve thousand largest private owners were expropriated. As a result, 110,000 sharecroppers and farm tenants gained title to the land. The minimum allotment for a family of five was set at 67 acres, with the right to purchase an additional hundred. In Camaguey province, 2.3 million acres were distributed in less than three weeks.

A second agrarian reform limited land holdings to 167 acres and expropriated ten thousand large farms. The large plantations and ranches were nationalized and turned into state farms. But the small peasant farmers—an estimated 45,000—were guaranteed that their properties would not be expropriated. Officials at the time and subsequently—with the transition from the nationalization of agriculture to collectivisation—stressed and constantly reiterated that the formation of state farms (and later production cooperatives or CPAS) was a purely voluntary process; that the peasant farmers would not be coerced into joining them, and that the principle of 'volunteerism' would be upheld and respected (Kay, 1989: 1254). Nevertheless, they were encouraged to sell their land voluntarily to state farms. But it is important to note that in Cuba there was no forced collectivization. But even so most of the land and agricultural production that had not been nationalized after 1975 was subsequently, albeit belatedly, collectivized. By the 1990s, only 15% of the land was held by private farmers (Canton Navarro, 2000: 258).

The Agrarian Law of 1959 also signalled the beginnings of what would turn out to be a long-term strategy reflected in a policy to nationalize production in the key sectors of the economy. But although the US companies and owners representing the most flagrant agencies of imperialist exploitation were taken over by the state early on and throughout the first year of the Revolution it was not until the following year that the government proceeded with a policy of renationalizing all of the key firms in the strategic sectors of the economy. This policy was implemented in the context of, and in response to, the virulent opposition to the Revolution by the US government and the machinations of the Cuban bourgeoisie.

Policy Measures for Equality 1960–1985

Economic inequalities may be defined as the differences in the distribution of income, in access to material and spiritual wellbeing and in consumer spending. As such, they are an expression of the different degree of resource availability and provision of means to meet the needs typical of different social groups. Within this trilogy (income, access to wellbeing, consumer spending), individual and family monetary income—operationally construed as the amount of money that an individual or family obtains from various sources (salaries, pensions, profits, informal sources, and illegal activities, etc.) during specific periods—constitutes the primary (not the only) indicator to measure inequalities, poverty and social disadvantage.

In the case of Cuba, during the first three decades of the Revolution the structural reforms and socioeconomic changes resulted in a significant reduction in income distribution disparities, because the most marked extremities (excluding exploitative elites, the unemployed, and those in extreme poverty) within the 'stratification pyramid' were eliminated. In 1953, the richest 10% of the population appropriated 38% of total income whereas the poorest 20% of the population received only 2.1%. In 1978, two decades on, this relation had changed significantly: the poorest 20% received 11% of total income while the share of the richest 20% was reduced to 27% (Martínez et al., 1997).

The trend towards greater equality in Cuba was clearly discernible though the 1970s. However, questions were raised as to whether the 1976–1986 turn towards material incentives and the introduction of new wage scales in 1980 affected this trend. Zimbalist and Brundenius (1989) addressed this question in a 1989 study. A comparison of income distribution estimates for 1986 with earlier estimates for 1962 and 1978 indicated that the trend towards an egalitarian income distribution had continued. Moreover, in January 22, 1987 another decree upgraded all wage earners in wage categories below 100 pesos a month to at least 100 pesos, a measure that improved the incomes of 186,000 people and further closed the income gap.

By 1985 at the cusp of an economic growth spurt,[3] when the rest of Latin America was mired in a devastating debt crisis, Cuba had achieved a level of social equality in income distribution that was unmatched. In Latin America generally, the poorest quintile of income earners at the time received barely 2% (2.3 it was estimated by ECLAC) of total income while in Cuba this share was estimated at 11.2%, five times greater (Zimbalist and Brundenius, 1989: 45). At the other extreme of income distribution, which in Cuba was comparatively flat, the richest 10% of households received 20% of total income in Cuba but 47.3% in Latin America as a whole. And it is important to remember that this comparison of inequality based on the distribution of money seriously underestimated the difference in purchasing power capacity because in Cuba healthcare and education was provided free to the entire population without exclusions and basic goods, as well as housing and rental costs were heavily subsidized by the state. Pay scales were set by the government in a centralised wage and salary system, rather than the labour market, and income to some degree lost its relative importance as a marker of social inequality.

The difference in social welfare was directly reflected in various indicators of 'human development': life expectancy at birth, the infant morality rate, literacy—and a comparison of the rate of urban

---

[3] From 1980 to 1985 the annual rate of per capita income growth in Cuba was 6.8% versus -1.8% in Latin America as a whole (Zimbalist and Brundenius, 1989: 46). However, in 1986 the engine of economic growth sputtered to a halt, with a growth rate of only 0.1% (and a decline of 4.4% in 1987). Even so, taking into account this economic downturn from 1960 to 1987 Cuba outperformed the rest of Latin America at the level of both economic growth and equality.

unemployment, another welfare measure. According to ECLAC (1986), in Cuba in the mid-1980s life expectancy already averaged 74 years, the highest in Latin America. In Mexico and Brazil, for example, life expectancy was only 59 and 63 respectively. As for infant mortality rates, a critical measure of the health factor in human development, the rate in Cuba was 13 (deaths by 1 year of age per 1000 births) versus 71 in Brazil, 82 in Mexico, 36 in Argentina, 24 in Chile, and 107 in Haiti (Zimbalist and Brundenius, 1989: 46). As for education, the rate of illiteracy in Cuba was estimated at 3.9% vs. 26% in Brazil, 17.4% in Mexico and Peru. Even in Argentina, Costa Rica and Uruguay, the countries in the region with the highest level of per capita incomes—and, apart from Cuba, with the lowest level of income disparities in the region—from 6 to 9% of the population were illiterate.

Consolidating the Transition

The transition from capitalism to socialism, a process begun in the 1960s and more or less completed by 1975, entailed an expansion of the public sector in the economy and resulted in a major change in both the source and the distribution of household and individuals incomes. The share of state employees in national income, relative to the working population as a whole, jumped from 8.8% in 1953 to 86% in 1970 and 94% in 1988 (Comité Estatal de Estadísticas, 1981; Oficina Nacional de Estadísticas, 1998).

The socialization of production and nationalization of employment was accompanied by the design and implementation of a uniform and centralized wage and salary system. The state displaced the labour market, in this regard, and assumed responsibility for designing a pay scale for different categories of work, establishing the upper and lower limits of earned income. The aim was to secure a more egalitarian distribution of income and ensure equal pay for equal work a (see Nerey and Brismart, 1999).

There were two main dimensions of this policy-induced improvement: earned income on work in the public sector employment had come to represent the major source of family and individual income, and the 1983 General Salary/Wage Reform allowed only one differentiation between maximum and minimum incomes in a range from 4.5 to 1 (Nerey and Brismart, 1999). As a result, the share of the poorest quintile of income earners had improved their share of total income from 2.1 to 11% (Martínez et al., 1997). This significant progress at the level of social equality is also reflected in the Gini coefficient. Brundenius (1984) calculates that by 1986, the Gini coefficient was 0.24, signifying one of the most equitable distributions of income in the world. In 1959, the Gini coefficient for Cuba was 0.57, in line with the high levels or depths of social inequality found in other parts of Latin America.

Another indicator of social equality, or egalitarianism, is the share of the lowest income earners (the bottom quintile, which in many contexts captures the rate of poverty) in total income. Arguably this is a much better measure of human development than the UNDP's measure of per capita income, which actually does not measure distribution at all; it is quite possible for an increase in per capita income to be accompanied with an increase in social inequality. In terms of this critical measure of human development—the share of the bottom quintile of income earners in total national income—Cuba had made considerable progress by 1975, when the Revolution had become fully institutionalized.

At the same time, it could be argued (Espina Prieto, 2005), that income had become less significant as an indicator of inequality. This is because of policies pursued by the government in improving access to healthcare, education, social security, food, sports, culture and other assets and services designed to meet the basic needs of all Cubans. In effect, with the expansion of these 'services' to most of the population, many of whom had been hitherto excluded, the relationship between material consumption or wellbeing and individual and family monetary income was reduced. It took a lot less income to provide for the population's material and spiritual needs. In either case, all indications are that the revolutionary government had made considerable progress in the direction of human development on the basis and in terms of its commitment to a policy of egalitarianism.

Until October 1960, the measures taken by the Revolution were not directed against capitalism per se. They entailed radical reform of the existing system rather than socialism. Nevertheless the aim was the creation of a new and better form of society in which there is no place for the opulence of the few at the expense of the misery of the others— where individuals, by virtue of their private property, can enrich themselves by exploiting labour, converting work from a means of self-realization into private profit, to benefit the owners rather than the workers.

Despite their apparent radicalism, the agrarian reform and the first nationalization measures continued to allow for a private sector and a market, and even presupposed capitalism as the fundamental systemic framework (88: 132). Not that the revolutionary leadership favoured capitalism over socialism as the best or most viable path towards national development—an issue that was widely contested at the time. In fact it was thought that the sugar agrarian-industrial bourgeoisie could play a positive role in the process of national development. However, the attitude and actions taken by this bourgeoisie, all with that associated with foreign capital, cut off this option and led to a radicalization of the revolutionary process. But the engine driving this process (and the ideology behind it) was not socialism (socialization of the means of production) but nationalisation and nationalism. In any case, both nationalization and socialization measures taken over this period (January 1959-September 1960) were taken when and where circumstances dictated and allowed.

From October 1960 to December 1962, nationalization was extended to commerce, but from that point on the expropriation of private property was used to advance the revolutionary process in a more explicitly socialist direction—expropriation without compensation and directed towards socializing rather than nationalizing the production apparatus. The entire process was completed by 1968 in the context of a major 'revolutionary offensive' that resulted in the elimination of all forms of private enterprise—small business as well as capitalism.

By 1970, the heyday of liberal reform in the context of the development paradigm, virtually all of the production apparatus was in the state sector. In this period the revolutionary process of socialist development was institutionalized if not yet consolidated. Aspects of this 'institutionalization' included the centralization of state and the institution of the Council of Ministers In 1976 a new Constitution established 'Popular Power' (OPP) as the 'supreme organ of state power', with the authority to pass annual and five-year plans (until these were disbanded with the crisis of the early 1990s), approve the national budget and make laws. It also officially exercised control over all governmental bodies and appointed members to the Council of State and the National Assembly of People's Power. At the base of this 'popular power' were 169 municipal assemblies that functioned as democratic local government bodies. Citizens in the respective districts chose their local Municipal Assembly delegates by secret ballot in multi-candidate elections in which the CCP was prohibited by law from participating. These locally elected officials had to 'render accounts' of their activities to people in their districts several times a year and hear citizen complaints, and were subject to recall if deemed irresponsible by their constituents.[4]

From a liberal perspective human development means putting people at the centre of development: about people realizing their potential, increasing their choices and enjoying the freedom to lead lives they value. From a social liberalist perspective this means expanding an individual's freedom of choice and capacitating them to take advantage of their opportunities. From a socialist perspective human development is a matter of overcoming the conflict between social life as it ought to be, an ideal state of freedom and equality.

Human Development and Work

To bring about an egalitarian social structure, and to generate the conditions of social equality, it was not enough for the revolutionary government to institute measures that would lead to increased opportunity, improving access to existing institutions and resources. It required a change in the social structure itself, not merely shifting the chairs on the deck, adjusting the position that individuals occupy in this structure, but to rebuild the deck.

Prior to January 1959 the social structure of Cuban society was a variation of a theme found across Latin America and indeed in all capitalist societies. Society in this system, based on the capitalist mode of production, is divided into two basic social classes: the capitalist class, and the working class, or proletariat, composed of all those, who, dispossessed from their means of production, are compelled to exchange their labour power against capital for a living wage. However, in any capitalist society there are different groups and categories of people who are not positioned within this structure (the capital-labour relation). Typically, and certainly in the case of pre-1959

---

[4] At the municipal level the OPP operated democratically in practice as well as theory. Elections, for one, resulted in considerable municipal delegate turnover. Between 1976 and 1984, for example, about half the delegates voted into office changed hands each election, and over a tenth of elected delegates were recalled for failing at their job. Second, electoral turnout tended to be exceptionally high. Third, municipal meetings during these years were filled, in some instances, with intense discussions of constituent concerns, which contributed to policy reforms.

Cuba, one can find a class of small proprietors—the petitbourgeoisie in Marxist lingo, as well as a class of small-scale producers or farmers ('peasants') that strictly speaking are not part of the capitalist system. In addition, depending on the degree of capitalist industrialization or modernization, there can be found what sociologists have termed a managerial-professional class, the upper stratum of 'the new middle class' that accompanies a process of capitalist industrialization and modernization.

Without a doubt Cuban society in the 1950s had assumed such a class form. However, without access to relevant data on different forms of property relations it is difficult to retrospectively reconstruct Cuban society on the basis, and with the tools, of this (Marxist) form of class analysis. It is easier to visualise and reconstruct the social structure of pre-revolution Cuban society in terms of the three alternative forms of analysis, methods and theory, widely used by sociologists and economists in their analysis of the 'social structure'. One is to group people by occupation, on the premise that 'work' is the most stable and fundamental institution of modern society, determining as it does an individual's socioeconomic status and 'life-chances'. The assumption made by those who use this form of *occupational class analysis* is that there is a close correspondence between one's 'occupational status' and the 'coefficient of wellbeing' accorded the individual in the distribution of income and other 'rewards' in return for talent and expended effort. Another approach is to group people according to their relationship not to production but to the market, which determines an individual's 'life chances', i.e. their level of material consumption of goods produced for the market. Basic categories of this type of *social class analysis*, which some sociologists associate with occupational group analysis, are upper, upper-middle, middle, lower-middle, and lower. This form of sociological analysis, which originates with Max Weber, can also be accommodated to the method used generally by economists to analyze the social structure of society: *income class*. The difference is that *income class analysis* is based on a statistical, rather than a social, grouping of the population.

Given the policy and efforts of the revolutionary government to bring about greater social equality by abolishing private property in the means of production, and thus breaking down the class structure underlying the distribution of wealth and income, it is useful to analyse the progress made in the direction of social equality in terms of a combined occupation-and-income class analysis. Given that a Marxist class analysis is inappropriate and indeed rather useless for an analysis of the social structure under post-revolution conditions we will employ this combined occupation-and income method in our analysis of the development dynamics of government policy.

In these terms it is evident that strong strides were taken, and considerable progress was made, by the Revolution. This progress will be traced out in the following section in terms of improvements in the distribution of income and in improved access of the hitherto excluded groups of the population to vital government services related to the provision of education, housing, healthcare and welfare. We reviewed the human development implications of these improvements in Chapters 6. In the following two sections of this chapter, the equality dimension of this development will be emphasized, with primary reference to improved income distribution.

Human Development at Work: Egalitarianism as a Socialist Work Ethic

The elimination of most private ownership in 1968, together with wage increases for the poorest paid workers and a guaranteed employment policy, served to equalize earnings. Indeed, these initiatives led Cuba to come to have the most egalitarian distribution of wealth in Latin America. And through rationing the government sought (beginning in 1962) to equalize consumption at prices affordable to all.

The egalitarian emphasis came with a promotion of Ché's vision of the 'new man (and woman)'. Workers were exhorted to labour for society rather than for personal gain. In place of material reward for overtime work and exceptional productivity, workers individually and collectively were to labour hard out of a sense of moral commitment. Rewards for 'socialist emulation' and 'fraternal competition' consisted of diplomas, pennants, flags, and titles. Sections, departments, and factories, as well as individuals, competed for these nonmaterial 'rewards'.

In a similar egalitarian and collectivistic spirit, the government expanded free social services. All education, medical care, social security, daycare, and much housing were provided free of charge, with access to them more equitable and need-based than ever before. Money lost much of its historical meaning in the process, as Marx argued it should in a utopian communist society.

Meanwhile, the government attacked social distinctions and privilege. Drawing on idealistic societal visions advanced by Marx, as well as by Cuba's independence hero José Martí, Castro urged the breakdown of barriers between manual and nonmanual labor. City dwellers, including professionals, were exhorted to volunteer for seasonal agriculture activity and other tasks. By 1970, 40 to 57% of the labour force worked part-time in agriculture, mainly in sugar-related activity.

The egalitarian, anti-elitist emphasis involved a campaign against bureaucracy as well. Bureaucratic problems—the proliferation of administrative personnel, bureaucratic inertia, and red tape, and the creation of a privileged stratum removed from the masses—were portrayed as 'unsavoury holdovers from the past' that were exacerbated by inexperience and by copying 'countries of the socialist camp that were weighed down with bureaucratism'.

Newly created state organizations facilitated the revolutionary offensive in 1968 as a 'push for communism'. Membership in the prestigious Vanguard Peasant Movement and in the Vanguard Worker Movement, for example, was restricted to private farmers and workers, respectively, who conformed with state-set norms. To become a Vanguard Worker, as 18% of the labour force had in 1969, workers were expected to over-fulfill their average daily production schedule, meet all standards of quality, contribute to a reduction of production costs, do voluntary work, belong to the militia, maintain 'correct behaviour', and have a positive attitude toward skill improvement and political involvement.

The 1980 wage reform was not the only policy associated with the 'retreat to socialism' that turned on labour. Already in 1971 an anti-loafing law had been promulgated that made work for men an obligation and no longer merely a 'socialist right'. The 1971 law also deprived workers guilty of absenteeism of vacations and social benefits (including the work canteen), and, in extreme cases, ordered their transfer to work camps.

And another law called for the repeal of a 1968 pension and retirement benefits decree. Meanwhile, survey data suggest that workers in the mid-1970s saw the main function of unions as improving production and educating members, not as defending workers' rights.

Between the mid-1970s and the mid-1980s several market-related reforms also were introduced. For one, a new management and planning system (the SDPE, the System of Economic Management and Planning) was initiated—modeled, in many respects, on 1965 Soviet reforms. Premised on self-financing, profit incentives, decentralization, and efficiency, it involved an incorporation of market features into the state sector. Profit incentives included a 'stimulation fund', which could be used for social and cultural purposes, small investments, and productivity-linked employee bonuses. Under the SDPE enterprises could also use up to 30% of their profits for purchases from the private sector, and managers could hire and fire workers (within limits) and employ workers on a piecework basis. Profit incentives were to serve as a corrective to the 'command economy' enterprise tendency to hoard labour and other resources. With the right to retain a portion of profits, managers in principle had an incentive to minimize their wage and supply bills.

Gender Matters: Equality at Issue

According to Marta Nuñez, a Cuban sociologist working at the Centre for Studies of International Migrations (CEMI) at the University of Havana, a critical feature of the Cuban Revolution from the very beginning was the concerted and successful efforts taken to advance the status and the increased participation of women, particularly as regards to educational opportunities and employment (Nuñez, 2007). The resulting transformative developments, such as the feminization of the labour force, were not unlike that in other countries at the time and since but with a number of distinct permutations. For example, from the beginning, the Revolution focused on women and children, and several sections of the Cuban Constitution refer explicitly to gender equality. Indeed, the infringement of the right to equal treatment is considered a criminal offence. The *Federación de Mujeres Cubanas* (FMC) was founded in 1960, spearheading the concerted drive to bring about a very different society in terms of social equality and egalitarian relations between men and women. In the context of the 'Revolution' Cuba, Nuñez emphasised, has uninterruptedly developed programs to eliminate all types of discrimination but the 'struggle against gender discrimination has been one of the most successful ones, much more than those aimed at eliminating racial taboos' (2007: 5).

The FMC grew from 400,000 members in 1962 to 3.2 million in 1990, and has influenced decision-making at all levels of society (Mehrotra, 2000b). Indeed, Nuñez notes, by means of the FMC in particular, '[w]omen have been the engines of [many of the] transformations [wrought in Cuban society]'. Among other things, the FMC promoted equal employment opportunities, maternity leave, and daycare centres, and has fought indefatigably—and, by and large, successfully—to advance the status of women in Cuban society.

As for the broader issues of great concern to women in particular (or more so than men) the Mother-Child Health Program is an example of how the government targeted its social programs on women and children. The prioritization of children can be seen, inter alia, in the building of daycare centres in and around all major workplaces, the training of primary school teachers and the implementation of vaccination campaigns. The government over the years has been particularly attentive to the needs of women, children, youth, and the elderly, with well over a hundred programmes targeted at these groups.

As Nuñez reconstructs it, programs to advance the status of women have functioned at two distinct but closely linked levels, that of public policies elaborated 'from above' and responses 'from below' (from women's organizations) to these policies, which, according to Nuñez, were seriously modified as a consequence. The FCM, for example, is granted special status under the Cuban Constitution and, as with all mass organizations,[5] peruses proposed, and initiates new, legislative and policy changes (Constitution of the Republic of Cuba, 1993).

These transformations, engineered from above and from below, were constituted as the result of distinct new policies, legal statutes and regulations, various economic measures, and new cultural patterns. The 1976 Constitution codified the government's public concern with women's rights—women's equal rights in marriage, employment, earnings, and education. Sex discrimination was made punishable by a withholding of ration rights and imprisonment.

The new institutional and policy framework instituted by the Revolution included a new Family Code, maternity leave within the Labour Code, free education from primary to postgraduate education, children's circles (*circulos infantiles*), dining rooms in the primary schools for the children of working mothers, scholarships for those who needed them, and guaranteed work placements upon graduation from vocational, technical, professional and university programs. Families are provided government subsidized or free public healthcare services, including access to abortion and family planning. Women are also guaranteed equal pay under the Constitution, and the Women's

---

[5] The major 'mass organizations' were the Committees for the Defense of the Revolution (CDR), the National Small Peasants Association (ANAP), the Cuban Women's Federation (FMC), and the Cuban Labour Confederation (CTC).

Commission on Employment operates to thwart discrimination in hiring and at the workplace. The Family Code included the specification that men were to share housework when women were gainfully employed.

These and other gender equality policy measures and actions instituted over the years were extended and reinforced in the wake of the UN's New Millennium Goals. The gender dimension of these transformative changes, in terms of the relation between women and men, and the improvement of conditions for women relative to men, are reflected in the following statistics. At the level of employment, the proportion of women in the labour force increased from 13% in 1959 to 39% in 1989. In the mid-1990s, the proportion of women in the labour force plateaued and then declined slightly, eventually recovering. In the latter half of the 1990s, it began to increase again. At present, more than 40% of the workforce is made up of women, constituting an estimated 60% of the upper echelons of technicians and 67% of professionals. Women constitute 61% of Prosecutors, 49% of Judges, 47% of Magistrates and 30% of State Administrators and Ministry Officials (Nuñez, 2007). Since 1978 women constitute over 50% of all professionals and technicians in the country and the female labour force is more educated than the male labour force. By 2002, 48% of all economically active women had completed grade 12 and 10% were university educated, versus 37% and 11% of men. Women today constitute 60% of all university students and 47% of professors; 52% of scientists are women as are 70% of medical students and 52% of medical doctors and 50% of lawyers.

At the level of the labour market and employment, gender-equalizing policies and the resulting feminization had a contradictory impact on gender relations and identity throughout Cuban society—and not just among women—with a resulting dramatic decrease in discrimination. Again, Nuñez emphasizes, Cuban women were the driving force of these changes and the advances made, and a traditional macho culture remained the main obstacle.

At the level of education, Cuba also has one of the highest rates of school enrolment of young girls in the world. Given that education is the major avenue of social mobility, empowerment and opportunities for self-advancement, these statistics are significant at the level of human development.

These and other statistics reflect the clear progress made by and for women in the Cuban Revolution as a result of public action—taken from above and below, and combined. But these advances and improvements do not by any means signify that full gender equality has been achieved. For one thing, besides the persistence of sexist attitudes and male chauvinism women are still under-represented in the higher echelons of power, particularly in the political sphere. Even so, Cuba performs well compared to other countries (Randall 1981). In terms of political representation of women, Cuba ranks first in the Americas (Lopez Vigil 1999: 157). As for the participation of women in the National Assembly—Cuba's parliament—Cuba places tenth in the world (Seager, 2000: 90, 96-97). Also, in recent years there has been a concerted effort to increase women's representation in the political, state and managerial structures and bodies, resulting, inter alia, in an increased empowerment of women. The UNDP (2010) in this connection reports that while Cuba ranks 51st out of all countries on the HDI it stands 29th on its 'women's empowerment index'.

In the 1998 national elections, the decline in the number of women delegates in the National Assembly was slightly reversed over the course of the Special Period, with women's membership rising to 27.6% (August 1999: 366). The 2003 elections saw women's parliamentary representation increase to 35.9%, and, according to Save the Children (2010: The Women's Index) and the UNDP (2010), today 43% of government positions are occupied by women. In the Council of State—the highest executive body—16% of members are women. Saney notes that as he was writing his study of the Cuban Revolution, women headed five ministries: Science, Technology and the Environment; Interior Commerce; Finance and Prices; Foreign Cooperation and Investment; and Auditing and Control. Women also occupy 52.5% of union leadership positions and comprise more than 30% of the active membership of the Communist Party. In addition, women constitute 31% of all managers in state enterprises. Thus, despite the challenges of the Special Period and the succession of economic reforms that it induced or help bring about it is evident that the policies of the Cuban Revolution continue to embody 'a clear willingness to achieve equality between men and women' (Lopez Vigil 1999: 173).

From a more critical perspective, sociological studies evidence the fact that Cuban women, like women elsewhere in both advanced and developing capitalist societies, also experience what has been termed the 'double shift' in the working day, dedicating on average up to 36 hours a week on domestic or household labour versus 12 for men (Nuñez, 2007). Also, because of the housing shortage it is not unusual to find up to three generations of family women and other family members living under the same roof. Remaining patriarchical attitudes among men and a macho culture that has survived all of the legislation thrown at it ensures that women not only continue to assume responsibility for the bulk of domestic labour [cocinar, limpiar, fregar y lavar] but have the primary responsibility for social reproduction. In this regard the status of women is clearly a cultural artifact that has survived the transformation of a capitalist into a socialist society.

Revolution and the Racial Divide[6]

That the Cuban Revolution was—and is—a fundamental watershed for Afro-Cubans is indisputable (De la Fuente 2001). A 1962 survey found that 80% of Afro-Cubans and the mixed population 'were wholly in favour of the revolution'. The corresponding figure for whites was 67% (de la Fuente 2001: 276). The Revolution challenged entrenched segregation, with Fidel Castro publicly raising the issue of racial discrimination in several speeches.

On 21 March 1959, he said: 'In all fairness, I must say that it is not only the aristocracy who practice discrimination. There are very humble people who also discriminate. There are workers who hold the same prejudices as any wealthy person, and this is what is most absurd and sad ... and should compel people to meditate on the problem.' (quoted in Serviat 1997: 87)

In another speech, Fidel added: 'Why do we not tackle this problem radically and with love, not in a spirit of division and hate? Why not educate and destroy the prejudice of centuries, the prejudice handed down to us from such an odious institution as slavery? We know that in the war of independence the integristas came and said that no revolution should take place because if we achieved independence it would be a republic ruled by blacks. Now they stir up the same fears today, fear of the black. Why? It was unfounded and false then. Why does anyone need to be alarmed when justice is sought through persuasion and reason, not force? It is a struggle we all wage together, all Cubans, against prejudice.' (quoted in Fernández Robaina 2000: 103)

---

[6] This section relies heavily on Saney (2004).

Castro stated that racism was anti-nation and singled out discrimination in employment and at the workplace as the worst manifestations. In a December 28, 1959, speech, Che Guevara discussed the role of universities: 'I have to say it should paint itself black, it should paint itself mulatto, not only its students but also its professors; that it paint itself worker and peasant, that it paint itself people, because the university is the heritage of none, it belongs to the Cuban people…and the people that have triumphed, that have been spoiled with triumph, that know their own strength and that they can overcome, that are here today at the doors of the university, the university must be flexible and paint itself black, mulatto, worker and peasant, or it will have no doors, the people will break them down and paint the university the colours they want' (quoted in Serviat 1997: 87).

The massive literacy campaign of 1961, the establishment of universal and free education and healthcare, the redistribution of land by the agrarian reforms of 1959 and 1963, the dramatic reduction of rents under urban reform and the building of new housing and recreational facilities, all of these, among others, radically and positively transformed the lives of the black population. The Revolution's commitment to promoting equity and providing equal access to society's resources was further demonstrated by the outlawing of racial discrimination, later enshrined in the Constitution: Article 42 declares: 'discrimination because of race, colour, sex or national origin is forbidden and is punished by law' (Constitution of the Republic of Cuba 1993). Article 295 of the Cuban criminal code establishes fines and sanctions of between six months and two years for discrimination and incitement of hatred on the basis of gender, race or national origin.

Thus, equal rights are mandated for all citizens. A black worker at a nickel refinery remarked: 'I am most proud of what the revolution has done for the workers and the campesinos—and not only at work. For example, Negroes couldn't go to a beach or to a good hotel, or be jefes (bosses) in industry, or work on the railroads or in public transportation in Santiago. This was because of their colour! They couldn't go to school or be in the political office, or have a good position in the economy either. They would wander in the streets without bread. They went out to look for work and couldn't get it. But now, no—all of us—we're equal: the white, the Negro, the mulatto'.

In the 1960s, an intense national discussion and debate on Cuban culture and history paralleled the revolutionary transformations.

The contributions of Afro-Cubans were increasingly outlined and popularized (de la Fuente 2001: 286). The non-racist reconstruction of Cuban culture and historiography was seen as essential to the creation of the New Cuba and was reflected in film and cultural institutions (De la Fuente 2001: 288–289). It was considered a necessary break with the bourgeois stage of the island's history, an indispensable and inevitable step on the road to socialism.

Before the onset of the Special Period, Cuba 'had achieved relatively high levels of equality and racial integration' (De la Fuente 2001: 318). Castro declared that Cubans were a Latin-African people, acknowledging the critical African role in Cuban history and culture. This ran counter to dominant Cuban historiography and challenged the conceptions that prevailed in the Cuban exile community, which was predominantly upper class, white and comprised of those who had fled the island in the wake of the Revolution. Increasingly, this valorization of Black Cuba was—and is—'anathema in the ethno-specific Cuban diaspora'.

Estimates—from both internal and external sources—of the proportion of the Cuban population that is black have ranged from the ridiculously low figure of 11% to the more realistic 75%. This wide and confusing range is based on, one, a conscious or unconscious obfuscation aimed at downplaying the role of blacks in Cuban history and in the contemporary period, and two, the elasticity of defining who is black. However, it is a fair estimate by Saney that at least 70–80% of the Cuban population is of African descent.

While the government in its public actions and policies had 'altered the dynamics', it had not eliminated the problem (Knight, 1996: 107). It also 'subordinated considerations of race to other, more explicitly articulated goals of the socialist society'. The equality of all citizens was accepted and understood as immanent, natural and inevitable in the social order of the New Cuba. This new order was established under a project of social justice based on the elimination of classes. Nevertheless, the Cuban government was unable to completely remove race—and for that matter gender and class considerations—from the daily life of the country (Saney, 2003: 116). Indeed, 'the weight of the racist superstructure of the past, conscious and subconscious ideological assumptions, and cultural patterns and social relations transcend the particular social formation which gave it life'.

While a persuasive case can be made that 'racism in its institutionalized forms had been eliminated in Cuba' (Cole, 1986: 15; quoted in

Saney, 2003), the state has not been able to regulate relations at the personal level (Knight, 1996: 116–117). Likewise, although the quantitative and qualitative changes in the material conditions of life for Cuban blacks had been immense, the process was—and is—incomplete. Enormous strides had been made in the transformation of the social and economic conditions that generated and sustained inequality, but complete equality and equity had not been achieved. For example, blacks continue to predominate in poorer neighbourhoods. Overall, this was reflective not only of the reality that a few decades is a very short time in which to alter social phenomena, structures and ideations which are the product of nearly five centuries of slavery, colonialism and imperialist domination, but also of the failing of government policy to comprehend the complexity of the situation facing Afro-Cubans and to appreciate that dealing with this inheritance required the active participation and intervention of the state in all spheres of society.

In 1986, the revolutionary government introduced new policies to directly address the issue of race and racial inequality. This represented a deviation from the orthodox or dogmatic Marxist position that understands race and racism as phenomena subordinate to class and class oppression. In the orthodox or dogmatic approach, racism is viewed as a problem that resolves itself naturally as society transforms its socioeconomic and political structures; racism and racial discrimination were conceptualized as 'remnants of the past that would disappear in due time' (de la Fuente 2001: 276). In short, they would wither away under socialism.

At the Third Congress of the Communist Party, in 1986, it was acknowledged that racial discrimination and racism had not been eliminated (Saney, 2003). Castro challenged the political structures and the entire society to address the issue, declaring: 'The hypocritical societies that promote racial discrimination are afraid to talk about this, but revolutionary societies are not' (quoted in De la Fuente 2001: 312).

A race, gender and youth affirmative action program was adopted, with the aim of bringing more Afro-Cubans, women and youth into the decision-making bodies of the Party and the government. Fidel Castro stated that it was necessary that leadership structures 'duly reflect the ethnic composition of our people' and that the process of promotion of blacks 'must not be left to chance' (Castro Ruz, 1988: 80). He further observed: 'The correction of historic injustice cannot be left to spontaneity. It is not enough to establish laws on equality and expect total equality. It has to be promoted in mass organizations, in party youth.....We cannot expect women, blacks, mixed-race people to be promoted spontaneously...We need to straighten out what history has twisted' (De la Fuente, 2001: 313).

Assata Shakur, a long-time African-American political exile in Cuba, in the midst of the Special Period observed: 'The first lesson I learned was that a revolution is a process, so I was not that shocked to find sexism had not totally disappeared in Cuba, nor had racism, but that although they had not totally disappeared, the Revolution was committed to struggling against racism and sexism in all their forms. It would be pure fantasy to think all the ills, such as racism, classism and sexism, could be dealt with in 30 years. But what is realistic is that it is much easier and much more possible to struggle against those ills in a country which is dedicated to social justice and to eliminating injustice' (Belton, 2007: 9).

The Urban-Rural Divide

One of the central objectives of revolutionary policy from the beginning was to bridge and ultimately eliminate 'the differences between urban and rural living' standards (Glazer 1989: 80). To fulfill this goal, the level and quality of services had to be equalized between the two areas. In order to provide services that had historically been denied in rural areas and also to optimize the use of resources, it was necessary 'to concentrate residents in communities that were large enough to make the services viable' (Glazer 1989: 80). Hence, new towns and communities were created in the countryside and were equipped with, for example, schools, clinics and libraries. Residents were given fully-furnished, rent-free homes (Glazer 1989: 80). From 1959 to 1964, the Cuban government directly built or sponsored 26,000 new homes in rural areas, representing approximately 47% of all new dwellings.

Before the Revolution, virtually all new housing had been constructed in urban areas, particularly Havana. 150 settlements, varying in size from several dozen houses to several hundred, were created. These new housing and community conditions were reflected in a new stability in rural employment. At the end of the fifth year of this first phase of housing construction and community development, 70% of agricultural workers had regular salaried positions (Glazer 1989: 80).

Development under colonialism and neo-colonialism—i.e. prior to the Revolution—had generated urban centres where wealth and services were concentrated and rural regions, particularly in the mountainous zones, where the absence of services and poverty reigned. The relationship between town and country was altered as the revolutionary government directly addressed the historical disparity in the allocation of resources. Rural needs were emphasized over urban needs, ensuring that rural areas would have priority in the allocation of material and labour resources. This policy was an integral element in Cuba's efforts to decentralize development by curtailing Havana's economic importance and share of resources.

The policy of the Revolution was relatively successful in stemming the flow of people into the large cities and in equalizing the quality of housing, healthcare, educational facilities and social services between urban and rural regions. Indeed, Saney points out that Havana has had the lowest rate of population growth of any Latin American or Caribbean capital. Between 1970 and 1988, Havana's population increased by less than 7% (Frank 1993: 79). Cuba has thus avoided the problems that have afflicted so many Third World cities. While Cuba today classifies 80% of its population of eleven million as urban, it must be borne in mind that over three million of these urban Cubans live in towns that may have fewer than a thousand residents (Frank 1993; 80 and Castro 1996a: 34). These are classified as urban zones by standards applied to the demography of developing countries because they have electricity, schools, water supplies, health clinics, cultural centres and other facilities (Frank 1993: 80, Stubbs 1989: 138).

Notwithstanding the policy thrust of the Revolution towards redressing the urban-rural divide, and the disparity of living conditions in different provinces and regions of the country, it is evident that regional disparities of one sort and another persist.

Conclusion

Equality, together with freedom and solidarity, is a fundamental value of socialist humanism. It is also the conceptual and ethical foundation of the Cuban Revolution—of socialist human development. Development as *equality*, one might conclude, as opposed to development as *freedom*. In the UNDP conception of human development as freedom equality appears not as a substantive social condition—an egalitarian society in which conditions are ideally equal for all, at least ideally—but as *equity*, an *equality of opportunity*, the essential condition of which is freedom rather than equality.

The difference is critical because capitalist societies are so structured as to render equality into an abstraction or a utopian ideal. Capitalism is fundamentally nonegalitarian, characterized by a class hierarchy of relations and conditions. It cannot satisfy the system requirements for human development at the level of equality or solidarity. On the other hand, socialism, a socialist conception of human development, is predicated on egalitarianism, a relatively egalitarian society in which ideally conditions are equal for all; i.e. equality is not merely a matter of opportunity but a fundamental right and a necessary condition.

Cuba undoubtedly falls short as a fully egalitarian society, but there is no doubt that social equality is a vital element of the revolutionary consciousness that has been promoted by public action and national policy over the years. It has also been a fundamental organizing principle of the Revolution. One of the very first actions taken and policy measures adopted by the revolutionary regime (in May 1960) was a radical land reform that reverted capitalism in the countryside and substantially improved conditions for 150,000 poor peasant farmers. In relatively short order (over the course of the first two years) relations of production both in the countryside and in the urban centres were at first nationalized, then socialized. In this socialist process of productive transformation, the property of the big landlords and capitalists, in both the agricultural and industrial sectors, were expropriated, but the small property holders were not. Unlike the experience in Russia the peasant farmers were not forcibly separated from their means of production, but were encouraged to freely combine their units of production into state farms or agricultural cooperatives. The nationalization and socialization process proceeded apace and was more or less completed by 1975, fifteen years into the Revolution, but under conditions of free choice or voluntary submission. The exception to this rule occurred in the revolutionary offensive of 1968 in which the petit-bourgeois service sector of small business was eliminated virtually overnight by administrative fiat. In this development both the market and the private sector were all but eliminated in a system of nationalized and socialized production, surviving only in the agricultural sector. With the nationalization and socialization of production, elimination of the labour market, improved access to food and housing via public subsidies, and the socialization of public services in the sectors of health and education, Cuba completed the transition from capitalism to socialism—from a class divided society characterized by relations and conditions of social equality to a relatively egalitarian socialist society. The transition was not easy or free from all sorts of mistakes and policy experiments, and shifts in economic strategy, but remarkably free from social conflict in comparison to the experience with capitalist or social development elsewhere or before.

CHAPTER EIGHT

SOCIALIST HUMAN DEVELOPMENT AS FREEDOM

Man is born free but everywhere he is in chains
—Jean-Jacques Rousseau, *The Social Contract* (1762)

Socialism [in the 21st century] is the search for a fully democratic society [based on] a culture that promotes...values such as solidarity, humanism, respect for difference, and protection of the environment and [that] turns its back on the view that hunger for profit and the laws of the market are the guiding principles of human activity.
—Marta Harnecker (2010)

In Chapter 4 it was argued (reference to Martínez Heredia, 2001) that the transition towards socialism would require—and in Cuba it did indeed meet—three conditions of revolutionary transformation: (1) the supremacy of politics over economics and the orientation of the latter towards meeting the needs of the population; (2) the elimination of any obstacles to that end, in particular and mainly capitalist private property; and, echoing Guevara (3) direct popular participation, organized with the revolutionary consciousness. In Chapter 4 we argued that the history of the Cuban Revolution, as de- and reconstructed in the chapter, established the first and second condition. In this chapter we will argue that the third condition (popular participation in the construction of socialism and the revolutionary process) is a defining characteristic of the Cuban model, and as such a critical factor of socialist human development.

As we see it, and expand upon below, this dimension of human development is fundamentally an issue of freedom, not freedom as conceived by Amartya Sen and other theorists in the philosophical tradition of social liberalism in which freedom is viewed essentially as a matter of the equal opportunity for individuals to realize their human potential ('capabilities', in Sen's formulation), but freedom as emancipation from exploitation and oppression, and the capacity for collective action in the public interest.

Development as Freedom

The first HDR in 1990 begins with the stirring words: 'An irresistible wave of human freedom is sweeping across many lands. Not only political systems but economic structures are beginning to change in countries where democratic forces had been long suppressed.' The Report continues: 'People are beginning to take charge of their own destiny… We are rediscovering the essential truth that people must be placed at the centre of development.'

The Report follows this rediscovery (the awareness of this truth was presumably lost in the post-war concern for re-activating the economic growth process) with the statement that the purpose of development is to 'offer people more options' such as 'access to income, a long life, knowledge, political freedom, personal security, community participation and guaranteed human rights.' This, in fact, turns out to be the UNDP's conception of development broadly defined as 'freedom'— development understood as the expansion of 'choice' and 'human capabilities', or 'enlarging the range of peoples' choices'. As the HDR-92 had it: freedom (and thus development) means 'increasing…opportunities for education, healthcare, income and employment' as well as a range of 'economic and political freedoms'.[1]

This vision of development as 'promoting people's freedom to lead the lives they [have reason to value and] choose' (HDR, 2009) naturally raises questions that the authors subsequently address: What are the barriers to freedom—the obstacles in the way of development and the actions that need to be taken? And what changes are needed to remove these obstacles?

Presumably the main obstacle has to do with the unequal distribution of opportunities, the inability of the poor to access the resources needed to take advantage of these opportunities. As the authors observe, without a note of irony, the 'choices of the poor are often constrained'. This, they note, 'can arise from underlying inequalities in their skills (a perceived deficit for which the poor themselves are presumably responsible) but also from policy and institutional barriers'

---

[1] This concept of freedom can be clearly differentiated from both the Marxist conception of freedom as emancipation (from exploitation and oppression) and the neoliberal conception of the freedom of individuals from constraint excercised in the public interest.

(UNDP, 2009: 108). The system underlying the institutions at issue is not questioned.

In this connection, i.e. regarding actions that need to be taken to remove the barriers to their freedom and thus level the playing field for the poor, the authors of the HDR-2009 defend themselves from the 'misconception' that human development is 'anti-growth'; that 'it concerns distribution rather than the generation of income, that it is a social rather than a developmental concern'. On this point the authors note that 'nothing could be further from the truth'.

So what is the truth? As the authors of the HDR-09 assert HD is *not* a matter of equality in social relations and conditions, a question of redistributing the product of collective action and creating conditions 'equal for all', as Marx and the advocates of socialism after him see it. Rather, HD is a matter of *equal rights* and the freedom of people to exercise these rights in the pursuit of opportunities to lead the 'lives they choose' and to realize the outcomes that they have reason to value. The concern is not for freedom from constraint but freedom of choice, the ability to exercise one's rights, and an equality of opportunity to do.

The point of the defensive assertion by the authors of the HDR-1990 that 'development' properly understood—i.e. as freedom—is multidimensional and cannot be measured merely as economic growth, i.e. in terms of an annual increase in the GDP per capita, nor as an improvement in the distribution of this growth, which is to say, progress in the direction of social equality. Development is a matter of freedom and equity, equal opportunity rather than social equality. For one thing, economic growth measured in the aggregate in per capita terms (as a statistical average) does not necessarily indicate 'improved access to income', one of several indicators of human development (weighted one third in the HDI). Nor would data on measured improvements in the distribution of income get us closer to measuring progress in the direction or at the level of HD. More relevant would be an expansion of choices and opportunities available to individuals. And even if the playing field were levelled by a more inclusive policy framework that facilitates action by the poor; and even if the government acts to remove the institutional barriers to the freedom of people to live the life of their choice, the poor and the 'hitherto excluded' need to be capacitated to act, empowered to make decisions on their own behalf.

Deconstructing in this way the notion of HD embodied in the HDRs leads us to question, first, the empirical indicators used to measure improvements in HD; second, the changes needed to bring about these improvements; and, thirdly, the perceived agency for these changes.

As for the first question, the UNDP economists involved with the preparation of the HDRs have operationalized their notion of HD—translated their theoretical definition into an empirical measure—in terms of an index composed of three unweighted variables: per capita income, defined in purchasing power parity terms, an annual increase viewed as progress; school enrolment, a crude measure of educational opportunity); and life expectancy, an indicator of the freedom from want and the illnesses and conditions that afflict the poor). However, their notion of HD is also reflected in, and indicated by, evidence of employment opportunities as well as a range of not so well defined (operationalized) 'economic and political freedoms'.

As for employment, explicitly identified as an issue of economic freedom, for some reason none of the HDRs measures or discusses the opportunities and conditions associated with it. Likewise housing, which like employment is also viewed essentially as a 'private sector activity', a commodity that should be accessed via the market rather than as a welfare issue for governments to assume responsibility. The likely reason for the difference in the way that health and education are viewed on the one hand, and housing and employment on the other, is that notwithstanding the professed concern of these UNDP economists for 'economic rights' as defined by the UN Charter of human rights, employment and housing within the capitalist system are generally and essentially viewed as commodities, and thus accessed with the assistance of the market, rather than as a social good, a constitutional right that the state has the obligation to provide for. Education and healthcare, on the other hand, are viewed by these economists (within the framework or with reference to the welfare state) as a social good and public responsibility more than a private activity. At the very least, education and healthcare are areas in which a 'better balance' between the state and the market is called for, with a presumptive responsibility and important role for the state (Ocampo, 2006, 2007).

This is not explicit but it can be deduced from the institutional framework established for the 'new social policy' under the post-Washington Consensus in the 1990s. Education and healthcare within this framework are singled out as matters of government responsibility, both in regards to 'investing in people' (strengthening human capital) and expanding the choices available to the poor and the hitherto excluded under conditions of equal opportunity (equity) that governments should support. Welfare or social assistance, another government responsibility, and a component of the social programs that correspond to the role of the State, was viewed as a matter of common or human decency, but not as a development issue. No government in Latin America, with the exception of Cuba (and Venezuela under its new constitution), viewed or view employment security and housing as human rights that require their inclusion in the 'new social policy' promoted with the post-Washington Consensus. To put this differently, the thinking of the economists associated with the UNDP, all of them social or reform liberals, is framed by the paradigmatic presupposition that capitalism provides HD its system requirements.

The one area where the HDRs have taken a position regarding human rights is that of political rights, particularly as concerns the freedom of expression, and the democratic right to vote and to organize in the free pursuit of one's beliefs. Although political rights are not measured by the HDI, human development as *political freedom* features significantly in a number of HDRs as a matter of principle and point of discussion. The issue as the authors of these HDRs see it is human development requires and only flourishes in conditions of economic and political freedom—economic freedom understood as the right of private sector firms to seek a return on their investments and a profit on their operations, and political freedom understood, in liberal democratic terms, as the rights of the individual. As we will argue below freedom is no less an issue in a socialist context but it is understood very differently.

Human development thus implies the opportunity and freedom of individuals to act in their own interest and citizens to participate in decision-making that relate to conditions that determine or affect fundamental conditions of their life and opportunity. In capitalist systems, especially in the form of laissez-faire capitalism or neoliberalism, freedom is a formal or legal right accorded to all, but it could be argued that it is only the private owners of capital and other means of social production—the so-called 'forces of economic freedom'—that are truly free, i.e. are able to take full advantage of their opportunities. Much or most of the rest of the population are only 'free' in a formal sense—equal in the eye of the law (and in their entitlement to vote). In practice the reality is that most people, especially the workers and the masses of the urban and rural poor, in most capitalist democracies on the margins and interstices of the world capitalist system are not 'free' in a substantive sense. Nor do they meaningfully 'participate' in the formulation of public policies. Apart from periodic voting rituals, the citizenry of capitalist democracies—and both capitalism and democracy assume very different forms—are nominally 'free to choose' their work or occupation and to make decisions regarding their personal lives, but the structure of their relations of production—and relations of power—viz. the objectively given social conditions of these relations prevent them from acting on the opportunity to pursue the 'lives [that] they choose'. Most people in Latin America, for example, constrained as they are by conditions not of their choosing and beyond their control, conditions that are generated by relations of production and power, are in no meaningful sense 'free to choose'. Virtually all except their most personal decisions and 'choices' are constrained and shaped by conditions that are well beyond their control, reducing their 'freedom' to an empty promise, an abstract right without any possibility of acting on it. This raises serious questions about the UNDP conception of *development as freedom* that we will explore below in the context of the Cuban Revolution.

Freedom as Emancipation

The profound value placed by Cubans on freedom, and the fundamental meaning of the Cuban Revolution in terms of freedom as a condition of human development, is expressed eloquently and powerfully by Fidel Castro in the *First Declaration of Havana*—in his passionate denunciations of 'Yanqui imperialism'—of the obscene profits obtained by American corporations at the price of undernourishment and infant mortality in Latin America.

To gauge the impact of Fidel's speech, and what it meant at the time not only for Cubans but for people across the region, it is useful to turn to a recent speech by Norman Girvan, a Jamaican economist and a member of the 'New World Group' founded by Lloyd Best, at his honorary doctorate acceptance speech at the University of Havana (December 3, 2008). In this speech, Girvan recounts the stirring words of Fidel at the time, which were 'still ringing in [his] ears' 50 years later. As he recounts his experience: 'The image of a million Cubans, assembled in one place as the National General Assembly of the People of Cuba, expressing their approval of the social and economic measures taken by the Revolution, and declaring their independence of foreign domination, was a transformative experience for me... It helped to shape my view of the world.'

In reconstructing the event (Fidel's speech, and the CR) Girvan recalls that Jamaica and the other West Indian territories were then preparing for national independence. In this context, he notes, 'the Cuban revolution was a source of inspiration to many of us [regarding] the ability of a small Caribbean country to chart its own course of social justice, economic transformation, and national independence by relying on the mobilization of the entire population, by relying on the will and energy of its people; with a leadership that trusted the mass of the population and refused to bow before threats, intimidation, economic punishment and counter-revolutionary violence from the greatest military power on the planet; just 140 kilometres from its shores.' He adds: 'It remains so to this day'.

Girvan's words captures the essence of the Revolution as a human development project of revolutionary transformation—to achieve freedom, independence, and bring about a social justice: in Girvan's words, for a country 'to chart its own course of social justice, economic transformation, and national independence by relying on the mobilization of the entire population...the will and energy of its people'.

It was in this spirit that Girvan some years later, in 1961 during the Bay of Pigs, as a student activist moved a resolution, seconded by Walter Rodney, the Guyanese revolutionary, in the University Students Council that 'condemn[ed] the shameless attempt to crush the Revolution by an illegal invasion launched from the territory of the United States'.

What the Cuban Revolution meant for Girvan's generation, and what it continues to mean for other peoples in the region, is also very well expressed by another Jamaican economist George Beckford, in his reflections on a visit to the island in 1965:

'First, the conspicuous absence of symptoms of unemployment (and underemployment); the signs of poverty are much less stark than elsewhere in the region—there is no prostitution and no begging of any kind, not even the covert kind of begging which produces 'tipping' in other places. Second, the omnipresence of education schemes—on radio and television, in the newspaper and factories, and throughout the length and breadth of the country. And, third, the obvious involvement of the people with matters affecting national life. The national and international awareness of the population at all levels and the general atmosphere of national cohesion, of public order, and of self-confidence are certainly not characteristic of the rest of the Caribbean' (Beckford, 'A Caribbean View of Cuba' (*New World Quarterly* II. 2: 271).

These words of two Jamaican economists, both of them well-known and highly respected development economists committed to the principle of HD, clearly express the essential meaning of the Cuban Revolution—a major testament to the struggle for freedom...for national independence and the enlightenment idea of a new society ('a new world' as Girvan and his compatriots at the time visualized it) characterized by freedom, equality and solidarity. These ideals and values, as Girvan notes, are deeply embedded in the socialist consciousness generated by the Cuban Revolution—a consciousness reflected not only in socialist practice but in Girvan's contact with Cubans as individuals: 'what has always stood out', in this contact is 'your professionalism, your discipline, your organization, your individual and national self-confidence combined with a total absence of a sense of superiority, your value system that is not driven by the worship of money and material objects, your willingness to share and your solidarity with others.'

In his reconstruction of his visit to Cuba, George Beckford also makes clear reference to another important dimension of the Cuban Revolution: overwhelming popular support for it. At issue in Beckford's remarks was a speech delivered by Fidel to an assembly of over 600,000 Cubans at Santa Clara (July 26, 1965). As Beckford notes, 'Let him take pictures, let him take films and see if in Washington, New York or anywhere else they can raise the enthusiasm of more than five hundred thousand citizens. Let's see if any of those puppet governments of Brazil, Guatemala, Nicaragua, Paraguay and other....if any one, or all of them together are capable of bringing together half a million people like those who are meeting here today...A crowd, large or small, can always be assembled by different means, but *what it is not possible to create is the enthusiasm of this crowd*. Any witness of the occasion (said Beckford) could not possibly disagree' (276).

What explains this 'enthusiasm'? The answer, according to Girvan, can be found in the active and transformative participation of so many Cubans in the revolutionary process—in the shared commitment to build a society based on freedom, equality and solidarity. As for freedom and equality, the working of these values and ideals on the consciousness of many Cubans is manifest in the evident active enthusiastic support for the Revolution's major achievements in building an education and a health system with few parallels in the developing world. As for the high value placed by the Cuban Revolution and many Cubans on solidarity it is reflected in the weakness, if not absence, of a deeply embedded culture of material consumption and the belief that 'greed is good', which leads to a view of others as mere means to one's own ends. But it is also evident in Cuba's astounding record of international solidarity—solidarity with the struggles of people all over the world to improve their lives in the face of grinding poverty and the machinations of class and imperialist exploitation.[2]

People's Power in the Cuban Socialist State

Chapter 8 argues that the idea of freedom is a critical element of socialist human development and a founding pillar of the conceptual and ethical foundation of the Cuban Revolution. However, it is not freedom as understood by the members of Pelerin Society, the neoliberal thought collective—an idea that underlies the project of a new world order installed in the 1980s.[3] Nor is it freedom as understood by Amartya Sen and others in the philosophical tradition of social liberalism. Essentially, freedom in a socialist context means emancipation from a system and institutions that violate the 'human essence', creating a conflict between the human and the social condition. At issue

---

[2] In the UNDP's corpus of Human Development Reports the only reference to 'solidarity' was in its 2007 report on the human development dynamics of climate change, and only in the Title and four brief references in the text to international cooperation. In this connection the Report makes two relevant statements. The first is that '[p]eople engaged in a daily struggle to improve their lives in the face of grinding poverty and hunger ought to have the first call on human solidarity' (p. 6). And the second: 'International cooperation...should be viewed not as an act of charity but as an expression of social justice, equity and human solidarity' (p. 194).

[3] The neoliberal conception is clearly represented in the Index of Economic Freedom constructed and published jointly by the Heritage Foundation, a prominent neoliberal think tank and policy forum, and The Wall Street Journal. In 2009 the Freedom Index (FI) ranked Hong Kong, a small city-state, as the freest country in the world, first out of 179 countries, while Haiti, on a descending scale, ranked 147th (because of government restrictions of starting up and doing business). Venezuela, because of its perceived (and measured) 'dictatorial' practices and repression vis-à-vis the private sector and the media, was ranked even lower as 174th. Cuba was ranked 177th, virtually the least free country in the world. By the UNDP's HDI Index Cuba ranked much higher on the freedom scale—freedom measured in terms of opportunities for self-realization.

here is a system based on class rule and imperialist exploitation—capitalism; and emancipation—liberation from exploitation (inequality) and oppression (unfreedom).

Fidel Castro and Che Guevara declared the Cuban Revolution to be fundamentally a struggle for national liberation—to liberate the country from imperialist exploitation and oppression—and a class struggle against class exploitation and the oppressive oligarchical regime set up to enforce this exploitation. At issue in this struggle was a struggle for national liberation and the emancipation of Cubans from an oppressive state and a system of class exploitation in which a ruling minority appropriated the lion's share of the social product, alienating most Cubans from their 'human essence' (freedom and equality).

Limia (2009) argues that the struggle for freedom—i.e. liberation from the yoke of 'imperialist exploitation'—should be traced back to its roots, to the 19th century struggle against American imperialism, and even earlier to the Spanish Empire and the struggle for freedom from slavery and colonialism.

In this context the Cuban nation was established with the 1869 Constitution but it soon gave way to a war of national independence, with its 'social-emancipadoras y dignificadoras de los humildes, trabajadores y excluidos....resistencia against slavery...primero, frente al colonizador español y al régimen de dominación capitalista neocolonial que impuso durante medio siglo el imperialismo norteamericano por medio de la oligarquía interna' (Bell Lara et al., 2006).

According to Limia, the triumph of the revolutionary forces led to the implantation of a new social and political paradigm embedded in the writings and practice of José Marti. Limia understands the new paradigm as a rupture with liberalism on key issues such as the nature of the human being, democracy, the need for a new sociality in regard to justice, and the pre-revolutionary (formally democratic) political system,[4] Above all, the Cuban Revolution represented a rupture with capitalism, the class-divided and -dominated system that underlies the institutionality of liberal democracy (hence the designation 'capitalist democracy') and other elements of the ideological superstructure. Liberalism, in this context, can be understood in ideological terms as an orientation towards social and political reform, viewing change as

---

[4] See: *Sociedad civil y participación en Cuba*, en *Teoría Sociopolítica. Selección de temas*. Tomo 2. Editorial "Félix Varela". La Habana, 2000, epígrafe 4, 2. (Colectivo de autores coordinado por Emilio Duharte).

progressive and liberating in the sense of equalizing opportunity for hitherto excluded groups and expanding choices available to individuals.

In this sense, the Cuban Revolution represented a rupture with capitalism as an economic system and liberalism as ideology. In effect, the Revolution can be seen as bringing about or instituting what might be termed a socialist, as opposed to capitalist, democracy based on mass participation. This is not to say that the Cuban revolutionaries turned from liberalism to socialism as an explicit ideology—an idealized vision of another world and a better future—to mobilize action and mass support. The ideological underpinnings of the Cuban revolution included *nationalism* ('la patria o muerte') and *human development*. Socialism as an ideological framework for mobilizing action, and Marxism as theory, would take immediate form as humanism and active social participation but another year of developments on the front of international relations to take form as Marxist Leninism.[5] As Limia has it: 'Marxism and Leninism would [come to] provide Cuban revolutionary thought a new 'sustancia cosmovisiva' under historical conditions created by imperialist domination—and a continuing hostility of the United States to the revolutionary regime'.[6]

According to Limia, the Provisional Revolutionary Government put into practice a form of socialist democracy, giving a voice to the people, guaranteeing popular participation in the discussion and decision-making on issues of transcendental significance. The key laws and political documents at the time, he argues, were subject to intense and open debate and popular approval ('aprobación populares') and their implementation was left to the 'new political actors formed from below' ('surgidos del pueblo').

Political power was achieved and defended by force, but Limia insists, it was built with 'popular participation and a broad consensus as to the importance of the common welfare and solidarity in a context

---

[5] It was not until the early nineteenth century that the idea began to emerge that human beings could themselves refashion society. It was only with the industrial revolution and the emergence of the modern working class that critics of society began to think in terms of a human transformation of social life. And it was with these developments that the idea of *socialism from below* emerged. But at the start, socialism was largely utopian, elitist and antidemocratic in character. It was only through decades of working class struggle that socialism took the form of a movement devoted to the self-emancipation of the oppressed and exploited. It was in this sense that the Cuban revolutionaries turned towards socialism as ideology and Marxism as theory.

[6] On this point Limea here cites Miranda Francisco (1999).

of a class struggle for national sovereignty and social emancipation'. More generally, he continues to argue, revolutionary political power acquired its significance in that for the first time political power was achieved and exercised in the name of 'the people', advanced to establish the sovereign right of the Cuban people to decide for themselves and manage their own affairs, and to do so with a government of their own making. This 'crucial historic fact', Limia argues, became a key feature and an essential element of a uniquely Cuban form of 'human development'. This is to say (and here write), the Cuban Revolution is profoundly democratic and participation is key to Cuba's democracy.

Having overthrown a bastion of the American empire in the hemisphere the main political task at the time (January 1959) was to construct 'a unity of the people', converting diverse segments of the popular movement—'workers, peasants, intellectuals, students, youth… women'—into a 'revolutionary mass surrounding the political vanguard of the Revolution' in the process of constructing socialism—and, Limia adds, 'el desarrollo humano masivo'—based on massive popular participation. In the process of this revolutionary process, Cubans 'laid the foundation of a new state, a different type of civil society, and a new relation between them'.

Institutional Dynamics of National Politics

In the wake of the 'revolutionary offensive' of 1968 the revolutionary leadership came to the conclusion that Cuban society could no longer operate on the basis of the existing institutional-policy framework. Consequently, there was a rethinking of the decision-making and policy formulation process—and a search for a new institutionality. In the early 1970s, Cuban political leaders announced their intention to begin what they called a 'process of institutionalization' of the state and the political system.

Thus, while the 1960s had been the time of 'taking heaven by storm', the 1970s were characterized by the institutionalization of the new economic, social and political order. The goal was now to establish stable regulatory forms and the formal institutional setting for popular input into national decision-making. This included the passage of a the new Cuban Constitution and the reorganization of the political system, administrative structures and the legal system in order to create a structure 'more suited to the ideology and practice of a socialist political economy' (see also Evenson, 1994: 13–14; August, 1999: 202; Fitzgerald, 1994: 56–95; Fuller, 1992: 172–191; Mesa-Lago, 1974). And this quest to institutionalize a Cuban form of participatory democracy also included a sub-system of local government in the form of the 'municipality', which, for José Marti was 'the root…of freedom' and for Harold Dilla (1991) 'an experience beyond the paradigms.[7]

The institutionalization of the Revolution in 1976 was formally marked by the ratification of a new Constitution via a popular referendum and the establishment of the Órganos Locales del Poder Popular (Local Bodies of People's Power, OLPP), the first municipal system in revolutionary Cuba and the Municipal (and National) Assembly of Peoples' Power.

Beyond Elections: Debating Democracy and Democracy in Cuba

Beyond Elections: Redefining Democracy in the Americas is an important documentary film that explores the vital question of 'What is democracy'? In its search for an answer the film takes us on a journey across the hemisphere from Venezuela's communal councils to Brazil's participatory budgeting process, from the emergence of constitutional assemblies within the indigenous communities of Bolivia to the formation of grassroots movements in the region, from the 'recovery' by Argentinean workers of their factories to the construction of cooperatives and alternative forms of economic production and social organization.

---

[7] [*Esa es la raíz, esa es la sal, de la libertad: el municipio* (José Marti)]. At the time, Cuban researchers and others researching Cuba began to interpret the likely contents of a new, more democratic system from a perspective that ranged from the democratic liberalism of Dominguez (1978) and Mesa Lago (1978) to the charged ideological hostility of Irving Horowitz (1977) who argued that the so-called institutionalization as well as the creation of local government was simply 'Stalinist, depoliticizing bureaucratic integration,' Jorge Dominguez in his classic *Cuba: Order and Revolution.* provided a more focused and objective diagnosis but even so with a theoretical and ideological liberalism that left little room for analytical flexibility. Mesa Lago's interpretation was in the same mold. The institutionalization of the Revolution, he noted, was characterized by 'central control, dogmatism, administrative-bureaucratic features and limited participation, in the Soviet mold'. In this interpretation, the new municipal governments had only a very subordinate role to play, not at all the democratically defining role that the Cuban leadership tried to give it and our own retrospective analysis accords.

A democratic wind, the filmmaker suggested, is blowing across Latin America in the form of experimenting with new forms of popular participation that go well beyond the electoral process of voting. Within the liberal democratic system democracy is defined formally in terms of the 'rule of law', on the basis of the political party apparatus and use of the electoral mechanism to secure a system of representation and participation in the making of decisions and public policy. However, as the film makes clear (and the UNDP has long argued) democracy is *much more than elections*. It is 'a long-term process of reorganizing the institutions of civil society....[the participation of people] in events and process that shape their lives' (UNDP, 1993: iii).

As for political democracy, Cuba has demonstrated that the institution of multi-party politics is not the only way of organizing democratic elections—that direct elections in the context of workplace and community councils can produce an alternate system that is highly representative and participatory, and thus arguably or tangibly democratic. As for the form that democracy is theorized to take at the level of respect for human rights and free elections, numerous political analysts—including notably Eduardo Galeano, Amy Goodman, Emir Sader, Martha Harnecker, Ward Churchill, and Leonardo Avritzer— have noted in Latin America the emergence of experimentation with different and new forms of participation and democracy. These exercises in democracy have ranged from participatory budgeting in Brazil to the formation, in Venezuela, of tens of thousands of self-organized communal councils on the model of Cuba's Organs of People's Power.

Across the world, by the UNDP's reckoning 120 countries now have at least the minimum trappings of democracy—the freedom to vote for all citizens or with few exclusions. But for many in the global south, this is just the beginning, not the end. Following decades of US-engineered or backed dictatorships, civil wars and devastating structural adjustment policies in the south, imperialism and corporate control, electoral corruption, and fraud, representative politics in the Americas is seriously at issue if not in crisis. People are choosing to redefine democracy in their own terms: *local, direct, and participatory—socialist.* In 1989, the Brazilian Worker's Party altered the concept of local government when they installed participatory budgeting in Porto Alegre, allowing residents to participate directly in the allocation of city funds. Ten years later, Hugo Chávez was swept into power with the promise of granting direct participation to the Venezuelan people. As it turned out diverse forms of popular participation, especially the Communal Council on the Cuban model, were subsequently formed both as an initiative 'from above' and spontaneously from below. In Argentina, a growing number of factories have been 'recovered' from their owners by the workers, and across Latin America social movements and popular assemblies have taken form, taking power away from the dominant class and the ruling elites and putting it directly into the hands of their members and citizens.

The debate continues, but it is arguable if not evident that these direct and local forms of 'citizen participation' have produced a more substantive form of 'democracy' than that which prevails in the capitalist democracies of the 'West', incorporating as they have masses of the hitherto excluded poor in the decision-making process. These experiments have also thrown light on the democratic nature of the system devised in Cuba for public action and citizen participation.

Arnold (1999), in this connection, argues that the Cuban approach to democracy has produced a system that is more representative than is generally the case in capitalist democracies, a system based on the guaranteed rights and the opportunity and freedom of all citizens to participate in the electoral process without the constraints (lack of money, for example) that surround elections in the capitalist democracies. The relative absence of such constraints on political participation in Cuba is reflected in the dynamics of political representation in the electoral process. In liberal democracies such as the US and Canada there is a notable divergence between the social type or groupings of individuals that have achieved political power by electoral means and the distribution of this type and these groups in society as a whole. In these systems there is a virtual if not total absence of any direct representation of the common worker, housewife, family farmer, etc. In Cuba, however, it is quite different. There is no such divergence between the characteristics of those holding power and the distribution of these characteristics in the general population. The Cuban electoral system, in which no party (i.e. the CCP) is allowed to participate in the process results in a system that is arguably democratic in terms of the right, and the freedom, of all citizens to actively participate, as well as the principles of representation and accountability.

Notwithstanding the UNDP's perennial concern with the 'density of the state' in Cuba, and the perception of so many non-Cuban liberal (or 'bourgeois') political scientists as to Cuba's 'democratic deficit'[8] Cuba's approach has resulted in an arguably 'democratic' system—a socialist democracy in which citizens are free to actively participate within the limits of respect for the system and the revolutionary process, i.e. the institutionality of the Cuban state. This of course is a basic principle of any democracy: that freedom does not extend to the right, and active efforts, to subvert the system or betray the people. But democracy, whether capitalist or socialist, should mean maximum freedom within these limits. As Marta Harnecker emphasized in a recent interview, 'socialism is the search for a *fully* democratic society'.

But this debate continues—and it could well be argued that the security concerns for the Cuba state results in undue restrictions on basic democratic rights—to freely express opinions, dissent and to organize. In this connection, there is nevertheless some basis for arguing a 'democratic deficit' in Cuba: the use of security concerns to stifle dissent.[9] On the other hand, it could be argued that in the capitalist democracies, under conditions that prevail in most countries the freedom to meaningfully participate in the political process is severely

---

[8] This perception of Cuba's 'democratic deficit' is widespread among non-Cuban scholars and cuts across the ideological spectrum from the 'far left' (Trotskyists) to the reactionary liberal or conservative right (Irving Horowitz). Within these two ideological extremes both liberal bourgeois and Marxist scholars have often converged in their criticism, if not outright condemnation of 'Castroism' (one-man rule), 'centralized bureaucracy' (Fitzgerald), lack of political freedom to organise and express support for alternative policies and programs, a measure of 'thought control' and an intolerance of any form of dissent and a crackdown on dissenters, including in this crackdown constructive critics as well as some in the pay or service of Washington. In Cuba's political system, it is argued, power is concentrated in the Communist Party, within the Party in the Central Committee, and within the Central Committee in the 'maximum leader' (Huberman and Sweezy, 219–220). This structure, the argument advanced by Marxists and constructive critics was built from the top down: first came the leader, then the Central Committee, then the regional and local organizers, and finally the membership. James Harris, in this connection, argues that 'the verticalism, bureaucratism, and vanguardism that characterize Cuba's single-party-dominated political system pose serious problems to the democratization of the country's centralized state apparatus.' Petras and Morley (1992: 23–24, 17) add that 'mass popular mobilizations' in this context should be understood not as expressions of social democracy but rather as devices used by the leadership to legitimize itself and 'attack middle levels of power'.

[9] The periodic crackdowns on dissent, and the imprisonment of dissenters remain a major concern for liberal democrats and the so-called 'international community'. Inside Cuba, hoever, there prevails a different view and understanding of this issue. Georgina Suárez Hernández (1992) puts it this way: 'The isolated groups that in Cuba demand the right to function as a political opposition have their social base in the United States....This opposition is synonymous with counter-revolution, and it has always been and will remain pro-imperialist and anti-patriotic.'

constrained, and that the freedom of expression does not mean much, if, as is usually the case, the means of mass communication are in the hands of a powerful elite and there are few meaningful opportunities to express dissent regarding the existing economic system. Although the mechanisms for manufacturing consent and stifling dissent in capitalist democracies are different, and less obvious and public, they are nonetheless as effective. As in Cuba when someone transgresses the limits of dissent (subversion or betrayal of the system of government) he or she is held in line, if not imprisoned or worse.

Even so, the apparent intolerance of Cuban officials—particularly members of the CCP, whose self-assigned role is to ensure respect for the socialist system and the revolutionary process (and to be on the watch for 'counterrevolutionaries')—remains an issue of concern that notwithstanding its human development achievements Cuba is not yet (or even far from) a 'fully democratic society'. Indeed, as argued by the economist Esteban Morales, a member of the Unión de Escritores y Artistas de Cuba (UNEAC) who was 'separated' from the CCP for public statements about official corruption), 'corruption is the true counterrevolution' and much more dangerous than the internal dissent that led to the 2003 crackdown (*La Jornada*, 15 July 2010).

Cuba's leadership, it should be pointed out, have acknowledged that the government and the CCP in this regard had made a serious error in placing too many restrictions on 'intellectual liberty'. For instance, the Minister of Culture Abel Prieto told the writers association, January 2007, that during the 1970s, hardliners in the regime conducted 'witch hunts', especially against homosexual intellectuals but also against artists and intellectuals too attuned to a worldview hostile to socialism and the Revolution. Many were apologized to and several persons once censored are now in leading positions. Some, such as Antón Arrufat and Miguel Barnet, have been awarded the national prize for literature. Nevertheless, it has to be said (or it could be argued) that in this respect the Cuban Revolution is still in a deficit situation.

The CDR: Security versus Freedom

In the liberal democratic tradition of political thought (John Locke, etc.) freedom is counterposed to security, and the state is viewed as a necessary evil, with which members of society express their willingness to sacrifice some degree of freedom in exchange for gaining in security. It is this exchange, and a presumed willing submission of citizens to the laws of the state, that explains the conundrum posed by Jacques Rousseau in his critique of the liberal democratic theory of the social contract: 'Man is born free but everywhere he is in chains'.

A similar counterpoint between freedom and security, it could be argued, can be found in the workings of the Committees for the Defense of the Revolution (*Comités de Defensa de la Revolución*, or CDR), a network of community-based organizations across the island, with an estimated membership of over 7.6 million. But the security exchanged in the process is social rather than political in form; i.e. just as the economic freedom of the individual is limited by the superior claims of equality and solidarity, the political rights and freedom of the individual is subordinated, within limits, to the security of the population as a whole and the freedom of the country—*la patria*.

The CDR system was formed on September 28, 1960, as 'a collective system of revolutionary vigilance' to report on 'Who lives on every block? What does each do? What relations does each have with tyrants? To what is each dedicated? In what activities is each involved? And, with whom does each meet?'[10] Set up as an organization designed to protect the Revolution—to prevent counterrevolutionaries from acting like termites to undermine the Revolution from within—the CDR has been the subject of considerable criticism and endless debate. From a liberal democratic perspective they are naturally enough viewed as neighborhood watch organizations formed to spy on neighbors, constituting not only a home security organization but a non-democratic means of silencing dissent and policing as well as monitoring behaviour. Needless to say, the revolutionary leadership sees it in a different light—as an essential organization for domestic and national security—to protect the hard-fought freedoms won by the revolution.

When the CDR system was set up, it raised questions then and ever since as to the dynamics of their actual functioning—whether or not and how they have changed over time as the presumed threat to internal and national security abated. Curiously, there have been very few social scientific 'studies' into the functioning of the CDR, and those that have been published invariably reflect the ideological bent of the authors of these studies. Foreign, mostly American, scholars tend to view them as a fundamental threat to essential freedoms, as restricting the capacity of Cubans in different walks of life from expressing their

---

[10] Fidel Castro's *CDR Speech*/YouTube (Archival video: audio of speech, in Spanish).

view and to organize freely—in the name of fighting counterterrorist activity but in effect functioning somewhat like the STASI, the Ministry for State Security in the German Democratic Republic.[11]

On the other hand, proponents of the CDR and many Cuban scholars tend to emphasize the important role played by the CDR not only in securing 'home security' (defense against the threat of natural disasters—hurricanes etc) but in promoting social and community-based local development projects, and organizing mass rallies to advance or in support of the revolutionary process. Proponents also emphasize that CDR put medical, educational, or other campaigns into national effect and that, being organized on a geographical basis, they also act as centres for many who do not work in farms or factories and hence include a large proportion of female membership (Thomas, 1971: 996).

In the context of the centrality of community-based neighbourhood organizations such as the CDR there has also in recent years surged a debate as to whether Cuba can be thought to have a 'civil society' or whether all such organizations are merely conduits for the government line on public policy and its view of proper thinking and behaviour (Marín-Dogan, Michelle (2008). This issue is discussed further below in the context of community-based agencies for local development.

Civil Society, the State and Democratic Politics

The functioning of the CDR and its role in the revolutionary process have raised the question as to whether the local community or

---

[11] CDR officials, it is noted, have the duty to monitor the activities of each person in their respective blocks. There is an individual file kept on each block resident, some of which reveal the internal dynamics of households. Critics such as A. Rivera Caro, a journalist for *El Nuevo Herald*, trace the CDR system's origins to Germany's 'committees of territorial vigilance', described as organizations of agents that Adolf Hitler established by 1935 and have likened CDR and the associated 'Young Pioneers' to the Hitler Youth (Fidel Castro's *CDR Speech*/YouTube (Archival video: Channel 41/ extended commentary, in Spanish). A 2006, Amnesty International report noted CDR involvement in repeated human rights violations that included verbal as well as physical violence. Repressive CDR activity, the authors of this Report and other critics point out, has often been euphemized as (acts of repudiation) against those targeted as 'counterrevolutionary'. Other opponents further indict Cuba's CDR system of informants and accompanying control of individuals with the breakdown of the family unit and for widespread human alienation and pervasive interpersonal mistrust. However, these ideas appear to be based more on ideology and abstracted political analysis than empirical research.

neighbourhood (los 'barrios') constitute a mechanism of government control over the population, ensuring that people 'toe the line', or, on the contrary, that they serve as a locus of civil society organization, a mechanism of social democracy or popular participation in public action. From the former perspective, critics have noted that it was the local committee of the PCC in the Havana municipality Playa that forced the expulsion of Esteban Morales (see the discussion above) to silence a voice that was raised not in dissent from the government line or the system, but as part of an internal debate on the nature and future of Cuban socialism—a debate that by any democratic account should be open and free. On the other hand, the CDR is by no means the only community- or barrio-based organizational expression of what some see as an organ of people's power if not a vibrant 'civil society'.

Indeed, research reported on and reviewed in Gray and Kapcia (2008) point to the growing importance of the *barrio* as the locus of a vibrant civil society, organizing for the promotion and to advance local development. As noted in Chapter 4 the municipal, provincial and national assemblies of People's Power were constituted in 1976 to provide real, regular and more systemic and systematic forms through which people could participate in running the society. The exercise of social and political democracy through elective state bodies is a necessity of the socialist model of development but in Cuba it was delayed after the triumph of 1959 and through the early declared socialist development (García Brigos, 2001: 13).

The popular assemblies of popular power constitute a distinctly Cuban form of democratic participation in the affairs of the country and decision-making at all levels of political organization. They were designed to function as an institutional form of social and political democracy, understood as self-government. In 1986, however, the institutional form of people's power was modified into the *People's Council*, the embryo for what was regarded as a superior form of self-government and democracy. Growing disillusion with the system of popular power led to reforms in democratic governance, beginning in Havana in 1989. New People's Councils, with full-time administrators to tend to local concerns, were introduced and in 1992 extended throughout the country. The revised Constitution of 1992 granted the electorate the right to elect directly Provincial Assembly delegates and National Assembly deputies, as well as municipal delegates. Incorporated into the 1992 Constitution as part of the state system, the People's Councils supplemented, rather than supplanted the OPP as a means of providing a more active approach to democratic political participation—to engage more fully ordinary citizens in the affairs of state and to strengthen popular participation. The People's Councils also created a broader group of social actors to coordinate the tasks of government. As such, they were linked to both the OPP and the mass organizations, which, in the view of some are merely adjuncts of the state apparatus while others see them as an expression of 'civil society'.[12]

The notion of civil society, as an amalgam of social organizations formed outside the state system is a concept of the 18th century 'Enlightenment', resurrected in the 1980s in a context of a movement to democratize capitalist development and the state—to engage civil society in taking responsibility for development and for ensuring governability and good governance (Bardham, 1997; OECD, 1997; UNDP, 1993; World Bank, 1994). To that date capitalist development had been notoriously undemocratic, with key decisions made by a small elite that controlled the institutions of economic and political power. National politics was nominally 'democratic' in the sense that powerholders were subjected to periodic democratic elections, but the power of the democratic vote cannot match the power of money in determining the policy-making choices available to people.

In this context it was argued that the only way to secure a substantive democracy, a more than formal participation, was to 'strengthen civil society'—to create an alternative organizational base for helping to shape or determine public decision-making. And indeed this has been the history of democracy in Latin America since the

---

[12] Portrayed by regime critics as a spy organization, the CDRs at the local level coordinate neighbourhood safety watch and community-support work. They also sponsor campaigns to improve health standards (e.g., blood donation and immunization drives), to enroll students in school, and to encourage people to work. The FMC, in turn, initially provided opportunities for women to learn work skills, as well as integrating women who had been economically and politically marginal into the Revolution. While not a feminist organization, it did address women's concerns. ANAP grouped small private farmers whose land was never collectivized, while the CTC grouped together members of sixteen industry-based unions. But, according to Eckstein while it was subject to state repression prior to the Revolution, it lost whatever autonomy it had as Fidel Castro consolidated power. Both organizations, she argues—the point is debateable, promoted by critics and rejected by supporters—came to serve as 'channels through which government directives affecting the respective constituencies were disseminated and support for those directives attained, even when antithetical to rank-and-file interests'.

mid-1980s—a struggle to strengthen and engage civil society in the process of public policy formation.

As noted above, the institutional basis for this process was a policy of decentralization that was mandated and widely implemented as the price of admission into the 'new world order'. The aim of the policy was to create the institutional framework for 'good governance', a more participatory and inclusive form of local development with the agency of community-based forms of organization and the strategic support of civil society (Mitlin, 1998).

Democratization of the (capitalist) state in the form of strengthening civil society, which reversed the understanding dominant among American social and political scientists as to the requirements and optimal conditions for promoting development, also shifted the terms of debate on democracy in Cuba—as to whether it was democratic or authoritarian. Hitherto the focus of the debate had always been on the institutional structure of the electoral process, specifically the absence of political parties in the role they played in democratic democracies. In the 1990s, however, in the wake of this renewed interest in civil society and in decentralizing governmental decision-making regarding development, the question became: Did Cuba have a civil society or not able to counter the weight of the state, and to allow for popular participation in decision-making and the formulation of public policy?

Answers to this question have been given by and large on ideological lines rather than based on empirical research and scientific analysis. Most American and European social scientists continue to view the mass organizations as part of the State, without the capacity of exerting a countervailing force on state officials and in opposition to and against the powerful interests that have such a powerful influence in capitalist democracies. However, a number of scholars, both Cuban and non-Cuban, have entered the fray to argue the contrary. See, for example, Dilla and Oxhorn (2002).

Democracy as Freedom

Democracy, like freedom, takes different forms but it is normally defined in terms of the principles of political representation and participation in public policy formation, as well as the institutional trappings of these principles. In the liberal tradition of representative democracy and electoral politics, political 'representation' is often merely the 'business of elites' while 'participation' is commonly reduced to the periodic electoral mobilization of isolated voters. But it could also be argued that the distinctive feature of representative democracy is not the holding of elections as such but an institutional setting that allows citizens to influence the dynamics of representative institutions on a continuous and regular basis. In these terms the critical democratic issue is the nature of the relation between the state and civil society, or, more precisely, the mediating structures that facilitate the participation of civil society 'actors' in the public policy arena.

As a means of understanding the different but distinct forms taken by civil society and participation (political participation, participatory development) Peruzzotti (Selee and Peruzzotti, 2009) has identified three main approaches, each advancing a different model for analysis: (i) the *social capital model*; (ii) the *public sphere* model; and (iii) the *pressure group politics model*. Each approach focuses on specific types of participation involving specific actors, although, to account for the diversity of civic initiatives that generally form civil society, these approaches, Peruzzotti argues, need to be brought together.

As for Cuba, analysis of the civil society-state relation, and the dynamics of popular participation in public policy, have generally been shaped by a combination or one of the public sphere and the social capital models. In terms of the former emphasis is placed on the construction, early on in the revolutionary process, of civic organizations in the workplace and the community linked to the state so as to allow for a two-way flow of information and policy inputs. Examples of such organization would be the CDR, the FMC and the UNEAC.

Mainstream scholars in the liberal bourgeois tradition of political science cast aspersion on these and other such organizations, which they generally regard as government set-ups. From this perspective the institutional channels and mediating structures between state and civil society in Cuba serve merely as conduits of government control—to pass down the government line on public policy. However, several studies (see, for example, Saney, 2003) suggest that these organizations are in fact legitimate functional expressions of an effective, if limited, civil society and that the link to the state does indeed constitute a two-way channel, allowing neighbourhoods and workers to influence and actively participate in public policymaking as well as receive and debate the government line on these policies.

In democratic discourse 'participation' has different meanings in the political sphere, ranging from episodic participation of citizens in periodic elections (to elect between or among alternative candidates for public office and political or policy program attached to them) to active discussion in workplaces or barrios of public policy options available to their elected representatives. The associated dynamics often enough are analyzed from an ideological as well as a theoretical standpoint. In the case of Cuba a number of studies in recent years have challenged the widely held view among American, Canadian and European political scientists that the claim to democracy in Cuba is a sham; that decisions are made at the top, in fact by the maximum leader (Fidel and then Raúl); and that the participation of civil society in the public policy process is limited to rubber stamping decisions made at the top.

El Barrio and the Dynamics of Participation and Local Development

Popular participation in the field of development studies—participatory development, in the development discourse, democratic governance in political discourse—generally (or since the 1980s, when it became a distinct field of study) can also be analyzed in terms of the state-civil society relation. In this context, participation is, in the view of some economists at ECLAC, viewed as the 'missing link' (in the development process) between 'productive transformation' and 'equity' (ECLAC, 1990).

To facilitate a participatory form of development the proponents of this approach, together with other exponents of a post-Washington Consensus in the search for a 'new development paradigm', argued the need for a new institutional and policy framework revolving around a policy of administrative decentralization. A decentralized institutional structure, the argument goes, would not only strengthen civil society but create conditions for a more participatory form of development, in which the 'hitherto excluded' (mostly rural poor) would be empowered to act for themselves in the development process (Wolfe, 1998). Scholars have problematized this approach from diverse theoretical perspectives, arguing that it was designed to divert the rural poor from challenging the power structure, to depoliticize the demand for change and the theorists and practitioners of 'development' from engaging with the broader issues of power and politics that shape outcomes in real life for the rural poor (Selee and Peruzzotti, 2009; Veltmeyer, 2007). Ordinary citizens, it is argued by these and other critics, should have the right to participate in and make social and political claims from governing powers. But in practice, the poor are enabled only to participate in the making of decisions that affect them directly in their local communities and livelihoods—in the making of decisions as to how to spend the poverty alleviation funds that might come their way with international cooperation. They are encouraged to seek change not by changing national policy and confronting the power structure but in the local spaces of this structure—local development (Albuquerque, 2001; Uriarte, 2008; Vazquez, 2007).[13]

Conclusion

Freedom is a vital requirement and condition of human development but it comes in different forms. Freedom as development has three different meanings, each associated with a particular form of democratic discourse and practice. From a social liberal perspective freedom refers to the capacity of individuals to make decisions in their own interest and on behalf of their fundamental right to development, and the expansion of choices available to these individuals. With the optics of socialist theory, freedom denotes a political condition of emancipation, liberation from the power relations of class rule and imperialist exploitation, and the capacity and power of collective or national self-determination. As for economic and political liberalism, freedom is not seen as a matter of development; rather, it is an issue of allowing economic agents to calculate and pursue their self-interest (to profit from their economic transaction with others), and to do with the minimum of social or political constraint; on the other hand it means to be accorded the freedom to pursue their inalienable democratic political rights—the freedom of expression, to organize and to participate in the political process.

Although freedom in the Cuban context implies emancipation and pursued fundamentally as a matter of independence and national

---

[13] On the dynamics of local development in the era of neoliberal globalization see Veltmeyer (2007). As for Cuba Peña Castellanos (2006) provides the perspective of Cuban academe ('una visión de la actualidad de la academia cubana') on the globalization-local development connection, seeing the latter as the paradoxical outcome of the former.

self-determination, in the context of human development theory and practice it should be understood in social and political liberal terms as a participatory democracy. In these terms it could be argued (and we do) that most Cubans are relatively free and equal in regard to their opportunities and the capacity to make fundamental choices in their lives, and in their capacity to participate in the dynamics of local and national decision-making, and in their power to influence and affect public policy. At the same time Cuba evidentially still suffers from what we might term a 'democratic deficit': it has not yet realized the socialist ideal of a 'fully democratic society'.[14]

Not that Cuba's critics are correct in viewing Cuba as non-democratic in the sense that decisions are made at the top without popular participation. Far from it. It is more a matter as to whether Cubans have the right and the opportunity to dissent, freely organise and express their views. In this regard Cuba's polity does not include the institutional trappings sanctified in democratic theory: an electoral system in which different political parties present the electorate with alternative slates of potential representatives and programs, and all citizens are presented with a clear choice and are free to vote their preferences.

Nevertheless, the Cuban political system is arguably 'democratic' but in a different form, allowing all citizens to freely elect by secret ballot their choice of representatives to the organs of political power, but to do so in their workplaces and communities rather than via the mechanism of competing parties. It is even possible to argue that at the level of the institutions that connect society to the state the Cuban

---

[14] Some, like Susan Eckstein—and she is no ideologue but a serious scholar, albeit inclined to liberalism—would go so far as to argue that notwithstanding the trappings of 'popular power' the average or ordinary Cuban has no influence on public policy. Of course this is also certainly true in capitalist democracies such as the US, where the power of the occasional vote is no match for the power of money. Eckstein sees ordinary people having influence on public policy and over policymakers, but only in the form of what Scott in a different context described as 'everyday resistance'. The role of 'ordinary people', Eckstein opines, is '[u]nderestimated in Communist studies in general, including of Cuba'. As for Cuba '[e]ven though citizens were never entirely free to organize on their own or to express their points of view in any Communist Party-run regime, in none did they simply march to state orders. They have influenced policy implementation, if not policy formation, informally and indirectly: through, for example, foot-dragging, pilferage, desertion, black-market and sideline activity, absenteeism, and hoarding. They have done so in patterned ways shaped by their traditions and everyday experiences' (2003: xiv).

system provides a superior form of democracy in terms of the principles of representation, participation and accountability (Harnecker, 1979).[15]

At the level of political practice, however, we found evidence of a democratic deficit. This deficit takes the form of undue restrictions on dissent from the government line and to freely organise and express one's views on public policy and the underlying socialist system—the revolutionary process itself. Arguably, every political system has built-in mechanisms for controlling dissent, and places restrictions on the freedom to organise and the freedom of expression. However, indications are that Cuban authorities are overly sensitive and controlling in this regard. The legitimate and understandable concern for US-instigated subversion is clearly behind this over-sensitivity, but it appears that this concern also serves as a pretext for controlling dissent and limiting internal debate. Although this point is debateable (some view the threats from the US as sufficient cause) there does not seem to be a sufficient justification for or the need to prohibit or inhibit internal debate or open discussion about the system itself—to question socialism and the Revolution. The achievements of the Revolution, and the superior ethics of socialist human development, should suffice to contain any fundamental internal threats to the system. External threats are another matter.

---

[15] The institution of the OPP was first examined in a substantial and very sympathetic way by Marta Harnecker in her widely-read study *Cuba: Dictatorship or Democracy?* Some of the more recent literature, however, is less sympathetic and more critical of the OPP as a democratic institution. For example, the nomination process is relatively open but candidates are not permitted to present any kind of political platform or to campaign around any ideas (or to campaign at all: this would be grounds for immediate disqualification). Of course, this would be anathema for liberal democrats. Another issue has to do with the fact that although the PCC cannot participate in the electoral process in 1989, in one account about 70% of the deputies of the National Assembly were members of the PCC or the Union of Young Communists. But what this likely means is that PCC and UCJ members are the most actively engaged and committed members of the electorate, and likely to be chosen for office by community members or work fellows for this very reason.

CHAPTER NINE

IN SOLIDARITY: A FUNDAMENTAL PRINCIPLE OF SOCIALIST HUMANISM

> Solidarity in the heart of a people is impossible without solidarity among all peoples
>
> —Fidel Castro

To bring about a 'better society' and progress at the level of social welfare, the French revolutionaries called for freedom, equality and solidarity. The American revolutionaries similarly called for a system that would secure the right of each member of society the freedom to pursue the inalienable human right to freedom and the pursuit of happiness. To bring about progress so conceived the revolutionaries entrenched in the Constitution of the new State the formal equality of each individual in the face of the law and the eyes of God, and the democratic right of each individual to enjoy a number of fundamental human rights, including the freedom of expression and political organization, and to be protected in these rights. What the Constitution did not guarantee, however, was that these rights would be given and secured by the State under conditions of social solidarity, i.e. in conditions that are 'equal for all'. And this for good reason. The State was founded on the principle of private property in the means of social production, thus guaranteeing the legal right of the owners of property to freely dispose of it in their own economic interest. For this reason, the democratic states and capitalist economies—capitalist democracies—so constituted gave institutional form to the principle of freedom, or prioritized economic and political *freedom* over social equality and solidarity in the scale of values. In any case, the resulting system and subsequent regimes were democratic in form and class-based and divided, resulting in conditions of substantive social inequality in access to the means of social production and the distribution of the social product. Under these conditions social solidarity is simply not possible.[1]

---

[1] This fundamental point of principle was not understood by Michel Camdessus, Executive-Director at the the time of the IMF, when, on an official visit to Mexico

In societies that are divided by relations of class—and capitalist societies are necessarily class divided—the poor often live on islands that are separated from the non-poor by oceans of wealth and privilege. Under these conditions social solidarity cannot exist except in the dreams and minds of reformist social liberals such as Michel Camdessus, concerned with the destabilizing effects of class division but unwilling to propose the abolition of class. At most, what is proposed is the attenuation of the inevitable inequalities in social conditions, providing avenues of social mobility, and overcoming the class divide by convincing the poor that the existing system of institutions and policies also benefits them, providing opportunities and pathways out of their poverty.

Democracy as Social Solidarity

In the modern world of capitalist development and liberal democracy, and especially in the United States, social solidarity, in the words of Joseph Swartz (2009), is the 'forgotten sibling' among the family of democratic values—'liberty, equality and fraternity'—that suffused the democratic social revolutions from the French Revolution onwards. While schoolchildren in the US are taught that the American Revolution fought for the rights to 'life, liberty and the pursuit of happiness' (or 'property' according to John Locke) the less liberal individualist and more democratic collectivist (proto-socialist?) French Revolution spoke of 'liberty, equality and fraternity'. The concept of 'fraternity' or 'solidarity' (in gender neutral terms) implies that in the course of constructing the enterprise of creating a better form of society and a more human form of development, people develop a capacity for empathy and trust in their fellow beings—social solidarity, we would say today, or, as Che Guevara would have it, a 'love of humanity'.

In capitalist or other forms of class-based and divided societies governed by hierarchical norms of class and status, social obligations and duties are set by customary practice and cultural tradition. In contrast, in community-based societies, or those oriented towards communalism

---

under Ernesto Zedillo's Presidency he announced that the Fund's policy regime was not based on neoliberalism (belief in the free market), but rather on three pillars: the invisible hand of the market; the visible hand of the state; and 'social solidarity between the rich and the poor'.

or socialism, such obligations and duties are based on a culture of solidarity, which, in turn is based on a system in which relations and conditions are relatively egalitarian, shared equitably in the interest of democratic or social justice. In these communities and such relatively egalitarian societies, even in the welfare states and social liberal democracies of Europe, the polity collectively regulates the social relationships established by economic and social life (Schwartz, 2009: 27).

Thus, all democratic societies, at a minimum—with the United States a possible exception—are at least nominally committed to ensuring that no citizen is so destitute or socially marginalized that he or she cannot meet his or her basic needs or participate in political life. Much of the historic and on-going struggle between the democratic Left and the Right in the class-divided but 'advanced' capitalist societies has revolved around the question of the extent to which social rights (as opposed to economic freedoms or political rights) or public provision should constrain the nonegalitarian outcomes of a capitalist economy (and also an allegedly meritocratic 'modern' educational system). By means of political conflict (rather than abstract philosophical argument capitalist 'democracies' have developed social policies and institutions designed to cushion individuals from the risk and vicissitudes of the capitalist marketplace. Thus, even the most classically liberal or most illiberal of capitalist democracies—the United States—provides a minimal level of universal insurance against disability, unemployment, abject poverty (and hunger, if not homelessness) and old age. In the words of that compassionate conservative (and pragmatic liberal), UK Tory leader David Cameron, 'my government always looks after the elderly, the frail, the poorest in our country' (*New York Times*, May 17, 2010).

The ultimate democratic trust, Schwartz (2009: 27) argues (with particular reference to the US (and also the revolutionary France of the 18th century) 'resides in the sharing of the burden of bearing of arms to defend the nation'. But in the context of revolutionary socialist Cuba, it is a matter of defending 'la patria' from the machinations of US imperialism. As for international solidarity (and the right to human or social development)—the principle of which is written into the constitution of the Cuban state—the issue is support for the struggles of people all over the world against oppression and exploitation. Specifically, Article 12 of the Cuban Constitution states that '[t]he Republic of Cuba espouses the principles of anti-imperialism and internationalism'. And Section (d) of Article 12 adds that Cuba 'advocates the unity of all Third World countries in the face of the neocolonialist and imperialist policy which seeks to limit and subordinate the sovereignty of our peoples, and worsen the economic conditions of exploitation and oppression of the underdeveloped nations'.

Behind this principle of solidarity codified in the Constitution itself is the notion of the moral (and instrumental) duty and the readiness of all members of society (both in Cuba and the world) to ensure the wellbeing of the collectivity and to share more equitably in the product of collective economic enterprise. Political theorists have long debated whether such an impulse derives from a universal human inclination to aid those less fortunate than ourselves (charity) or from human engagement in activities that construct social bonds of mutual support among the members of societies 'on the road to economic and political integration for the attainment of true independence' (Cuba. The Constitution, Article 12d). The classic example of such an ethic is the shared burden of work symbolized by the trade union motto 'an injury to one is an injury to all'. A more contemporary example is found in subcomandante Marcos' declaration that no one is free while some people elsewhere remain oppressed. Fidel Castro himself in this connection declared that internationalism is integral to socialist development and that '[s]olidarity in the heart of a people is impossible without solidarity among all peoples'.

The concern for social solidarity is not just a matter of theoretical debate. In Cuba it is a matter of constitutional principle and political practice. At this level it is possible to discern major differences in the value placed on solidarity as a fundamental principle of social organization, and the institutionalization of this value as a matter of revolutionary consciousness—a *cultural* revolution, one might argue. A 'culture' is a complex of values and corresponding beliefs. For a value to be converted from an organizational principle into a tradition, it must take form as a belief that has been long-held, consented to by members of society and deeply entrenched in institutional practice. Lying somewhere between a tradition and a principle, a value suggests the kind of belief that if seriously challenged would overturn the prevailing worldview: something for which no law is needed because it would be freely enforced by social consensus.

Emile Durkheim, a founder of sociology as an academic discipline, argued that any social order is predicated on some form of social solidarity, or ties of mutual obligation and shared morality. Thus, he argued, even class-divided societies based on an extended division of labour and a high degree of individuation have a moral basis and are constituted as a moral order. Thus, the difference between inherently unequal class-divided societies (capitalism, for example) and those that are more egalitarian in form is not just in the mode of production and the associated social structure but in the prevalent form of organization—whether it is communal or associational in form.[2]

On this issue there is a long-standing sociological debate on the impact of modernization on the dominant form of social organization, and the finding that modernization generally brings about a transformation in the dominant form of social organization, replacing communal forms of organization based on norms of reciprocal exchange and a culture of social solidarity, with an associational-type organization and a modern form of (capitalist) society based on a rational calculus of shared self-interest and commercial transactions.

With reference to this view it could be argued that social solidarity as a value is a victim of modernization, the casualty of the great transformation of a precapitalist and traditional form of agrarian society into a modern industrial capitalist system. At the same time it is evident that certain political practices and forms of development can serve to revive the 'spirit of community' weakened by the forces of structural change. For example, the new paradigm of local development promoted by the theorists of 'another development' in the 1990s is predicated on the existence or the rebuilding of a culture of social solidarity in local communities. Whether communities in this sense— as people bound together by a culture of mutual obligation and social bonds—still exist or might be found is very much at issue (Durston, 1998). The key issue here is the penetration of capitalism in the countryside, with its inevitable solidarity-destroying class relations (Veltmeyer and O'Malley, 2001). But the entire thrust of current development thinking and practice is towards the institutionalization of community-based forms of local development based on the accumulation of 'social capital', the one asset that the poor are deemed to have in abundance and thus a potential source of participatory

---

[2] Solidarity as an organizational principle or value is seen by Schwartz (2009: 29) to originate within the fellow-feeling of particularist organizations such as the guilds of medieval or feudalist societies. In the modern world this fellow-feeling (or spirit of community) is found in rural or indigenous communities, self-help organizations with their basis in ethnic, immigrant, racial or gender solidarity, or in the antiglobalization movement of organizations formed in solidarity with people all over the world in their resistance and struggles against the dynamics of global capitalism.

development—empowering the rural poor to act for themselves in the quest to alleviate their poverty and sustain their livelihoods on the basis of a culture and economy of 'solidarity' (Razeto, 1988, 1993).

It is assumed by these theorists and practitioners that capitalism, rather than socialism, provides the system requirements for this 'development'. And in Bolivia, the advent to state power of Evo Morales, the political representative of a popular movement of indigenous communities, has led to a political project to create a solidarity-based national economy—to reconstruct the process of national development on a communalist model of social organization ('communalism is our political practice'). As to whether this development process can or will proceed on a capitalist or a socialist path is unclear. But what is clear—or what we argue in this chapter—is that social solidarity is a fundamental principle of organization and human development for the Cuban Revolution.

Solidarity within the Revolution

One of the major differences between capitalist and socialist regimes of human development is in the fundamental value attached to social solidarity and a corresponding revolutionary consciousness. Human development in the UNDP model and the associated discourse is predicated on the value and organizational principle of *equality*, conceived of as a matter of 'opportunity' or 'equity'; and *freedom*, conceived of in the same terms, i.e. as the capacity for individual self-realization. For the Cuban revolutionaries, however, the concepts of equality and freedom only acquire meaning with the implementation of policies designed to assure social solidarity—the identification and mutual support of all members of society viewed and treated as equals. As for social solidarity or cohesion it is predicated on substantive equality within a relatively egalitarian society, i.e. egalitarian relations and an equality of social condition, equal access to society's productive resources and opportunities for collective development, and an equitable sharing of the product of collective labour. Inequality in this regard when structured (i.e. based on institutionalised practice) is fundamentally destructive of social solidarity or cohesion, as concluded by some ECLAC economists, after reviewing Latin America's long and 'bitter experience of inequality', that 'it is time for equality' (ECLAC, 2010).

'Growth', the authors of this ECLAC study argue (with reference to the dominant economic development strategies pursued over the past five decades), 'has a negative effect on social inclusion and cohesion when its benefits...[are] concentrated.... As the expectations gap widens, social conflict increases and erodes the legitimacy of governments, thereby jeopardizing the sustainability of growth.' They add; 'A society that shares out educational opportunities and access to formal employment in a more egalitarian way [i.e. not as a commodity traded on the labour market] will have a workforce with greater capabilities and will optimize both the use of those capabilities to make progress with...the use of fiscal resources for productive investment and social protection' (ECLAC, 2010: 41). The authors conclude from their study of the 'inequality predicament' that '[a] society which universalizes timely access to healthcare and nutrition will reduce the costs associated with disease and malnutrition, from lower productivity to sickness-related expenditure'. Furthermore, '[a] society with a higher level of equity will...incur fewer costs related to...the quality of democracy' (ibid.). They could have added, which they did in another part of the study without being explicit, that social equality is a fundamental principle of human development.

ECLAC theorists came to the conclusion that 'it is time for equality' after five decades of 'bitter experience with inequality' under conditions of state-led and then market-friendly national 'development'. The Cuban revolutionaries, however, came to this very same conclusion at the very beginning of this development process, as the result—they would, and did, argue—of the revolutionary struggle itself. Thus the decision was made very early in Cuba's revolutionary process to give the land back to the tiller and to socialise the means of production; to secure a relative equality of income distribution via the mechanism of a relatively flat pay scale for different categories of work and social contributions; to universalise access to essential public services regarding human welfare and development, and to 'share... out educational opportunities and access to formal employment'.

International Solidarity: Human Development as the Export of Human Capital

'Before focusing hopeful eyes on the future, you must be grounded in reality. And the reality of international cooperation is fundamentally perverse, and that's why it must be changed' (Ximena de la Barra, International Consultant, United Nations). 'This,' Fidel Castro has declared, 'is the battle of solidarity against egoism'.

The Preamble of Cuba's Constitution includes a commitment to 'proletarian internationalism, on the fraternal friendship, aid, cooperation and solidarity of the peoples of the world'. In Cuba's 2004 report to the United Nation's Millennium Development Goals, adopted in 2000 by 189 heads of state, it demonstrated that is had met three of the eight humanitarian goals designed towards eliminating extreme poverty by 2015, and that it was on track with the rest. Cuba's foreign policy is, in fact, based upon the eighth goal: 'Develop a global partnership for development'.

In 2006, 25,000 of the nation's 70,000 doctors and several thousand other medical personnel were serving in 68 countries, and a similar number of teachers and technicians were serving the cause of Cuban internationalism in a total of 100 countries. In 2008, 38,524 Cuban healthcare workers (including 17,697 doctors) served this cause in 73 countries (Saney, 2009). Of these 29,594 (76.8%) did so in the health sector.

In addition to this export of 'human capital' via these 'internationalist missions', 27,235 young people from 120 countries are now studying in Cuba, 80.6% of them with the intent of becoming general practitioners in the areas of greatest need in their countries. Since 1961, Cuba has graduated 45,352 medical students from 129 countries (66.4% from sub-Saharan Africa and 19.2% from 18 Latin American countries).

Cuba is also building a medical university in Venezuela, and over the last three decades it has built such centres in Equatorial Guinea, Ethiopia, Uganda, Ghana, Gambia, Yemen, Guinea Bissau Guyana and Haiti.

In addition to providing healthcare and education, thousands of Cubans are also working abroad to assist 24 of the most underdeveloped nations with technical advice and aid to HIV victims. In this connection, in June 2001, the UN General Assembly met to discuss AIDS and Cuba offered doctors, teachers, psychologists, and other specialists needed to assess and collaborate with the campaigns to prevent AIDS and other illnesses; diagnostic equipment and kits necessary for the basic prevention programs and retrovirus treatment for 30,000 patients—without charge, proposing to pay the salary of these professionals in its national currency. But under pressure from the US the offer was rejected—'democracy' over health being the issue. Nevertheless, eight African and six Latin American countries accepted Cuba's AIDS intervention project, offering education programs and treatment of 200,000 patients, and the training of half a million health workers.

The export of 'human capital', as the Cuban government characterizes these missions, is generally provided to individual recipients free of charge. In most cases, however, the states that receive aid from Cuba do pay in some form such as bartering oil and other resources and manufactured products.

Cuba's commitment to serving the poor, the sick and victims of natural catastrophes is a glaring contrast to the typical response of the US government—even to the human disaster caused in August 2005 by Hurricane Katrina in New Orleans and Mississippi and Alabama. In this case Cuba immediately offered to help save survivors with a specially formed Henry Reeves International Team of Medical Specialists in Disasters and Epidemics. Fifteen hundred medical professionals committed themselves to assist Katrina's victims, each equipped with 50 pounds of medicines—a total of 36 tons of medical supplies—and field hospital equipment. These missionaries had an average of ten years clinical experience and had served in 43 countries. But the George W. Bush regime did not even have the decency to reply to the humanitarian offer. Instead it 'absorbed the loss' of 1,800 people, who died simply for lack of aid and treatment (Petras and Veltmeyer, 2010).

Henry Reeves teams were instead sent to aid Pakistani earthquake victims and Guatemalans affected by Hurricanes Stan and Wilma. Most of the 2,500 doctors and paramedics served half-a-year in Pakistan. By April 2006, they had treated 1.5 million patients—73% of patients hit by the disaster—performed 13,000 surgical operations, trained 660 Pakistani medics and turned over the 32 field hospitals they brought with them. The Cuban government also donated 241 tonnes of medicines and surgical instruments, and 275 tonnes of hospital equipment.

The Cubans were most noted for taking on the toughest assignments, climbing mountainous areas and working with the poorest of the poor who had never been visited by a doctor. Dictator Pervez Musharraf, a close ally and friend of Bush, officially thanked Cuba and acknowledged that it had sent more disaster aid than any other country, including the United States.

In 2006, Henry Reeves volunteers numbered 3,000. They were required to speak at least two languages and be competent in epidemiology. The mission's namesake was taken from the US Civil War veteran who served in Cuba's first war of independence from Spain. Reeves, a New Yorker, earned the rank of brigadier general. He died in battle, in 1876, after having fought in 400 battles. 'Recognition of Cuban expertise in disaster preparedness and response' promoted the UN Development Program and Association of Caribbean States to select Havana as headquarters for the new Cross Cultural Network for Disaster Risk Reduction, which is to facilitate regional cooperation in disaster management, wrote MEDICC Review, summer 2005.

In 2004, Cuban doctors began to apply what their associate scientists had created, a simple surgery that cures many forms of blindness within two to three days. By mid-2006, a quarter million people in 24 countries had been cured of cataracts, retractile disorders, corneal glaucoma, myopias and strabismus. Cuba had 14,000 doctors working in poor areas, and many conservative Venezuelan doctors complained of the free competition but refused to attend to the poor themselves. One hundred thousand Venezuelans regained their eyesight in the first year of Cuba's Operation Miracle program.

Fidel Castro and Hugo Chávez, in this context, agreed to provide funds, medicines and medical personnel to treat those suffering from these eye afflictions caused by malnutrition. Over one million Latin Americans are affected by this disease annually, and the two governments planned to operate on that many patients each year over a decade. In this Cuban medical missionaries carrying backpacks with hospital equipment and medicines have reached into the most remote areas and marginalized communities in the far corners of Latin America to perform the surgeries. 'The world has never witnessed anything equal to this health program', commented Ralph Gonsalves, Prime Minister of San Vicente-Granada, upon landing in Havana in 2006. Gonsalves came to thank Cuba for having cured 1,000 blind citizens in yet another foreign aid program—Operation Miracle. In the case of San Vicente-Granada, only a few personnel could arrive at a time in small aircraft since there is no international airport for larger craft. Thus Cuba and Venezuela agreed to build one through their ALBA cooperative trade pact, and tens of thousands of blind patients not treated where they live were transported to Havana for the surgeries. This program was also funded through ALBA. The largest numbers came from Venezuela but they also came from the entire continent and the Caribbean. And poor blind people in the US are also eligible.

Since the beginning of the Revolution, Cuba's foreign policy has been oriented to assist all Third World countries, especially in Latin America, Caribbean and Africa, to escape foreign domination, which, the Cubans argue, keeps people in poverty, ignorance and ill health. In this connection it is probably the only country in the world whose foreign policy is governed by the UNDP's dictum that '[i]nternational cooperation...should be viewed not as an act of charity but as an expression of social justice, equity and human solidarity'.

La Patria Es Humanidad: *Internationalism as a Reservoir of Socialist Values*

In a review of Cuba's extraordinary record of solidarity with the emancipatory struggles of people in other parts of the world, Saney (2009) notes that 'Cuba's internationalism has been treated as epiphenomenal to the trajectory of the Cuban Revolution rather than as a central component'. In this epiphenomenal perspective Cuba's internationalist missions, whether medical, educational, or military, are 'divorced from the domestic sphere', ignoring their critical function in consolidating socialist consciousness. But, as Saney emphasises, 'the role of internationalism cannot be ...underestimated. It is a[n important] reservoir of socialist values and revolutionary fervour'—and as such a vital connection to the homeland of the Cuban Revolution (*La Patria*), namely, humanity as a whole (*la humanidad*).

The fundamental role of international solidarity in maintaining revolutionary consciousness can be traced out in the history of military missions that preceded the contemporary program of educational and medical missions (*misiones*) in the health and educational brigades sent to Africa, Asia, and Latin America—missions formed to the purpose of lending support to the struggles for national liberation in other parts of the global south. From its inception, the revolutionary government extended civilian and military assistance to numerous countries,[3] the most dramatic example being the struggle waged in Angola against South Africa's racist regime. Cuba's longest and largest internationalist

---

[3] They include Chile, Algeria, Yemen.
For a full summary of this period, see Kirk & Erisman (2009) "Introduction".

mission, it lasted from 1975 to 1991 and involved 330,000 participants and 2,000 deaths. The Angolan mission has assumed legendary status on the island, holding a privileged position in the pantheon of Cuba's internationalism. The sheer numbers involved in the contemporary internationalist effort highlight the continuing significance of internationalism for the Cuban Revolution.

While there is a growing literature on the various internationalist missions of the Cuban Revolution (e.g. ¡Salud!, 2009; Kirk and Erisman, 2009), there has been little discussion of their connection to the consolidation of the revolutionary project of independence and the construction of socialism—an important part of the ideological and ideational struggle to build socialism. Most of the discussion of Cuba's internationalism as official government policy and practice under the Revolution focuses on its impact in the international arena and its role in meeting the nation's foreign policy objectives—a means of revolutionary self-defense. In this connection, both Fidel Castro and Che Guevara emphasized internationalism as part of the 'inescapable necessity' of 'globaliz[ing] the revolutionary struggle against the United States'. However, it is evident that Cuba's international solidarity missions over the years, as argued by Cantón Navarro (2000: 246) and as Fidel himself makes clear in diverse allusions and speeches, were conducted not in the expectation of some financial or political return—as is sometimes argued, an investment in the goodwill and support of other countries for Cuba in various international arenas and forums—but as a matter of principle, a fundamental commitment to the value attached by the Revolution to solidarity. This point, and the significance of Cuban selfless internationalism as a source of inspiration for other revolutionary struggles, is expressed most clearly by Nelson Mandela in his state visit to Cuba in July 1991, his first visit overseas after his release from prison and made at a 'decisive hour when the Cuba people have resolved to defend at all costs the revolution, socialism and the homeland' (Cuba, Council of State, 1991: 72).

In Mandela's words: 'The Cuban people hold a special place in the hearts of the people of Africa. The Cuban internationalists have made a contribution to African independence, freedom and justice unparalleled for its principled and selfless character...We admire the sacrifices of the Cuban people in maintaining their independence and sovereignty in the face of a vicious imperialist-orchestrated campaign to destroy the impressive gains made in the Cuban Revolution' (1991: 18).

A FUNDAMENTAL PRINCIPLE OF SOCIALIST HUMANISM   249

The gloss provided by Mandela on Cuba's heroic Angola mission is a clear testament to the inspirational value of selfless internationalism as a socialist ethic, a value that some analysts (Petras, for example) argue needs to be balanced against the more fundamental value of ensuring a better quality of life for all Cubans. However, looking at this internationalism from the inside as it were—from inside Cuba—points to another feature: the role of internationalism in consolidating *la conciencia*, or revolutionary consciousness (see previous discussion in Chapter 5). From this perspective international solidarity is not, as suggested by some analysts, at the expense of domestic solidarity.

Saney elaborates on this point as follows: 'Cuban society...is suffused with the recollections of the *internacionalistas*, and these recollections [have become] part of the Cuban meta-narrative. The purchase of the war in Angola on Cuban popular consciousness is indicated by the popularity of books on the subject, which tend to sell out very quickly and are often very difficult to find' (2009: 116).[4]

There have also been several very popular documentaries. *La repuesta a la escalada de Sud-Africa*, which dealt with the final battles in Angola in 1988, was rebroadcast several times by popular demand. In 2007 a 22-episode television series on the internationalist mission in Angola, *La epopeya de Angola*, gripped the attention of Cubans. In addition to the books and documentaries, there have been numerous commemorations. The main organizer of many of these events has been the *Asociación de Combatientes de la Revolución* (Association of the Combatants of the Revolution), founded in 1993 and made up of those who fought in the revolutionary war, against the Escambray insurgency in the 1960s, and in foreign campaigns. One of its primary objectives is to preserve the historical memory of Cuba's various internationalist military missions.

In November 2005 Fidel Castro addressed a major event marking the thirtieth anniversary of Cuba's military intervention in Angola (Castro Ruz, 2005a). On March 24, 2008, Raúl Castro presided over a

---

[4] The considerable output of such books is indicated by this far from complete sample identified by Saney: *Secretos de generale* (Baez, 1996); *Al encuentro de los desconocidos* (del Valle, 2005); *Angola: Relatos desde las alturas* (González, 2003); *La guerra de Angola* (Editora Politica, 1989); *La paz de Cuito Cuanavale: Documentos de un proceso* (Editora Politica, 1989); *Angola: Un abril como girón* (Ortiz, 1979); *Angola: Fin del mito de los mercenarios* (Valdes, 1976); *Angola: Saeta del norte* (Fernández and Garciga, 2005); *Operación Carlota: Pasajes de una epopeya* (Díaz, 2006); *Cangamba* (Blandino, 2006); and *Victoria al Sur de Angola* (Campos, 2006).

ceremony that celebrated the internationalist mission in Angola as a defining moment in the trajectory of the Cuban Revolution (Núñez Betancourt, 2008). Every year in Havana on May 4, the *Organización de Solidaridad de los Pueblos de África, Asia y América Latina* (Organization of Solidarity with the Peoples of Africa, Asia, and Latin America) organizes an event commemorating the 1978 massacre of hundreds of Namibian refugees by South African troops in the Angolan town of Kassinga. This event is attended by representatives from Angola, Namibia, South Africa, and Cuba and receives wide coverage in the Cuban media. A central theme of this annual event is the Cuban contribution to the defeat of the apartheid regime.

It was during the crisis of the 1990s, Saney (2009: 116–117) suggests, that internationalism had its most decisive impact *inside* Cuba. 'As the Cuban Revolution was caught in the maelstrom that ensued from the collapse of the Soviet Union and the Eastern bloc, its very legitimacy and relevance were called into question. The ideological pressures on the island were intense. Internationalism was one of the factors that contributed to the resilience of the Revolution, particularly Cuba's role in the defeat of the apartheid regime.'[5]

Cubans took considerable pride in their country's victory. This pride was not only expressed by soldiers, who often spoke about 'returning to Cuba with victory in our hands'. Samuel Fure Davis, who was in Havana at the time, was quoted by Saney (interview, May 4, 2007) to have said: 'There was lots of excitement about the battle. Word of victory was received with elation. I remember vividly the celebrations of the victory'. Cubans took pride not only in their victory but in the altruism that characterized the Angolan mission. Nacyra Gomez stated, 'Some do not understand our presence in a country out of solidarity. We are not there to kill but to defend another people, to fight for others and to die for others' (Bravo, 1990). Poignantly, one mother said that she was able to cope with the pain of her son's death only because he 'did something for others, and especially for Africa' (Bravo, 1990).

But the Cuban armed forces returned victorious. The status of the Cuba armed forces in the popular consciousness, already high, was

---

[5] During a series of battles in Angola in 1987–1988, Cuba's Fuerzas Armadas Revolucionario (Revolutionary Armed Forces—FAR) decisively defeated the South African armed forces at the town of Cuito Cuanavale, altering the balance of power in the region and forcing Pretoria to negotiate with the antiapartheid forces. This eventually led to the dissolution of apartheid (Saney, 2006).

thus enhanced. As Saney notes, their high standing among the people was important during the Special Period as the military assumed an expanded role throughout the economy and society. It was one of the principal organizations mobilized to preserve ideological and political unity. The values of self-sacrifice and social solidarity that were the leadership's watchwords in the early 1990s were the values that the FAR embodied: values crystallized in the internacionalistas, who had operationalized them in Angola and now reinforced them in Cuba.

As Saney (2009: 118) notes in his reflections on the domestic impact of Cuba's costly Angola mission no political or ideological crisis developed. The contribution of the island's internationalist record (especially in Angola) to avoiding just such a crisis should not be underestimated. As the revolution was being portrayed as a relic with no meaningful role in the world, Cuba's crucial contribution to the South African transformation was a potent counter. It fortified belief in the Revolution's relevance and legitimacy in a world that was radically different from the one in which it was born and had developed. Perhaps the most poignant deployment of internationalism in defense of the Cuban Revolution was Fidel Castro's 2003 May Day speech. The context for the speech was the intense criticism of Cuba for the arrest of 75 opposition figures and the execution of three armed hijackers in March and April 2003, when several prominent intellectuals and personalities publicly broke with and condemned the revolution. In response, Castro delivered a speech that encompassed the island's extensive internationalist missions, particularly its assistance to national liberation movements. The war in Angola was given special attention. The speech amounted to a comprehensive presentation of the revolution's curriculum vitae; it was a riposte to those who condemned and dismissed it. Thus, what the Cuban Revolution had done—and continued to do—on a world scale was presented as unequivocally establishing its legitimacy and validity

Conclusion

Human development in the discourse of liberalism, embodied in the UNDP's *Human Development Report*, is predicated on a belief in the need for institutional reform in the direction of freedom and equality—in the institutionalized value of freedom understood as the right and capacity of individual members of society to flourish in the pursuit of their opportunities for self-realization. Freedom and equality, however, in a socialist context only makes sense in terms of the value attached to solidarity.

In socialist discourse, human development is based on the belief for more radical change, a fundamental reorganization in the direction of a 'new man and woman', a culture of social and international solidarity brought about in a revolutionary process.

This is to say, in the hierarchy of socialist values solidarity is preeminent, defining the meaning that socialists attach to freedom and equality. The value attached to solidarity as an organizational principle is embodied in the history of the Cuban Revolution, evidenced by the socialist conception of human development as an on-going revolutionary process. In this there is a fundamental difference between the Cuban Revolution and the Russian and Chinese—in the historic process through which socialism in some form was actualised in these countries in the 20th Century. Both the Russian and the Chinese Revolutions, like the French Revolution in the 18th Century, are generally regarded as a *social revolution* in that the process entailed a restructuring of the nation at the social as well as political level—of the society as well as the state. And the organizing principle of reorganization was equality—the socialization of production and an egalitarian distribution of the social product. But the revolution was not on-going, nor was it based on a systematic overhaul of the cultural foundations of the society and polity—creating a new man and woman, a new society based on social solidarity. There was a belated attempt in China, in the 1960s, to bring about a 'cultural revolution', but as in Russia the people were not engaged in the process as active participants under conditions of freedom. The hallmark of the Cuban Revolution, a fundamental defining feature, was its concern for human development under conditions of freedom, equality and solidarity.

PART III

A SOCIALIST ISLAND IN A SEA OF CAPITALISM

CHAPTER TEN

HUMAN DEVELOPMENT IN AN ERA OF GLOBALIZATION

In the mid-1980s, at a time when most of Latin America was in crisis and under the sway of the new 'economic model' (neoliberal globalization), Cuba's engine of economic growth slowed down and began to sputter, leading the government to stay the course of socialist development but to 'rectify' its policy stance and adjust its human development strategy. However, this 'rectification' campaign failed to turn things around or to stave of an impending crisis, which resulted from conditions well beyond the capacity of the Cuban government to control. Behind these conditions were political conditions in the Soviet Union and the socialist bloc in Eastern Europe that led to the collapse of socialism in this part of the world system, and with it the near collapse of the Cuban economy, By 1991 the output of the Cuban economy dropped by as much as 35%, creating conditions of a major production crisis that threatened the survival of the Revolution. Other dimensions of this production and development crisis, dubbed by the regime a Special Period, included pressures from the US which chose the moment as an opportunity to tightening the noose of its economic blockade.

In the vortex of these 'developments', Cuba entered a 'special period' in its development process. This chapter reviews the major dynamics and dimensions of this process in order to explain how Cuba managed to survive the challenge to the revolutionary project of the external threats to it and the structural adjustments that the regime was forced to make to the forces of neoliberal globalization. In other parts of Latin America and the world 'human development in the era of globalization' (Boyce et al., 2006) was studied with reference to the post-Washington Consensus and the 'new development paradigm'. In Cuba, however, the human development project needs to be understood as a combined effort of the government and ordinary Cubans to adjust to the forces of change unleashed by the capitalist development process while defending the hard-earned gains and achievements of the Revolution.

Cuba in the Vortex of a Crisis: The Revolution under Siege

The 1990s, according to Mesa-Lago (2000: 289ff.), saw the fourth major shift in the country's basic development strategy since the successful conquest of state power in 1959. At this point the ideological pendulum that Mesa-Lago uses to mark these shifts in economic organization and strategy had moved closer to the market than ever before, with the opening and paralleled concessions to foreign capitalist investment, trade and technology. These actions, taken in reluctant response to the worst crisis experienced by the Revolution, clearly eroded the foundations of Cuban socialism laid over four decades of struggle and public action: the socialization of the means of production, an appreciable equality of social conditions, full employment and universal free access to essential social services. Some foreign 'experts'—'many', according to Mesa-Lago, and 'probably a good part of the Cuban people'—questioned whether the Revolution and socialism are 'still alive or dead on the island' (2000: 289). However, the leaders—and many other observers and analysts, it might be added—'nevertheless insist[ed] that such dramatic changes do not constitute a transition to capitalism, but undesired albeit necessary tactical steps to save both socialism and crucial revolutionary gains'. This section of the chapter will focus on this issue and seek to assess the truth of the matter.

The conditions that led to this phase of the Revolution are diverse. *First,* the Rectification Process (RP) had failed to arrest a trend towards a slowdown of the economy after five years of rapid growth in the early 1980s. In fact, according to Mesa-Lago the RP was responsible for this 'fiasco'. However, here he ignores the fact that other 'socialist' countries were undergoing the same slowdown without anything like the RP. *Second*, the Food Program, a keystone of the RP, was predicated on continued aid from and trade with the USSR and the COMECON countries, but by 1993 Fidel was forced to admit that 'all was lost' on this front. *Third,* the collapse of socialism in the USSR and Eastern Europe, the dissolution of the former and the disappearance of CMEA, led to a drastic reduction of trade with former allies and a disastrous end to crucial oil deliveries on which both industry and transportation was highly dependent. *Fourth*, the collapse of socialism and trade with the socialist bloc led to severe scarcities in Cuba of foodstuffs, fuel, fertilizers, chemicals, spare parts needed for agricultural and industrial production, provoking drastic cuts in transportation services, industry and mining and some agricultural activities. *Fifth,* the enactment of the Cuban Democracy Act (the Torricelli Law) in 1992 and, particularly, the Helms-Burton Act (1996) tightened the noose of the US embargo, rendered more effective in its aim at strangling the Cuban economy precisely because of the lack of aid from and trade with the socialist bloc countries. Under these conditions, the leadership and the country faced a disastrous collapse of the economy, an estimated 35% fall in production and with it the very survival of socialism in any form. This situation was described by the leadership as a 'special period' of extraordinary challenges, forcing on the country and a most reluctant regime the need for a major 'structural adjustment' to the new world order of neoliberal globalization (Lara, 1999; Monreal, 2001).

Faced with the desperate need of the small island economy to reinsert itself into the market of the world capitalist system, a few Cuban economists in 1990 began to consider market-friendly oriented reform as the lesser of two evils (the collapse of socialism being the second). There was an intensive internal and largely unpublicized debate (see below) about the possibility of combining a socialist institutional framework with the market, which, in any case, was not exclusive of and limited to capitalism. In fact, it was evident that the issue was not whether the market would have to be restored but to what degree, in what form and under what conditions—how to embed the market in a socialist system without provoking forces and conditions that could render socialism asunder and threaten the revolutionary process.

Most Cuban economists, policymakers and technicians, understandably enough had serious reservations about the 'market mechanism', derived not only from their clear understanding of the dynamics of capitalist development and its foundation in greed and possessive individualism, but the adverse consequences of market reform as in the Soviet Union and Eastern Europe. At the same time, it was recognized that the market and the private sector do not equate to capitalism—that in eliminating the market and the private sector the government had, to a degree, thrown out the baby (the market) with the bathwater (capitalism); and that the market and the private sector could as well be harnessed to socialism as to capitalism. The problem was to find the right formula—resolve the crisis while holding capitalism at bay, preserving the socialist achievements of the Revolution. Of particular concern was to prevent the tearing of the Revolution's advances in health and education, the laboriously constructed safety net and welfare programs; and, most importantly, to prevent the breakdown of the fabric of social equality that had kept the Cubans together in support of the revolutionary process and a commitment to socialism. This was to be a challenge of a lifetime; and an analysis of how it was met—how Cuba managed to preserve socialism and the achievements in human development—is a major aim and purpose of this volume.

How Far to Go in the Direction of the Market?

At the time of the onset of the 'special period' of war in peacetime the chief stumbling block to the reversion to the market and market-oriented reform appeared to be—at least to close observers and analysts like Mesa-Lago—Fidel's opposition to the type of reform implemented in China and Vietnam (economic liberalization plus strong political control), which clearly placed both countries on a capitalist path notwithstanding continued lip-service to 'socialism' or 'communism'. In a number of speeches from 1990 to 1992 Fidel Castro rejected any move towards privatization, even of small noncapitalist enterprises; contracts between state farms and factories with families and groups of workers; free farmers' markets or self-employed small owner-operated businesses or street vendors. Indeed he insisted that the Revolution would resist the overtures and siren song of foreign capital and continue along a socialist path, the path of further socialization and state enterprise. In this vein he criticised those individuals and groups within Cuba who were 'sceptical', 'disaffected', 'critical', 'defeatists' and 'cowards', not to mention (in regard to proponents of market reform) 'imperialist puppets', 'pseudo-revolutionaries', 'fifth columnists' and 'traitors'. As late as April 1992, in the throes of a deep production crisis, he publicly stated:

'[Some] think that the problems [we have] are the results of stupid acts committed by ... cadres ... [and that we and they] do not understand anything about the market economy...[But we] must engage in all out war against those who ignore the facts...True revolutionaries never surrender, never sell out, never betray. That is for cowards, traitors and opportunists. None of us want that trash that [capitalists] are offering us. We prefer any sacrifice, any fate to that of capitalism.

Even so, the crisis was of such magnitude and depth that the government had to launch an emergency adjustment program. The government, it would appear from a review of the debates leading up the reform process, also reluctantly began to accept the idea that the resolution of the crisis would necessitate a carefully controlled 'opening' to foreign investment and a strategy of promoting foreign tourism as a means of earning for the country crucially needed reserves in hard currency, even though this strategy would undoubtedly bring all sorts of problems for the Revolution.

The fourth PCC Congress in 1991 ratified the RP (Rectification Program) and FP (Food Program), even though neither was particularly successful or could even be said to have failed. At the same time, under conditions of the time—and after broad consultation (see the discussion on workers' parliaments below) it approved a more flexible foreign investment policy. A constitutional amendment in 1992 also made possible the creation of mixed enterprises and joint ventures with the participation of foreign investors, but neither this amendment or the new foreign investment policy were sufficient or worked to stop a deepening of the crisis.

Several events in the summer of 1993, convinced the government—Fidel Castro, in the perception of Mesa-Lago, who totally ignores the popular consultative process leading up to the economic reform policy—of the need to introduce domestic market reforms in addition to the external opening: (1) a 39% drop in sugar production costing the state US$ 700 million in lost export revenues; (2) continuous production declines in other sectors both in agriculture, mining and industry; (3) a severe shortage of fuel that forced the closing down of more factories, sugar mills and transportation, and resulted in long electricity black- and brown-outs; (4) a huge budgetary deficit and excess money in circulation; a boom in the black market and a rapid devaluation of the currency, all of which created serious production disincentives and labour problems (Mesa-Lago, 2000: 292).

At this point a general consensus was achieved among political leaders, economists and technocrats—and the general population after an extended series of open debates both behind closed doors and in workplaces, and neighbourhood communities across the island—in what have aptly been termed 'workers' parliaments' (see below on the political dynamics of these parliaments as a form of 'public action'). The policy and political hard-liners, led by Fidel Castro, in this debate and resulting consensus advocated and argued for a cautious and gradual minimal reform approach. They opposed deeper-cutting reforms that might undo the Revolution's major achievements at the level of equality and equity, and indeed possibly provoke a political chain reaction and a collapse similar to what occurred in the Soviet Union and Eastern Europe (sceptical observers of these internal debates inclined to the latter interpretation). The second position, held by a sizeable albeit loose group of academics and technocrats, relatively young (mostly in their forties and fifties, and many trained or educated abroad) and without political power, as it turned out was supported by many workers in their 'parliaments'.

This group advocated a 'mixed economy' and pushed for a more comprehensive 'structural' reform that would get to the 'roots of the problems'. Specifically, they recommended: (i) ending the overwhelming predominance of the state in ownership of the means of social production in favour of a more balanced combination of state, cooperative and private ownership; (ii) replacing the use of central planning with a state regulated market; (iii) competition for capital and other resources, and the allocation of these resources by means of mixed system of state and market mechanisms; (iv) an income distribution that avoids both extreme egalitarianism and extreme inequality, which, in practice would mean setting the prices of consumer goods above the cost of production (ending state subsidies), material incentives and some degree of profit-making, rewarding workers according to their productivity, skill and effort—and, of course, social assistance to the needy; and (v) the retention, by the government, of enough power to promote basic economic and social development and secure a relative 'equity' in the distribution of the social product among different groups and individuals across the entire population.

These reforms meant combining the workings of a regulated market with an 'authoritative' allocation of resources to different factors of production: a strong and effective state committed to 'equity' rather than socialist 'egalitarianism' but decentralized to allow for the workings of a dynamic private sector as well as the popular participation in local development (which, of course was *not* a feature of social democratic forms of socialism). No one in this group advocated a full restoration of free market capitalism but rather a mixed system somewhere between socialism and capitalism along the lines perhaps of a Scandinavian-type welfare state/social democracy, a Chinese-Vietnam type reform, or even the 'post-Washington Consensus' on the need for 'greater balance between the state and the market' (González, 1992; Carranza, Gutiérrez and Monreal, 1995).

In the public debate, Fidel made reference to this group in the following terms: 'There are 1,000 political economic schools now…and

[each] has a plan or formula for solving our economic problems.... But they did not go to Harvard where capitalist economics is taught. They went over there [the Soviet Union and Eastern Europe]...and I ask myself: How can we use socialist economics in our situation?' (Mesa-Lago, 2000: 293). However, when a number of foreign economists (of 'diverse ideological orientations', according to Mesa-Lago but in fact all committed to neoliberalism) invited into the country in 1993-1994 to give their opinions and advice essentially and unanimously gave similar if not the same advice—deepen the market reforms—the government softened its tone and began to change its policy line.[1]

Yielding to the economic crisis but lacking a viable alternative, the government in August 1993 introduced a series of market-oriented reforms: (i) the legalisation of the possession of hard currency (including remittances from Cubans living abroad) and opening state 'dollar shops' to the local population; (ii) authorization of specific types of self-employment; (iii) transformation of state farms into a new type of cooperative and granting small land parcels to families; (iv) the reintroduction of free agricultural markets as well as artisan markets; (v) fiscal measures to reduce the budget deficit such as new taxes, increased utility rates and some cuts in state subsidies and other pubic expenditures (not in essential social services, however), and a rise in the price of non-essential consumer goods; (vi) creation of a 'convertible' peso and the opening of foreign exchange agencies; (vii) a new foreign investment law with incentives for foreign capital, and the creation of free trade zones.

Although these policies were subjected to diverse restrictions, regulations and state controls, by 1994-1995 they seemed to have stemmed the tide of economic decline, reduced the fiscal deficit and excess

---

[1] These economists, neoliberals all despite Mesa-Lago's characterization of them as 'ideologically diverse', included Jude Waninski, a founder of 'Reaganomics'; Carlos Solchaga, Spain's former Minister of Economics in Felipe Gonzalez's socialist government; and several IMF officials—all of whom could have been expected to argue in favour of neoliberal market reforms. Also in 1994 an MA program in market or capitalist economics was offered by Carleton University at the University of Havana. Although very few outside those involved in the faculty exchange deemed this program to be a 'success', unlike a subsequent MA program offered by the Public Administration program of Carleton University (the professors of which had more of a socialist or social democratic orientation focused on Keynesian economics and the welfare state) the program did introduce economics students at the university and government officials to capitalist economics.

money in circulation, and attracted some foreign capital from Canada and Europe. By mid-1995 the government appeared to have a strong hold on the economic situation and the pace of reform began to slow down.

Grappling with Inequality

The Special Period marked a radical change in the relatively egalitarian distribution of individual and household incomes. First, the pay scale for work, which determined the socioeconomic status and standards of living of the vast majority of Cubans, was allowed to widen, leading to a widening of income levels for state workers. Secondly, the average income of self-employed workers increased at a faster rate than the incomes of state wage earners, and the opportunities to earn or receive income by other means (such as productivity incentives) increased. Thirdly, the introduction of a dollarized economy in relation to tourism, with wages paid and earnings, including tips, received in dollars, unhinged the existing structure of the work-income relation, creating a dual or segmented labour market and a significant new source of growing social inequalities, excluding of large 'population segments' (paid only in pesos) from new consumer goods markets (Togores, 1999). Fourthly, according to Espina (1999), changing conditions and the new government policy generated a 'restratification' process, resulting in a polarisation of incomes to the extreme of generating a 'worker elite' at one pole and a substantive category of 'income poor' (the impoverishment of vast social sectors) at the other. And fifthly, the collapse of exports produced a major strain on the government's capacity to fully fund its social and human development programs. Even though reportedly not one school or clinic was closed down there is no doubt about the erosion and quantitative and qualitative weakening of social services provision, and also a serious decline in the monetary value (or basic needs coverage) of the ration card (Nerey and Brismart, 1999).

An Economic Income-Class Analysis of Inequality

The structure of income distribution resulting from these changed conditions in the occupational class structure is presented with available statistics in Table 7. The Table provides a statistical representation of the social structure of income distribution in 1995 in the depth of the country's worst economic crisis, which threatened the very pillars of the Revolution' as a planned program for sustainable human development such as egalitarianism. Although the authors identify 10 income classes (groups of income earners) and these data can be interpreted differently, the Table points to three broad groups of the population according to socioeconomic status (or Max Weber's 'life chances'):

- Those with higher than average or superior incomes (650–6000 pesos on average)—some 10% of all income earners;
- Those with average incomes (150–400 pesos on average)—48.5% of income earners: Cuba's 'middle class' in Weberian terms of an individual's 'life chances' vis-à-vis the capacity for material consumption; and
- Those with a lower than average or low income (40–150 pesos on average)—around 40% of the population.

Presumably 18.3% of the total number of Cubans are in the 'lower class' category or income poor (earning 40 pesos on average) while some 4% (1000+ pesos on average) might be deemed a relatively elite group, including a small category of individuals (0.4%) who might in Weberian terms be deemed to be 'positively (or relatively) privileged).

Table 7. Income Distribution, 1995

	Income range	Avg. monthly income	% of population
I	0–50	40	19.3
II	51–100	75	22.7
III	101–200	150	25.0
	201–300	250	12.5
IV	301–500	400	11.0
	501–800	650	5.5
	801–1200	1000	2.4
V	1201–1500	1350	0.7
	1501–2000	1750	0.5
	20001+	6000	0.4

Source: Espina Prieto (2005: 221)

This pattern of income distribution in 1995 is difficult to compare with precision relative to previous years for which data are available, in part because the underlying structure (and source of income) had changed. Nevertheless, it is evident that the level of egalitarianism in the distribution of national income—a hallmark and major achievement of the Revolution—had been seriously eroded to the point of putting at risk of poverty (in a state of deprivation) a significant segment of the population.

As to how deep or extensive this issue of poverty tore into the fabric of Cuban society is not easy to precisely determine. For one thing, we would need to sort out and measure the income and non-income conditions of 'poverty'—issues on which there are no precise data or relevant studies. Certain estimations can nevertheless be made on the basis of anecdotal evidence collected by the authors at the time during several short annual visits and study tours.

If we assume: (1) that the average household had two income earners and 1.5 dependents, thus access to 3.5 ration-cards; and (2) that each ration-card in 1995 cost around 30 pesos and provided access to 70% of a individual's requirements for food nutrients and comestibles, then individuals and households in Income Class I–II (very low, low) would be hard pressed to meet all of their basic needs and might well go to bed hungry or be undernourished. What is needed is more precise information on the geographical distribution of the income poor (the urban poor would have little or less access to supplementary food) and the accessibility of school- or workplace-provided meals. Nevertheless, based on our own interview data and indirect evidence of malnutrition we can safely assume that the caloric intake of a substantial number of Cubans was forcibly reduced (due to low income) to an undesired or inadvisable level. These individuals—perhaps some 40% of the population, as per Income Class I–II—could well be regarded as 'poor'.

Cubans in Income Class III (even IV) might well have a relatively low capacity for material consumption but strictly speaking they cannot be defined or reasonably regarded as 'poor'. Even those individuals in Class I, who at the level of income might well be defined as 'poor' in relative if not in absolute terms, were not poor, or as poor, as those in other parts of Latin America—an estimated 40% of the population at the time—who were deprived not only of access to nutritious food but a broad range of essential services. The difference between the two classes of income poor (in Cuba, other Latin America) is mainly a matter of commodification (the degree to which income determines access) or social exclusion (access to public provisioning of basic needs).

Recent studies (see Ferriol, 2002) point towards the reproduction, even an extension and deepening, of the income class structure identified by ONE economists (2001) in terms of five income class categories:

I   (<50 pesos);
II   (51–100 pesos);
III   (101–150 pesos);
IV   (151–200); and
V   (201> pesos).

According to Espina Prieto (2005) in 1995 Classes I–II accounted for 42% of the economically active population at the lower end of the income distribution; Classes III–IV accounted for 25%, representing what in the Cuban context might be viewed as the 'middle class' in terms of 'life chances' and economic interests; and Class V, representing a population with an above average or superior level of material consumption, accounts for another 33% (Espina Prieto, 2005: 221).

At the lower level of the income class or social structure (Class I), encompassing some 18.3% of the economically active population in 1995, could be found the poor, which, unlike other Latin American countries, were predominantly urban. Zabala (2002) estimates that 14.7% of the urban population in 1995 was poor or at risk, which compares to 6.3% in 1985 and, according to Ferriol (2002), up to 20% in 2000. By some accounts this social structure of income distribution was maintained into the new millennium, even with an economic recovery trend that can be traced back to 1998 but that accelerated after 2002 under conditions of a global primary commodities boom.

Recent studies suggest that the percentage of Cubans that can be placed in the 'low income' category of the social structure today is at the same level as it was in 1995 but that today low income does not have the poverty effects (malnutrition, etc.) that it did then. To the degree that poor can be identified today as a category of the Cuban population it is a matter of relative, rather than absolute or extreme, poverty. That is, it is a matter not so much of 'life-chances' or 'wellbeing'—a state of deprivation—as it is of material consumption.

According to the data constructed in recent studies, personal and household incomes in the aggregate have steadily increased, commensurate with the rate of economic growth. However, for most Cubans the increase in their earned income or consumption capacity (re the value of their wage) has been minimal if not negative. This is because of the trend towards structural differentiation in the source and levels of income in different sectors of the economy. Although the government has continued to maintain the basic pay scale for different categories of work, with periodic adjustments for inflation, earned incomes have risen in the most dynamic sectors of economic growth, particularly in the agricultural sector where incomes are not confined by the Ministry of Labour's pay scale, or in the expanding and increasingly diversified private sector of the self-employed worker or independent small business operator. In addition, remittances since the mid-1990s constitute an important source of income for a substantial number of households—possibly one-third.

The greatest source of income differentiation, accounting for most of the aggregate increase in per capita incomes over the past decade, has been the expansion of the dollarized economy. In other words, the critical factor in increased income and consumption capacity of a category (albeit not a class) has been access to US dollars.

For some analysts, the foreign exchange payment system, instituted as a necessary means of acquiring hard currency, has not only created a dual economy but an important source of social inequality, undermining a core value of Cuban socialism and thus the revolutionary process. Espina Prieto (p. 221), in this connection, concludes from her studies that the structural changes regarding income have resulted in the emergence, since the mid-1990s, of a considerably more diversified income structure with a marked 'restratification'—an increase in the range and number of income levels. She and her colleagues calculate that as a consequence of this new social structure the Gini Index of income inequality increased from .24 in 1986 to .38 in 1999. If this calculation is correct, this would represent a serious regression in regard to development as equality.[2]

Public Action Dynamics of Human Development in a Crisis

In July 1992, the 1976 constitution was amended to limit state ownership to the 'fundamental' (rather than 'all') means of production (e.g. land, mines, water) and to allow: (1) the transfer of state rights to individuals and enterprises by approval of the Council of Ministries),

---

[2] A more qualitative case study of Havana by Iñiguez and other studies that rely on small samples and in-depth interviews, point in the same direction—of a structure in which the income in the top income group/category is ten times that of the bottom group—in comparison to a differentiation of 4.2 to 1 in the income structure formed in the 1980s.

provided they contribute to economic development and do not conflict with public goals; (2) ownership by mixed enterprises, economic associations such as joint ventures; and (3) the creation of quasi-private foreign trade enterprises engaged in exports and imports. The President of the National Assembly, however, warned (see Mesa-Lago, 2000: 295 on this point) that this amendment did not constitute a retreat from socialism or a transition to capitalism. For one thing, in regard to the *sociedades anónimas* facilitated by the constitutional amendment the capital is provided by the state, not private investors with the capacity for conversion into a capitalist class. Similarly, the state is able to dispose of the profits generated by these enterprises for the good of society as a whole, not for personal enrichment or capital accumulation.

In effect capital (also production technologies) could not be owned, invested or disposed of as 'profit' by private 'interests' for the purpose of capital accumulation. Cuban citizens cannot be associated directly with foreign capital but only through the state. Thus there was no privatization or private property in the means of social production, nor the possibility of capital accumulation on the basis of the capital-labour relation, i.e. exploitation of labour; only the right of usufruct (the use and exploitation of land and resources for productive purposes) via contracts or long-term leases for specific or indefinite periods. Thus the fundamental pillars of socialist production remain intact, to the dismay or scorn of capitalist economists (for example, Mesa-Lago, who judges the entire reform process in this regard to be a sham or a scam (p. 295)).

The most important change in ownership related to the organization of production has been the transformation of state firms into a new type of production cooperative termed Basic Units of Cooperative Production (UBPC), and the granting of public uncultivated parcels of land to groups and families for their economic use. Tantamount to a third agrarian reform, the law that brought about or facilitated this change were enacted in the last quarter of 1993. In agreement with the government, workers on a state farm can sign a contract for an indefinite period in order to form a UBPC under the following conditions: (i) the land can be exploited under the right of usufructs, not ownership, and is rent free; (ii) the production technology and equipment is turned over by the state to the cooperative for collective use, and for the purpose of productive investment the National Bank will provide capital on credit with a three-year grace period and at 4% annual interest thereafter; (iii) the obligation to plant certain crops and to sell most of the product to the state (*acopio*) at process set in pesos by the government and not by the market; (iv) allocation of a part of the land (7%) for self-consumption and family subsistence; (v) any crop surplus left after meeting *acopio* obligations can be sold on the free market reintroduced in September 1994 (for this purpose individuals were also authorized to own trucks for transportation); (vi) UBPCs can and should elect their own manager but are subject to state auditing; (vii) UBPC members are to be paid out of co-op revenues after all other costs are met (state farm workers are guaranteed a set wage); and (viii) the UBPC decides how to use any remaining profit (e.g. reinvest it, build homes for members, distribute it among members).

Short of a systematic assessment of this policy and the new production unit in terms of its output and contribution to expanded production of agricultural goods, in overcoming the shortage of food and meeting the growing domestic demand, Mesa-Lago (2000: 296) points to several inherent deficiencies in the UBPC system. The problem is that unlike similar agricultural production units set up in China in the late 1970s, the UBPC does not have private property ownership rights in regard to what to produce, to whom the crop should be sold to, and at what price set by the market. As a result, the UBPC members have an incentive to minimise production sold to the state (paid in pesos and at low prices) and to maximize their own consumption. More to the point (Mesa-Lago's argument on the previous point is not logically consistent) if the direct sale of the agricultural surplus on the free market is impeded by the *acopio* obligation then UBPC members can turn to middlemen or sell it on the black market at a much higher price. If these alternatives are not available, then, Mesa-Lago (2002: 296) argues, 'they can simply reduce their labour effort'.

The problem with this assessment is that these alternatives (to market the surplus product or consume it) do not in any way reduce the *acopio* obligation, meaning that there *is* in fact an incentive for UBPC members to expand production and increase their labour effort, especially given the moral pressures that each member is under from the collective—a dimension of noncapitalist cooperative production that Mesa-Lago ignores.

In any case, what cannot be ignored is the impact of the 'third agrarian reform law' on the structure of production. In 1989, state farms worked 78% of arable land; 18.7% was organised in cooperative form; and 3.3% was in small private farms. At the end of 1994 only 33.1%

of non-sugar cane production took the form of state farms; 61.8% was organised in the cooperative sector—40.6% as UBPCs; and an estimated 5.1% of the land was used productively by small private farms or used as family plots (CEE, AEC, 1989a; Deere, 1995; Dilla, 1993).[3]

The thrust towards egalitarianism under the RP was somewhat muted in this period and phase of the Revolution—'the special period in a time of peace'. Fidel himself at the end of 1993 acknowledged that an overly egalitarian approach to economic development (social development was an entirely different matter) was ill advised, particularly in a 'situation of poverty' (Castro, 1993b). In fact, Fidel continues, '[t]he more poverty there is the less egalitarianism works'. Thus, 'the changes [made in the 'special period] were inevitable', notwithstanding their negative effects regarding social equality and the possibility, even probability, that these changes and others that will have to be made, will 'foster individualism, selfishness…and generate alienating effects'—not unlike capitalist development, Fidel could have added. In this sense, the reforms and actions taken by the government—reluctantly, and in a process of broad consultation and public action with considerable 'popular participation' (the workers' parliaments, etc.)—could be seen as a setback to the Revolution, but even so as unavoidable, a necessary evil.

The trade union newspaper echoed this view in declaring that 'egalitarianism went too far, beyond the nation's economic capacity' (*Trabajadores*, November 22, 1993, p. 2). In a similar vein (the negative impact of market reforms was decried although seen as unavoidable), the Party newspaper *Granma* (January 4, 1995, p. 4), some thirteen months further into the 'special period' of crisis and reform, declared that 'it has become evident that there is a process of unequal distribution of income'.

The driving force behind this development is not difficult to discern. For one thing, social inequalities in the distribution of income had expanded with the introduction of dollar economy associated with foreign tourism, in parallel with but totally disconnected from the peso economy. The dual economy created a major divide in earning and purchasing power in that while a majority of the population had no

---

[3] See Mesa-Lago (2000: 297) for an assessment of the efficacy of this agrarian reform from its institution in October 1993 to 1996.

access to dollars a sizeable minority received remittances, food and medicine from relatives abroad while another group had access to hard currency through their connection to foreign tourism. Employees working in the tourist sector or for foreign companies and in strategic sectors such as tobacco, mining and docks could earn a part of their salary or a bonus in dollars or receive packages of goods.

While a minority of employees were able to buy all sorts of consumer goods in dollar stores and the market they were totally out of range for most workers in the peso economy. On our visits and conversations we collected a lot of anecdotal evidence and stories about university professors and other professionals decamping to the tourist sector as hotel staff in the quest for hard currency income, which even in the form of tips was greater in terms of its purchasing power than their professional salaries paid in pesos. The social inequality and other negative effects of this dual economy (on the psyche of many Cubans having to live with an exceedingly low and even dismal level of material consumption and austerity), no matter how necessary the policy as a means of bringing in vital foreign exchange reserves for the government, cannot be overemphasized.

Other sources of growing inequality at the time include the fact that the self-employed and farmers earned several times the average wage in the state sector. Middlemen and truck owners can make major gains in the agricultural market and the black market in pilfered goods of all sorts is by some accounts ubiquitous, providing opportunities for black-marketers to enrich themselves. These and other contradictions and market 'distortions' had a major cumulative effect on the structure of income distribution and thus the condition of equality in Cuba.

The data on income distribution available for Cuba at that stage are scarce but all indications are that inequalities in disposable income, access to consumer goods and even some services expanded significantly. Access to education and health, however, was universal and continued to be more or less equal. It was significant that in the depth of the crisis not one school was closed, not one hospital or clinic closed— although there is evidence that the quality of service in these areas deteriorated, in some cases badly for lack of supplies and equipment.

Freedom and Democracy in a Crisis

After an initial period of ups and downs and shifting reforms (1959– 1968), mostly in the direction of reverting the existing social structure of income / wealth distribution and nationalization—and then the socialization of production and consumption—the Cuban economy stabilized and entered a period of slow but fairly steady growth (in the late 1970s) that peaked in the mid-1980s, at a point when other countries in the region were deeply into a debt crisis and a decade lost to development. But, as in the rest of the socialist world, for some reason (a combination of factors have been adjudged to be responsible—including the inherent problems of overly centralized planning, a failure in productive investments / the incorporation of new production technologies, and a supply crisis) by 1985 this engine of growth began to sputter and slow down to a crawl, creating conditions—in the USSR and East Europe anyway—of a political crisis that eventually led to the collapse of 'actually existing socialism'. But Cuba weathered this storm, as well as the pressures and forces unleashed by the collapse of the socialist bloc together with a tightening of the noose of US imperialism, leading to the most serious challenge ever faced by the Cuban Revolution. Even so it managed to survive against all odds, raising questions as to what helped Cuba recover from the worst crisis in the history of the Revolution.

Although not necessarily determinant it is evident—or at least, we choose to argue—that one of the reasons that the Revolution survived while socialism collapsed elsewhere was precisely the workings in Cuba of what we might term [a neighbourhood- and workplace-based] 'participatory' development and a 'socialist' democracy. While the lack of popular support, indeed widespread opposition, led to a political crisis and a collapse or the abandonment of socialism, the democracy installed and functioning in Cuba at the time helped maintain essential support for the Revolution and the socialist regime.

A recent book by Henry Taylor provides some insight into the process. Taylor's book, based on 15 years of research, describes two Cubas, one viewed from the inside, the other from the outside—this a rather one-dimensional view of Cuba that many people 'discover' through tourism or from the writings of anti-Castro political propagandists and in the mass media. The other Cuba, Taylor asserts, viewed from within is a more complex and multi-dimensional Cuba, where people live in a highly stable and deeply organized society and exercise considerable control over the development of neighbourhoods (los barrios) and communities that are imbued with a participatory socialist democracy and deep reservoirs of social capital. It is this Cuba, Taylor argues, that sustained the country (and the government) through hard times and severe economic hardship, and continues to do so. On this point Taylor writes that, '[n]o iron wall exists between these two Cubas but people rarely get insight into the world inside el barrio'—the world that he explores in his book.[4]

Taylor and his research team spent a great deal of time visiting Havana's neighbourhoods and interviewing people (conducting 398 household interviews) between 1989 and 2006, a period marked by the abrupt collapse of the Soviet Union and the socialist bloc, plunging Cuba into near economic catastrophe marked by unprecedented financial hardship, a marked increase in social tension and the emigration of thousands.

Taylor noted that he and his team learned to appreciate the importance of local communities or neighbourhoods in shaping everyday life and culture, and he found that the social networks and neighbourhoods, so important to the way the socialist system operates on the ground in Cuba, were critical factors in sustaining the socialist regime under conditions that led to the collapse of socialism elsewhere. In 1989, when the Soviet Union and the East European Community Bloc were on the brink of collapse, Cuba was plunged into a deep economic crisis that spawned unprecedented hardship and generated great social tensions within and across the country. But Taylor points out what is well known albeit not well understood—that notwithstanding this development neither the government or socialism collapsed. Where were the demands for regime change and a resurrection of capitalism that surfaced elsewhere and that the US government attempted to induce via a tightening the screws and the noose of the blockade? Not only did the regime survive this challenge and imperialist offensive but, Taylor notes, 'the bearded one remained as defiant as ever'. In searching for an explanation he found it in the culture of everyday life in the poorest neighbourhoods.[5] In his words:

> What I discovered is that the Cubans developed a strong system of community development, which was informed by a strategy of building communities that were highly developed social units that must function in

---

[4] 'One of the most important things I learned is that it takes time before most Cubans will befriend you, speak to you in frank terms and carry you into their world. Without this frankness it is easy for a foreigner to be misled, misinterpret conversations and form false impressions'

[5] This emphasis on the centrality of culture in the dynamics of local transformation is echoed in the writings of Linares on local development (2006).

an efficient and effective manner in order to produce desirable social outcomes (Taylor, 2009)

To make this happen, he notes, the government encouraged the development of participatory democracy inside the neighbourhoods to unleash the creative powers of residents and to make them partners in the quest to recover from the economic crisis. The result, is that 'Cuban neighbourhoods are hyper-stable and hyper-organized communities in which residents exercise considerable control over neighbourhood life and culture, albeit in an environment of scarcity'.

Social Participation and Local Development in an Era of Neoliberal Globalization

The glimpse provided by Taylor into the roots of Cuban socialism places into perspective an important feature of the Cuban Revolution at the time. In retrospect it is evident that the painful economic reforms that the government were compelled to introduce under these circumstances in the event succeeded in staving off a fundamental threat to the Revolution and Cuban socialism. However, the significant aspect of these reforms—and, we argue, a major reason that the Revolution and the socialist model of human development managed to survive—is widespread popular participation in the reform process in the form of 'workers' parliaments' set up to debate the way out of the crisis. Notwithstanding the appearance to many observers from outside the country that the decisions as to how to respond to the crisis came from above, with the strong hand and loud voice of Fidel, decisions as to what economic reforms would be needed and were indeed implemented were thoroughly aired, debated and decided upon in a multitude of workplaces across the country that in effect were converted into policy forums. Unlike the many forums set up in Washington and elsewhere to inform and direct policymakers in office—forums that without exception are restricted to insiders and the economic and the political elite—the 'workers' parliaments' set up in Cuba to debate 'what was to be done' were paragons of popular participation and social democracy, allowing ordinary Cubans of all walks of life to actively participate in public decision-making.

But public action is not only a matter of popular participation in public policy. It is also, and especially so in Cuba, a matter of government participation in community-based actions or local development.

Nothing illustrates this point as clearly as what came to be known as the 'Cayo Hueso Intervention'.

Community-based 'local development' initiatives such as the Cayo Hueso Intervention did not originate with the Special Period. Indeed, as argued earlier they were encouraged from the outset and facilitated by the institutionality of people's power. However, and perhaps paradoxically, the conditions for local development, according to Peña Castellanos (2006), were improved by the forces of globalization. As he constructs it globalization created or imposed on Cuba as it did elsewhere conditions that encouraged and led to the adoption and widespread implementation of a municipality-based local development strategy (Guzón, 2003; Peña Castellanos, 2006: 17). Although there was 'international collaboration' in the design and implementation of this strategy, particularly from the UNDP and CIDA it was grounded in the 'structures of people's power', and, according to Cecilia Linares (2006), in the 'culture' cultivated by these structures.[6] In this connection—and to explain therewith the surge of municipality-based initiatives discussed by Guzón (2006: 64–90)—Linares sees local development as a 'cultural construction' and as such, as described by Boisier (2003), a 'systemic emergency', as well as more generally a specific social and political response to globalization. In this connection, Vazquez (2007) argues that local development is a 'strategy for times of crisis'.

As for the UNDP it moved into Cuba in the mid-1990s, at a time in which Cuba was adjusting to the demands of the neoliberal world order, and the UNDP itself was heavily engaged in a search for government sponsors of its model of sustainable human development.[7] For other countries in the region this model mandated holding the neoliberal line on macroeconomic policy, a new social policy targeting the poor, greater social inclusion in the area of essential services and human development infrastructure, a policy of administrative decentralization, a good governance regime based on social participation, and a new development paradigm based on local development (Albuquerque, 2001).

---

[6] On the 'centrality of culture in the dynamics of local transformation' see Linares (2006) as well as Rey (2006). A similar conception of culture as the base of contemporary development has also been articulated by Amartya Sen (2006).

[7] The UNDP entered Cuba by sponsoring several studies into the state of human development in Cuba under conditions of its adjustment to the external forces of neoliberal globalization (UNDP, 1997, 2000).

But in Cuba structural adjustment took a very different form. The Washington-mandated program of 'structural' or policy reforms (privatization, liberalization, deregulation, decentralization) was the price that any country had to pay for admission into the new world order of neoliberal globalization. Under conditions of this adjustment a local development process was unleashed throughout the region in the 1990s, leading a number of economists with the UNDP and CEPAL—and, it turns out, also in Cuba—to conclude that globalization and neoliberalism were propitious for local development, opening up space for local actors and social participation (Boisier, 2005; Hernández, 2004; Peña Castellanos, 2006). Indeed, as pointed out by the Cuban scholars of 'local economic development' (LED), conditions for local development were more favourable in Cuba than elsewhere precisely because of the institutional framework of people's power and a culture of social participation and collaborative social action. In Cuba local development did not require government legislation of administrative decentralization, or, as in the case of Bolivia, popular participation.

Conclusion

The most surprising fact about the Cuban Revolution in the 1990s, in the crisis phase of its development, was that it survived. As the UNDP (2010) notes in its first *Regional Human Development Report* for Latin America, 'Despite the restrictions and the changes that occurred in the 1990s Cuba's socioeconomic strategy maintained its essential objectives in the social sphere' and managed to stay on track as regards its fundamental human development agenda in the face of external and internal 'challenges'. Most surprising for the authors of the report was the ability of the regime to achieve such a broad consensus on the need to 'assimilate the external adjustment and confront the internal economic transformations' (PNUD, 2010: xv). The 'State [throughout] maintained its defense of social equity on the basis of universality and free basic social services of education and health' and indeed, the authors add, 'the complexity of these services went well beyond those that are internationally considered as basic' (PNUD, 2010: xv). Indeed the Report goes on, no activities related to basic social services were privatized, and, the authors add, 'it should be kept in mind that [over this period] no other country in the world registered as great an advance [in terms of human development as Cuba]—improving its HDI ranking by eight positions'.

The solution to this enigma was not hard to find, even though it eluded the UNDP in both its 1996 Report on Human Development in Cuba and its 2000 award-winning report on 'human development and equity in Cuba', both of which focused on the strategic responses to 'neoliberal globalization' ('the external adjustment') by the government and the people ('the State and social participation'). The explanation of Cuba's successful navigation of those troubled waters can be found in the dynamics of 'social participation'—in the 'workers' parliaments' and other forms of popular participation in decision-making and the public policy process. It is this feature of the Cuban Revolution more than any other that explains the resilience of the Revolution in confronting the challenges from without and within.

CHAPTER ELEVEN

CONTINUITY AND CHANGE: THE REVOLUTION IN THE NEW MILLENNIUM

The Cuban revolution with its socialist economy has demonstrated unprecedented resilience in the face of enormous political obstacles and challenges. It successfully defied a US-orchestrated invasion, naval blockade, hundreds of terrorist attacks and a long-standing and continuing boycott (Morley, 1987). Cuba was able to withstand the system-threatening fallout from the collapse of the USSR and the Eastern European 'socialist' regimes, and it has managed to adjust to the new world order—and China and Indo-China's transit to capitalism—without abandoning its socialist path to national development.

As many scholars and political leaders—including adversaries—have noted, Cuba has developed a very advanced and well functioning social welfare program characterized by free, universal, quality health coverage and education from kindergarten through advanced university education, and delivering a high level of human development on a very limited economic base. In its foreign as well as domestic policies Cuba has successfully developed economic and diplomatic relations with countries across the world despite a comprehensive US embargo and political pressures. On issues of national and personal security Cuba is a world leader. Crime rates are low and violent offenses are rare. Terrorist threats and acts (emanating from the US and its Cuban exile proxies), have declined and are less a danger to the Cuban population than to the US or Europe.

But it is precisely the successes of the Cuban Revolution, and its ability to withstand external threats that would have brought down most governments, that have now created a series of major challenges that require urgent attention if the Revolution as we know it is to advance further into the 21st century. These challenges are a result of persisting external constraints as well as internal developments. Some are the inevitable consequences of emergency measures and structural reforms introduced in the 'special period' but that are now pressing for immediate solution if not radical change. This chapter will elaborate on the human development dynamics and implications of these challenges to the Cuban Revolution in the current conjuncture of worldwide forces and conditions of change.

Holding the Line on Socialism

After a decade and near the official end of Cuba's Special Period in Time of Peace, Menno Vellinga published an essay based on a review of two retrospective studies on the thinking of Che Guevara, and three book-length studies of the dynamics of change and continuity within the Cuban Revolution. Each of these studies in its own way addressed questions that have animated Cuba watchers and scholars over the past two decades: How to understand developments in Cuba over this period? How it changed in adjusting to the forces released by the process of capitalist development in the latest phase of neoliberal globalization (conditions and the responses to which were discussed in the previous chapter)? How did the Revolution survive as a system against overwhelming odds? And how has it been able to continue to generate considerable support among the Cuban population despite the sacrifices and austerity that Cubans have had to bear for so long?

On these questions Antoni Kapcia, in his *Island of Dreams* (2000) offers a perspective based on a review of the entire revolutionary process, with a focus on developments in the realm of ideology. He traces the emergence of the ideological complex of *cubanía*, which includes the construction of a politico-historical mythology of a heroic past, which took Kapcia back to the origins of the Revolution (la 'conciencia') and the fundamental contributions of Che Guevara, described by García and Sola and explored in more theoretical terms by Casteñeda. However, in seeking to establish a link from Cuba's heroic past to a projected socialist future, Kapcia raised questions that he was unable to answer—in terms of conditions that prevailed at the time and the strategic and tactical responses to these conditions. One of the aims of this chapter is to return to these questions, with reference to developments that have unfolded in the subsequent decade, and in the context of advancing the thesis of this study.

Marifeli Pérez-Stable (1999) in her study of the Cuban Revolution also raised questions about the efficacy of the ideological complex constructed over these years, and the impact of the Special Period on this ideology, embedded in what we have viewed as a 'revolutionary consciousness'. We have argued that this 'conciencia'—reflected in a commitment to the principles and values of equality, freedom and solidarity—is a defining feature of socialism in the Cuban context, i.e. as a project of human development, and also in explaining the survival of the socialist project with so many forces against it. We further argue that the reconstruction of this 'conciencia' is the major challenge faced by the Cuban leadership in securing the continuity of the revolutionary project of humanist socialism.

From the standpoint of developments in the 1990s, and a retrospective gaze over the decade, Pérez-Stable suggested that the Fidelista-Guevarista 'project' in regard to the workings of the revolutionary 'myth'—that reflected the commitment of Cubans in general to the ideals of egalitarianism and solidarity—was put in jeopardy by the reforms that the regime was forced to introduce as well as the cumulative effects of decades of austerity. She maintained that the 'Fidel-patria-revolución' formula for governance had begun to lose its appeal, leading to 'schizophrenic situations' for a growing numbers of Cuban citizens, who in public would express conformance to the public discourse while 'privately dissenting, [albeit] without...the security of possible alternatives'. The size of this group or population segment she estimated—without any evidence, it might be noted—to be at around a third of all Cubans. The segment of those actively committed to the Revolution she also estimated at one third. This included the older generation (with memories of the pre-1959 situation), party members, UJC and CDR activists, workers in the education and public service sectors and the population in the rural areas in the provinces outside Havana. Those in opposition—those unquestioningly opposed to the system, albeit unorganized and silent—by her estimation might amount to another third. In addition, the dollarization of the economy and the stagnating purchasing power of those completely dependent upon the Peso-based system, she suggested, were creating tensions, undermining communal solidarity and causing Cubans to shift to the 'opposition' camp.

However, the extent of such a shift was—and still is—not known, and, as Velinga (2001: 141) noted, 'it may even be that the slight improvements of the last few years have helped to maintain the active and passive support for the system'. In any case, Velinga adds, there was little evidence that 'the Castro-led system' was any more threatened than it was before at the outset of the Special Period. Kapcia explained this continuity in terms of *cubanuía* ('la concienica'), the role it played in sustaining the system with all its complexities and contradictions. A part of this, he noted, was the code of *solidarismo* and the system of reciprocity and mutual help (social capital) that on the local level cushioned the impact of economic downturns and the ensuing scarcities, and that sustained a deeply embedded culture of solidarity. The urge to persevere and to survive as a system, Kapcia argued, was supported by the guerrilla myth: stories of battling against all odds, snatching victory from apparent defeats, and the emergence of a growing community of shared struggle, suffering and victory, through acts of daily and often unsung heroism and sacrifice.

How valid is this explanation? Velinga for one, argues that notwithstanding the evident importance of the ideological factor Kapcia overemphasizes the impact of the cubanía complex and its influence on the Cuban population—on their motivation and disposition to persevere through all the trials and tribulations of the various phases of the revolutionary process. In his view, Kapcia underestimated the pragmatism with which many Cubans have learned to survive, adapting to changing conditions without weakening their intense feelings of patriotism, which, he added, 'have remained surprisingly strong among all sectors of the Cuban population, irrespective of their personal attitudes towards the Revolution'.

Pérez-Stable (1999) in this regard underlined the importance of this element of revolutionary consciousness in the reaction of the Cuban population towards the US embargo and the Torricelli and Helms-Burton legislation. In the eyes of the Cuban people, these foreign dictates would never be the motor of a change toward democracy. However, Velinga also argued that Kapcia underestimated the impact of the 'elaborate system of political control that will act immediately in the event actions pass the limits of solidarity to the Revolution as defined by the revolutionary leadership'. In that situation, he argued, any dissidence would have to operate against almost insurmountable odds.

However, in retrospect it is evident that both Velinga and Kapcia underestimate, or fail to take into account and analyze, the diverse ways in which Cubans continue to actively participate in the revolutionary process. Just two examples should suffice to make this point. First, beginning in November and continuing throughout December of 2008, meetings were held at workplaces throughout the country giving workers a chance to participate in the formulation of the 2009 budget and Economic Plan. In a subsequent meeting of the country's 19 national unions Luis Manuel Castanedo, a member of the CTC National Secretariat, gave the following details of these national 'discussions'. By December, he noted, more than 38,000 workplace assemblies had been held, 46% of those planned, with the participation of 1.5 million workers. However, he also noted several lingering problems such as the need to make the meetings more participative and to improve the quality of the reports presented for analysis (*Granma*, December 10, 2008). These consultations were preceded in 1993–1994 by national deliberations aimed at formulating the first policy response to Cuba's dire economic situation following the collapse of the USSR (Saney, 2003: 51). And around the same time the national leadership of the Committees for the Defense of the Revolution called on the general population to take part in a program of volunteer work to coincide with the Sixth CDR Congress. The volunteer work in neighborhoods and rural communities embraced the continuing recovery effort from the hurricanes, both in food production, cleanup and building projects. It is easy enough to dismiss the CDR as an extension of the State (to mobilize support for the government's programs, including public health action) but it is by far the country's largest parastatal organization, actively engaged in the defense of socialism 'with unity and combativeness', with an impact on the popular consciousness that should not be underestimated.

Advances, Virtues and Vices

The great virtue of the Cuban revolution is that it survived, maintaining many of its positive social achievements when many previous and subsequent reformist or revolutionary regimes were defeated or overthrown or collapsed. The US and its allies overthrew the reformist regimes of Arbenz in Guatemala (1954), Mossadegh in Iran (1953), Allende of Chile (1973), Lumumba in the Congo and many others. The White House ousted the Sandinista Government in Nicaragua in 1989, the Aristide regime in 1992 and 2004 and many others. But Cuba managed to defeat a US-sponsored invasion in 1961, resisted a US naval blockade in 1962, rebuffed hundreds of CIA-organized assassination attempts and terrorist attacks over a half-century, and endures a worldwide economic boycott to stay a socialist course under adverse conditions of neoliberal globalization.

At the outset, thanks to some astute diplomacy, Cuba had secured favourable and opportune trade and aid agreements with the former USSR and Eastern Europe. By the end of the 20th century, notwithstanding the US boycott, Cuba had diplomatic and economic relations with almost the entire world. In 2001 Cuba even broke the US trade embargo by importing (albeit on unfavourable, one-sided terms) food and medicine from US exporters and farmers. However, the sudden collapse of the USSR and the conversion of Russia and Eastern Europe into capitalist dependencies were devastating blows to the Cuban economy. The loss of trading partners led to a precipitous decline of production.[1] And with China's transition to capitalism for Cuba there was no alternative but to navigate the turbulent disorder of neoliberal globalization. The Cuban government adopted an emergency economic strategy, inaugurating therewith a 'special period' of forced austerity and structural adjustment that spread the pain of economic recovery throughout Cuban society—unlike the experience in the capitalist countries where the pain and 'transitional' social costs of 'adjustment' were inevitably and disproportionately borne by the working class and the poor.[2]

Between 1990 and 2000, Cuba reconstructed the economy to meet the new exigencies while retaining its social safety net and social programs, an unprecedented accomplishment. Not one hospital or school was privatized or closed down in the Special Period.[3] Already in 1999 the economy began to recover, a process that was accelerated in 2003,

---

[1] In the period 1990–1994, the GDP contracted upwards of 35%. The enormity of this economic dislocation, derived largely from the disintegration of the USSR that had accounted for 87% of Cuba's trade relations, meant that Cuba needed to make a major economic adjustment. In short, Cuba had to stabilize its economy that by 1994 was severely distorted, as a result of which was that the Cuban peso that had virtually lost all of its value. At the same time, the country had to make the appropriate 'structural' changes to its economy in order to reinsert itself in the competitive world market.

[2] It is worth noting—particularly in the face of the misconceived idea that national policy in Cuba is entirely shaped by decisions at the top by the maxium leader, Fidel Castro until recently, Rául Castro since—that the government's first austerity plan by the National Assembly in 1993 was rejected by the populace, leading to subsequent mass national consultations and what have been termed 'Worker's Parliaments' to formulate a new austerity plan, one that was eventually adopted by the government (Saney, 2003: 51).

[3] This was a rather extraordinary feat that contradicts the finding of the OECD Development Centre (2010), in regard to Latin American countries generally (excluding Cuba) that social expenduitures (on health, education, etc.) follow a cyclical pattern that tracks the ups and downs of the economy: 'Spending tends to rise above trend during economic expansions and contract pro-cyclically during recessions' (Table 0.1).

under conditions of a global primary commodity boom. The economy recovered, with annual rates of economic growth that climbed to 11.8% in 2005 and 12.5% in 2006 before levelling off at 7.0% in 2007 and then down to 1.3%, in 2009, in the new conditions of a boom gone bust (ECLAC, 2007b; 2009).

It appears that Cuba weathered what might have been viewed a 'perfect storm' on the high seas of global capitalism and US imperialism—with a massive assault on the country's capacity to survive. Cuba's survival and recovery were based on what in retrospect can be seen as a successful strategic and policy response to forces and winds of change in the new world order.

Several elements of this strategy can be readily identified: rapid and comprehensive development of the tourist sector through large-scale, long-term investments in association with European and Latin American and multinationals; massive investments in biotechnology to stimulate research and the development for export of pharmaceutical products; long-term, large-scale trade and investment agreements with Venezuela involving Cuban medical teams and medical facilities in exchange for petroleum products on favourable terms; joint ventures with Canadian and European firms to develop and export nickel, rum, tobacco and citrus products; and food import agreements with US and Canadian agribusiness corporations. The majority of Cuba's sugar mills were closed down in response to a free-fall in sugar prices, sharply reduced sugar production and reconverting cane fields to alternative crop production on a limited scale. Major investments in new advanced schools of computer science ($200 million dollars), medical tourism and external humanitarian projects continued.

This economic strategy, combined with favourable external conditions (high world prices for commodities such as nickel, the radicalization of Venezuelan President Hugo Chávez, the shift from far-right wing to moderate centre-right neoliberal regimes in Latin America) and the apparently willing sacrifice of the majority of the Cuban people, led to a gradual but steady economic recovery from 1999 on, followed by accelerated growth as of 2003 (Parts I–II; ECLAC, 2007).

From deep depression to economic recovery the Cuban Government maintained the basic structure of its social network and welfare provisions. All of the major health and educational programs continued to be free and open to the public. Workers displaced as a result of economic restructuring continued to receive their wages and were offered state-funded jobs and retraining programs—no workers were abandoned to fend for themselves. Rents and charges for public utilities remained low. Pension payments continued. Food subsidies and rationing of basic items continued, providing a measure of food and economic security. Cultural, sports and recreational activities progressed despite sharp cutbacks in funding. Despite general scarcities, low consumption and social deprivation crime rates remained far below Latin American and US levels.

National security institutions successfully protected the Cuban public from US-backed terrorist attacks and domestic destabilization efforts sponsored by White House-funded 'dissident' organizations. Despite Cuba's greater economic vulnerability it rejected US and European Union attempts to dictate domestic security and economic policies.[4] Cuba rejected Washington's attempt to convert Cuba into a free market satellite similar to the Eastern European, Caucasian and Russian examples and it pursued its own independent path, maintaining intact, albeit somewhat battered, the socialist model.

Unlike the formerly communist countries of the USSR, Eastern Europe and Asia, Cuba's transition to a new economy did not result in monstrous inequalities with which a tiny group of billionaires and multi-millionaires seized control of public assets and resources, leaving the rest of the population poor and jobless and facing skyrocketing rents, with inaccessible privatized health and education and miserable pensions. The government also retained the majority share and control over most (if not all) joint ventures with foreign capital (Parts IV, VI), in contrast to the situation in East Europe and elsewhere in Latin America where US and European companies and banks have taken over almost every major enterprise in the manufacturing, financial, media and commercial sectors of the economy.

Even more noteworthy, unlike Eastern Europe and the USSR Cuba did not suffer the massive outward transfer of profits, rents and illegal earnings from large-scale networks of prostitution, narcotics and arms sales. Nor was Cuba's transition to a mixed economy accompanied by

---

[4] Interview by James Petras with Felipe Perez Roque, Cuban Foreign Minister, February 4, 2004. Results of this and other interview with government officials and Cuban scholars are summarized in Chapter 5 of Petras and Veltmeyer (2009).

organized criminal syndicates, which played such a major role in the making and unmaking of electoral outcomes in Bulgaria, Poland, Romania, Albania and the rest of the new capitalist democracies (Klebnikov, 2000; Hoffman, 2003).

Cuba's success in overcoming an array of major structural and political obstacles to its survival, its striking economic recovery and formidable national defense force reflects a successful economic strategy and the ability to tack with each change in the turbulent winds that prevail in the world market.[5] But it is due in large part to a combination of popular perseverance, loyalty to revolutionary leaders and the continued embrace of shared socialist values of egalitarianism, solidarity, national dignity and independence. Even so, as mentioned above, the very success of the Cuban government in meeting and overcoming the obstacles resulting from the US embargo and collapse of the USSR has created a new set of challenges and contradictions.

Challenges of the 'Post-Special Period'

Promotion of tourism as an engine of economic recovery was the fastest, easiest and most rational use of Cuba's natural endowment to compensate for the economic depression, scarcity of capital and political isolation. Moreover, it was the tourist sector that most interested prospective foreign investment partners. Tourism generated scarce

---

[5] One instance and demonstration of this willingness to 'correct' errors in policy or adjust to changing conditions was the 'rectifications' in economic strategy implemented by the government in the mid-1980s in response to a drastic fall in the GDP from an 8.5% annual growth rate in 1980-1985 to barely 0.7% from 1986 to 1989 (UNDP, 2000: 57). The rectification process included policies that restricted market activity in the state sector and in the private sphere. Farmer's markets that had been introduced in the previous era were abolished. Private activity in the service sector, construction and petty commerce were also eliminated. The reasons for government restrictions on private market activity were twofold. Firstly, market measures had produced inequalities. Secondly, in allowing for market measures in the private sector and state sector, the government had lost much-needed fiscal revenue. Much of the private activity was at the state's expense. For example, in the agricultural sector, private farmers would sell the state its worst quality products in order to save the best products for personal profit on the farmers markets. The government's policy of supplying cheap credit, machinery and inputs to farmers also aggravated the state's financial burden. In the urban private economy, many workers would steal resources from state jobs in order to sell in the private market. As well as they absented themselves from their state jobs in order to profit from private initiatives, while still retaining their official wages and benefits.

hard currency with which to import essential commodities, especially petroleum and manufactured products, medical supplies and food.

But over time, as is well known, tourism led to major distortions in the economy: unskilled or semi-skilled tourism-connected employment earnings or purchasing power capacity far exceeded those of highly-trained scientists, doctors, skilled workers and agricultural workers among others. Moreover, the 'mixed enterprises' in the tourist sector led to the emergence of a new and relatively well-off bureaucratic social stratum and the growth of social inequalities, particularly in the distribution of income (see Chapter 10). Then-President Fidel Castro here emphasized the point that the Revolution faced its principal danger from within (see below).

Equally troubling, and potentially damaging, is that the massive influx of tourists led to the growth of a lumpen-proletariat, prostitutes, drug pushers and other forms of non-productive 'hustlers', whose illicit earnings exceeded those of workers, employees and professionals. This group developed networks with hotel, restaurant and nightclub managers, which encouraged corruption and challenged the revolutionary ethos. Continued scarcity, low real purchasing power and the absence of desired consumer goods weakened the government's campaigns to 'moralize' tourist activity without driving out the tourists.

Large-scale, long-term investments in tourist infrastructure—hotels, restaurants, imported furniture and food—diverted funds from agriculture. Agricultural production, especially in foodstuffs for the local population declined significantly, encouraging the spread of black, gray and 'free' markets. Cuba became a food-dependent country, a problem of significant proportions in the emerging new global economy in which food inflation is becoming a critical issue (Castro, 2007).[6] Raúl Castro, Fidel's brother who was delegated the

---

[6] On this point see the address for the Presidential Summit 'Sovereignty and Food Security: Food for Life' by Esteban Lazo Hernandez, Vice-President of Cuba's Council of State, 7 May, 2008, Managua, Nicaragua. 'The facts speak clearly for themselves. In 2005, we used to pay $250 for every ton of rice we imported; now we pay $1,050, four times as much. For a ton of wheat, we used to pay $132; now we pay $330, two and a half times as much. For a ton of corn, we used to pay $82; now we pay $230, nearly three times as much. For a ton of powdered milk, we used to pay $2,200; now it is $4,800. This is a perverse and unsustainable trend. This phenomenon undermines the internal markets of most countries in our region and around the world, affecting the population directly, particularly the poorest sectors, bringing poverty to millions of people. A few decades ago, there were countries that grew their own rice and corn. But, following the neoliberal recipes of the IMF, they liberalized the market and began to

responsibility of head of state by the leadership on Fidel's illness, here emphasized the need for greater domestic agricultural production, especially of foodstuffs for local consumption, pointing to 'structural deficiencies'.

A critical dimension of this issue—other issues include food insecurity and a weakening of the local food production sector—is the fact that already up to one third of government revenues generated in the tourist sector are needed and used to pay for food imports. While tourism has attracted hard currency, hundreds of millions of dollars were spent on importing food from the US, Canada, Argentina, the Dominican Republic and elsewhere. Food dependency on the US increased Cuba's vulnerability to any tightening of the export embargo. Thus it could be argued that Cuba's national security was weakened by the government's paying hard currency upfront, as required by the US Treasury Department, for an increasing proportion of US food imports.

While tourism served as a needed immediate strategy in the Special Period, unfortunately it has become an entrenched and strategic growth sector of the economy. Thus Cuba continues to follow its traditional cycle of 'monoculture' dependency—shifting from sugar export to the US and then to the USSR and Eastern Europe, then to tourism for Canadians and Europeans. The problem with the new dependency (as with the old) is that it provides a 'short term' solution while deepening long-term structural problems, including a misallocation of human resources (architects becoming bellboys, professors as taxicab drivers) and the lack of a diversified economy with resiliency to cope with the inevitable economic cycles endemic to the world capitalist market.[7]

Cuba's growing food dependency, reflected in the increased importation of rice, beans, poultry, pork, beef and other essentials

---

import subsidized US and European cereals, eradicating domestic production. With the rise in prices at the pace we have mentioned, a growing number of people can no longer afford to eat these basic food products. It comes as no surprise, thus, that they should resort to protests and that they should take to the streets to find whatever means they can to feed their children'.

[7] This and other structural and social problems deriving from the strategy of tourists development are serious enough and need to be dealt with. Nevertheless, positive factors in the government's implentation of this strategy included the provision of a majority government stake in the industry and the eventual assumption of full infrastructure ownership by the state after a minimum 15–20 year profit agreements with investors. Also, the misallocation of human resources in the personal decision of many professionals to enter the tourist sector as a means of improving their earned income also reflects Cuba's over-production of professionals, a problem which is partially relieved through the emphasis on the export of eduational and health services.

(including, at times, sugar) in the Cuban diet, is becoming acute. In his July 26, 2007 speech, Raúl Castro pointed to the enormous increase in prices of imported food, citing the threefold increase in the cost of powdered milk in the previous three years; the 10% increase in the price of milled rice between 2006 and 2007 and a doubling of the price of chicken.

Cuba's agricultural production is directed in large part toward the tourist and export market: tobacco, citrus, tropical fruit, and sugar (barely). Much of the quality fruit, meat, produce and poultry is sold in the private 'farmers' markets, or in the special stores which trade in dollars or 'convertible' currency. As a result, there is a scarcity of products at the state-subsidized neighbourhood stores. The development of 'urban gardens' has been one solution for certain neighborhoods—providing fresh quality 'organic' produce—but fail to cover much of the population's needs.

The decline in food production, especially rice (Cuba imports over 75% of its rice!) is striking. This is in part due to a lack of agricultural workers willing to farm rice—a labour-intensive crop—at least for the pay offered in comparison to employment in other sectors, especially the 'fast money' to be found in any official or informal work associated with tourism. With its low birth rate and very highly educated population, and despite the relatively high incomes and superior working conditions, Cuba is in need of greater numbers of agricultural workers, and the government seems uninterested in worker emigration from countries, such as Haiti, with a surplus of skilled agricultural workers. Paradoxically, Cuba possesses abundance of resources, agronomists and agricultural extension operators. In 2009–2010, the government initiated major agricultural reforms that involve the distribution of land in usufruct to thousands of would-be new farmers.[8] More than 1.2-million hectares of heretofore unproductive land is intended to be distributed. Change in the agricultural sector remains a challenge, however, as the 2009–2010 production in agriculture declined by 7.5% even with the new lands in production.[9]

---

[8] Decreto-Ley No. 259, del Consejo de Estado, de la República de Cuba, del 10 de julio del 2008

[9] "Cuba intenta reducir importación de alimentos," - *Notimex / El Porvenir*. Viernes, 16 de Julio de 2010.

While Cuba channelled large-scale capital investments into tourism, biotechnology and other productive sectors it relatively neglected its housing sector, creating a huge deficit, reflected in a 10-year housing waiting list for over a million families. Although the government is clearly aware of the problem and has begun to redress it, by some accounts and also anecdotal evidence, the housing deficit is a source of social discontent, even among mid-level party and government officials who have to live with their in-laws. In addition, current housing is in great disrepair, a problem that is especially pronounced in old Havana.[10]

While the government has announced a program to build 100,000 homes and apartments a year, the program suffers from bureaucratic delays and mismanagement, the pilfering of building materials by officials, low labour productivity, an inadequate supply of building materials and the not-insignificant effects of hurricane damage, which destroyed homes across the island in 2004 as four storms ravaged the island in the space of three months.[11] Notwithstanding recent policy moves in this area,[12] housing has not received the priority that the hotel-building tourist sector received in the 1990s. The emphasis on 'economic recovery' during the Special Period has led to an under-emphasis on basic consumer needs in the housing sector, creating a major deficit vis-à-vis the socialist human development model (housing as a fundamental human right) used to guide government policy.

The prioritization of short-term production over consumption is leading to what could turn into long-term problems of discontent among a sector of Cubans who have all the markers of a middle-class standard of living except for an exceedingly low level of material consumption. Cuban demographers have noted the absolute decline in

---

[10] For an excellent exploration of the housing situation in Cuba, see Taylor (2009).

[11] See *Juventude Rebelde* (June 18, 2007) in Arreola (2007). According to the trade union publication, Trabajadores, of 8,934 housing units approved for 2005 only 1,445 had been built by 2007.

[12] Notwithstanding the obvious and acknowledged housing deficit, Oris Silvia Fernández Hernández, first vice-president of the National Institute of Housing (INV), on December 17, 2007 announced that by the close of 2007 some 52,000 houses will have been completed in our country and some 180,000 repairs and renovations will have been carried out. 'This is a very accurate forecast', she said, 'although these figures won't mean the 100% execution of the strategic program of house building that the country has been implementing since the end of 2005…2007 will be the third year that Cuba has achieved important results in such a vital activity, though the larger quantity of finished houses was achieved the year before with 110,000 and, before that, with 57,000.'

Cuba's population as well as an aging population, lowering the number of people available for productive work.

According to Cuban population analysts the key socioeconomic factors that account for the demographic crisis is the lack of housing and the high cost of living (Oficina Nacional de Estadísticas—ONE, 2007). It has been argued that Cuba's economic development from this point forward, in regard to both human development and political legitimacy, require that top priority be given to homebuilding, repair and rehabilitation (Xinhua, 2007).

As for transportation, Cuba's purchase of a thousand buses from China provided some alleviation of a long-standing problem but the continuing reliance of many workers on hitchhiking testifies to the continued deficit in this area of human welfare. Likewise the 'losses', which occur during the transport of goods from producers to consumers, in recent years have generated chronic shortages of foodstuffs, building materials and petroleum.[13] Corruption, widespread theft, lack of coordination, inadequate managerial supervision are largely to blame—as well as (arguably) the lack of mechanisms for political control by consumers and conscientious workers. In sectors where the state has set high priorities, such as tourism, nickel and pharmaceuticals, the transport system seems to be functioning in a reasonably efficient manner.

The transport problem is not simply a lack of political will. The government's announcement in November 2005 that over 50% of gasoline was being pilfered, siphoned and sold on the black market is indicative of the breakdown of administrative oversight and the weakening in the government's authority, and thus, to some degree, the revolutionary ethic and culture of social solidarity (Castro, 2005).[14]

To overcome this lapse in socialist morality and regenerate a revolutionary consciousness—to motivate workers and others to work for the collective benefit—socio-political education, moral exhortation and citation of exemplary historic leaders (traditional motivational devices) are necessary but obviously insufficient in the context of continuing and renewed austerity, and the absence of decent wages and salary levels, problems of which the government is painfully aware.

---

[13] Castro, July 26, 2007 Speech at Camaguey. Raúl here cites the example of the waste of petroleum in the transport of milk from dairies to processing plants back to consumers living next to the same dairies.

[14] Fidel Castro speech, November, 2005—University of Havana (*Granma*, November 19, 2005).

Raúl Castro in this regard in his July 26, 2007 speech in Camagüey pointed out that:

> We are also aware that because of the extreme objective difficulties that we face, wages today are clearly insufficient to satisfy all needs and have thus ceased to play a role in ensuring the socialist principle that each should contribute according to their capacity and receive according to their work or contribution. This has bred forms of social indiscipline and tolerance, which having taken root proved difficult to eradicate even after the objective causes behind them have been removed (Castro, 2007).

Thus, one of the first policy moves made by Raúl Castro as President was to raise wages although ('with realism').[15]

Low wages—weak motivation—lack of work discipline—low productivity have affected services, manufacturing and agriculture in a vicious cycle. Over the past three years, wages were unfrozen after almost two decades and some relatively substantial increases were granted, supplemented by several announced further increments. Even so, relative to the substantial increases in charges for home electricity use, food (a substantial proportion of which is purchased in the 'free' market), clothing and other necessities, these pay increases are less than what would be necessary to stimulate greater productivity.

While greater effective consumer purchasing power is needed, so is the greater availability of consumer items at competitive prices. Salary and wage increases in the face of scarcity leads to more money pursuing fewer goods and informal price increases, thus eroding the nominal 'raises'. In view of these issues, Petras and Veltmeyer (2009: Chap. 5) argue that the economy needs to balance increased production and imports of consumer goods with investments in capital goods and production for export. They add that investments in tourist facilities need to be balanced with capital investments and exports. The gap between luxurious facilities for tourists and the poor state of workers' housing grew enormously during the 'special period'—a contradiction with serious human development as well as political implications and possible repercussions if not corrected. Also, continuation of foreign tourism's expansion during the decade and a half of recovery could erode the socialist ethos as much as the inequalities resulting from a

---

[15] 'Regardless of our great wishes to solve every problem we cannot spend in excess of what we have' (Raúl Castro, July 26 Moncado Day speech).

structural adjustment to globalization, and the theft of public resources—a major problem and another emerging contradiction.

Increased inequalities in the distribution of income is a major downside of the Special Period structural reforms, the social cost of 'market friendly' economic reforms implemented, with great reluctance by the government, as a desperate measure to salvage the economy. But according to various unofficial accounts, inequalities have also widened because of unofficial 'bonuses' to top officials engaged in joint ventures, foreign trade and the dollar (now Euro) economy. A new incomes policy in itself could contribute to greater incentives for productivity if combined with greater direct participation of all workers in the organization and administration of the workplace as well as the opening of multiple spaces to discuss the restructuring of the economy.[16]

James Petras, a long-time analyst of the Cuban Revolution and also a constructive critic, has analysed in some depth some of the shortcomings of current policy in regard to socialist human development (Petras, 2007). A revised income policy, he argues, should be directed toward promoting growth and development in the strategic sectors of the economy. However, stimulating growth in the sectors of agriculture, manufacturing and applied information systems require a change in the direction of government policy, particularly in regard to educational and professional training programs.

While most Asian and Latin American countries lagged behind Cuba in the 1960s, Petras observes, they have far surpassed Cuba in diversifying their economies, developing competitive export manufacturing sectors and lessening their export dependence on a narrow group of exports. By adding value to their products, Asian countries have increased earnings, which has led to higher wages and a better 'fit'

---

[16] On this point, the following remarks in Raúl Castro's speech on Moncada Day (July 26) 2008 are apropos (and, it is hoped, acted upon): 'The process of study and consultation with all of the workers will begin next September, prior to the adoption of the Bill by the National Assembly on December. That procedure will be useful to clarify every doubt and offer the opportunity to volunteer any criteria. Everybody will be attentively listened to, whether their views coincide or not with those of the majority, the same as we have done with the views expressed during the process of reflection on the last July 26th speech. We do not aspire to unanimity that is usually fictitious, on this or any other subject....The main problems and tasks we shall continue to analyze with the people, particularly with the workers, with the same transparency and confidence we've always had. We shall seek for the best solutions mindless of those who abroad try to take advantage of such debates. Sooner or later the truth prevails.'

between advanced education and occupational opportunities. Cuba's economy, Petras opines, is marked by a serious disjunction between a highly developed educational system and an economy that is not sufficiently diversified as to provide jobs appropriate to this system. Cuba, he argues, needs to adjust its education to train graduates to manage and run industrial and agricultural activity that mass-produces goods for mass popular consumption as well as trained scientists in medical services.

Both economic growth and social equality, Petras (2007) continues, have been significantly affected by the high level of theft of public property. Fidel Castro, while still in command, himself pointed to one indicator of this: the loss of 50% of earnings in the distribution of petrol sold on the black market. Official corruption and public theft, Petras observes, concentrates income in the hands of the black market operators, so increasing inequality and eroding a socialist work ethos.

The institution of joint ventures in economic enterprise, with a consequent reappearance of the social inequalities, was a necessary means of attracting needed capital during the years of systemic crisis. However, what was seen at the time as a tactical retreat has become entrenched with—Petras argues—far-reaching results. Indeed, social inequalities have created what Fidel himself has termed a 'class of newly rich' who are more disposed to embrace liberalism. The public sector in Cuba is still dominant and politically powerful,[17] but if it were to fail in coming to grips with the continuing scarcities and to provide for an adequate (or desired) level of material consumption, the government could become increasingly vulnerable to 'market socialists' who will tend to argue that the solution to scarcity is greater space for capitalist investors and commercial interests, both domestic and foreign.

However, it could be argued that social inequalities are not just the result of market forces, corruption and tourism, and an inequitable social structure. The concentration of political power is another factor. To curtail the growth of a nouveau riche requires more than periodic popular mobilizations—such as social workers taking over the gas stations—or a renewal of moral exhortations (which are nevertheless

---

[17] On the predominance of state property despite the inroads of joint ventures see the pronouncements of Economy Minister Jose Luis Rodriguez in Gerardo Arreola, "Firme en Cuba el predominio de la propriedad estatal: ministro de Economía" (La Jornada May 30, 2007) for a detailed discussion.

important!). Petras believes the prevention of new class formation requires a new system of elected representatives to oversee the allocation of the budget to the various ministries and the power to summon responsible officials to televised hearings for a strict public accounting, when necessary.

Another potential source of social discontent—other than the continuing scarcity of essential consumer products—Petras argues, is the disproportion between foreign humanitarian aid (internationalism) and the scarcity of goods in the domestic market. No one in Cuba, to all appearances, is calling for an end to solidarity with the global poor but Petras suggests—based on admittedly anecdotal evidence—that given the scarcities of consumer goods at home many Cubans do not necessarily support the current allocation of resources to the campaign for international solidarity.

Nevertheless, Petras insists that objections have been raised about Cuba's medical and educational internationalism and overseas commitments, some viewing it as an issue of misplaced priorities. For some (Petras, for example), who view Cuba's policy of exporting 'human capital' with the lens and optics of economic planning or social welfare rather than a matter of fundamental principle (international solidarity), regard the policy as a misplaced priority. Petras, in this connection, argues that Cuba's international health programs in some if not many cases (for Venezuela and Bolivia this is not an issue) are not reciprocated by favourable diplomatic or political responses by the regimes in the recipient countries. In fact, he writes that Cuban health spending allows some reactionary pro-US regimes to allocate funds for incentives to foreign investors or the purchase military weapons—as in the cases of Honduras, Pakistan, and in Africa and elsewhere—taking popular pressure off the national governments to provide social services. No doubt, Petras continues, Cuba gains the goodwill of the poor of these countries through this 'export of human capital', but it also threatens to provoke resentment on the home front.

On the other hand, it could well be argued that the 'export of human capital' is not just a matter of misplaced priorities in the allocation of scarce resources—international solidarity at the expense of domestic solidarity; that medical and educational internationalism is not based on the allocation of scarce resources; that Cuba has an abundance of human capital; and that, apart from the fundamental principle involved (international solidarity), the export of this capital at one and the same time relieves the pressures of a domestic oversupply of these resources (high-level qualified professional services) and, as in the case of Venezuela, allows for an equitable if not equal[18] international exchange.[19] A positive example of balanced reciprocal relations is Cuba's socioeconomic exchanges with Venezuela: oil at a discounted price (vis-à-vis the world market), investments and trade from Caracas in exchange for large-scale medical, educational and social services from Cuba's highly trained workforce.[20]

Economic Reforms and Human Development Matters

In 1990, when the socialist world was collapsing, the capitalist world order was in disarray, and Cuba was entering a system-threatening 'special period', the UNDP launched its flagship annual publication, the *Human Development Report*, designed to measure and rank countries according to their success in achieving 'human development'.[21] Cuba in this report was ranked 62nd out of 130 countries on its 'human development index (HDI). Two years later, Cuba ranking dropped as low as 81st (61st in the category of 'developing countries'), a clear reflection of the drastic reduction in the GDP and thus per capita income. In 1993, reflecting both realities in Cuba and possibly

---

[18] ALBA is not based on the capitalist principle of commercial exchange, but takes into account the developmental situation and needs of different countries

[19] The matter of Cuba's international solidarity programmes and the debate on the costs and benefits are explored in Kirk and Erisman (2009) *Cuban Medical Internationalism: Origins, Evolution and Goals.*

[20] In 2007 Cuba 'service' exports rose dramatically for the third consecutive year—to $8.36 billion in 2007, more than twice the level reported in 2004. This expansion of service exports was largely the product of an exchange with Venezuela for medical and educational services (tourism revenues stagnated for a second year at $2.2 billion). Cuba reported 39,000 of its citizens worked in Venezuela last year, 30,000 of them in the health sector. Cuba has also increased the export of services to Caribbean countries under Venezuela's Petrocaribe plan, which provides preferential financing for oil at 1% interest over 24 years if the saved revenues are used for economic and social development, often with Cuban participation. Revenues from joint pharmaceutical ventures in countries as varied as Iran, Russia, India, Malaysia and China fall under the service export category, as well as Cuban projects to build and staff eye clinics in various countries in Latin America, Asia, Africa and the Middle East.

[21] 'The basic purpose of development is to enlarge people's choices. In principle, these choices can be infinite and can change over time. People often value achievements that do not show up at all, or not immediately, in income or growth figures: greater access to knowledge, better nutrition and health services, more secure livelihoods, security against crime and physical violence, satisfying leisure hours, political and cultural freedoms and sense of participation in community activities. The objective of development is to create an enabling environment for people to enjoy long, healthy and creative lives'—Mahbub ul Haq, Founder UNDP Human Development Report.

methodological irregularities, Cuba was ranked 75th on the HDI vis-à-vis other 'developing countries' but 100th overall, while just a year later, Cuba's ranking returned to 89th and 108th (out of an enlarged group of 173 countries). In terms of the UNDP's 'capability poverty' measure Cuba ranked 10th out of all developing countries, not nearly as high as one might expect but then the country was at the nadir of a devastating economic crisis.

From 1994 to 2000 when Cuba introduced a series of major reform measures designed to restructure the economy out of the crisis, a slow but persistent trend towards an improvement in socioeconomic conditions could be detected notwithstanding increasing inequalities. This trend was reflected in a steady improvement in the HDI ranking from 88th in 1994 to 58th in 1999, 56th in 2000 and 51st in 2009, placing it well up into the 'high human development category'.

The 2001 HDR did not rank Cuba because of the 'lack of reliable data', but in 2002 it ranked 55th on the HDI (6th in the region) with a score of .795 (a hair breath below the arbitrary .80 medium to high threshold), and a difference of 35 in its ranking on the GDP per capita index. In the UNDP's supplementary Human Poverty Index (HIPI), which for some reason was not factored or integrated into the HDI (despite the need, stated as early as 1991, to 'make the HDI sensitive to income distribution') Cuba was ranked 4th out of all 'developing countries' (behind Uruguay, Costa Rica, Chile). In 2003, when Cuba's economic reforms began to bear fruit in the form of economic growth Cuba's HDI ranking improved three points to 52nd (.806), pushing it past the high-income threshold, even though its per capita income ranking slipped three points (to 38th). Only three Latin American countries—Argentina, Costa Rica, and Chile were ranked higher, and this because of the per capita income factor—considerably higher in these countries than in Cuba.

As for the Human Poverty Index (HIPI), Cuba's ranking fell one point—now 5th in the 'developing country' category. In 2004, at the threshold of a sustained economic upturn, Cuba retained its ranking on both the HDI and HPI, as it did in 2005. But in 2006 Cuba broke another threshold (a 50th ranking on the HDI), which provoked the President of the World Bank to grudgingly concede that 'Cuba was… doing something right…' (Lobe, 2001).[22] Cuba had succeeded in

---

[22] During a 2001 visit to participate in the conference on globalization organized annually by the association of Cuban economists, World Bank President James

achieving a relatively (and surprisingly) high level of human development not only on a low-income base but in the context of the worst crisis in its history and system-threatening challenges.

This 'accomplishment' begs a number of critical questions that require a closer look. What specific measures and structural reforms were taken to bring about this development while keeping the economy on a socialist track? That is, what crisis countermeasures did the government take in responding to the challenges confronting the country? More to the point, what do the noted improvements in Cuba's ranking on the UNDP's measure of human development mean for the average Cuban? Did the government's response to the pressures of neoliberal globalization and the challenges of the special period impact most Cubans in the same way or were there discernable or measurable differences in the distribution of associated costs and benefits? Elsewhere in Latin America adjustments to the requirements of the new world order increased social inequalities in the distribution of wealth and income, at an exceedingly high social cost borne by most working people. Was this the case in Cuba? What is the connection between the dynamics of income growth/distribution and other dimensions of human development?

Income-Based Social Welfare[23]

The level of 'real' or inflation-adjusted wage levels in Cuba collapsed catastrophically in the economic meltdown of 1989–1993. Even in Cuba, where the state provides substantially for social welfare, wage-based income is an important factor in determining the quality of life for most Cubans. Thus the capacity of the Cuban economy and government to counteract and reverse this meltdown is critical. The question as to whether or not the 'alleged economic recovery from 1994 to 2010' has been sufficient for Cuba to remedy this situation was the focus of a recent study by Arch Ritter (2010) on the Cuban economy.

Figure 3, based on calculations made by Pavel Vidal Alejandro, an analyst in Cuba's primary economic research institute (the *Centro de Estudios sobre la Economia Cubana*—CEEC), and presented by Ritter,

---

Wolfensohn remarked that 'Cuba has done a great job on education and health…they have done a good job, and it doesn't embarrass me to admit it'.

[23] The data and analysis in this section are based on Ritter (2010).

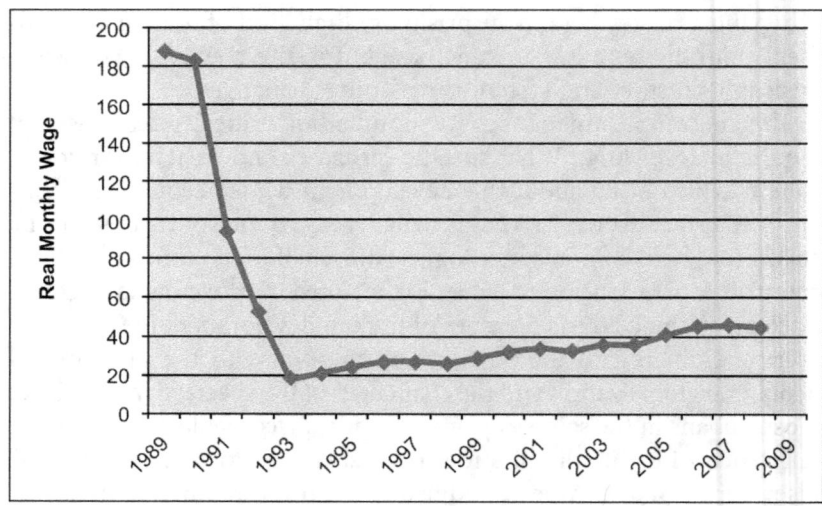

Figure 3. Cuba Real Monthly Wages, 1989–2009
Source: Ritter (2010)

shows that real wage levels did indeed steadily increase after 1994 but even so they are still but a small fraction of their pre-melt-down level.

According to these data, Cuba's real wage collapsed from a high of around 190 pesos to a low of 20 pesos in 1993, recovering gradually to 2008 (Figure 4). For those who observed this collapse in the early 1990s, these figures, as Ritter notes, 'are indeed credible'. How Cubans reliant upon peso incomes survived through this catastrophic decline constitutes, he notes, 'several million stories of endurance and innovation—or the practices encapsulated by the Special Period terms *resolver, luchar, conseguir* and *inventar*'.

Even so, although it would seem that the Cuban economy has fully recovered, surpassing the 1989 level by about 20% in GDP per capita terms, real wages on average are only at about 22 to 25% of the 1989 level (Table 8). This seeming contradiction raises a question that Ritter subsequently addresses: how have Cubans lived this contradiction? His answer: by seeking in many ways to make up the income deficit—including pilfering and the expansion of an underground economy; remittances from abroad; illegal but tolerated salary supplements for employees of joint foreign-state enterprises; legal forms of self-employment; 'income-in-kind' supplements (lunches for workers, food supplements for seniors, special access of some to transportation and housing); and the growth of a social economy in which

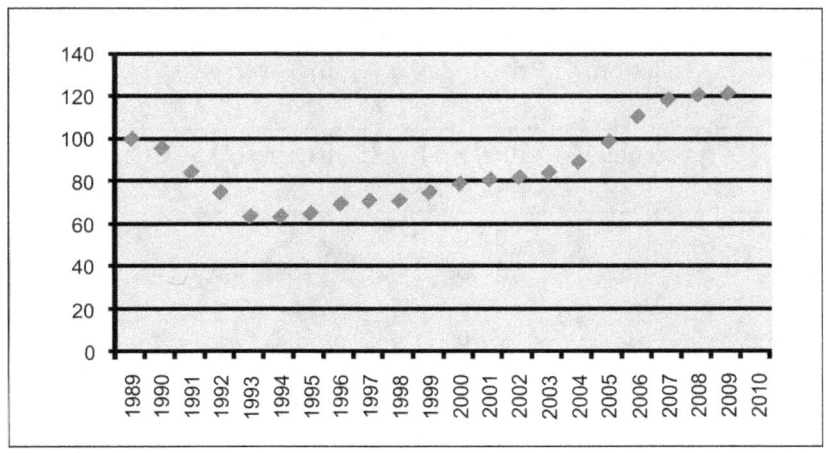

Figure 4. Cuba GDP per Capita, 1989–2009 (1989=100.0)
Source: Ritter (2010)

home-produced goods and services are exchanged with friends and neighbours (Ritter, 2010).

Ritter opines that if Cubans are able to tap these other sources of income—and it would seem that most can and do—they 'can survive reasonably well'. Those that cannot—some pensioners; workers in the state sector outside the major cities; some agricultural workers—are likely to be 'in dire straits' (i.e. income poor). However, it would seem that most Cubans by one means or another, and often some combination of them, are able to share in the increased social product—in the proceeds of the economic recovery.

The Scope of Raul's Economic Reforms

> The revolution has done and will continue to do anything within its power to continue to advance and to reduce to the minimum the unavoidable consequences of the present international crisis for our people. Yet, we should timely explain to our people the difficulties so that we can be better prepared to face them. We must get used to receiving not only good news….We are aware of the great amount of problems waiting to be solved, most of which weigh heavily and directly on the population. Nevertheless, it should be recognized that lately the limited resources the nation has been able to additionally deliver to the eastern region have been quickly put to good use.
> —President Raúl Castro, Moncada Day Speech, 2008

Table 8. Cuba—estimated Real Wages (pesos)

Year	Inflation	Price index	Nominal average salary	Real average salary
	(percentage)	(1989 = 1)	(Cuban pesos)	Cuban pesos 1989
1989		1.00	188	188
1990	2.6	1.03	187	182
1991	91.5	1.96	185	94
1992	76.0	3.46	182	53
1993	183.0	9.78	182	19
1994	−8.5	8.95	185	21
1995	−11.5	7.92	194	24
1996	−4.9	7.54	202	27
1997	1.9	7.68	206	27
1998	2.9	7.90	207	26
1999	−2.9	7.67	222	29
2000	−2.3	7.50	238	32
2001	−1.4	7.39	252	34
2002	7.3	7.93	261	33
2003	−3.8	7.63	273	36
2004	2.9	7.85	284	36
2005	3.7	8.14	330	41
2006	5.7	8.61	387	45
2007	2.8	8.85	408	46
2008	4.9	9.25	414	45

Source: Ritter (2010)

When Fidel Castro fell sick the popular sport (among foreign 'observers') of speculating on the 'post-Fidel transition'—on what would happen to Cuba once Fidel was constrained to step down from the driver's seat of state power—was renewed with vigour and some glee. In retrospect, however, what struck (and in some corners, disappointed) most observers was how 'smooth' the 'transfer of power' was. 'Unity at home', the message went, 'is the best defense against the only external power Cuba still regards as a threat—the United States.' These are not the words of a revolutionary or Cuba supporter but of

Julia Sweig, an academic spokesperson for the Corporate Global Empire (CGE).[24]

'None of what Washington and the [Cuban] exiles anticipated', Sweig writes, 'has come to pass'. Even as Cuba-watchers speculate about how much longer the ailing Fidel would survive, 'the post-Fidel transition is already well under way. Power has been successfully transferred to a new set of leaders, whose priority is to preserve the system while permitting only very gradual reforms'. In this context, Sweig notes, 'Cubans have not revolted, and their national identity remains tied to the defence of the homeland against US attacks on its sovereignty'. She adds: 'Not one violent episode in Cuban streets; no massive exodus of refugees...a stunning display of orderliness and seriousness'. She concludes that '[d]espite Fidel's overwhelming personal authority and Raúl's critical institution-building abilities, the government rests on far more than just the charisma, authority, and legend of these two figures'. Indeed, '[Cuba] is a functioning country with highly opinioned citizens...Although plagued by worsening corruption, Cuban institutions are staffed by an educated civil service, battle-tested military officers... and a skilled workforce'. Moreover, 'Cuban citizens are highly literate, cosmopolitan, endlessly entrepreneurial, and by global standards quite healthy'.

Beyond this issue of a peaceful 'transfer of power' as emphasized by the Cuban journalist Manuel E. Yepe (2008), 'the Cuban Revolution [since the transfer of power from Fidel to Raúl] has been characterized by its pragmatism within the context of very firm ethical principles'. The ability to 'correct errors and negative tendencies, without losing sight of the fundamental path', Yepe notes, 'has been a big factor in the survival of the Cuban vision of social revolution, which

---

[24] An axisoflogic.com label for the world's hegemonists in the form of the Rockefellers, ruling class members of the Empire and founders of the CGE. David and Nelson Rockefeller. Sweig is a Rockefeller Senior Fellow and the director of Latin America Studies at the Council of Foreign Relations (CFR), a major foreign policy forum for the US segment of the 'global ruling class'. The CFR has published the bi-monthly journal Foreign Affairs since 1922. Eleven secretaries of state, including John Foster Dulles and Henry Kissinger, have been part of its stable. Sweig's article, 'Fidel's Final Victory', in the January-February 2007 issue, is worth citing because it does what security-intelligence agencies are supposed to do: provide information to CGE's politicians so that they can make 'realistic' decisions about how to deal with their enemies, i.e. terrorists, socialists, revolutionaries and, generally, defenders of national sovereignty when this is anathema to CGE economic-political interests.

for a half century has faced very complex tests in the midst of great dangers'.

Yepe is almost certainly correct in this view of the Cuban Revolution—that its resilience and survival is based on a continuous process of reform and adjustment to changing conditions as well as a healthy and active internal debate. Raúl Castro, immediately upon assuming office in 2007 initiated another round of internal debates on the direction of the Revolution, a debate that resulted in another round of reform measures ('Raúl's reforms'!), the meaning of which has engaged the attention of Cuba watchers within and outside the country.

Some of the reforms have been announced publically, eliciting the most diverse interpretations;[25] others, as evidenced by Yepe in his review of recent and ongoing reforms to Cuba's food production process, were acted on without fanfare and few comments by outside observers like ourselves, who come in all kinds of ideological shades.

Wage and Income Reforms

Under *Labour and Social Security Resolution 9*, signed in February 2008 although not published in the official Gazette, the limits that had been placed on a state employee earnings were lifted. For the first time in decades, there would be no limits on employee earnings, state-television reported on April 10, 2008: 'For the first time it is clearly and precisely stated that a salary (or wage) does not have a limit, that the roof of a salary [will] depend on productivity', economic commentator Ariel Terrero noted, with reference to a new policy measures designed to improve the country's economic performance, revamping the state wage system to create more incentive by allowing workers to earn as much as they can.

Currently the Cuban state controls about 90% of economic activity and employs the vast majority of the labour force, often setting wages from offices in Havana. Cuba has always prided itself on its relatively flat pay scale system, ensuring a relatively equal distribution of the social product and national income—in a range of 4 to 1 from top to

---

[25] On this diversity of interpretations, the normal accompaniment to any announced reform measure, and the rather jaundiced and ideological responses of the foreign press and many outside Cuba watchers, see Walter Lippmann, Editor-in-Chief, CubaNews, July 27/2008).

bottom, versus a range of 12–18 to 1 that prevails in Latin America generally.

However, Cuba's egalitarian approach has come under fire in recent years for holding back production. 'One reason for low productivity is there is little wage incentive and this breaks productivity and stops bigger salaries', Terrero said. The LSC Resolution 9 was aimed at breaking the cycle while yet respecting the socialist principle, 'to each according to his work, from each according to his ability'. Raúl Castro, in this connection, upon taking over from an ailing Fidel in February, promised to make wages better reflect one's work, a major complaint of the population. 'It is our strategic objective today to advance in an articulate, sound and well-thought-out manner until the wages recover their role and everyone's living standard corresponds directly with their legally earned incomes'.

Raúl also launched a major reform of the agricultural sector to create conditions for state and private farmers to legally earn as much as they can from their efforts after meeting state quotas. It is an old problem. 'There is no reason to fear someone earning lots of money if it really is due to their work', Adalberto Torres, a Havana retiree, was reported to have said. 'It is the same with farmers. Give them land, let them work, it is not important how much they make. It is good because it means they are producing'.[26]

In addition, the ban on the sale of computers, DVD players, other consumer goods, cellphones, and on Cubans staying at tourist hotels, was also lifted. However, the problem here was that the vast majority of Cubans lacked the purchasing power to consume these goods or take advantage of the new opportunities for increased material consumption. One strategy of the Cuban government since the 1990s was to obtain foreign currency through their citizens who receive monetary gifts from relatives abroad. Behind this problem is the dual currency system instituted in the context of the Special Period as an adjustment to the economic conditions. When the fall of the Soviet Union plunged Cuba into its worst crisis in the early 1990s then-President Fidel Castro bitterly announced that the US dollar would become legal tender alongside the Cuban peso. He said at the time that the government had no choice if Cuban socialism were to survive,

---

[26] Frank, Mark. (2008) "Cuba removes wage limits in latest reform," Reuters. 10 April. http://www.reuters.com/article/idUSN1032792120080410

notwithstanding the inequality and social problems the measures would create.

As a result of the dual currency system and economy, the goods and services made available under the new policy could only be purchased by Cubans who have the hard currency to pay for them in convertible pesos, or CUCs, worth 20 times more than the Cuban pesos that most wages and salaries are paid in. By putting them on legal sale, it will make life easier for those Cubans with access to CUCs, which are pegged at $1.08. But it also highlights the inequalities in a country where the average wage is equivalent to about $17 a month in pesos.

Espina Prieto (2004), a Cuban academic specializing in matters of social inequality, notes that Cuba's Gini index of income inequality rose from .24 in 1986 to .38 in 2000 (perfect equality = 0, total inequality = .99). The index is an international standard widely used to measure inequality, though it excludes health care and education. Since these two elements are universal and free in Cuba, the country's Gini coefficient is typically underestimated. Cuba's Gini index is generally considered to have risen since 2000. Despite the dearth of updated figures, Cuba's standing remains above its neighbours in Latin America, which overall lie between .50 and .60 on the index.

While professionals such as doctors and teachers have very low state salaries, Cubans who receive remittances from family overseas, tips from tourists, run small businesses, go on government missions abroad, receive CUC bonuses, or sell goods on the black market have access to dollars with considerably higher purchasing power.

Currency Reforms—29 May 2008

The dual currency policy was undoubtedly functional and perhaps necessary at the time, but it had an exceedingly high social cost in generating a degree and forms of social inequality—even a class divide—that contradicted and placed a serious strain on one of most fundamental principles of socialism and the Revolution. Thus it was inevitable that the system would have to be dismantled sooner or later—when conditions allowed.

Osvaldo Martinez, President of the Commission for Economic Affairs of the National Assembly on a state visit to Madrid, acknowledged the problem and the plan to abolish the dual currency system. 'The government's policy is elimination of the dual currency, which in some way hurt the national self-esteem, but we need a minimum of monetary reserves for a normal exchange rate'. The government did not propose to eliminate the peso, the national currency, because it lacked the foreign reserves to back and circulate only CUCs. As for the US dollar, which circulated in Cuba from the mid 1990s on, it was removed from circulation late in 2004 because of the growing class divide and social discontent that it spawned. Today whenever a dollar is converted into CUCs, the government charges a 10% tax, which provides a minimal addition to the government's fiscal resources.

Pension Reforms—April 27, 2008

Barely two weeks after the announced labour code reform,[27] the government under the new Raúl Castro regime announced a policy reforming the pension system. In this regard, '[o]ne of the Revolution's invariable principles is to raise workers' wages and pensions, starting from those with the lowest, in the just aspiration of reducing social inequalities and reaching the point of all Cubans being able to live off their work or pensions'. Needless to say, the pension system, like the ration card, no longer fully supports this principle, the value of pensions having been significantly reduced over a decade and more of economic adjustments to the 'new economic reality'. The announced reform was designed to compensate for this loss in value on the basis of the fiscal resources made available by five years of recovered export-led growth.

'The revolutionary government, it was announced, 'has decided to increase social security and assistance pensions, in a fair acknowledgement to millions of men and women who have devoted a large part of their lives to creative work over nearly 50 years of building a new society and who are still firmly defending our socialism.'

The government similarly decided to increase the salaries of workers in the island's courts and public prosecutors offices—some two million (2,163,496 to be precise).[28] In 2005, economic realities (three years

---

[27] For details see "Información a la población: Decide el Gobierno Revolucionario el incremento de las pensiones de la Seguridad y la Asistencia Social," Juventud Rebelde.

[28] The rationale for including this sector of public workers in the new legislation was 'their dedication to fulfilling their duties and obligations, their ethics and professionalism in imparting justice, the role that they are playing in the battle against crime, social indiscipline and anti-social behaviour, and in preserving public order, security and tranquillity on the basis of socialist legislation'.

of economic growth) allowed income increases for more than five million workers, retirees and people dependent on social security and assistance, almost 50% of the population. At the time Cubans were informed that 'as economic realities, the fruit of hard work, savings, productivity and efficiency permitted, wages and pensions would continue to increase'.

Wage and salary raises were designed and applied by sector and priority, always with 'a rigorous assessment of economic and financial conditions as a premise for their implementation'. Thus, the government noted in its announcement that for that reason 'it is not currently possible to apply across-the-board wage increases, as the country does not as yet have the necessary resources'.

The improvement in pension benefits came into effect on the 1st of May and cover all social security retirees receiving pensions of up to 400 pesos, more than 99% of the total. The minimum social security pension was also increased from 164 to 200 pesos, retirees receiving pensions from 202 to 360 pesos received a 40 peso increase, and those on pensions of 361–399 pesos received 400 pesos. Families covered by social assistance received an increase of 25 pesos each, bringing the minimum up from 122 to 147 pesos, a 20% increase. These increases, by the government account, benefited 2,154,426 people, almost the same number of beneficiaries of the salary raise for workers in the People's Supreme Court and the Public Prosecutors Office.

International agencies acknowledge that more than half of the world's population still has no guarantee of social security. But in Cuba social security is assumed by the state as a human right, and on this basis the government channels a significant part of its fiscal resources to provide a measure of social security to the entire population, protecting people unable to work on account of age, disability, sickness or maternity. In the case of the death of a worker, similar protection is guaranteed to his/her family and, via social assistance, to senior citizens without resources or homes, as well as all people unable to work and who do not have relatives in a position to help them.

Together with its health and education programs, the social security provided by the state to the entire population is a major achievement of the Revolution, and undoubtedly a major policy reason for Cuba's high rate of human development—including life expectancy and infant mortality rates at levels common to the most economically advanced and wealthiest countries in the world—a theoretical anomaly as well as a major policy and political achievement.

The new 'economic realities' of the 'Special Period in Peacetime' (basically the entire decade of the 1990s) put this and other achievements of the Revolution at serious risk. Probably the most outstanding achievement of the Cuban Revolution was its ability to withstand the forces of change and survive a production crisis of such historic proportions, with its basic structure of economic and social policies intact; notwithstanding the enormous pressure of extremely scarce financial and economic resources not one school or hospital was closed; resources were stretched to their limits, and the requirements and pressures of economic adjustment led the government to institute reforms that themselves threatened to undo the entire system.

This provides a background for the recent post-Fidel reforms instituted by the government under the Presidency of Raúl Castro. As for the context that gave rise to these reforms and in which they were instituted, it is in the new conditions of global trade—a primary commodities boom. Although Cuba's exports in the new millennium are increasingly taking the form of tourism, health and educational services, and value-added manufactured goods, it is evident that the country has not managed to construct a sufficiently diversified economy.

However, in the context of a primary commodities boom lasting from 2003 to 2008 Cuba also benefited from the turn in the global economy and the ascension of China. This was particularly the case in regard to nickel, which accounted for 35.4% of exports in 2000 but as much as 46% in 2005. The economic recovery, and the high rates of growth recorded in recent years, were driven less by increased productivity growth based on productive investment than by the growing demand in Asia for primary commodities. Today 75% of Cuba's exports are still in the form of primary commodities—both a boon (in the context of a growing demand for these products) and a major structural problem, which was evident when the boom went bust in 2008.

Back to the Food Production Crisis—July 26, 2008

Even though there have not been and major public announcements on it, nor comments by the legion of Cuban watchers and the capitalist media, no reform is as important—or very few of them are—as the current efforts to reform Cuba's food production system under the terms of Decree Law 259, touching as these reforms do on 'a matter of national security for the revolutionary process' (Yepe, 2008).[29]

This reform process in terms of its 'far-reaching economic and social scope' and implications, were compared by Yepe to the agrarian reforms of the early years of the revolutionary process. As we argued above, it was a monumental mistake for the revolutionary regime to sacrifice food security to gain a comparative advantage on the capitalist world market—a problem that came home to roost in the current global context of dramatically rising food prices.[30] In this context, food imports in 2007 cost the country $1.6 billion and likely to rise thereafter, placing a serious constraint on national development as well a local consumption crisis in terms of domestic food costs.

One of the most significant changes wrought by *Decree Law 259* was to turn over idle land for use by state entities, cooperatives, and any Cuban citizen physically fit for agricultural labour. The aim of the decree was to reverse the decline in the acreage of cultivated land, which had fallen some 33% from 1998 to 2007. After the decree went into effect, farmers were brought together through their local organizations to describe their needs in terms of machinery, spare parts, irrigation equipment, ploughs, windmills, and other inputs needed to make the best possible use of the land.

A short time earlier there had been a reorganization of the agricultural sector, aimed at moving decision-making as close to the fields as possible by eliminating intermediary layers. In the context of what might be described as 'administrative decentralization' and local

---

[29] The agricultural sector—vegetable, dairy and cattle farming—means foodstuffs, a business on which Cuba spent $1.7 billion in 2007. Increasing production and productivity in this sector is a vital problem, particularly in the current context of rising food prices on the world market and the strategic importance of food production. This importance relates to the 'multiplying effect' of food production. It generates raw materials, raw foods, exportable goods and is a significant source of employment that provides jobs or about 24% of the nation's workforce. Given the dependence of Cuba on food imports (from a third to a half of what it needs) reforms in this sector have a dual dimension: to satisfy the needs of the population at acceptable prices and to achieve alimentary sovereignty, reducing dependence on the international market to a minimum, now that prices will undoubtedly continue to rise.

[30] Over 15 years ago, Raúl Castro, then Minister of the Revolutionary Armed Forces, had warned that in regard to national security and the continuation of the revolution, the availability of food for the population is as important as the weapons that the country requires for its defense—and sometimes even more important. From his new post as chief of state he has stressed the importance of securing the country's food supply as a high-priority national security issue, at a time when the world situation makes the food question more pressing, serious, and urgent.

development, the municipal delegations of the Ministry of Agriculture took over many of the functions that had been centralized, including servicing the private farmers and those organized in cooperatives. In addition, state food purchasing companies, which buy between 70 and 80% of the crops harvested by private farmers, increased the prices for the food products paid for (the remainder of their produce is sold directly to the public on the open market). The state farms and farmers' cooperatives would presumably experience a similar price increase, allowing them to productively invest some of the proceeds as well as improve the livelihoods of farm households. Farmers and farm workers are being remunerated for their labour at levels well above prevailing pay scales in the urban centres, under working conditions that are vastly improved from conditions that prevail in the region.

More than a few have objected to the prominence that the measure cedes to private property in the context of a socialist project that theoretically is wedded to social property and that therefore would assign a minor role to individual property and market production. However, factors relating to the survival of the revolutionary process have led to a convincing case made in favour of the measure, which, as Yepe notes, in a review of the ongoing reform process, 'borrows elements of the market economy to use to serve a pressing socialist objective'.

The ultimate aim of the reform process in the food production system is to increase food security as well as contributing to national development and an improved livelihood for the farm population in Cuba. The as-yet open and unsettled question is whether the reform process activated by *Decree Law 259* will bring about this development, and what effect it will have on Cuba's socialist path to national development. At issue here is what capitalist institutions (if any) can be, or need to be for the sake of national development, incorporated into a fundamentally socialist system. The issue: socialism or capitalism—or what possible combination?

Private Sector and Employment Reforms (August 2010)

At the point of this writing (August 12, 2010) President Raúl Castro announced the imminence of another round of economic reforms designed to absorb the surplus labour to be shed from the state sector—perhaps as much as a hundred thousand jobs. Already over the past few years since assuming power the regime shed hundreds of thousands of state sector jobs, and the only way to manage this contraction of the public sector in terms of employment without reneging on the responsibility of the state to deliver on the right of all Cubans to a decent job or adequately remunerated economic activity is to expand the private sector. This is the aim of the latest round of reforms instituted under Raúl's Presidency.

Contradictions and Problems, Options and Solutions[31]

Cuba's success in overcoming the collapse of its main trading partners in Eastern Europe and the ex-USSR, and restructuring its economy is one of the most dramatic developments in contemporary history. Likewise, Cuba's national security system's ability to defeat every effort by the world's biggest superpower to destroy the Revolution is also unprecedented.

Cuba's success in adjusting to changing economic conditions while sustaining its social programs distinguishes Cuba from the rest of the world where economic restructuring was accompanied by a reduction in fiscal expenditures and investments on social services. The changes engineered by the revolutionary government, however, have created important contradictions, which as yet are not system threatening but could become so if neglected. There are processes, practices, policies and structures that are gradually eroding the basis of mass support and should be addressed with some urgency while they are still solvable.

Positive reforms in this regard included:

More balanced economic planning and worker-consumer oversight of administration and participation in joint decision making;

1. Publication for public scrutiny of accounts, income, expenditures of all ministry officials;
2. Publication of expense accounts, transport, housing, private gifts and assets, overseas purchases, of all top officials;
3. More open and public debates, and referendums on major national policy issues such as investment priorities, overseas aid versus domestic programs in healthcare, housing, food and transport. This would bring popular participation and people's power to bear on macroeconomic policy as well as local development issues.

---

[31] This section leans heavily on points made in Petras and Veltmeyer (2009: Chap. 5).

Two of the biggest mistakes made by Cuban policy-makers in past years (and of course hindsight is useful here) are the closing down of small business operations for the domestic market and the failure to prioritize domestic food production and food security. In regard to the first, the decision in 1968 to close down approximately 50,000 small businesses in hindsight was a colossal error, which has not been sufficiently rectified by recent reforms designed to restore a limited private sector and local markets. Small enterprises such as cafes, bars and restaurants, and in the retail sales and service sector, provide a variety and quality of services that the state cannot, and they make a significant contribution to the quality and sociality of life—an important condition of human development!

Petras (2007) suggests that Cuba has over-extended its overseas medical aid programs at the expense of maintaining hospitals, clinics and health service at home. He observes that while outside observers rightly compare Cuba's vast superiority to the poor US public health system Cubans have begun to complain of delays and waits in treatment due to the overseas assignments of medical staff.

It might be an issue of competing values and commitments—international solidarity versus essential social services. In any case, in its efforts to recreate the internal dynamics of the Revolution the Cuban government should probably continue to prioritize basic needs but it should also address the desires and demands of the Cuban people for more consumer goods. The evident desire for more and better consumer goods cannot be indefinitely put off with an appeal to solidarity with the Revolution's basic values. The production of an adequate level of consumer goods is also a social welfare issue and thus a human development concern. Although President Raúl Castro, in his Moncada Day speech on July 26, 2008, was correct in emphasizing the enormous challenge of meeting the entire population's basic needs and its demands on the basis of very limited resources, this challenge can be met with an energetic application of the right policy and strategy (on this see the discussion above on the meaning of Raúl Castro's reforms). As argued by Petras (2007) it could also be accomplished by redressing the imbalances between the export and domestic sectors, the development of advanced training and the practical needs of the economy, and increased investment of the society's productive resources. In this connection, the current regime's emphasis on infrastructural development and productive investment in the industrialization of the country's non-renewable and particularly renewable resources would seem to be on the right track (*La Jornada*, July 27, 2008).[32]

Cuba has demonstrated a capacity to resolve internal contradictions and correct errors in economic policy—tacking with different shifts in the winds of change with 'the courage to rectify the mistakes made on the side of idealism in the management of our economy' (Fidel Castro, July 26, 1973). The current contradictions and problems, such as the importation of food products that should and could be produced by Cuba, are not irresolvable, but they do require a serious rethinking of current priorities, strategies and structures. An open debate among all anti-imperialist Cubans is a necessary means for deepening and sustaining the achievements of the Revolution.

In this connection, Petras (2007) could well be correct in warning that any new dogmas and some entrenched bureaucrats, as well as the posturing of apolitical and politically liberal artists, writers and filmmakers, could be as much an obstacle to winning or maintaining the support of the Cuban people for the Revolution as the social inequalities that have emerged. While efforts must be made to ensure that these inequalities are not entrenched, and indeed reversed, the critical factor in the successful management of the country's persistent and new contradictions is to fully engage the population in the project. This was the recipe of successful socialist development and for advancing the revolutionary process in the past; it is the key to the current predicament of the government.

In the same connection (how to advance the revolutionary process) the Cuban Revolution and its leadership can count on an enormous

---

[32] 'A work of special significance ... is advancing at a good pace: the reconstruction and expansion of the aqueduct ... by 2011 the renovation of the El Cobre and El Cristo aqueducts shall be completed ... and the construction of the 15.6 miles of water pipeline ... So far, 231.2 miles of major water networks and 370.6 miles of secondary water networks have been completed ... Likewise, the modernization of the Quintero Uno ...[and] work is being done on several water transfer systems throughout the country ...heavy polyethylene pipes ... increased with the construction of factories in Holguín and Havana City....This is an enormous investment that we are carrying out looking not only into the present but especially into the future.....A special place among the new investments undertaken in cooperation with Venezuela is taken by petrochemicals: the increase of oil refining, the production of fertilizers and the manufacturing of synthetic resins....At the same time, a major expansion has been undertaken—in some cases with our own resources and in others with foreign companies—in the area of nickel, cement and mining....these works will be spread all over the country. For example, the expansion of the Hermanos Diaz oil refinery has been planned to exceed twice its capacity; at that point it will be in a position to supply oil to the entire eastern part of the country' (Castro, July 26, 2008).

reservoir of good will, solidarity and loyalty from the vast majority of Afro- and Euro-Cubans. But there are limits in time and patience: Cubans' desire for a better life is pressing for solutions to everyday needs. Delays and constant postponements in meeting basic needs in housing, transportation, income and food only lends support to the liberal counter-revolutionaries who argue or clamour for greater market and political freedoms. Moral appeals and disciplinary measures, in this connection, are necessary but insufficient if they are not accompanied by a more active engagement of Cubans from all walks of life in the revolutionary process, greater popular oversight and the improved availability of material goods and incentives, affordable quality and varied food and available housing for each family generation. The future of the Revolution is now, not in their lifetime but this year. Nothing less than the future of the Cuban Revolution is at stake as the current wide-reaching debate over strategy, social structures and political action proceeds.

Culture as a Pillar of the Revolution: Critics Within and Without

A pillar of the Revolution and a critical factor in explaining its surprising longevity is the extent and depth of the loyalty to the project and its leadership, a loyalty that extends into several generations removed from direct participation in the initial experience and an appreciation of pre-revolutionary conditions. It is clearly difficult for any revolutionary process to maintain a revolutionary élan from one generation to the next—to maintain the essential support for the Revolution against threats, which can come from both within and the outside. The capacity of the revolutionary leadership to instil and maintain this loyalty has been a major achievement, due in good part to the success in bringing about a 'cultural revolution' and in the ability of the regime to sustain this culture against diverse threats and direct attacks against it from the advocates of liberalism and capitalism.

The neoliberal threat comes from several sources. The most obvious 'hard threat' comes from the US empire—from the government and its pseudo-nongovernmental organizations (NGOs) mass propaganda and entertainment media as well as from informal sources like relatives and sports recruiters. This 'hardline' animosity to the Cuban Revolution, however, as is well known, is a powerful force but not in the least effective, mainly because it is so clearly identified in Fidel's speeches and revolutionary discourse, embedded in 'la conciencia' and widely understood and embraced.

Fidel Castro on Revolutionary Morality and Education

> This country can self-destruct; this Revolution can destroy itself, but they [the US] can never destroy us; we can destroy ourselves, and it would be our fault
>
> —Fidel Castro, November 17, 2005

In his speech at the University of Havana, on the 60th anniversary of his enrollment at the University, Fidel for the first time publicly referred to the ultimate consequence of a failed effort to develop a revolutionary consciousness among the population as a whole. A disillusioned populace, he observed, one that pursues individual greed-consumerism, can destroy the Cuban revolutionary 'project', something that the enemy cannot. That would mean that the key goal—'The ultimate and most important revolutionary aspiration: to see man liberated from alienation' (Che's motto)—had not progressed sufficiently.

That Fidel would make this reflection public is a clear admission of the greatest actual challenge for the Revolution. The ethical root to this dilemma—selfishness and greed, reflected in a culture of possessive individualism and consumerism that underpins and is promoted by capitalism—'is, in fact, at the core of existence for the human race and the planet'. Progressive or revolutionary readers, and supporters of Cuba, must not—Fidel admonished—'shun our own reflection on this decisive question' A united, conscientious people, he continued, can withstand the strongest enemy even when hungry—such as did the Vietnamese against China, France and the United States—but 'a morally disillusioned people cannot, not even with full stomachs'.

Democratic freedom, as the 'bourgeois capitalists' would have it, is based upon an appeal to individualism and coated with the surrendering supposition that humankind is born sinful, guilty, greedy, egoistic, and even evil. But, Fidel argues, 'the best that can be said about us is that we are born neutral and given a caring environment we can develop into a loving, and thus sharing and peaceful, race'.

As 'an advocate of and sometimes participant in socialist revolution', Fidel added, 'I, alongside many Cubans, work for the human race's development into Che's *new man*, or Jesus Christ's *love thy neighbor* human beings'. In this connection, '[w]e hope that not too many

Cubans sink into the quagmire of individualism, into the *American Dream* of individualist opportunities for wealth'. This ideology, he argued, 'is as powerful a weapon for capitalism-imperialism as is their police-military violence. It has captured the majority of working classes in most countries'.

In this regard, Fidel noted, 'the Cuban people have braved the rigours of US imperialism. They have struggled up from the darkest days of the collapse of European state socialism, they have continued the egalitarian social network for all inhabitants and continue offering their *human capital* to poorer countries.' On the other hand, 'their lack of allies and the Special Period reforms have also caused large numbers of people—including but not exclusively the new rich sector—to shun revolutionary morality'. To this frank admission of a major problem confronted by the Revolution—how to retain a revolutionary consciousness in the conditions of the 'special period'—Fidel adds the comment: 'As I was often told by several Cubans earlier this year, *We can't eat morality*'.

At this point in his analysis of a fundamental problem faced by the Revolution ('the unique survival of Cuba and revolutionary consciousness'), Fidel quotes Heinz Dietrich, a well-known Latin American Marxist intellectual, as follows:

> During the long heroic phase of the Revolution, the overwhelming majority of the population fully identified with the process. But this identification is much more qualified today...for several reasons: Generational change, the fall of the USSR, the scientific and technological revolution, with its resulting processes of intensive accumulation and globalization, and the hampering effects of imperialist aggression on Cuba's endogenous economic and political development.

The admission or the argument that the support of Cubans for the Revolution, or solidarity, might be flagging in some Leftist circles led to charges of 'betrayal', providing grist for the mill of anti-Cuba propaganda, allowing Cuba's many enemies to sow the seeds of discontent and reap the harvest—'to divide people and thus allow the enemy to conquer them'. However, Fidel himself confronted the problem pragmatically rather than ideologically. Notwithstanding the 'vital need of shaping and maintaining unity' (which 'Cuban leaders have always stressed') 'if we ignore the reality of disillusionment, we do nothing to avert its consequences'. As Dietrich notes in this connection: 'We should have learned this already, especially with the fall of state socialism, which was accomplished with hardly a whimper'. The working class in this case had 'lost its revolutionary morality and turned its back on so-called socialism'.

Addressing the question of the possible reversibility of the Revolution—a heresy for some dogmatic leftists unable to confront their demons but discussed by Fidel in his speech—Dietrich for his part proclaims: 'The Cuban Revolution, for me, must succeed, not only for eleven million Cubans but as our beacon of hope for a better world. If Cuba self-destructs hundreds of millions will be lost in depression.' He adds: 'The world's monster [US imperialism] realizes this. That is why it is so imperative for it to destroy the "bad example of the good example". And that is why we must confront our warts.'

And indeed, that is what Dietrich proceeds to do ('So, let's look at the problems!'). When the Special Period in Times of Peace was launched in September 1990, and set fast with the July 26, 1993, declaration by a solemn Fidel of the need for a 'dual economy', he acknowledged being 'afraid that inequalities would lead not only to a new rich but to a class society'. Dietrich began writing about this worry in some left media, but *Prensa Latina*, where he worked, would not publish such 'subversive' thinking. He noted that many foreign supporters of Cuba accused him of betraying the Revolution—not unlike the response of a number of Leftist supporters of Cuba (and some Cubans) to the 'constructive' criticisms leveled by Petras against some of the policies pursued by the current regime and its hypersensitivity to criticism, using national security as an excuse for eluding open debate on the mounting problem of a decline in socialist morality.

As for Fidel himself, on November 24, 2005, on a popular roundtable TV program he made direct reference to this decline in socialist morality, speaking of the associated problems of selfish behaviour, theft of public property and corruption in terms of a 'new class': 'We are well aware', he asserted, 'that today there is a new class, in virtue of the phenomena [the Special Period] that the Revolution has had to go through'. But in another speech, on November 17, he argued that the new rich would not win against socialism: 'I can assure you with absolute certainty that this battle against waste, theft, the illegal diverting of resources and other generalized vices has been won in advance'.

Fidel praised the revolutionary efforts of the mass organizations and the new youth brigades—social workers—established to watch thievery by the working class and the petty bourgeoisie. Thousands of students, wearing blue T-shirts with white lettering that read 'social workers', had taken the place of workers at gas stations. Fidel explained: 'Certain vices can be very deep-seated. We started with Pinar del Rio to ascertain what was happening in the gas stations that sell gas in dollars. We soon discovered that there was as much gas being stolen as sold...in some places more than half'.

'Well, what is happening in Havana?' Fidel continued. 'Will they mend their ways? Not really, everything is fun and games'. In Havana Province, 'people learned to steal like crazy. Today, the social workers are in the refineries; they get on board the tanker trucks that carry 20,000 or 30,000 litres, and they watch, more or less, where that truck goes, and how much of the oil is rerouted. They have discovered private gas stations supplied with oil from these trucks.'

French journalist-sociologist Danielle Bleitrach wrote an analysis of Fidel's November 17 speech[33] in which she noted some of the results of the measures adopted to combat the epidemic corruption and the decline in socialist morality. 'The sweep is deep. A number gives a good idea: in 2005, the Party rid itself of 2,900 members and several company directors and ministers were dismissed. In the workers assemblies, workers were invited to reflect on everything, to figure out the real cost of the robberies. The consequences were sanctions and expulsions but also jail sentences or transfers to sectors less in play'. Some cases were made public, but in general the measures were taken discreetly in the work centres. She defined Fidel's speech as being in 'perfect synchrony with the Cuban mentality'. The debate starts from a concrete fact, how to leave the Special Period, and ends with an investigation of socialism and the future of humanity.

Socialist Consciousness and the Battle of Ideas

Recognition by the Cuban government of the seriousness of the alienation among some sectors of the population from the ideals of the Revolution, and the problem of maintaining intergenerational support for the socialist project led to new policy directions. The 'battle of ideas' is one such effort, waged in a context of evident discontent in order to revive a flagging social ethic, to repair the breach caused by the construction of a dual economy, market reforms, and continuing austerity.

---

[33] See "Que pasa en Cuba", www.rebelion.org, May 18, 2006, and in English published by www. walterlippmann.com July 3, 2006.

Font (2008) provides one of the more comprehensive studies of the 'Battle of Ideas' initiative, which is in many ways a catch-all umbrella for a variety of components, categorized as:

1. An emphasis on human and social development (taking precedence over economic growth)
2. Educational reform
3. Emphasis on consciousness and values
4. National campaigns (e.g., the effort to free Elian González; the Energy Revolution, etc.)
5. Emphasis on mass mobilization
6. Recentralization and the economic role of the state
7. Reaffirmation of socialist norms and concepts in the economy
8. New internationalism

Font sees parallels with the 'Battle of Ideas' in the rectification program of the late 1980s, consolidating core support and authority in the state. He sees the initiative as being tightly connected to the active participation of former President Fidel Castro, with an ebb during Castro's illness and relinquishing power in 2006 and a rise again with Castro's prominence in the publication of the Comandante's (later Compañero's) *Reflexiones* in Cuban media:

> the more ambitious aims and hopes of the Battle of Ideas may not be sustained, several specific programs and tendencies (for example, educational institutions and programs, some entitlements, and the like) seem to have better short-term prospects. A turning point beyond the current stalemate with the hardliners will ultimately hinge on the reformers' willingness and ability to confront and transcend the traditional orthodoxy of state socialism (p. 65)

As the 'Battle of Ideas' is seen as less prominent in official discourse of late, there remain the various initiatives, each with a differing capacity to endure (and some, such as the Elian González saga, come to a definitive end).

Education and the Battle of Ideas

Cuba's educational program from the beginning was oriented towards achieving social justice under conditions of 'full equality'. This commitment has continued to evolve. For example, since the beginning of this century, illiteracy having been vanquished, the government has conducted a campaign known as the 'Battle of Ideas'. The campaign is based on Cuba's liberation hero José Martí's ideal that 'no social justice is possible without educational equality'. Che Guevara, as noted in Chapter 4 interpreted this ideal by considering the whole of Cuba as one great university.

The 'Battle of Ideas' aims to promote and reinforce a revolutionary consciousness of the need for social solidarity, especially in light of the efforts of the United States, to counter the emphasis and the value placed by Cuba on social solidarity with liberal individualism. The campaign begins in daycare centres with the 'Educate Your Child' program, using non-formal ways of training that include the use of television programs, and continues into tertiary or university programming.

Cuba today has five television stations as opposed to two a decade ago. Two of these channels are oriented towards educational programming. Teachers use these channels video programs. Children also learn computer skills in primary school. English is taught from the third grade onward. Primary classes were down to a student-teacher ratio of 1 to 20, and even a lower ratio for 428 schools for children with disabilities. Classrooms had been organized in hospitals and in children's homes taught by peripatetic teachers. Pre-university education had been expanded and the student-teacher ratio reduced to 1-30. All teachers are trained to become educators responsible for the all-round education of a set number of students. A new group of peripatetic teachers, the José Martí Contingent, included 4,000 art instructors teaching visual arts, music, theater and dance in all communities. Another program, Study As Work, provided three hours of classes four days a week and part-time jobs to 150,000 young people, who had neither studied nor worked. Fifty thousand new teachers, who would otherwise not have become teachers, graduated through these work-study courses in the past three years. Cuba has the most teachers per capita in the world: one to every 37 inhabitants. Another 20,000 secondary school graduates were trained as social workers while pursuing a university education. These 'doctors with souls' deal with human problems. They frequent homes where families have special needs, such as: elderly people, those with disabilities and social behavioural problems.

The 'Battle of Ideas' campaign also seeks to universalize higher education. The universalization of higher education was supported, if not assured, in 2006 by a doubling of state educational expenditures—one-fifth of the national budget. The Minister of Education, Juan Vela Valdes, reported on July 19, 2006, that Cuba's network of university classes was functioning in 3,150 localities covering all the country's 169 municipalities. Four hundred thousand people were studying at university level in this way. Many were take courses part-time while working. Another 86,000 students were studying full-time at Cuba's 65 universities. All together these one-half million people studying at a university level represented 4.5% of the population.

At the time of the revolutionary victory, Cuba had only three state universities and one private. Total enrolment was 20,000. Since the revolutionary victory, Cuba has graduated 800,000 university students. Former Minister of Education, Dr. Luis Gómez Gutiérrez, explained Cuba's Battle of Ideas to participants of the World Conference on Basic Literacy Training held in Havana, February 2005, in this way: 'The idea is to reach everybody, that no-one is ever abandoned or unattended. Education reaches everyone from early childhood and throughout life…excluding no one. We pin our hopes on this utopia and the results we have obtained breathe life into our optimism. We are building the fairest, most equal society that has ever been known to the history of humankind'.

Conclusion

The first decade of the new millenium brought innumerable new challenges and opportunities to Cuba. Despite an improving economic context built upon the successful cultivation of the tourism industry, biotechnology and nickel exports (among others), and a GDP that is in the neighbourhood of pre-Special Period figures, Cuba also was faced with internal distortions brought about by structural changes in the economy, the cultural/consumerist influence of some two-million tourists per year and a general weariness of the population which has endured material deprivations for an extended period. The fact that the country remains highly stable in a sociopolitical sense in spite of continuing economic repercussions (long-term arising from the Special Period; short-term arising out of the global economic crisis) is a testament to the groundwork laid over the previous five decades.

CHAPTER TWELVE

CONCLUSION

The first step in the construction of our argument was to deconstruct the concept of human development as presented in the prevailing 'development' discourse and to reconstruct it in socialist terms. In these terms 'human development' was redefined with reference to three revolutionary ideals, each constituting a fundamental value and organizational principle of socialist human development: equality, freedom, solidarity.

With reference to these ideals and values we then identified the following steps in the evolution of the human development idea. First, we had the liberal conception of freedom and equality, expressed in economic and political terms. In economic terms Adam Smith conceived of the free play of market forces as the ideal that made the pursuit of individual interests compatible with the greater good of society. Subsequent liberals, in the 19th Century elevated the rational calculation by each and all individuals of their self-interest into a social virtue, transmuting the ideal of equality (within the framework of the market) into the notion of *equity*, secured by social and political reforms to the economic and political systems. It was the utopian socialists and then Marx who criticized this conception of equity, arriving at the conclusion that it an equitable social order required a new form of social organization and an overhaul of both systems.

Some hundred and fifty years later, the idea of social equality, and the principles of equity and social justice, put forward in socialist thought crystallized in the form of social liberalism and socialism. In social liberal terms the principles of equity and social justice took form as the idea of human development. In socialist terms, they were embodied in and most consistently advanced by the Cuban Revolution in the notion of socialist human development.

The advance of socialism in these terms took place in the context of what could be termed 'the globalization of solidarity' versus the dynamics of neoliberal globalization, which, by its very nature, impedes the achievement of human development, allowing only for 'structural adjustment with a human face'.

Human Development Dynamics of Capitalism and Socialism

The idea of human development, to all intents and purposes (or in regard to the post-World War II development projects of international cooperation, decolonization and nation-building) can be traced back to the ideas of freedom, equality and fraternity (solidarity)—rallying cries for revolutionary change in the eighteenth century and the declared goals of the post-war efforts to bring about improvements in the social condition of people and nations across a global development and ideological divide.

Over time these ideas were acted upon in different ways, giving form to different conditions and diverse forms of social change and development. Development can be viewed in both structural terms (as the result of the normal functioning of the system) and in strategic terms (the result of actions on values and beliefs consciously directed towards a defined goal), but in terms of the latter, we identified the following major 'moments' in the dialectic of the idea (human development, or freedom and equality):

- Elaboration of two ideologies (liberalism and socialism) to mobilize the forces of progressive change in the directions of freedom and equality
- Construction of the *welfare state* under conditions of a major capitalist crisis and a socialist state under conditions of a 'proletarian revolution' in Russia
- The declaration of the UN Charter of fundamental human rights
- Formation of a developmental state within the institutional framework of a new world order (the Bretton Woods system) and the fusion of the ideas of 'progress, 'equality' and 'freedom' as 'development'
- Formation of a socialist state in Cuba based on humanist principles
- Construction of the Basic Needs development paradigm based on a program of state-led social reforms to the operating economic system
- Construction of a model for bringing about a process of 'sustainable human development'
- Implementation of a development strategy based on a Washington Consensus on the superiority of free market capitalism, followed by a post-Washington Consensus on the need to 'bring the state back in' to create conditions for a more socially inclusive and

participatory development based on the empowerment of the poor, a policy of decentralization and 'good governance'
- A strategic public action' response within the Cuban Revolution to a major crisis in the socialist system of production
- Reformulation of the UNDP view of human development in terms of the dynamics of human development in Cuba in a context of crisis and globalization
- Emergence of a movement towards the 'socialism of the 21st century' based on a culture that promotes unity around values such as solidarity and humanism.

Revolution as Human Development

In the post Second World War context, development, whether viewed in structural or strategic terms, unfolded within the institutional framework of two distinct systems—capitalism and socialism. The project of international cooperation for development was designed to ensure that the developing and undeveloped countries of the so-called 'third world' would not fall prey to the lure of communism and that they would pursue a capitalist line of national development. Pressures for revolutionary change in the 1950s and 1960s, and the demonstration effect of the Soviet model of socialist development, led to the formation of diverse welfare and economic development regimes, and a broad program of state-led social reforms to the capitalist system. The high costs of these programs led to a counterattack against the forces of progressive change and the construction of a new world order in which the 'forces of economic freedom' were released from the regulatory constraints of the welfare-development state.

In the face of this 'counterrevolution' the proponents of progressive reform advanced diverse ideas for bringing about alternative forms of development that are socially inclusive and participatory, human in scale and form, constructed from below rather than from above, people-led and-centred, equitable and empowering of women and the poor, and sustainable in terms of the environment and rural livelihoods. While the Washington Consensus on the need for free market capitalism took form as a new economic model of neoliberal globalization and a program of market-friendly 'structural reforms', proponents of progressive change and government intervention designed and placed on the policy agenda a model to guide policy in the direction of sustainable human development.

Throughout the post-Second World War period and until the 1990s development unfolded in two different systemic contexts, providing developing countries that were formally non-aligned room and opportunities to opt for but also to manoeuvre between a capitalist and a socialist path. In the historic context of US imperialism and an oppressive class rule power, and the specific conjuncture of growing resistance to imperialist exploitation and oppressive class rule, Cuban revolutionaries turned towards socialism to provide the system requirements for their human development project. Throughout the 1960s and subsequent decades Cuba proceeded along this path, tacking to the winds of change.

Changing conditions in the 1980s and 1990s created different context for human development in both its capitalist and socialist form. A capitalist form of human development was advanced and promoted by the economists at the UNDP, with variable degrees of success. Human development in this form throughout the 1980s and 1990s and beyond, bound by the institutional and social structures of a capitalist society and economy, had to contend with conditions generated by contradictions inherent in the system. The major contradiction is that under a private property regime, and given the power of capital and its relation to the state, the freedom accorded the capitalist class in the pursuit of profit undermines the ability of workers and people in the subjugated popular sector to pursue lives that they have reason to value. The freedom of capital is the unfreedom of labour; the forces of capital accumulation, even when regulated by the state in the public interest, militate against human development, providing opportunities for some to accumulate wealth at the expense of many others, limiting their opportunities for self-advancement and exposing them to forces that prevent many of them from even meeting their basic needs.

A corollary of this conclusion—that capitalism does not satisfy the system requirement of human development for freedom and equality; that capitalism at the level of both freedom and equality is inherently inhumane; and that giving capitalist development a human face does not change this fact—is that socialism should provide better system requirements. This is because socialism by definition, in theory if not in practice, is geared to the values of freedom and equality, and commits a governing regime or State to the institutionalization of these values not just as a formal or legal right but as a substantive human condition—under conditions that are equal for all. In this respect Marx formulated the dictum that 'the free development of each is the condition for the free development of all'. We might also hypothesize, and here state as a guiding principle, that 'the free development of all is the condition for the free development of each'. This corollary in subsequent chapters is formulated as a hypothesis and a guiding principle—to give direction to our study into the dynamics of socialist human development in Cuba.

Human Development as Revolutionary Consciousness

The demand for more equitable and sustainable forms of human development is a critical factor in a growing worldwide rebellion against the institutions and agents of global capitalism—the global ruling class and their international financial institutions and global corporations. But this movement needs a vision that conceives of these institutions and their policies as part of an exploitative system: capitalism. And it needs a framework for the debate, reconciliation, and realization of alternative pathways and strategies for negating the power of capital over the conditions of human development. That framework is socialism. Towards these ends, it could be argued that Marx's vision and political project remains 'the most thoroughgoing and self-consistent project of social emancipation and hence…worth studying as such' (Chattopadhyay, 1986: 91).

Another project that warrants a closer look and further study in this regard is the way in which the Cuban Revolution exemplifies this vision, advancing and acting on it in the form of a cultural revolution that created the ethical and conceptual foundation of a socialist form of human development.

Human Development as Social Welfare

The most surprising feature of developments in Cuba from 1959 to 1989 was the level of human development in terms of social welfare achieved with relatively low levels of per capita GDP and sluggish rates of economic growth. Throughout the 1960s and 1970s annual growth of the GDP per capita was unpredictable as the Revolution's leaders implemented economic plans that changed the structure of Cuba's economy. At the same time the key indicators of human development, particularly in regard to health and education but also employment and housing, point towards a significant improvement in social welfare, not just for certain groups but for the population generally.

Normally—or rather, in development theory—indicators of economic and social development are closely correlated, the second generally tracking the first. But not so in Cuba. And there can be no doubt as to the agency of this development. Rather than prioritizing economic growth, and assuming that economic growth will inevitably or naturally bring with it an improvement in social conditions (from the workings of the market), the revolutionary regime prioritized social development and used the agency of the state to bring it about. This conclusion has important implications for human development theory, viz. the centrality of public action and the role of the state.

Not that another conclusion could not be drawn from our findings. The superior performance of the Cuban state to the economy might well be interpreted by economists and policymakers working within the orthodox paradigm of economic development that there is an inevitable trade-off between 'pro-growth' and 'pro-distribution', and that in consideration of the higher rates of economic growth achieved by regimes that prioritized growth a 'growth first' policy is nevertheless justified both theoretically and programatically. The response to this view that we would give on the basis of our findings is that it depends on how development is conceived—as a political project consciously directed towards a desired end, or as an undirected process—and the priorities of the government: whether these be oriented towards economic growth, the fruits of which are unevenly distributed under conditions of social inequality; or whether they are designed to advanced the level of human development under conditions 'equal for all'.

Another conclusion is that in the context of the economic model used to guide economic and social policy across the developing world, the strategy pursued by the Cuban government could well be described as 'growth with equity'. Of course, Cuba was not the only government at the time to pursue a *growth with equity* strategy. The government of Kerala certainly did as did other governments such as Sri Lanka and Costa Rica, in these cases as part of a capitalist economic regime. What this strategy meant was an orientation of the government's fiscal resources and expenditures towards an investment in people and on social infrastructure (human capital formation) as well as productive transformation and economic growth. And it also meant that economic growth must be included in the mix of human development policies; that efforts should be made to ensure an equitable or fair distribution of this growth; and that the government is the agency of these efforts. As for economic growth it is evident that governments have a role to play but our study does not address the broader questions at the centre of the economic development debate about the preferred relationship between the public and private sector, and how to balance the role of the market and the state in this regard.

Human Development as Equality

Equality, together with freedom and solidarity, is a fundamental value of socialist humanism. It is also the conceptual and ethical foundation of the Cuban Revolution—of socialist human development. Development as *equality*, one might conclude, as opposed to development as *freedom*. In the UNDP conception of human development as freedom equality appears not as a substantive social condition—an egalitarian society in which conditions are ideally equal for all, at least ideally— but as *equity*, an *equality of opportunity*, the essential condition of which is freedom rather than equality.

The difference is critical because capitalist societies are so structured as to render equality into an abstraction or a utopian ideal. Capitalism is fundamentally inegalitarian, characterized by a class hierarchy of relations and conditions. It cannot satisfy the system requirements for human development at the level of equality or solidarity. On the other hand, socialism, a socialist conception of human development, is predicated on egalitarianism, a relatively egalitarian society in which ideally conditions are equal for all; i.e. equality is not merely a matter of opportunity but a fundamental right and a necessary condition.

Cuba undoubtedly falls short as a fully egalitarian society, but there is no doubt that social equality is a vital element of the revolutionary consciousness that has been promoted by public action and national policy over the years. It has also been a fundamental organizing principle of the Revolution. One of the very first actions taken and policy measures adopted by the revolutionary regime (in May 1960) was a radical land reform that reverted capitalism in the countryside and substantially improved conditions for 150,000 poor peasant farmers. In relatively short order (over the course of the first two years) relations of production both in the countryside and in the urban centres were at first nationalized, then socialized. In this socialist process of productive transformation, the property of the big landlords and capitalists, in both the agricultural and industrial sectors, were expropriated, but the small property holders were not. Unlike the experience in

Russia the peasant farmers were not forcibly separated from their means of production, but were encouraged to freely combine their units of production into state farms or agricultural cooperatives. The nationalization and socialization process proceeded apace and was more or less completed by 1975, fifteen years into the Revolution, but under conditions of free choice or voluntary submission. The exception to this rule occurred in the revolutionary offensive of 1968 in which the petit-bourgeois service sector of small business was eliminated virtually overnight by administrative fiat. In this development both the market and the private sector were all but eliminated in a system of nationalized and socialized production, surviving only in the agricultural sector. With the nationalization and socialization of production, elimination of the labour market, improved access to food and housing via public subsidies, and the socialization of public services in the sectors of health and education, Cuba completed the transition from capitalism to socialism—from a class-divided society characterized by relations and conditions of social equality to a relatively egalitarian socialist society. The transition was not easy or free from all sorts of mistakes and policy experiments, and shifts in economic strategy, but remarkably free from social conflict in comparison to the experience with capitalist or social development elsewhere or before.

Human Development as Freedom

Freedom is a vital condition of human development but it comes in different forms. Freedom as development has three different meanings, each associated with a particular form of democratic discourse and practice. From a social liberal perspective freedom refers to the capacity of individuals to make decisions in their own interest and on behalf of their fundamental right to development, and the expansion of choices available to these individuals. With the optics of socialist theory, freedom denotes a political condition of emancipation, liberation from the power relations of class rule and imperialist exploitation, and the capacity and power of collective or national self-determination. As for economic and political liberalism, freedom is not seen as matter of development; rather, it is an issue of allowing economic agents to calculate and pursue their self-interest (to profit from their economic transaction with others), and to do with the minimum of social or political constraint; on the other hand it means to be accorded the freedom to pursue their inalienable democratic political rights—the freedom of expression, to organise and to participate in the political process.

Although freedom in the Cuban context basically implies emancipation and pursued fundamentally as an issue of national self-determination, in the context of human development theory and practice it should be understood in social and political liberal terms as well. In these terms it could be argued that most Cubans are relatively free and equal in regard to their opportunities and the capacity to make fundamental choices in their lives, and also in their power to influence and affect public policy, but that Cuba still suffers from what we might term a 'democratic deficit'—that it has not yet realised the socialist ideal of a 'fully democratic society'.

Not that Cuba's critics are correct in viewing Cuba as non-democratic in the sense that decisions are made at the top, without popular participation, and not according Cubans the right to dissent, freely organise and express their views. Certainly Cuba's polity does not include the institutional trappings of liberal democracy—an electoral system in which political parties present the electorate with alternative slates of potential representatives and programs, and all citizens are presented with a clear choice and are free to vote their preferences.

But the Cuban political system is 'democratic' in its own way, allowing all citizens to freely elect by secret ballot their choice of representatives to the organs of political power, but to do so in their workplaces and communities rather than the mechanism of competing parties. It is even possible to argue that at the level of the institutions that connect society to the state the Cuban system provides a superior form of democracy in terms of the principles of representation, participation and accountability.

At the level of political practice, however, we found evidence of a democratic deficit. This deficit takes the form of undue restrictions on dissent from the government line, and to freely organise and express one's views on public policy and the underlying socialist system—the revolutionary process itself. Arguably, every political system has built-in mechanisms for controlling dissent, and places restrictions on the freedom to organise and the freedom of expression. However, indications are that Cuban authorities are overly sensitive and controlling in this regard. The legitimate and understandable concern for US-instigated subversion is clearly behind this over-sensitivity, but it appears that this concern also serves as a pretext for controlling dissent and limiting internal debate. Although this point is debateable (some view the threats from the US as sufficient cause) there does not seem to be a sufficient justification for, or the need to, prohibit or inhibit internal debate or open discussion about the system itself—to question socialism and the Revolution. The achievements of the Revolution, and the superior ethics of socialist human development, should suffice to contain any fundamental internal threats to the system.

Human Development as Solidarity

The liberalist discourse on human development, embodied most clearly and emphatically in the UNDP's *Human Development Report*, is predicated on a belief in the need for institutional reform in the direction of freedom and equality—the institutionalized value of freedom understood as the right and capacity of individual members of society to flourish in the pursuit of a life that they reason to value and in their opportunities for self-realization. But by way of contrast in socialist discourse, human development is based on the belief for more radical change, a fundamental reorganization in the direction of a 'new man and woman', a culture of social and international solidarity brought about in a process of revolutionary transformation.

In the hierarchy of socialist values solidarity is preeminent, defining the meaning that socialists attach to freedom and equality. The value attached to solidarity as an organizational principle is embodied in the Cuban Revolution, evidenced by the conception of human development as an on-going revolutionary process. In this there is a fundamental difference between the Cuban Revolution and the Russian and Chinese—in the historic process through which socialism in some form was actualised in these countries in the 20th Century. Both the Russian and the Chinese Revolutions, like the French Revolution in the 18th Century, are generally regarded as a *social revolution* in that the process entailed a restructuring of the nation at the social as well as political level—of the society as well as the state. And the organising principle of reorganization was equality—the socialization of production and an egalitarian distribution of the social product. But the revolution was not on-going, nor was it based on a systematic overhaul of the cultural foundations of the society and polity—creating a new man and woman, a new society based on social solidarity. There was a belated attempt in China, in the 1960s, to bring about a 'cultural revolution', but as in Russia the people were not engaged in the process as active participants under conditions of freedom. The hallmark of the Cuban Revolution, a fundamentally defining feature, was its concern for human development under conditions of freedom, equality and solidarity.

Socialism in an Era of Neoliberal Globalization

The most surprising fact about the Cuban Revolution in the 1990s, in the crisis phase of its development, was that it survived. As the UNDP (2010) notes in its first *Regional Human Development Report* for Latin America, 'Despite the restrictions and the changes that occurred in the 1990s Cuba's socioeconomic strategy maintained its essential objectives in the social sphere' and managed to stay on track as regards its fundamental human development agenda in the face of external and internal 'challenges'. Most surprising for the authors of the report was the ability of the regime to achieve such a broad consensus on the need to 'assimilate the external adjustment and confront the internal economic transformations' [PNUD, 2010: xv]. The 'State [throughout] maintained its defense of social equity on the basis of universality and free basic social services of education and health' and indeed, the authors add, 'the complexity of these services went well beyond those that are internationally considered as basic' (PNUD, 2010: xv). Indeed the Report goes on, no activity related to basic social services were privatized, and, the authors add, 'it should be kept in mind that [over this period] no other country in the world registered as great an advance [in terms of human development as Cuba]—improving its HDI ranking by eight positions'.

The solution to this enigma was not hard to find, even though it eluded the UNDP in both its 1996 Report on Human Development in Cuba and its 2000 award-winning report on 'human development and equity in Cuba', both of which focused on the strategic responses to 'neoliberal globalization' ('the external adjustment') by the government and he people ('the State and social participation'). The explanation of Cuba's successful navigation of those troubled waters can be found in the dynamics of 'social participation'—in the 'workers' parliaments' and other forms of popular participation in decision-making and the public policy process. It is this feature of the Cuban Revolution more than any other that explains the resilience of the Revolution in confronting the challenges from without and within.

Socialism and Revolution in the New Millennium

A revolutionary consciousness, forged in a process of active social participation in public action, is a defining feature of Cuban socialism and a critical factor in the successful management of the most severe threat to the survival of the system over some thirty-five years of socialist development. However, what was and remains a major source of strength, still is a major point of vulnerability: the difficulty of reproducing this revolutionary consciousness, and the socialist ethic embodied in it, under conditions of an intergenerational distance from the actual experience of conditions that dictated a revolutionary response, and the growth of social inequalities and continuing austerity under conditions of global capitalist development. How the revolutionary regime and the Cuban people responds to this challenge will have a meaning and an impact that will resonate well beyond this small island state.

BIBLIOGRAPHY

[A] *The Theory and Practice of Human Development*

Adelman, I. (1986). "A Poverty Focused Approach to Development Policy," in Lewis, J.P. and Kallab, *Development Strategies Reconsidered*. Reprinted in Wilber, C.K. *The Political Economy of Underdevelopment*. 4th ed., pp. 493-507.
Albuquerque, Fernando (2000). La importancia del enfoque del desarrollo económico local. Available at: http://www.scribd.com/doc/13299630/1-AlburquerqueLa Importancia-del-Desarrollo-Economico-Local.
———. (2001). Desarrollo económico local y cooperación descentralizada para el desarrollo: Desarrollar lo local para una globalización alternativa. San Sebastion: HEGOA, Euskal Fondoa, Octubre.
Alkire, S. and S. Deneulin (2009). "The Human Development and Capability Approach," in S. Deneulin with L. Shahani (eds), *An Introduction to the Human Development and Capability Approach*. London: Earthscan.
Alonso, Aurelio (2002). "La pobreza vista en tres escalas. Reflexiones sobre el Caribe hispano," Seminario Internacional Estrategias de Reducción de la Pobreza en el Caribe: los Actores Externos y su Impacto, CLACSO-CROP, La Habana, mimeo.
Álvarez, Sonia (2005). "Los discursos minimistas sobre las necesidades básicas y los umbrales de ciudadanía como reproductores de la pobreza," in Álvarez, S. (comp.) *Trabajo y reproducción de la pobreza en Latinoamérica y el Caribe. Estructuras, discursos y actors* Buenos Aires: CLACSO-CROP.
Amsden, A.H. (1989). *Asia's Next Giant: South Korea and Late Industrialization*. New York: Oxford University Press.
Anand, Sudhir and Amartya Sen (2000). "The Income Component of the Human Development Index," *Journal of Human Development*, 1 (1): 17-23.
Anand, Sudhir and Ravi Kanbur (1993). "Inequality and Development: A Critique," *Journal of Development Economics*, 41, June.
ANC—African National Congress (2007). "A capable state to build a new nation," *Umrabulo*, No. 30, November.
Andrew, Glyn (ed.) (2003). *Social Democracy in Neoliberal Times: The Left and Economic Policy since 1980*. Oxford: Oxford University Press.
Apple, M.W. (1982). *Education and Power*. Boston: Ark Paperbacks.
Arias Duran, I. (1996). *El Proceso Social de la Participación Popular: Problemas y potencialidades*. La Paz: SNPP.
Arocena, J. (1995). *El desarrollo local: un desafío contemporáneo*. Nueva Sociedad, Caracas.
Auerbach, Paul and Peter Skott (1993). "Capitalist Trends and Socialist Priorities," *Science & Society*, 57, No. 2 (Summer).
Banco Mundial (1997). *El Estado en un mundo en transformaciones*. Washington DC.
———. (2000). "*Caribbean economic overview 2000, Informe N° 20.460*. Washington DC.
Bardhan, Pranab (1997). *The Role of Governance in Economic Development*. Paris: OECD, Development Centre.
Bardhan, Pranab and John Roemer (eds.) (1993). *Market Socialism: The Current Debate*. Oxford: Oxford University Press.
BID-Banco Interamericano de Desarrollo (1992). *Reducing Poverty in Latin America and the Caribbean: An agenda for Action*. Washington DC.

Bigman, D. (ed.) (2002). *Globalization and the Developing Countries: Emerging Strategies for Rural Development and Poverty Alleviation*. The Hague: CAB Publishing.
Blair, H. (1995). "Assessing Democratic Decentralization," CDIE Concept Paper. Washington DC: USAID.
Boyce, J.K., S. Cullenberg, P. Pattanaik and R. Poolin (eds.) (2006). *Human Development in the Era of Globalization*. Cheltenham UK: Edgar Elgar
——. (2003). "¿Y si el desarrollo fuese una emergencia sistémica?" *Comunicación Jornadas Desarrollo* [Chile: Universidad de General Sarmiento], Febrero.
Boisier, Sergio. (2005). "¿Hay espacio para el desarrollo local en la globalización?" *Revista de la CEPAL*, No. 86, agosto, Santiago de Chile, pp. 47-62.
Boisier, S. et al. (1992). *La descentralización: el eslabón perdido de la cadena transformación productiva con equidad y sustentabilidad*. Santiago: Cuadernos de CEPAL.
Boltvinik, Julio (1992). "La medición de la pobreza en América Latina," *Comercio Exterior*, N° 42.
Borja, Jordi et al. (1985). *Descentralización del estado, movimiento social y gestión local*. Santiago: FLACSO.
Borón, Atilo A. (1995). *State, Capitalism and Democracy in Latin America*. London: Lynne Rienner.
——. (2000). *Tras el Búho de Minerva. Mercado contra democracia en el capitalismo de fin de siglo*. Buenos Aires: CLACSO/Fondo de Cultura Económica.
——. (2003). "Sobre mercados y utopías. La victoria ideológico-cultural del neoliberalismo," *Caminos*, N° 29-30.
Borón, Atilio, Javier Amadeo and Sabrina González. (2007). *A Teoria Marxista Hoje: Problemas e Perspectivas*. São Paulo: Expressão Popular.
Braathen, Einar and Hartley Dean (2003). "Anti-globalization and Anti-statism: emergent Challenges to the Role of the State in Poverty Reduction," Seminario Internacional El Papel del Estado en la Lucha contra la Pobreza, CLACSO/CROP, Recife, mimeo.
Braverman, Harry (1974). *Labour and Monopoly Capital: The Degradation of Work in the Twentieth Century*. New York / London: Monthly Review Press.
Brenner, Robert (2000). *The Economics of Global Turbulence*. London: Verso.
Brenner, Robert and Mark Glick (1991). "The Regulation School and the West's Economic Impasse," *New Left Review*, 188, pp. 45-120.
Brus, Włodzimierz (1972). *The Market in a Socialist Economy*. London: Routledge and Kegan Paul.
——. (1973). *The Economics and Politics of Socialism: Collected Essays*. London: Routledge and Kegan Paul.
——. (1975). *Socialist Ownership and Political Systems*. London: Routledge and Kegan Paul.
Bulmer-Thomas, Victor (1996). *The New Economic Model in Latin America and its Impact on Income Distribution and Power*. New York: St. Martin's Press.
Burguete, Ricardo (1976). *La teoría marxista de las clases sociales y la estructura de la sociedad contemporánea*. La Habana: Ciencias Sociales.
Calderón, Fernando G. et al., eds. (1985). *Descentralización y democracia: Gobiernos locales en America Latina*. Santiago: CLACSO/SUR.
Caminotti, Mariana et al. (2002). "El capital social en el marco de las nuevas estrategias del Banco Mundial para la reducción de la pobreza" en *Pensamiento Propio* (Managua) N° 16.
Campbell, Al and Mehmet Ufuk Tutan (2008). "Transformation Beyond Capitalism," *Studies in Political Economy*, 82, Autumn.
Castellani, Ana Gabriela (2002). "Implementación del modelo neoliberal y restricciones al desarrollo en la Argentina contemporánea," in Schorr, Martín et al. *Más*

allá del pensamiento único. Hacia una renovación de las ideas económicas en América Latina y el Caribe. Buenos Aires: CLACSO.
Castillo, Marcelina (2003). "Conceptualización de la pobreza desde la perspectiva de género," Población y desarrollo. Argonautas y caminantes [Tegucigalpa] N° 1.
CEPAL (1987). "Proyecto Inter-Institucional de la Pobreza Crítica en America Latina," elaborated in 1983 (CIEM, 1983) and published in 1987 [provided the framework for Rodriguéz and Carrazo (1990)].
——. (1990). Transformación productiva con equidad. Santiago de Chile: Naciones Unidas.
——. (1992). "Renovadas orientaciones y tendencias de los programas de compensación social en la región", Tercera Conferencia Regional sobre la Pobreza en América Latina, Santiago de Chile, mimeo.
——. (1994). Panorama social de América Latina 1994. Santiago de Chile: Naciones Unidas).
——. (1998). El Pacto Fiscal. Fortalezas, debilidades y desafíos. Santiago de Chile: Naciones Unidas.
——. (2001). Panorama social de América Latina y el Caribe 2000. Santiago de Chile: Naciones Unidas.
——. (2004). Panorama social de América Latina 2002-2003. Santiago de Chile: Naciones Unidas.
——. (2006). Panorama social de América Latina. Santiago de Chile: Naciones Unidas.
Chalmers, Johnson (1995). Japan: Who Governs? The Rise of the Developmental State.
Chambers, R. (1994). Paradigm Shifts and the Practice of Participatory Research and Development. Brighton: Institute for Development Studies.
Chattopadhyay, Paresh (1986). "Socialism: Utopian and Feasible," Monthly Review, Vol. 37, No. 10 (March).
Cohen, G.A. (2000). Karl Marx's Theory of History: A Defense, 2nd. Edition, Oxford: Oxford University Press.
——. (2009). Why Not Socialism? Princeton NJ: Princeton University Press.
Coraggio, José Luis (1999). "¿Es posible pensar alternativas a la política social neoliberal?" Nueva Sociedad, N° 164.
——. (1997). "Descentralización: el día después…" Cuadernos de postgrado. Buenos Aires: Universidad de Buenos Aires. Available at: <http://www.corragioeconomia.org/jlc_ publicaciones_d.htm>.
Cornia, Andrea, Richard Jolly and Frances Stewart (1987). Ajuste con Rostro Humano. Madrid: Siglo XXI-UNICEF.
Craig, D. and D. Porter (2006). Development Beyond Neoliberalism? Governance, Poverty Reduction and Political Economy. Abingdon Oxon: Routledge.
Davis, Mike (2006). A Planet of Slums. London: Verso.
De Vroey, Michel (1984). "A Regulation Approach [to an] Interpretation of [the] Contemporary Crisis," Capital & Class, 23, Summer.
Deneulin, S. and L. Shahani (eds.) (2009). An Introduction to the Human Development and Capabilities Approach: Freedom and Agency. London: Earthscan / IDRC.
Desai, Meghnad (2002). Marx's Revenge: The Resurgence of Capitalism and the Death of Statist Socialism. London: Verso.
Díaz-Salazar, R. (ed.) (2002). Justicia global. Las alternativas de los movimientos del Foro de Porto Alegre, Intermón/Icaria, Barcelona.
Dijkstra, Geske (2005). The PRSP Approach and the Illusion of Improved Aid Effectiveness: Lessons from Bolivia, Honduras and Nicaragua. Development Policy Review, Vol. 23, No. 4, Pp. 443–464, July.
Dominguez, J. and A. Lowenthal, eds. (1996). Constructing Democratic Governance, Baltimore: John Hopkins University Press.
Dos Santos, Teothonio (1998). "La teoría de la dependencia," in López Segrera, Francisco (ed.) Los retos de la globalización. Caracas: Nueva Sociedad.

Drèze J. and Sen, A.K. (1989). *Hunger and Public Action*. Oxford University Press.
Duarte, Marisa (2002). "El Consenso de Washington y su correlato en la reforma del estado en la Argentina: los efectos de la privatización" en Schorr, Martín et al. *Más allá del pensamiento único. Hacia una renovación de las ideas económicas en América Latina y el Caribe*. Buenos Aires: CLACSO.
Durston, J. (1998). "Building Social Capital in Rural Communities (Where it Doesn't Exist);' Santiago: ECLAC.
ECLAC—Economic Commission for Latin America and the Caribbean (1990). *Productive Transformation with Equity*. Santiago: ECLAC.
———. (2007b) see page 285.
———. (2008). *Statistical Yearbook for Latin America and the Caribbean*. Santiago: ECLAC.
———. (2010). *Time for Equality: Closing Gaps, Opening Trails*. Santiago, Chile: ECLAC.
Economist, The (2010). *Criminal Justice: Glorious Failures*. Special Report. August 13.
Engels, Frederick (1939). *Anti-Dühring*. New York: International Publishers.
Ellerman, David P. (1992). *Property and Contract Economics: The Case for Economic Democracy*. Cambridge MA: Blackwell Publishers.
Ellison, C. and G. Gereffi (1990). "Explaining Strategies and Patterns of Industrial Development," in G. Gereffi and D.I. Wyman (eds), *Manufacturing Miracles. Paths of Industrialization in Latin America and East Asia*. Princeton NJ: Princeton University Press.
Escobar, Arturo (1991). "Imaginando el futuro: pensamiento crítico, desarrollo y movimientos sociales," in López Maya, Margarita (ed.). *Desarrollo y democracia*. Caracas: Nueva Sociedad.
———. 1996 (1995). *La invención del Tercer Mundo. Construcción y deconstrucción del desarrollo*. Bogotá: Norma.
Esping-Andersen, Gosta (1999). "Después de la Edad de Oro: el futuro del estado benefactor en el Nuevo Orden Mundial," *Desarrollo Económico* [Buenos Aires] Vol. 36, No. 142.
———. (2006). "After the Golden Age? Welfare State Dilemmas in a Global Economy," in Esping-Andersen Gosta (ed.), *Welfare States in Transition: National Adaptations in Global Economies*. London: Sage Publications.
Espinoza, Vicente 2002 La movilidad ocupacional en el Cono Sur. Acerca e las raíces estructurales de la desigualdad social (Santiago de Chile: Instituto de Estudios Avanzados).
Evans, Peter (1995). *Embedded Autonomy: States and Industrial Transformation*. Princeton: Princeton University Press.
Faletto, Enzo (1993). "Política social, desarrollo y democracia en América Latina. Las funciones del Estado," *Fermentum* [Mérida] Año 3, Nos. 6-7.
Falk, Richard (2000). "The Quest for human Governance in an era of Globalization," in D. Kalb, et al. (ed.), *The End of Globalization, Bringing Society back In*. Lanham, Rowland & Littlefield.
Figueroa Albelo, V.M. y otros (2006) La Economía Política de la Construcción del Socialismo Edición electrónica. www.eumed.net/libros/2006b/vmfa/
Filgueira, Carlos (2000). *La actualidad de viejas temáticas: sobre los estudios de clase, estratificación y movilidad social en América Latina*. Santiago de Chile: CEPAL
Foladori, G. and R. Delgado Wise (2011). "Contemporary Capitalism: Development in an Era of Neoliberal Globalization," in H. Veltmeyer (ed.). *The Critical Development Studies Handbook*. Halifax: Fernwood Publishing.
Francis, Paul (2001). "Participatory Development at the World Bank: The Primacy of Process," in B. Cooke and U. Kothari (eds.) *Participation: The New Tyranny*? London and New York: Zed Books.
Freire, Paulo (1970). *Pedagogy of the Oppressed*. New York: Continuum.

Fukuda-Parr, Sakiko and A.K. Shiva Kumar (ed.) (2004). *Readings in Human Development Concepts, Measures and Policies for a Development Paradigm*. OUP.
Fukuyama, Francis (1992). *The End of History and the Last Man*. London: Penguin
Girvan, Norman (2008). *The Debt Is Unpayable* (Honorary Doctorate acceptance speech, University of Havana). Accessed at: http://www.normangirvan.info/wp-content/uploads/2009/01/girvanthe-debt-is-unpayable1.pdf
Glynn, A, A. Hughes, A. Lipietz & A. Singh (1990). "The Rise and Fall of the Golden Age," in Stephen Marglin & Juliet Schor (eds.), *The Golden Age of Capitalism: Re-interpreting the Post-War Experience*. Oxford: Clarendon Press.
González Casanova, Pablo (1992). "Crisis del Estado y lucha por la democracia en América Latina," in *Estado, nuevo orden económico y democracia en América Latina*. Caracas: Nueva Sociedad.
Gordon, David and Paul Spicker (eds.) (1999). *The International Glossary on Poverty*. Bergen: CROP.
Gosfroguel, Ramón (2003). "Cambios conceptuales desde la perspectiva del sistema-mundo. Del cepalismo al neoliberalismo," *Nueva Sociedad*, N° 183.
Gottlieb, Roger S. (1989). *An Anthology of Western Marxism: From Lukács and Gramsci to Socialist-Feminism*. Oxford University Press.
Goulet, Denis (1989). "Participation in Development: New Avenues," *World Development* 17 (2): 165-178.
Granma 2004, 13 de noviembre.
Gray, Patricia (2002) *Latin America: Its Future in the Global Economy*. London: Palgrave
Gray, Molina and Mark Purser (2010). "Human Development Trends Since 1970: A Social Convergence Story," Human Development Research Paper 2010/02. UNDP.
Greenspan, Alan (1998). "Income Inequality: Issues and Policy Options," Remarks by Chairman Alan Greenspan, Symposium sponsored by the he Federal Reserve Bank of Kansas City, Jackson Hole, Wyoming, August 28.
Griffin, K. (1989). "Pensamiento sobre el desarrollo: la visión más amblia," *Desarrollo*, n° 15, Madrid. pp. 3-5.
Griffin, K. and J. Gurley (1986). "Análisis radicales del Tercer Mundo y la transición al socialismo: una panorámica," *Información Comercial Española*, N° 651, Agosto-Septiembre, Madrid, pp. 229-273.
Griffin, Keith and John Knight (1989). "Human development in the 1980s and Beyond," *Journal of Development Planning*, No. 19: 9-40.
Griffin, Keith and Terry McKinley (1994). *Implementing a Human Development Strategy*. New York: St. Martin's Press.
Gunder Frank, André (1973). *América Latina: subdesarrollo o revolución*. México DF: Era.
Haq, Mahbub Ul (1994). Foreword (pp. vii-ix), in Griffin, K. & T. McKinnley, *Implementing a Human Development Strategy*. London: Macmillan.
——. ([1995], 2000). *Reflections on Human Development*. New York: Oxford University Press.
Harvey, David (2005) *A Brief History of Neoliberalism*. Oxford: Oxford University Press.
Hay, Colin, Michael Lister and David Marsh, eds. (2006). *The State: Theories and Issues*. Nueva York: Palgrave McMillan.
Hicks, Douglas A. (1997). "The Inequality-Adjusted Human Development Index: A Constructive Proposal," *World Development*, Vol. 25, No. 8, August: 1283-98.
Horvat, Branko (1982). *The Political Economy of Socialism: A Marxist Social Theory*. Armonk NY: M.E. Sharpe.
Hunt, Diana (1989). *Economic Theories of Development: An Analysis of Competing Paradigms*. New York: Harvester Wheatsheaf.

Iansi, Mauro Luis (2006). *As Metamorfoses da Consciência de Classe: O PT entre a negação e o consentimento*, São Paulo: Expressão Popular.
——. (2007). *Ensaios Sobre Consciência e Emancipação*. São Paulo: Expressão Popular.
IFPI (2007). Taking Action for the World's Poor and Hungry People, Conference, Beijing China, 17-18 October.
Isaac, T.M. with Richard Franke (2000). *Local Democracy and Development: People's Campaign for Decentralized Planning in Kerala*. New Delhi: Left World Press.
Ivo, Anete (2003). "Las nuevas políticas sociales de combate a la pobreza en América Latina: dilemas y paradojas," Seminario Internacional El Papel del Estado en la Lucha contra la Pobreza. CLACSO/CROP, Recife, mimeo.
James, Wendy (1999). "Empowering Ambiguities," in *The Anthropology of Power*. ASA Monograph 26, Routledge.
Jessop, Bob (1991). *State Theory: Putting the Capitalist State in its Place*. Cambridge: Polity.
——. (2003). *The Future of the Capitalist State*. Cambridge: Polity.
Kamat, Sangeeta (2003). "NGOs and the New Democracy: The False Saviours of International Development," *Harvard International Review*, Spring.
Kaufmann, D., A. Kraay and P. Zoido-Lobatón (1999). *Governance Matters*. Washington DC: World Bank.
Kliksberg, Bernardo (2002). "Diez falacias sobre los problemas sociales en América Latina", Seminario Internacional Gobernabilidad y Desarrollo en América Latina y el Caribe, MOST-UNESCO, Montevideo, mimeo.
Kucynski, P.P. and J. Williamson (eds.) (2003). *After the Washington Consensus: Restarting Growth and Reform in Latin America*. IEI, Washington.
Lebowitz, Michael A. (2007). "Human Development and Practice," Opening comments at Conference on Participation, Change and Human Development at Centro International Miranda in Caracas, Venezuela, 27 March 2007).
Lechner, Norbert (1997). "Tres formas de coordinación social," *Revista de la CEPAL*, Nº 61.
Lenin, Vladimir Ilich (1963 [1918]). *El Estado y la revolución*. La Habana: Editora Política.
——. (1981 [1919]). "El marxismo acerca del Estado," *La Sociedad Socialista* Moscú: Progreso.
Levy, Bettina (2002). "Una introducción a los estudios actuales sobre la política, el conflicto y el estado en América Latina y el Caribe" en Levy, Bettina (comp.) *Crisis y conflicto en el capitalismo latinoamericano*. Buenos Aires: CLACSO.
Lima, Ana Luiza (2003). "Combate a pobreza na América Latina: una abordagem comparada," in *Pobreza e desigualdades sociais*. Bahia: Superintendencia de Estudos Económicos e Sociais.
Lipietz, Alain (1987) *Mirages and Miracles: The Crisis in Global Fordism*. London: Verso.
Lopez, Humberto (2004). *World Bank Pro-Poor Growth: A Review of What We Know (and of What We Don't)*. Washington DC: World Bank.
Mançano Fernandez, Bernardo (2009). "Agrarian Transformation / social movements / territorial development," *CDS: Tools for Change*. London: Zed Books.
Marglin, Stephen and Juliet Schor (eds) (1990). *The Golden Age of Capitalism: Reinterpreting the Postwar Experience*. Oxford, Clarendon Press.
Marini, Ruy Mauro (1979). *Dialéctica de la dependencia*. México DF: Era.
Martinez, J.A. (1996). *Municipios y participación popular en América Latina: Un modelo de desarrollo*. La Paz: IAF/SEMILLA/CEBIAE.
Martinussen, J. (2004). *Society, State and Market*. Pretoria: HSRC Publishers.
Marx, Karl (1966). *Critique of the Gotha Programme*. New York: International Publishers.

Marx, Karl (1967). *Writings of the Young Marx on Philosophy and Society.* New York: Doubleday & Co.
Marx, Karl (1968). *Theories of Surplus Value*, Part 2. Moscow: Progress Publishers.
Marx, Karl (1971). *Theories of Surplus Value*, Part 3. Moscow: Progress Publishers.
Marx, Karl (1973). *Grundrisse, Foundations of the Critique of Political Economy.* Harmondsworth, England: Penguin.
Marx, Karl (1976). *Value, Price and Profit.* New York: International Publishers.
Marx, Karl and Fredrick Engels (1968). *The German Ideology.* Moscow: Progress Publishers.
Marx, Karl and Fredrick Engels (1976). *Collected Works*, Vol. 3. New York: International.
Marx, Karl and Fredrick Engels (1985). *On the Paris Commune.* Moscow: Progress Publishers.
Marx, Karl and Fredrick Engels (1989). *Collected Works, Karl Marx and Frederick Engels*, vol. 24. New York: International Publishers.
Marx, Karl and Frederick Engels (1994). *Collected Works*, Vol. 34. New York: International Publishers.
McNally, David (1993). *Against the Market: Political Economy, Market Socialism and the Marxist Critique.* London: Verso.
McNally, David. (1997). Socialism from Below - Part I. 2nd Edition. New Socialist Group. Availalable online: http://www.newsocialist.org/index.php?option=com_content&view=article&id=138&Itemid=75
McNeish, J. (2002). "Globalization and the Reinvention of Andean Tradition: The Politics of Community and Ethnicity in Highland Bolivia," *Journal of Peasant Studies*, Vol. 29, No 3/4 April/July,
Medina, Alejandro (2002) "Mitos y lecciones para enfrentar la pobreza en América Latina" en Burgos, Nilsa (ed.) *Política social y trabajo social* (San Juan de Puerto Rico: Universidad de Puerto Rico).
Mehrotra, S. and R. Jolly (eds.) (2000). *Development with a Human Face.* Oxford: Oxford University Press.
Milenkovitch, D.D. (1971). *The Worker-Managed Enterprise.* Princeton: Yale University Press.
Mirowski, P. and D. Plehwe (2009). *The Road to Mont Pelerin: The Making of the Neoliberal Thought Collective.* Cambridge University Press
Mitlin, Diana (1998). "The NGO Sector and its Role in Strengthening Civil Society and Securing Good Governance," in Armanda Bernard, Henry Helmich and Percy Lehning (eds.), *Civil Society and International Development.* Paris: OECD Development Centre.
Moe, J. (1997). *Implementing Bolivia's Law on Popular Participation and Administrative Decentralization: Progress and Challenges.* Washington: IADB.
Mohan, G. and K. Stokke (2000). "Participatory Development and Empowerment: The Dangers of Localism," *Third World Quarterly* Vol. 21, No. 2: 247-268.
Molina, María Lorena 2002). "Políticas sociales y seguridad social: reflexiones para la investigación," in Burgos, Nilsa (ed.) *Política social y trabajo social.* San Juan de Puerto Rico: Universidad de Puerto Rico).
Monk, Heidi (2010). Human Development and Limited Economic Activity: Government Expenditure and Health in Cuba and Kerala. MA Thesis. Halifax: International Development Studies, Saint Mary's University.
Montano, J.A. (1996). *Municipios y Participación Popular: Un modelo de desarrollo en América Latina.* La Paz: Producción Educativa.
Naciones Unidas (1995). "Declaración de la Cumbre de Desarrollo Social," Copenhague, 6-12 de marzo.
Navarro, Pablo (1994). *El holograma social. Una ontología de la socialidad humana.* Madrid: Siglo XXI.

Nelson, N. and S. Wright (1995). *Power and Participatory Development: Theory and Practice*. London: Intermediate Technology.
New Internationalist (2003) "The Liberation of Latin America," May.
Nickson, R.A. (1997). *Local Government in Latin America*. New York: Lynne Reiner Publications.
Noel, Alain (1987). "Accumulation, Regulation, and Social Change: an Essay on French Political Economy," *International Organization*, 41 (2), Spring.
Nove, Alec (1986). *Socialism, Economics and Development*, London: Allen and Unwin.
——. (1991). *The Economics of Feasible Socialism*, London: Harpur Collins Academic.
Ocampo, José Antonio. 1998. "Beyond the Washington Consensus: An ECLAC Perspective." *CEPAL Review* (66), December: 7–28.
——. (2005). *Más allá del Consenso de Washington: Una agenda de desarrollo para América Latina*, Serie Estudios y Perspectivas, N° 26, Naciónes Unidas-CEPAL, México.
——. (2006). "Latin America and the World Economy in the Long Twentieth Century," in Jomo K.S. (ed.) *The Great Divergence: Hegemony, Uneven Development, and Global Inequality*. New York: Oxford University Press.
——. (2007). "Markets. Social Cohesion and Democracy," pp. 1-31 in J.A. Ocampo, K.S. Jomo and S. Khna (eds.). *Policy Matters: Economic and Social Policies to Sustain Equitable Development*. London: Zed Books (in association with the UN).
OECD (1997). *Final Report of the DAC Ad Hoc Working Group on Participatory Development and Good Governance*. Paris.
OECD (2010). *Perspectives on Global Development 2010*. Paris: OECD.
Ojeda Lautero, S. (1988). *Políticas de bienestar social y participación popular en el Ecuador*. Ecuador: ILDIS.
Olave, Patricia (2003). *Chile: neoliberalismo, pobreza y desigualdad social*. México: UNAM.
Osorio, Jaime (2003). "El neoestructuralismo y el subdesarrollo. Una visión crítica," *Nueva Sociedad*, N° 183.
Ospina, C.M. (ed.) (1997). *Procesos y Tendencias de la Descentralización en Colombia*. Bogota: Fundación Universidad Central.
Palma Caravajal, E. (1995). "Decentralization and Democracy: the New Latin American Municipality," *CEPAL* 55, 39-53.
Paramio, L. (ed.) (2006). *Una nueva agenda de reformas políticas en América Latina*, Fundación Carolina-Siglo XXI, Madrid.
Parodi, Carlos (2001) "Perú: pobreza y políticas sociales en la década de los noventa" en Revista de Ciencias Sociales (Lima) Vol. VII, N° 3.
Pastor Jr., M. and A. Zimbalist (1987). *The International Monetary Fund and Latin America: Economic Stabilization and Class Conflict*. Boulder: Westview Press.
Patel, Surendra J. (2004). "In Tribute to the Golden Age of South's Development," *IDS Working Paper No. 91.5*, Saint Mary's University.
Petras, J. and H. Veltmeyer (2001). *Globalization Unmasked: Imperialism in the 21st Century*. London: ZED Press / Halifax: Fernwood Publishing.
Petras, J. and H. Veltmeyer (2003). *System in Crisis: The Dynamics of Free Market Capitalism*. London: Zed Books / Halifax: Fernwood Books.
Petras, J. and H. Veltmeyer (2005). *Social Movements and the State: Argentina, Bolivia, Brazil, Ecuador*. London: Pluto Press.
Petras, J. and H. Veltmeyer (2009). *What's Left in Latin America*. Ashgate Publishing UK.
Petras, J. and H. Veltmeyer (2010) *Social Movements in an Era of Neoliberal Globalization: The People Strike Back*. Basingstoke (London): Palgrave Macmillan.
Pierson, Christopher (1995). *Socialism After Communism: The New Market Socialism*. Cambridge: Polity Press.

Pinker, Paul (1999). "Do Poverty Definitions Matter?" in Gordon, David y Spicker, Paul (eds.) *The International Glossary on Poverty*. Bergen: CROP.
Portes, Alejandro and Kelly Hoffman (2003). "Las estructuras de clase en América Latina: composición y cambios durante la época neoliberal," *Políticas Sociales*, No. 68, CEPAL, División de Desarrollo Social. Santiago.
Prebisch, Raúl (1994 [1949]). "El desarrollo económico de América Latina y algunos de sus principales problemas," in *La teoría social latinoamericana. Textos escogidos*. México: UNAM.
Puerto Sanz, Luis Miguel (ed.) (2008). *Economía para el desarrollo: Lecturas desde una perspectiva crítica*. Madrid: Catarata / Instituto Universitario de Desarrollo y Cooperación (IUDC).
Ranis, G. and F. Stewart (1999). *Strategies for Success in Human Development*. New York, Presented at the First Global Forum on Human Development, 29-31 July.
Rao, V. (2002). *Community Driven Development: A Brief Review of the Research*. Washington DC: World Bank.
Rapley, John (2004). *Globalization and Inequality: Neoliberalism's Downward Spiral*. London: Lynne Reinner Publishers.
Razeto, Luis (1988). *Economía de solidaridad y mercado democratico*. Vol. 3. Santiago: Programa de Economía del Trabajo (PET), Academia de Humanismo Cristiano.
Razeto, Luis (1993). *De la economía popular a la economía de solidaridad en un proyecto de desarrollo alternativo*. Santiago: Programa de Economía del Trabajo (PET).
Rey, Germán (2006). "Cultura y desarrollo humano: unas relaciones que se trasladan», en *Boletines InterCambios*," Año 6, No. 64. <http://www.rimisp.org/boletines/bol64/>.
Reygadas, Luis (2004). "Las redes de la desigualdad: Un enfoque multidimensional," *Política y Cultura* [México], No. 22.
Rodrik, Dani (1997). *Has Globalization Gone Too Far*? Washington DC: Institute for International Economics, Harvard University.
Roemer, John (1982). *A General Theory of Exploitation and Class*. Cambridge, Mass: Harvard University Press.
Rondinelli, D.A., J. McCullough and W. Johnson (1989). "Analyzing Decentralization Policies in Developing Countries: A Political Economy Framework," *Development and Change*, 20 (1): 57-87.
Rondinelli, D.A., J.R. Nellis and G.S. Cheema (1983). "Decentralization in Developing Countries: A Review of Recent Experience," *World Bank Staff Paper*, No. 581. Washington DC: World Bank.
Saad-Fihlo, Alfredo (2005). "From Washington to Post-Washington Consensus," pp. 113-119 in Alfredo Saad-Fhilo & Debora Johnston (eds.) *Neoliberalism: A Critical Reader*.
Salles, Vania and Rodolfo Tuirán (1995). *The Human Cost of Women's Poverty*. México DF: Naciones Unidas/UNIFEM.
Sandbrook, Richard, Marc Edelman, Patrick Heller, and Judith Teichman (2007). *Social Democracy in the Global Periphery: Origins, Challenges, and Prospects*. Cambridge: Cambridge University Press.
Sané, Pierre (2001). "Las ciencias sociales y humanas en la lucha contra la pobreza," *Boletín de MOST* [París] N° 10.
Santos, Boaventura de Sousa (2005). *Reinventar la democracia. Reinventar el Estado*. La Habana: José Martí.
Sautié Mederos, Félix (2007). *Socialismo y reconciliación en Cuba: Una Mirada desde adentro*.
Saxe-Fernández, John (2002). *La Compra Venta de México*. México: Plaza James.
Schwartz, Joseph (2009). *The Future of Democratic Equality*. New York and London: Routledge.

Selee, Andrew and Enrique Peruzzotti, eds. (2009). *Participatory Innovation and Representative Democracy in Latin America*. Woodrow Wilson Center Press.
Sen, Amartya (1989). "Development as Capability Expansion," *Journal of Development Expansion*, No. 19: 41-58.
———. (1992). "Sobre conceptos y medidas de la pobreza," *Comercio Exterior*, Vol. 42, N° 4.
———. (1995). *Nuevo examen de la desigualdad*, Madrid, Alianza, Madrid.
———. (1999). *Development as Freedom*. New York: Alfred & Knopf.
———. (2001). "Las teorías del desarrollo en el siglo XXI," *Leviatán*, N° 84, Verano. Madrid, pp. 65-84.
———. (2006). "La cultura como base del desarrollo contemporáneo," *Boletines InterCambios*, Año 6, No. 64, Julio. <http://www.rimisp.org/boletines/bol64/>.
———.(2010). "As Biko Knew, Powerless in actual lives is the hurdle justice must clear," *Guardian*, March 23 [guardianco.uk].
Sen, Gita, Aditi Iyer and Chandan Mukherjee (2009). "A Methodology to Analyse the Intersections of Social Inequalities in Health," *Journal of Human Development and Capabilities*, Vol. 10, No. 3: 397-415
SNPP (1996). *Apre(he)ndiendo la Participación Popular: Análisis y Reflexiones sobre el modelo boliviano de descentralización*. La Paz: Ministerio de Desarrollo Humano, Bolivia.
Sojo, Ana (2001). "El combate a la pobreza y la diversificación de riesgos: equidad y lógicas del aseguramiento en América Latina," *Sociales* [Buenos Aires] Vol. 5.
Spicker, Paul (1999). "Definitions of poverty: eleven clusters of meaning," in Gordon, David and Spicker, Paul (eds.). *The International Glossary on Poverty*. Bergen: CROP.
Stewart, Francis (2008). Human Development as an Alternative Development Paradigm," UNDP http://hdr.undp.org/en/media/1 (accessed March 16, 2008).
Stiefel, M. and A. Pearce (1982). *UNRISD's Popular Participation Programme. An Inquiry into Power, Conflict and Social Change*, Assignment Children 59/60: 145-162.
Stiefel, M. and M. Wolfe (1998). *A Voice for the Excluded: Popular Participation in Development: Utopia or Necessity?* UNRISD.
Stiglitz, Joseph (1998). "More Instruments and Broader Goals: Moving Beyond the Post-Washington Consensus," *Wider Annual Lectures*. 2, Helsinki: WIDER.
Streeten, Paul (1981). *Lo primero es lo primero. Satisfacer las necesidades humanas básicas en los países en desarrollo*. Madrid: Tecnos.
———. (1984). "Basic Needs: Some Unsettled Questions," *World Development*, Vol. 12, No. 9.
Sunkel, Osvaldo (1990). "Neo-structuralism and Neo-liberalism," *CEPAL Review*, No. 42.
———. (ed.) (1993). *Development From Within: Towards a Neostructuralist Approach to Latin America*.
Szeleny, Ivan (1978). "Social Inequalities in State Socialist Redistributive Economies: Dilemmas for Social Policy in Contemporary Socialist Societies of Eastern Europe," *International Journal of Comparative Sociology* 19, Nos. 1–2: 63–87.
Tavares, Laura (1999). *Ajuste neoliberal e desajuste social na America Latina*. Río de Janeiro: UFRJ.
———. (2002b). "La reproducción ampliada de la pobreza en América Latina: el debate de las causas y de las alternativas de solución", Seminario Internacional Estrategias de Reducción de la Pobreza en el Caribe: los Actores Externos y su Impacto. CLACSO-CROP, La Habana, mimeo.
Thwaites Rey, Mabel and José Castillo 1999 "Poder estatal y capital global" en Boron, Atilio et al. (comp.) *Tiempos violentos. Neoliberalismo, globalización y desigualdad en América Latina*. Buenos Aires: CLACSO/EUDEBA.
Toye, John (1987). *Dilemmas of Development*. Blackwell.

Trputec, Zoran (2001). "Conceptualisation of poverty and struggle against it. Lessons from Central America", Tegucigalpa, Programa Latinoamericano de Trabajo Social / Universidad Autónoma de Honduras, Informe de Investigación.
——. (2002). "Desafíos de la gestión de desarrollo y toma de decisions," Programa Latinoamericano de Trabajo Social. Universidad Autónoma de Honduras, Tegucigalpa, mimeo.
UNDP (1993). *Human Development Report: People's Participation*. New York: Oxford University Press.
——. (1996). "*Good Governance and Sustainable Human Development,*" Governance Policy Paper. http://magnet.undp.org/policy.
——. (1997). *Governance and Democratic Development in Latin America and the Caribbean*. New York: UNDP.
——. (1997a). "Governance for Sustainable Human Development," *Policy Document*. New York: UNDP.
——. (1997b). "Participatory Local Governance," *Policy Document*. New York: UNDP.
——. (1997c). "The Shrinking State: Governance and Sustainable Human Development," *Policy Document*. New York: UNDP.
——. (2000). "The UNDP Role in Decentralisation and Local Governance," UNDP Evaluation Office, February.
——. (2002a). *Human Development Programmes at the Local Level*. Report, January, Edinfodec Project.
——. (2002b). *Bolivia: Progress on the Millennium Development Goals*, 2nd. Report, New York: UNDP.
——. (2003) *Human Development Report. Millennium Development Goals: A Compact Among Nations to End Human Poverty* New York: OUP.
——. (2005). *Democracy In Latin America: Towards a Citizen's Democracy*, United Nations.
Veltmeyer, H. (1978). "Marx's Two Methods of Social Analysis: A Critique," *Sociological Inquiry*, Vol. 48, No. 3.
——. (2007). *Illusions and Opportunities: Civil Society in the Quest for Social Change*. Halifax: Fernwood.
——. (ed.). (2010a). *Imperialism, Crisis and Class Struggle: The Verities of Capitalism*. Leiden and Boston: Brill Publishers.
——. (ed.) (2010b). *Critical Development Studies: Tools for Change*. Halifax and London: Fernwood Books and Pluto Books.
Veltmeyer, H. and A, O'Malley (2001). *Transcending Neoliberalism: Community-Based Development*. West Hartford CT: Kumarian Press.
Veltmeyer, Henry and James Petras (1997). *Economic Liberalism and Class Conflict in Latin America*. London: MacMillan Press.
——. (2007). *Dynamics of Social Change in Latin America*. Toronto: Broadview Press.
——. (2010a). *Social Movements in Latin America: Neoliberalism and Popular Resistance*. Basingstoke (London): Palgrave Macmillan.
Wade, Robert (2003). "What Strategies are Viable for Developing Countries Today? The World Trade Organization and The Shrinking of 'Development Space,'" *Review of International Political Economy*. 10 (4), pp. 621-644.
——. (2004). *Governing the Market: Economic Theory and the Role of Government in East Asian Industrialization*. Princeton University Press.
Wallace, Tina (2003). "NGO Dilemmas: Trojan Horses for Global Neoliberalism?" *Socialist Register 2004*. London: Merlin Press.
Webster, N. and Engberg Pedersen, L. (2002). *In the Name of the Poor: Contesting Political Space for Poverty Reduction*. London: Zed Books.
Wehle, Beatriz (1999). "Trabajo, inclusión y exclusión social. De la globalización de la economía a la globalización de la pobreza," *Nueva Sociedad*, N° 164.

Weiss, Linda (2000). "Developmental States in Transition: Adapting, Dismantling, Innovating, not Normalising," *Pacific Review*. 13(1): 21-55.
Williamson, J. (ed.) (1990). *Latin American Adjustment. How Much Has Happened?* Washington DC, Institute for International Economics.
Woo-Cumings, Meredith (1999). *The Developmental State*. Cornell University Press.
World Bank (1994). *Governance. The World Bank Experience*. Washington DC: World Bank.
———. (1994a). *The World Bank and Participation*. Washington DC: World Bank, Operations Policy Department.
———. (1995). *World Development Report: Workers in an Integrating World*. Oxford: Oxford University Press.
———. (1996). "Poverty Reduction and Human Development in the Caribbean: A Cross-Country Survey, *Discussion Paper* No. 366. Washington DC: World Bank.
———. (2000). *World Development Report 2000/2001*. New York: Oxford University Press www.worldbank.org/poverty/wdrpoverty/ report/index.html.
———. (2007). *Meeting the Challenges of Global Development: A Long-Term Strategic Exercise for the World Bank Group*. Washington DC: The World Bank, October 12
Yun Tae Kim (1999). "Neoliberalism and the Decline of the Developmental State," *Journal of Contemporary Asia*, 29 (4).

[B] *The Cuban Revolution in Theory and Practice*

Abbassi, J. (1997). "The Role of the 1990s Food Markets in the Decentralization of Cuban Agriculture," *Cuban Studies*, Vol. 27, pp. 21-39. Pittsburgh & London: University of Pittsburgh Press.
Acosta Santana, José (1973). "La revolución agraria en Cuba y el desarrollo económico," *Economía y Desarrollo*, No. 17, mayo-junio 1973.
Acosta, D. (2008). "Cuba: Economic Changes, Not If or When, but How." Available online.
Agarwal, C. (2004). "Cuba's Path to a Market Economy: Washington Consensus, Doi Moi, or Reforma á la Cubana?" Proceedings of the Fourteenth Annual Meeting of the Association for the Study of the Cuban Economy: *Cuba in Transition*, 2004.
Aguirre, B.E. (2002). "Social Control in Cuba." *Latin American Politics and Society* 44, No. 2: 67-98.
Aitken, S.C. (1990). "Local Evaluations of Neighborhood Change," *Annals of the Association of American Geographers* 80, No. 2: 247-67.
Allen, E. (ed.) (2002). *José Martí: Selected Writings*. London: Penguin.
Alvarez González, E. (1998). "Cuba: Un Modelo de Desarrollo con Justicia Social," *Cuba: Investigación Económica*, Año 4, No. 2, Abril-Junio, INIE.
Álvarez, Elena (2000). "Descentralización y diversificación en la economía cubana: nuevas bases para la cooperación internacional," *Cuba Investigación Económica*, Año 6, N° 1.
Alvarez, J. (2004). "Overview of Cuba's Food Rationing System," *Extension Data Information Source*. (EDIS) FE482: 1-6.
———. (2001). "Rationed Products and Something Else: Food Availability and Distribution in 2000 Cuba." Proceedings of the Eleventh Annual Meeting of the Association for the Study of the Cuban Economy: *Cuba in Transition*.
Álvarez, Mayda (2000). "Mujer y poder en Cuba," in Monereo, Manuel et al. (coord.) *Cuba construyendo futuro*. Madrid: El Viejo Topo.
Añé, Lía (2000). "La reforma económica y la economía familiar en Cuba," De Miranda, Mauricio (ed.) *Reforma económica y cambio social en América Latina y el Caribe*. Cali: T/M.
Araujo, M.F. (1976). "The Cuban School in the Countryside," *Prospects* 6 (1): 127-31.

Argüelles, Félix (1989). *La seguridad social en Cuba*. (La Habana: Ciencias Sociales).
Arnould, E.J., and C.J. Thompson (2005). "Consumer Culture Theory (CCT): Twenty Years of Research," *The Journal of Consumer Research* 31, No. 4: 868-82.
August, Arnold (1999). *Democracy in Cuba and the 1997-98 Elections*. Habana: Editorial Jose Marti.
Arocena, José (1995). *El desarrollo local: un desarrollo contemporáneo*. Caracas: Editorial Nueva Sociedad/CLAEH).
Azcri, Max (1988). *Cuba: Politics, Economics and Society*. London: Pinter.
——. (2000). *Cuba Today and Tomorrow: Reinventing Socialism*. Miami: University Press of Florida.
Banco Nacional de Cuba (1995, 1996, 1999). *Informe Económico*. Havana.
Barbería, Lorena (2003). "Remittances to Cuba: An Evaluation of Cuban and US Government Policy Measures," Rockefeller Center for Latin American Studies/Harvard University, Boston. Working Paper.
Barberia, Lorena, Xavier de Souza Briggs and Míren Uriarte (2004). "The End of Egalitarianism? Economic Inequality and the Future of Social Policy in Cuba," pp. 297-318 in Jorgé Domínguez, et al., *The Cuban Economy at the Start of the Twenty-First Century*. Cambridge, Mass: Harvard University Press.
Barkin, David (1972). "La redistribución del consumo en Cuba," *Comercio Exterior de Mexico*, No.7, Julio.
Baró Herrera, Silvio (1996a). "De la integración a la globalización," *Revista Economía y Desarrollo*, No. 2, Junio.
——. (1996b). "El desarrollo sostenible: desafío para la humanidad," *Revista Economía y Desarrollo*, No. 1, Marzo.
Beckford, George (1966). "A Caribbean View of Cuba," *New World Quarterly* II. 2: 271.
Bell Lara, José et al. (1999). *Cuba in the 1990s*. Habana: Instituto Cubano Del Libro.
Bell Lara, José, Delia Luisa López and Tania Caram (2006). *Documentos de la Revolución Cubana*. La Habana: Editorial Ciencias Sociales.
Belton, Brian A. (2007). *Assata Shakur: A Voice from the Palenques in Black Routes: Legacy of African Diaspora*. Hansib Publications.
Bengelsdorf, Carollee (1994). *The Problem of Democracy in Cuba: Between Vision and Reality*. Oxford: Oxford University Press.
Betancourt, R.R. (2001). "Felipe Pazos, Institutions and Retrospective View of 'Problemas Económicos de Cuba en El Periodo de Transicion" Proceedings of the Eleventh Annual Meeting of the Association for the Study of the Cuban Economy: *Cuba in Transition*.
Bettleheim, Charles (1964). "Formas y métoos de la plaanificación socialista y nivel de desarrollo de las fuerzas productivas," *Cuba Socialista*, No. 32, Abril.
Binns, P. and Gonzalez, M. (1981). *Castro, Cuba and Socialism: The Economics of State Capitalism*. Cleveland: Hera Press.
Blum, Denise (2008). "Socialist Consciousness Raising and Cuba's School to the Countryside Program," *Anthropology and Education Quarterly*, Vol. 39(2), June.
Bravo, Estella (1990). *After the Battle*. [Documentary]. Havana and London: Granma/Nexus and Channel 4 Television U.K.
Bray, D.W., and M.W. Bray (2002). "Introduction: The Cuban Revolution and World Change," *Latin American Perspectives*, 29, No. 3: 3-17.
Brenner, Philip, Marguerite R. Jiménez, John M. Kirk and William M. LeoGrande, eds. (2008). *A Contemporary Cuban Reader. Reinventing the Revolution*. Lanham MD: Rowman & Littlefield.
Brundenius, Claes (1981). *Economic Growth, Basic Needs, and Income Distribution in Revolutionary Cuba*. Lund, Sweden: Lund University Research Policy Institute.
——. (1982). "Development Strategies and Basic Needs in Revolutionary Cuba," in C. Brundenius and M. Lundahl (eds), *Development Strategies and Basic Needs in Latin America. Challenges for the 1980s*. Boulder: Westview Press.

———. (1984). *Crecimiento con equidad. Cuba 1959-1984.* Managua: INIES-CRIES.
———. (1984). *Revolutionary Cuba: The Challenge of Economic Growth with Equity.* Boulder: Westview Press.
———. (2002a). "Whither the Cuban Economy after Recovery?" *Journal of Latin American Studies* 34 (Spring).
———. (2002b). "Cuba: the Retreat From Entitlement," pp. 331-48 in Abel, Christopher and Colin Lewi (ed.) *Exclusion and Engagement: Social Policy in Latin America.*
Brundenius, Claes and Andrew Zimbalist (1985). "Cuban Economic Growth One More Time: A Response to 'Imbroglios,'" *Comparative Economic Studies* 27, No. 3 (Fall): 115–31.
———. (1985). "Recent Studies on Cuban Economic Growth: A Review," *Comparative Economic Studies* 27, No. 1, (Spring): 21–45.
Brundenius, Claes and John Weeks (eds.) (2001). *Globalization and Third World Socialism.* Basingstoke: Palgrave.
Brundenius, Claes and M. Lundahl (1982). *Development Strategies and Basic Needs in Latin America: Challenges for the 1980s.* Boulder, CO: Westview Press.
Bueno Sánchez, Eramis, Fidel Márquez Sánchez and Enrique Berros Padilla (1991-02). "La deuda social. La violenta extensión de la pobreza," *Revista Cuba Económica,* Año 2, No. 3, Octubre-Marzo.
Bunck, J.M. (1994). *Fidel Castro and the Quest for a Revolutionary Culture in Cuba.* University Park: Pennsylvania State University Press.
Burawoy, M., and J. Lukacs (1985). "Mythologies of Work: A Comparison of Firms in State Socialism and Advanced Capitalism." *American Sociological Review* 50, No. 6: 723-37.
Burchardt, H.J. (2002). "Contours of the Future: The New Social Dynamics in Cuba." *Latin American Perspectives* 29, No. 3: 57-74.
Cabrero, Olga (1977). *Guiteras: El Programa de la Jóven Cuba.* Havana: Editorial de Ciencias Sociales.
Canton Navarro, Jose (2000) *History of Cuba: The Challenge of the Yoke and the Star.* Havana, Cuba: Editorial SI-MAR.
Caño, María del Carmen (2004). "Cuba, desarrollo local en los 90," in Fuentes Ruiz, Reina and Miguel Márquez (eds.), *Desarrollo humano local.* La Habana: Cátedra UNESCO de desarrollo sostenible/Universidad de la Habana.
Carmona Báez, Antonio (2004). *State Resistance to Globalization in Cuba.* London: Pluto.
Carranza Valdes, Julio (1992). "Reform and the Future of Cuban Socialism," in Centro de Estudios Sobre America, ed., *The Cuban Revolution into the 1990s* (Boulder CO: Westview Press.
———. (1995). "La crisis: Un diagnóstico. Los retos de la economía cubana," In Hoffmann, Bert (ed.) *Cuba: apertura y reforma económica. Perfil de un debate.* Caracas: Nueva Sociedad.
Carranza Valdés, Julio, L. Gutiérrez and P. Monreal González (1995). *Cuba. La Restructuración de la economia. Propuesta para un debate.* La Habana: Editorial de Ciencias Sociales.
Carranza, Julio and P. Monreal, P. (2000). "Los Retos Actuales del Desarrollo en Cuba," *Revista Problemas del Desarrollo,* Vol. 31, No. 122. México, IIEc- UNAM, Julio-Septiembre.
Carriazo Moreno, George (1994). "Cuba: apertura y adaptación a una nueva realidad," *Boletín Informativo Economía Cubana.* No. 15, CIEM.
Casanova Montero, Alfonso and Ismael Zuaznábar Morales (1991-92). "Un modelo alternativo," *Revista Cuba Económica,* Año 2, No. 3, Octubre-Marzo.
Casanova, A. et al. (2002). "Estructura Económica de Cuba," Capítulo 3, *Aspectos Globales. Antecedentes Macroeconómicos.* La Habana: Editorial Félix Varela.
Castro Díaz-Balart, Fidel (2001). *Ciencia, tecnología y sociedad.* Editora Política, La Habana.

——. (1953). History will absolve me. (Online). Retrieved April 15, 2010, from http://www.marxists.org/history/cuba/archive/castro/1953/10/16.htm.
Castro Ruz, Fidel (1961). *La historia me absolverá*. La Habana: Imprenta Nacional de Cuba. Also *History Will Absolve Me*. New York: Lyle Stuart,
——. (1962). "The Role of Revolutionary Instructors in Cuba: School of Revolutionary Instruction," June 30. *Castro Speech Data Base*, Latin American Network Information Center.
——. (1981a). *Cuba's Internationalist Foreign Policy, 1975–1980*. New York: Pathfinder Press.
——. (1981b). *Second Congress of the Communist Party of Cuba: Documents and Speeches*. Havana: Editora Política.
——. (1988). *Por el camino correcto*. La Habana: Editora Política.
——. (2002). Discurso en la Conferencia Internacional sobre Financiamiento para el Desarrollo. Monterrey. México, 21 marzo 2002. http://www.cuba.cu/gobierno / discursos/.
——. (2005a). *Speech at the Ceremony Commemorating the 30th Anniversary of the Cuban Military Mission in Angola and the 49th Anniversary of the Landing of the Granma, Revolutionary Armed Forces Day*. Havana: Council of State.
——. (2005b). Speech at the University of Havana, November 17, *Granma*, November 18.
Castro, Raúl (2007a). "Year 49 of the Revolution," Speech in Camaguey, July 26.
——. (2007b). Speech at Camaguey, Speech July 26.
——. (2008). Speech as President of the State Council and the Council of Ministers, at Closing Session of the National Assembly of People's Power, Havana," February. Available online.
Centro de Estudios Sobre América (1996). *La democracia en Cuba y el diferendo con los Estados Unidos*. Ediciones CEA, Editorial de Ciencias Sociales.
CEPAL—Comisión Económica para América Latina y el Caribe (1980). *Cuba: Estilo de desarrollo y políticas sociales*. Mexicio: Siglo Ventiuo.
——. (1996). *Cuba: Evolución Económica durante 1995*. Mexico City.
——. (1997a). *La Economía Cubana. Reformas estructurales y desempeño en los años noventa*. Ciudad de México: Fondo de Cultura Económica.
——. (1997b). *Cuba: Evolución Económica durante 1996*. Mexico City.
——. (1998a). "Seminario de CEPAL sobre la Evolución Económica de Cuba y sus Perspectivas, Mexico City, 2-21 October 1997. Havana: Ministerio de Economía y Planificación.
——. (1998b). "Tablas Estadísticas," *Boletín Informativo de Economía Cubana*, No. 33. CIEM. Havana, Cuba.
——. (2000). *La economía cubana. Reformas estructurales y desempeño en los noventa*. México DF: Fondo de Cultura Económica.
——. (2004). *Balance preliminar de las economías de América Latina y el Caribe*. Santiago de Chile.
——. (1997). *La economía cubana. Reformas estructurales y desempeño en los 90*. Fondo de Cultura Económica, México.
César, María Auxiliadora (2005). *Mujer y política social en Cuba: el contrapunto socialista al bienestar capitalista*. Ciudad de Panamá: Mercie.
Chávez, Ernesto 2003 "El combate contra la pobreza en Cuba. Políticas sociales y estrategias familiares". Ponencia presentada en el Seminario Internacional Papel del Estado en la lucha contra la pobreza, CLACSO-CROP/FJN, Recife.
CIDEA (1997). *Cuba: medio ambiente y desarrollo; datos e informaciones*. La Habana, Ediciones Geo.
CIEM—Centro de Investigaciónes de la Economía Mundial (1983). *Estudio acerca la eradicación de la pobreza en Cuba*.
——. (1998). "Economía Cubana," *Boletín informativo*, No. 33, January-March, Havana.

———. (1997). *Investigación sobre Desarrollo Humano en Cuba 1996*. La Habana, Caguayo S.A.
Colantonio, A., and R.B. Potter (2006). *Urban Tourism and Development in the Socialist State: Havana during the 'Special Period.'* Aldershot, England: Ashgate.
Cole, Johnetta (1986). *Race Toward Equality*. Havana: José Martí Publishing.
Cole, Ken (1998). *Cuba: From Revolution to Development*. London: Pinter.
———. (2002). "Cuba: The Process of Socialist Development," *Latin American Perspectives* 29, No. 3: 40-56.
Comisión Nacional del Sistema de Dirección de la Economía 1988 "Decisiones adoptadas sobre algunos elementos del sistema de dirección de la economía" en Cuba, Economía Planificada (La Habana) Año 3, N° 3.
Constitution of the Republic of Cuba (1992). Accessed at http://www.parlamentocubano.cu/index.php?option=com_content&view=article&id=53&Itemid=84
CEE–Comité Estatal de Estadísticas (1969). *Anuario estadistico de Cuba*. Habana: Editorial Estadística.
———. (1974). *Anuario estadístico de Cuba*. Habana: Editorial Estadística.
———. (1979). *Anuario estadístico de Cuba*. Habana: Editorial Estadística.
———. (1981). *Encuesta*. Habana: Editorial Estadística.
———. (1984). *Anuario estadístico de Cuba*. Habana: Editorial Estadística.
———. (1985). *Anuario estadístico de Cuba*. Habana: Editorial Estadística.
———. (1987). *Anuario estadístico de Cuba*. La Habana. Editorial Estadística.
———. (1989). *Anuario estadístico de Cuba*. Havana: CEE.
Corrales, J. (2004). "The Gatekeeper State: Limited Economic Reforms and Regime Survival in Cuba, 1989-2002," *Latin American Research Review*, 39 (2).
Corzo, M.A.G. (2005). "Housing Cooperatives: Possible Roles in Havana's Residential Sector." Proceedings of the Fifteenth Annual Meeting of the Association for the Study of Cuban Economy: *Cuba in Transition*.
Coyula, M., R. Oliveras, and M. Coyula (2002). *Hacia un Nuevo Tipo de Comunidad en La Habana: Los Talleres De Transformacion Integral Del Barrio*. Havana: GDIC.
Cuba (1997). *Programa Nacional de Acción para el Cumplimiento de los Acuerdos de la Cumbre Mundial de la Infancia. Sexto Informe de Seguimiento y Evaluación*. La Habana, (s/e).
Cuba Project (2007). "Basic Needs Survey: SPSS Online Database." Buffalo: El Barrio Household Survey Center for Urban Studies, University at Buffalo.
Cuba: Revolución y Economía 1959-1960. Editorial Ciencias Sociales.
Cuban Council of State (1991). "An eloquent testimony of the solidarity between our two peoples: Resolution of the Cuban Council of State," pp. 71–73 in Nelson Mandela and Fidel Castro. *How Far We Slaves Have Come!* New York: Pathfinder Press.
Cuesta Braniella, José M. (1997). *La resistencia cívica en la guerra de liberación de Cuba*. La Habana: Editorial de Ciencias Sociales.
———. (1997). *La Resistencia Cívica en la Guerra de Liberación de Cuba* (Havana: Editorial de Ciencias Sociales).
D'Angelo, Ovidio (2004). "¿La autogestión local como vía para la transformación social?" *Temas*, N° 36.
De la Fuente, A. (1994). *A Nation for All: Race, Inequality and Politics in Twentieth Century Cuba*. Chapel Hill: University of North Carolina Press.
———. (2001). *A Nation for All: Race, Inequality, and Politics in Twentieth-Century Cuba*. Chapel Hill: University of North Carolina Press.
De Miranda, Mauricio, (ed.) (2003). "Cuba Reestructuración económica y globalización," *Desarrollo*, No. 2, Junio.
De Rivero, Oswaldo (2001). *The Myth of Development: The Non-Viable Economies of the 21st Century*. London: Zed.
Deere, C.D. (1997). "Reforming Cuban Agriculture," *Development and Change*, Vol. 28, No. 4, October.

Deere, C.D., P. Antrobus, L. Bolles, E. Melendez, P. Phillips, M. Rivera, and H. Safa (1990). *In the Shadows of the Sun: Caribbean Development Alternatives and U.S. Policy.* Boulder CO: Westview.
Departamento de Estudios sobre Familia-CIPS (2001). "Familia y cambios socioeconómicos a las puertas del nuevo milenio." La Habana,
Deutschmann, David (ed.) (1987). *Ché Guevara and the Cuban Revolution.* Sydney: Pathfinder.
Devine, P. (1992). "Market Socialism or Participatory Planning?" *Review of Radical Political Economics*, Vol. 24, No. 3.
Diaz-Briquets, S. (1983). *The Health Revolution in Cuba.* Austin: University of Texas Press.
Díaz Castañón, María del Pilar (2001). *Ideología y Revolución: Cuba, 1959-1962.* Havana: Editorial de Ciencias Sociales.
Díaz González, Elena (1999). "Cuban Socialism: Adjustments and Paradoxes," in José Bell Lara (ed.), *Cuba in the 1990s.* Havana: Editorial José Martí.
Diaz-Briquets, S., Casals and Associates (1994). "Emigrant Remittances in the Cuban Economy: Their significance during and after the Castro Regime," *Cuba in Transition*, Vol. 4, proceedings of the fourth annual meeting of the Association for the study of the Cuban Economy (ASCE), 1-14 August 1994, Miami. http://lanic.utexas.edu/la/cb/cuba/asce/ cuba4/diaz.htm.
Diaz, Beatrice (1992). "Cuba, modelo de desarrollo con equidad," Sistemas políticos. Poder y sociedad. Estudios de caso en América Latina. Caracas: Nueva Sociedad.
Dilla Alfonso, Haroldo (1993). "Cuba: la crisis y la rearticulación del consenso político (notas para un debate socialista)," *Cuadernos de Nuestra América*, Vol. 10, No.º 10.
Dilla Alfonso, Haroldo with Gerardo González Núñez (1997). "Participation and Development in Cuban Municipalities," in Community Power and Grassroots democracy: The Transformation of Social Life, Edited by *Michael Kaufman and Haroldo Dilla Alfonso.* London: Zed Books.
Dilla Alfonso, H., and P. Oxhorn (2002). "The Virtues and Misfortunes of Civil Society in Cuba," *Latin American Perspectives* 29, No. 4: 11-30.
Domínguez, Francisco (2008). "The Rise of the Private Sector in Cuba," pp. 65-89 in Alexander Gray and Antoni Kapcia (2008). *The Changing Dynamic of Cuban Civil Society.* University Press of Florida.
Dominguez, Jorge (1978). *Cuba: Order and Revolution.* Cambridge MA: Harvard University Press.
——. (2004). "Cuba's Economic Transition: Successes, Deficiencies, and Challenges," in Jorgé Domínguez, et al. *The Cuban Economy at the Start of the Twenty-First Century.* Cambridge, Mass: Harvard University Press.
Domínguez, Jorgé, Omar Everleny Pérez Villanueva and Lorena Barberia, eds. (2004). *The Cuban Economy at the Start of the Twenty-First Century.* Cambridge, Mass: Harvard University Press.
Domínguez, María Isabel and María del Rosario Díaz (1997). "Reproducción social y acceso a la educación en Cuba," *Informe de investigación*, Centro de Investigaciones Psicológicas y Sociológicas, La Habana.
Duharte, Emilio (ed.) (2000). *Sociedad civil y participación en Cuba,* en Teoría Sociopolítica. Selección de Temas. Tomo 2. La Habana: Editorial Félix Varela.
Echevaria, Oscar (2007). "Current Cuban Economy: Challenges and Prospects," Paper presented at Workshop on the Human Development Experience of Kerala and Cuba, Havana, December 4.
Echevarría, Dayma (2004). "Mujer, empleo y dirección en Cuba: algo más que estadísticas," *15 Años del Centro de Estudios de la Economía Cubana*, ed. Feliz Varela, La Habana.
Eckstein, Susan. (1980). "Capitalist Constraints on Cuban Socialist Development," *Comparative Politics* 12, No. 3: 253-74.

———. (1986). "The Impact of the Cuban Revolution: A Comparative Perspective," *Comparative Studies in Society and History* 28, No. 3 (July): 506.
———. (1992). "Commentary: Bases of Disagreements about Cuban Economic Performance: A Sociological Perspective," in *Cuban Studies Since the Revolution*, (ed.) Damian Fernández. Gainesville: University Press of Florida.
———. ([1994] 2003). *Back from the Future: Cuba under Castro*. Princeton NJ: Princeton University Press, 2nd. edn.
EIU—Economist Intelligence Unit (various years). *Country Report Cuba*, London: EIU.
———. (1997). "Reassessing Cuba. Emerging Opportunities and Operating Challenges," *Research Report*. London: EIU and Arthur Andersen.
———. (2000). Cuba, Country Profile 1999-2000. London: EIU.
Elson, D. (1988). "Market Socialism or Socialization of the Market?" *New Left Review*, No. 172, Nov-Dec.
Espina Prieto, Mayra Paula (1994). "Reproducción socioestructural en Cuba," Tesis de Doctorado, Centro de Investigaciones Psicológicas y Sociológicas, La Habana.
———. (2001). "The Effects of the Reform on Cuba's Social Structure," *Socialism and Democracy*, Vol. 15, No.1, Spring-Summer: 23-40.
———. (2003a). "Efectos sociales del reajuste económico: igualdad, desigualdad y procesos de complejización en la sociedad cubana," Congreso de LASA, Dallas, mimeo.
———. (2003b). "Territorialización de las desigualdades y reestratificación de los ingresos. Nuevos escenarios y retos para laseguridad social en Cuba," in Witte, Lothar (ed.) *Seguridad social en Cuba. Diagnósticos, retos y perspectivas*. Caracas: Nueva Sociedad.
———. (2004). "Social Effects of Economic Adjustment: Equality, Inequality and Trends Towards greater Complexity in Cuba Society," pp. 209-244 in Jorgé Domínguez, et al., *The Cuban Economy at the Start of the Twenty-First Century*. Cambridge, Mass: Harvard University Press.
———. (2005). "Poverty, Inequality and Development: The Role of the State in the Cuban experience," pp. 199-218 in Alberto Cimadamore, Jorge Siqueira and Hartley Dean (eds.) *The Poverty of the State: Reconsidering the Role of the State in the Struggle Against Global Poverty*. Buenos Aires: CLACSO.
———. (2008a). "Políticas de atención a la pobreza y la desigualdad. Examinando el rol del Estado en la experiencia cubana," CLACSO / CROP, Buenos Aires.
———. (2008b). "Viejas y nuevas desigualdades en Cuba: Ambivalencias y perspectivas de la reestratificación social," *Nueva Sociedad*, No. 216, Julio-agosto. <www.nuso.org>.
Espina Prieto, Mayra Paula, et al. (1994). "Reproducción de la estructura socioclasista cubana: cinco tesis acerca de sus rasgos generales," en Valdés Paz, Juan et al. *La transición socialista en Cuba. Estudio sociopolítico*. La Habana: Ciencias Sociales.
Espina Prieto, Mayra Paula et al. (2002). "Componentes sociestructurales y distancias sociales en la ciudad." *Informe de Investigación*, La Habana, Centro de Investigaciones Psicológicas y Sociológicas,
Espina Prieto, Mayra Paula, et al. (2003). "Componentes socioestructurales y distancias sociales en la ciudad," *Informe de investigación*. CIPS.
Espina, Rodrigo and Pablo Rodríguez (2004). "Raza y desigualdad en la Cuba actual", Taller Pobreza y Política Social en Cuba: los Retos del Cambio Económico y Social, Centro de Estudios Latinoamericanos David Rockefeller/Universidad de Harvard/ Centro de Investigaciones Psicológicas y Sociológicas. La Habana, mimeo.
Espinosa Martínez, Eugenio (1996). "Globalización e integración: desafíos y oportunidades para América Latina, el Caribe y Cuba," *Revista Economía y Desarrollo*, No. 1, Marzo.
Espinosa, J.C. (1995). "Markets Redux: The Politics of Farmers' Markets in Cuba," Proceedings of the Fifth Annual Meeting of the Association for the Study of the Cuban Economy: *Cuba in Transition*.

Ezcurra, Ana María (1999). "Intervención estatal y globalización neoliberal" en *Caminos*. La Habana, N° 15-16.
Fabienke, Rikke (2001). "Labour Markets and Income Distribution during Crisis and Reform," pp. 102-28 in Brundenius, Claes and John Weeks (eds.).
Fernández, Flor María and Mirtha Yordi (2002). "Estado y seguridad social: experiencia cubana" en Burgos, Nilsa (ed.) *Política social y trabajo social*. San Juan de Puerto Rico: Universidad de Puerto Rico.
Fernández, M. (1998). "Algunas Reflexiones sobre el Período Especial," *Revista Bimestre Cubana*, No. 8. SEAP, C. Havana. Cuba.
Fernández, Olga (1993). "Cuba: Reevaluate Democracy From a Third World Perspective," Havana: Instituto de Filosofia. Unpublished.
Fernández, R. and H. Dilla (1990). "Cultura política y participación popular en Cuba," *Cuadernos de Nuestra América*, Vol. III, July-December.
Ferrer Sánchez, Pedro (1995). "El enfoque social de la economía cubana en 1994. Nuevos escenarios y retos," *Boletín Cuba: Economía y Administración*, Año 2, No. 3, Enero-Marzo.
Ferriol Muruaga, Angela (1994). *Situación social en el ajuste económico*. La Habana: INIE.
———. (1995). "Situación social en el ajuste económico," *Cuba Investigación Económica*, Año 1, No. 1, Epoca II, Marzo, INIE.
———. (1996). "El empleo en Cuba 1980-1995," *Cuba Investigación Económica*, Año 2, No. 1, Epoca II, Enero-Marzo, INIE.
———. (1996). *Cuba, crisis, ajuste y Situación Social 1990-1996*. La Habana: Editorial de Ciencias Social.
———. (1998). "Política social cubana: situación y transformaciones," *Temas*, No. 11, Jul-September, pp. 88-99, Havana.
———. (1998a). "La reforma económica en Cuba en los 90 [Economic Reform in Cuba in the 1990s]," *Pensamiento Propio*, 7: 5–24.
———. (1998b). "Política social cubana: situación y transformaciones," *Temas* N° 11.
———. (2002). "Explorando nuevas estrategias para reducir la pobreza en el actual contexto internacional", Seminario Internacional Estrategias de Reducción de la Pobreza en el Caribe: los Actores Externos y su Impacto, CLACSO-CROP. La Habana, mimeo.
———. (2003a). "Acercamiento al estudio de la pobreza en Cuba," Taller Aproximaciones Metodológicas al Estudio de la Pobreza y la Política Social, Centro de Estudios Latinoamericanos David Rockefeller/Universidad de Harvard, Boston, mimeo.
———. (2003b). "Ingresos y desigualdad en la sociedad cubana actual," in Manuel Menéndez, (ed. comp.). Los cambios en la estructura socioclasista en Cuba. La Habana: Ciencias Sociales.
———. (2004a). "Política social y desarrollo. Un aproximación global," *Política social y reformas estructurales: Cuba a principios del siglo XXI*. Cepal / INIE/PNUD, México.
———. (2004b). "Reforma económica y población en riesgo en Ciudad de La Habana," Informe de Investigación. La Habana, Instituto Nacional de Investigaciones Económicas,.
Ferriol, Angela and Alfredo González (1995). "La política social: Enfoque y análisis," *Cuba Investigación Económica*, No. 4.
Ferriol, Ángela et al. (1997). Efectos de políticas macroeconómicas y sociales sobre los niveles de pobreza. El caso de Cuba en los años 90. La Habana: INIE-CIEM.
Ferriol, A. et al. (1998). *Efectos de políticas macroeconómicas y sociales sobre los niveles de pobreza: el caso de Cuba en los noventa*," in Ganuza, E., L, Taylor and S. Morley, *Política macroeconómica y pobreza en América Latina y el Caribe*. Madrid, Ediciones Mundi-Prensa.
Ferriol, Ángela, Maribel Ramos and Lía Añé (2004). "¿Pobreza en la capital?" INIE-Cepde / ONE, La Habana.

Figueras, Miguel Alejandro (1990). "Cambios estructurales en la economía cubana," *Cuadernos de Nuestra América*, Vol. VII, No. 15.
Figueras, Miguel Alejandro (1965). "Aspectos y problemas del Desarrollo Económico Cubano," *Revista Nuestra Industria*, Año 3, Febrero.
———. (1990). "Fundamentos de la concepción del Che sobre el sistema de dirección," *Revista Economía y Desarrollo*, No. 1, Enero - Febrero.
———. (2001). "Globalization, the Multilateral Agreement on Investment and Nationalization in Cuba," pp. 71-85 in Brundenius, Claes and John Weeks (eds.).
Fitzgerald, Frank T. (1994). *The Cuban Revolution in Crisis: From Managing Socialism to Managing Survival*. New York: Monthly Review Press.
Font, Mauricio A. (1997). "Crisis and Reform in Cuba," in M.A. Centeno and M. Font (eds.) *Toward a New Cuba? Legacies of a Revolution*. Boulder and London: Lynne Rienner Publishers.
———. (2008). "Cuba and Castro: Beyond the 'Battle of Ideas'," in Mauricio Font (Ed.) *Changing Cuba / Changing World*. New York: Bildner Centre for Western Hemisphere Studies. Ch.4. pp. 43-72.
Frank, Mark (2008) "Cuba removes wage limits in latest reform," *Reuters*. 10 April. http://www.reuters.com/article/idUSN1032792120080410
Fuller, Linda (1992). *Work and Democracy in Socialist Cuba*. Philadelphia: Temple University Press.
Gaceta Oficial de la República de Cuba (1999). "Preamble: Ley 88/99 Ley de Protección de la Independencia Nacional y de la Economía de Cuba," March 4.
García Álvarez, Anicia and Viviana Togores González (2002). "El acceso al consumo en Cuba y su repercusión en la vida cotidiana," CEEC, La Habana.
García Brigos, Jesús Pastor (2001). "People's Power in the Organization of the Cuban Socialist State," *Socialism and Democracy*, Vol. 15, No. 1, Spring-Summer: 113-36.
García Pino, Orlando et al. (1990). "Acerca del desarrollo del nivel de vida material y cultural en Cuba" in Mayra Paula Espina Prieto and Gunnar Winkler (coords.) Objetivos sociales y condiciones del desarrollo económico. Estudio comparativo RDA-Cuba (La Habana: Academia).
García Pino, Orlando et al. (1991). "Aspectos diferenciados de la política social en Cuba," La Habana, Centro de Investigaciones Psicológicas y Sociológicas, Informe de Investigación.
Garfield, R. and S. Santana (1997). "The Impact of the Economic Crisis and the US embargo on Health in Cuba," *American Journal of Public Health*, Vol. 87, No.1: 15-20.
Gasperini, Lavinia (1999). "The Cuban education system: lessons and dilemmas," Washington DC: World Bank, Paper Series N° 48.
Glazer, Howard L. (1989) "Architecture and the Building Industry in Contemporary Cuba," in *Cuba, A Different America*. Wilber A. Chaffee, Gary Prevost (eds.). London: Rowman and Littlefield.
González, Alfredo (2000). "Plan y mercado: aspectos estratégicos en el perfeccionamiento del modelo de planificación" in Cuba Investigación Económica (La Habana) Año 6, N° 3.
———. (2002). "Socialismo y mercado," *Temas* [La Habana] N° 30.
González, Alfredo and Ángela Ferriol (1995). "Cuba: política social en el ajuste económico" in Dagmar Guardiola et al., La política social entre los nuevos desafíos. Cuba / Puerto Rico. San Juan de Puerto Rico: Publicaciones Puertorriqueñas.
Gorry, Conner. (2005). "MDGs & Health Equity in Cuba," *MEDICC Review*. vol. 7, no. 9. Acccessed at http://www.medicc.org/publications/medicc_review/0905/spotlight.html
Gott, Richard (2004). *Cuba: A New History*. New Haven CT: Yale University Press.
Granma (1996). "Informe sobre los resultados económicos de 1996 y el plan económico y social para 1997 presentado ante la Asamblea Nacional por Jose Luis Rodríguez, Ministro de Economía y Planificación," *Granma*, 26 December 1996, pp. 4-5.

Gray, Alexander (2008). "The Genesis of NGO Participation in Contemporary Cuba," pp. 160-182 in Alexander Gray and Antoní Kapcia (2008). *The Changing Dynamic of Cuban Civil* Society. University Press of Florida.
Gray, Alexander and Antoní Kapcia (2008). *The Changing Dynamic of Cuban Civil Society*. University Press of Florida.
Guevara, Ernesto 'Che' (1964). "La planificación socialista: Su significado," *Cuba Socialista*, No, 34, Junio.
———. (1965 [2005]). "Socialism and Man in Cuba," in David Deutschmann (ed.) *The Che Guevara Reader*. New York: Ocean Press Books. Also available online at: http://www.marxists.org/archive/guevara/1965/03/man-socialism.htm
———. (1982). "Reminiscences of the Cuban Revolutionary War," pp. 173-185 in Gérard Chaliand (ed.) *Guerrilla Strategies: An Historical Anthology from the Long March to Afghanistan*. Berkeley: University of California Press.
———. (2006). *El Gran Debate sobre la economia en Cuba*. Melbourne and New York: Ocean Press.
Guevara, Ernesto 'Che' and Raúl Castro (1996). *La conquista de la esperanza. Diarios inéditos de la guerrilla cubana diciembre de 1956-febrero de 1957*. La Habna: Casa Editorial Abril.
Guzón, Ada (2003). "Potencialidades de los municipios cubanos para el desarrollo local," Tesis de Maestría. La Habana, Junio.
———. (2006). *Desarrollo local en Cuba*. La Habana: Editorial Academia.
Halebsky, Sandor and John M. Kirk, (eds.) (1985). *Twenty-Five Years of Revolution: Cuba 1959 to 1984*. New York: Praeger.
Harnecker, Marta (1979). *Cuba: Dictatorship or Democracy?* Westport: Lawrence Hill.
———. (2000). *La izquierda en el Umbral del Siglo XXI: Haciendo Posible lo Imposible* (Madrid: Siglo XXI).
Harnecker, Marta. (2010). "Latin America and Twenty-First Century Socialism," *Monthly Review*, v. 62, no. 3 (July-August). Accessed online at: http://monthlyreview.org/2010/07/01/conclusion
HDR–Human Development Report (various years). United Nations Development Programme.
Hernández, Aymara (2004a). "¿De que desarrollo local estamos hablando?" in Fuentes Ruiz, Reina and Márquez, Miguel, eds. *Desarrollo Humano Local*. La Habana: Cátedra UNESCO de desarrollo sostenible/Universidad de la Habana. CNI/SESI) No. 24.
———. (2004b). "Neoliberalismo y localismo, ¿una asociación posible de desmentir?" enen Linares, Cecilia et al. (comp.) La participación. Diálogo y debate en el contexto cubano (La Habana: Centro de Investigación y Desarrollo de la Cultura Cubana Juan Marinello).
Hernandez, Rafael., H. Dilla, J.D. Abbassi and J. Díaz (1991). "Political Culture and Popular Participation in Cuba." *Latin American Perspectives* 18, No. 2: 38-54.
Hernández, R. and H. Dilla (1990) "Cultura política y participación popular en Cuba" en Cuadernos de Nuestra América [La Habana) Vol. VII, N° 15.
Herrera, R., and P. Nakatani (2004). "De-Dollarizing Cuba." *International Journal of Political Economy* 34, No. 4: 84-95.
Hinkelammert, Franz (1999). *Ensayos*. La Habana: Caminos.
Hirschfeld, K. (2007). *Health, Politics and Revolution in Cuba since 1898*. New Jersey: Transaction Publishers.
Historiador de la Ciudad de la Habana (1998). "Programa para el Desarrollo Humano a Nivel Local: La Habana Vieja, Pinar Del Rio." *Granma*.
Horowitz, Irving (1977). "Institutionalization as Integration: The Cuban Revolution at Age Twenty," *Cuban Studies*, July 1977.
Huberman, Leo and Paul M. Sweezy (1960). *Cuba: Anatomy of a Revolution*. New York: Monthly Review Press.
———.(1969). *Socialism in Cuba*. New York.

Iñiguez Rojas, Luisa (1999). "Desigualdades Espaciales del Bienestar y la Salud en América Latina. Problemas Éticos y Metodológicos," in *Salud y Equidad: Una mirada desde las Ciencias Sociales*. Ed. FIOCRUZ / Social Science and Medicine, FLACSO Venezuela.
———. (2004). "Desigualdades espaciales en Cuba: entre herencias y emergencias," Centro de Estudio de Salud y Bienestar Humanos, Universidad de la Habana
Iñiguez, Luisa and Omar Everleny Pérez Villanueva (2004). "Espacio, territorio, y desigualdades sociales en Cuba. Precedencia y sobreimposiciones" in *Reflexiones sobre economía cubana*. La Habana: Editorial de Ciencias Sociales.
Iñiguez, Luisa y Mariana Ravenet (1999). "Desigualdades espaciales del bienestar en Cuba," La Habana: Centro de Estudios de Salud y Bienestar Humano, Informe de Investigación.
Iñiguez Rojas, Luisa and Omar Everleny Pérez Villanueva, (eds.) (2005). *Heterogeneidad Social en la Cuba actual*. Centro de Estudios de Salud y Bienestar Humanos. La Habana: Centro de Estudios Demográficos, Universidad de La Habana.
Jatar-Hausmann, A.J. (1999). *The Cuban Way: Capitalism, Communism and Confrontation*. West Hartford, CT: Kumarian Press.
Kapcia, Antoní (2000). *Cuba: Island of Dreams*. New York: Berg.
———. (2005). "Educational Revolution and Revolutionary Morality in Cuba: The 'New Man', Youth, and the New 'Battle of Ideas,'" *Journal of Moral Education* 34, No. 4: 399-412.
———. (2008). "Setting the Stage for a Discussion of Cuban Civil Society," pp. 20-39 in Alexander Gray and Antoní Kapcia, (eds.) *The Changing Dynamic of Cuban Civil Society*. University Press of Florida.
Kapur, T., and A. Smith (2002). "Housing Policy in Castro's Cuba." Boston, Joint Center for Housing Studies, Graduate School of Design, Kennedy School of Government, Harvard University.
Kay, Cristóbal (1988). "Cuban Economic Reforms and Collectivisation," *Third World Quarterly*, Vol. 10 (3), July: 1239-66.
———. (2004). "Community Development in Cuba: The Case of San Isidro." Buffalo: Department of Urban and Regional Planning, University at Buffalo.
Kirk, John M. and H. Michael Erisman. (2009) *Cuban Medical Internationalism: Origins, Evolution, and Goals*. New York: Palgrave MacMillan.
Kohan, Néstor (2007). *Introducción al pensamiento socialista*. Melbourne: Ocean Press.
Knight, Franklin W. (1996). "Ethnicity and Social Structure in Contemporary Cuba." In Gert Oostinde (ed.) *Ethnicity in the Caribbean*. London: Macmillan Education.
Koont, Sinan (2004). "Food Security in Cuba," *Monthly Review*, 55 (8). http://monthlyreview.org/0104koont.htm.
Lage Dávila, Carlos (1992). *El desafío económico de Cuba*. La Habana. Ediciones Entorno.
Lataste Hoffer, Alban (1968). *Cuba ¿Hacia una nueva economía política del socialismo?* Santiago: Editorial Universitaria.
Lebowitz, Michael (2005). *Lecciones de la Autogestión Yugoslava*. Caracas: La Burbuja, Instituto Municipa de Publicaciones de la Alcaldía de Caracas.
Leftwich, A. (1992). "Is There A Socialist Path to Socialism?" *Third World Quarterly*, vol.13, no.1.
Levya, R. (1972). "Health and Revolution in Cuba," pp. 456-96 in R. Bonachea and N. Valdes, eds., *Cuba in Revolution*. New York: Anchor Books.
Leogrande, William M. and Julie M. Thomas. (2002). "Cuba's Quest for Economic Independence," *Journal of Latin American Studies*. Vol. 34, No. 2., May. pp. 325-363.
Lieuwen, Edwin and Nelson P. Valdés (1971). *The Cuban Revolution: A Research Guide 1959-1969*. Albequerque.
Li, Tania (2007). *The Will to Improve: Governability, Development, and the Practice of Politics*. Durham: Duke University Press.

Limia, Miguel (1997). "Sociedad civil y participación en Cuba," *Informe de Investigación*. La Habana: Universidad de Habana, Instituto de Filosofía, Octubre.
Limia, Miguel (2010) *Working paper* for the "Cuba and Human Development" project workshop, FLACSO, Havana, March. (unpublished)
Linares, Cecilia, Sonia Correa and Pedro Mora (1996): *Participation: Solution or Problem*. Research and Development Center for Culture Juan Marinello.
Linares, Cecilia, et al. (2006). *La participación. Diálogo y debate en el contexto cubano*. La Habana: CIDCC.
Lobe, Jim (2001). "Learn from Cuba, Says World Bank," *Inter Press Services*, April 30.
Lockwood, Lee (1969). *Castro's Cuba, Cuba's Fidel*. New York: Vintage.
López, C. (1994). "*Indice de Desarrollo Humano: el caso Cuba*," Boletín del Ateneo Juan César García, 2: 2-37, (Representación en Cuba de la OPS/OMS).
——. (1996). "Indice de Desarrollo Humano: una propuesta para su perfeccionamiento," *Economía y Desarrollo*, 119: 141-175.
——. (1999). *Iniquidades en el desarrollo humano y en especial en salud en América Latina*
Lopez García, Delia Luisa (1999). "Economic Crisis, Adjustments and Democracy in Cuba." *Cuba in the 1990s*. Havana: Editorial José Martí.
Lopez Vigil, Maria (1999). *Cuba: Neither Heaven Nor Hell*. Washington: Epica.
Lorimer, Doug (2000). *The Cuban Revolution and Its Leadership*. Newtown, Australia: Resistance.
Lowy Michael (1971). *El pensamiento del Che Guevara*. Editorial Siglo XXI. Mexico.
Lutjens, Sheryl L. (1992). "Democracy and Socialist Cuba," in Halebsky and Kirk, et al, eds., *Cuba in Transition*.
MacDonald, T. (1999). *A Developmental Analysis of Cuba's Health Care System since 1959*. New York: Edwin Mellen Press.
MacEwan, Arthur (1981). *Revolution and Economic Development in Cuba*. London: Macmillan.
Malinowitz, S. (1997). "Public and Private Services and the Municipal Economy in Cuba," *Cuban Studies*. No. 27, pp. 68±89. Pittsburgh and London: University of Pittsburgh Press.
Mandel, Ernest, (1967) "El debate económico en Cuba durante el periodo 1963-1964." *Partisans* [Paris], No. 37.
Mandel, Ernesto (1971). "Mercantile Categories in the Period of Transition" in B. Silverman (ed.). Man and Socialism in Cuba: The Great Debate, New York: Atheneum.
Mandela, Nelson (1991). "We will ensure that the poor and rightless will rule the land of their birth," pp. 17-28 in Nelson Mandela and Fidel Castro, *How Far We Slaves Have Come!* New York: Pathfinder Press.
Marín-Dogan, Michelle (2008). "Civil Society: The Cuban Debate," pp. 40-64 in Alexander Gray and Antoní Kapcia (2008). *The Changing Dynamic of Cuban Civil Society*. University Press of Florida.
Marshall, J.H. (1998). "The Political Viability of Free Market Experimentation in Cuba. Evidence from Los Mercados Agropecuarios," World *Development*, Vol. 26, No. 2.
Martí, José (1977). *Our America: Writings on Latin America and the Struggle for Cuban Independence*. New York: Monthly Review.
Martí, José (1999). *José Martí Reader: Writings on the Americas*. Melbourne: Ocean.
Martín Fernández, Mariana and Ricardo Torres Pérez (2004). "La economía del conocimiento. Evolución de las tendencias mundiales y experiencias para Cuba," Trabajo de diploma, Facultad de Economía.
Martin, José Luis (2004). "La participación en la economía. Algunas reflexiones para el debate" en Linares, Cecilia et al. (comp.) *La participación. Diálogo y debate en el contexto cubano*. La Habana: Centro de Investigación y Desarrollo de la Cultura Cubana Juan Marinello.

Martínez, Antonio (1964). "El plan de la economía nacional para 1964," *Cuba Socialista*, N° 31.
Martínez, Osvaldo. (1991). "Cuba: Experiencias en desarrollo humano," *Revista Comercio Exterior*, Vol. 41, No. 6, México, Junio.
———. (1991). "Desarrollo humano: la experiencia cubana," *Revista Cuba Económica*, Año 1, No. 1, Abril-Mayo-Junio.
———. (1991-92). "Contradicciones del discurso neoliberal," *Revista Cuba Económica*, Año 2, No. 3, Octubre-Marzo.
———. (1996). "Globalización de la economía mundial: la realidad y el mito," *Revista Cuba Socialista*, No. 2.
———. (2007). Intervención en la sesión de la Asamblea Nacional del Poder Popular., La Habana, diciembre de 2006, mimeo.
Martínez, Osvaldo, et al. (1997). *Investigación sobre el desarrollo humano en Cuba 1996*. La Habana: Caguayo.
Martínez, Osvaldo, et al. (2000). *Investigación sobre desarrollo humano y equidad en Cuba 1999*. La Habana: Caguayo.
Martínez Carrera, R. (1990). "Cuba, crecimiento económico e inestabilidad externa," *Economía y Desarrollo*, No. 1. Havana: Facultad de Economía," Habana.
Martínez Heredia, Fernando (1988). *Desafíos del socialismo cubano*. La Habana: Centro de Estudios sobre América.
———. (1991). "Cuba: problemas de la liberación, la democracia, el socialismo," *Síntesis* [Madrid] N° 15.
———. (2001). "La alternativa cubana," *El corrimiento hacia el rojo*. La Habana: Letras Cubanas.
Martinez-Saenz, M. (2004). "Che Guevara's New Man: Embodying a Communitarian Attitude," *Latin American Perspectives* 31, No. 6: 15-30.
Matthews, Herbert L. (1975). *Revolution in Cuba: An Essay in Understanding*. New York: Charles Scribner's Sons.
Mazarr, M.J. (1989). "Prospects for Revolution in Post-Castro Cuba," *Journal of Interamerican Studies and World Affairs* 31, No. 4: 61-90.
Medín, Tzivi (1990). *Cuba, The Shaping of a Revolutionary Consciousness*. Boulder: Lynne Reinner Publishers.
Mehrotra, Santosh (2000). "Human Development in Cuba: Growing Risk of Reversal," in Jolly, Richard and Santosh Mehrotra (2000). *Development with A Human Face: Experiences in Social Achievement and Economic Growth*. Oxford University Press.
Mencía, Mario (2006). *El Moncada. La respuesta necesaria*. La Habana: Oficina de Publicaciones del Consejo de Estado.
Méndez, Elier (2004). "Desarrollo Territorial y Local en Cuba," *Observatorio de la Economía Latinoamericana*, No. 30, Septiembre. http://www.eumed.net/cursecon/ecolat/cu/emd-dtlc.htm
Méndez, Elier and María del Carmen Lloret (2005). "Índice de Desarrollo Humano a nivel territorial en Cuba. Periodo 1985-2000," *Revista Cubana de Salud Pública*, Vol. 31, No.2.
Mesa-Lago, Carmelo (1969). "Availability and Reliability of Statistics in Socialist Cuba," *Latin American Research Review* 4, No. 1 (Winter): 53-91.
———. (ed.) (1971). *Revolutionary Change in Cuba*. Pittsburgh: University of Pittsburgh Press.
———. (1974) see page 223
———. (1978). *Cuba in the 1970s. Pragmatism and Institutionalization*. Albuquerque: University of New Mexico Press.
Mesa-Lago, Carmelo (1981). *The Economy of Socialist Cuba: A Two Decade-Appraisal*. Albuquerque, University of New Mexico Press.
———. (1982). "Los planes quinquenales de desarrollo de Cuba (1976-80 y 1981-85): Comparación, evaluación y perspectivas," *Desarrollo Económico*. (Buenos Aires), No. 87 (octubre-diciembre): 375-408.

——. (1990). "Cuba's Economic Counter-Reform (Rectificación): Causes, Policies and Effects," pp.98-139 in *Cuba After Thirty Years: Rectification and the Revolution*, R. Gillespie (ed.). London: Frank Cass.
——. (ed.) (1993). *Cuba After the Cold War*. Pittsburgh, University of Pittsburgh Press.
——. (1995). "Prospective Dollar Remittances and the Cuban Economy," in A. Ritter and J. Kirk (eds.). *Cuba in the International System. Normalization and Integration*. New York: St Martin's Press.
——. (1998). "Assessing Economic and Social Performance in the Cuban Transition of the 1990s," *World Development*, Vol. 26, No. pp. 857-76.
——. (2000). *Market, Socialist and Mixed Economies: Comparative Policy and Performance–Chile, Cuba and Costa Rica*. Baltimore MD: John Hopkins University Press.
——. (2002). "La Reforma Estructural de las Pensiones de Seguridad Social en América Latina: Modelos, Características, Resultados y Lecciones," *Economía y Sociedad*. (San José), No. 19 (May-August): 75-91.
——. (2005). "Cuba's Ranking in the Human Development Index of 2005," *Focal Point*, October. http://www.cubanuestra.nu/web/article.asp?artID=2923
Mesa-Lago, Carmelo and Jorge Pérez-López (1985). "Imbroglios on the Cuban Economy: A Reply to Brundenius and Zimbalist," *Comparative Economic Studies* 27, No. 1 (Spring): 21–45.
Mesa-Lago, Carmelo and Jorge Pérez-Lopez (2005). *Cuba's Aborted Reform*. University Press of Florida.
Mills. C. Wright (1960). *Listen Yankee: The Revolution in Cuba*. New York, Ballantine Books.
Ministerio de Finanzas y Precios (various years) Anuario Estadístico, Havana.
Ministerio de Economia y Planifiacación (1997, 1998). *Cuba: Economic Report*. Havana.
Ministerio de Salud Pública (2009). *Anuario Estadistico de Salud 2009*. Havana: Gobierno Cubano.
Ministerio de Trabajo y Seguridad Social (1996). Resolución conjunta No. 1 MTSS-MFP sobre el ejercicio del trabajo por cuenta propia, April, Havana.
MINSAP (1998). *Salud en el tiempo*. La Habana, MINSAP.
Miranda Francisco, Olivia (1999). *La articulación del marxismo y el leninismo y las tradiciones nacionales en Cuba*. Unpublished manuscript.
Monreal, Pedro (1999). "Migraciones y Remesas Familiares: Notas e Hipótesis Sobre el Caso de Cuba, Havana: Centro de Investigaciones de Economía International (CIEI), mimeo.
——. (2001). "Cuba: The Challenges of Being Global and Socialist...at the Same Time," *Socialism and Democracy*, Vol. 15, No.1, Spring-Summer: 5-22.
——. (2002). "La globalización y los dilemas de las trayectorias económicas de Cuba," *Temas*, N° 30.
——.. (ed.) (2002). *Development Prospects in Cuba: An Agenda in the Making*. London: Institute for Latin American Studies.
Monreal, Pedro and Julio Carranza (2000). "Los retos del desarrollo en Cuba: realidades, mitos y conceptos," in Manuel Monereo et al. (coord.), Cuba construyendo futuro. Madrid: El Viejo Topo.
Morley, Morris H. (1987). *Imperial State and Revolution: The United States and Cuba, 1952–1986*. Cambridge: Cambridge University Press.
Moses, C. (2000). *Real Life in Castro's Cuba*. Wilmington, DE: Scholarly Resources.
Nerey, Boris (2004). "Empleo, seguridad social y el Estado revolucionario cubano", Taller Pobreza y Política Social en Cuba: los Retos del Cambio Económico y Social, Centro de Estudios Latinoamericanos David Rockefeller/Universidad de Harvard/ Centro de Investigaciones Psicológicas y Sociológicas. La Habana, mimeo.
Nerey, Boris y Brismart, Nivia (1999). "Estructura social y estructura salarial en Cuba. Encuentros y desencuentros," Trabajo de Curso, Maestría en Sociología. Universidad de La Habana, La Habana.

Notimex (2010). "Cuba intenta reducir importación de alimentos," *El Porvenir*. Viernes, 16 de Julio de 2010. Accessed at: http://www.elporvenir.com.mx/notas.asp?nota_id =413849
Nuñez Sarmiento, Marta (2007). "A Gender Approach to an Impossible Transition," Presentation to IDS/metropolis Project, Saint Mary's University, Halifax, September 14.
O'Connor, James (1970). *The Origins of Cuban Socialism*. Ithaca.
ONE—Oficina Nacional de Estadisticas (1996). *Anuario demográfico de Cuba 1995*. La Habana.
———. (1997). *Estadísticas seleccionadas de Cuba 1996*. La Habana.
———. (1998a). *Anuario Estadístico de Cuba*. La Habana.
———. (1998b). *Anuario estadístico de Cuba 1996*. La Habana.
———. (1999). *Perfil estadístico de la mujer cubana en el umbral del siglo XXI*. La Habana.
———. (2001). *Cuba en cifras 2000*. La Habana.
———. (2002). *Anuario Estadístico de Cuba*. La Habana.
———. (2005). *Estudio Y Datos Sobre La Población Cubana*, Publicación No. 35. República de Cuba, Centro de Estudios de Población y Desarrollo.
———. (2006). *Anuario Estadístico de Cuba*. La Habana.
———. (2001). "Encuesta sobre el uso del tiempo". Disponible en: <www.one.cu/ publicaciones/ enfoquegenero/ tiempo/eut.pdf>.
Oppenheimer, Andrés (1992). *Castro's Final Hour*. New York: Simon and Schuster.
Otero, Gerardo and Janice O'Bryan (2002) "Cuba in Transition? The Civil Sphere's Challenge to the Castro Regime," *Latin American Politics and Society*, Vol. 44, No. 4, Winter. Pp. 29-57.
Partido Comunista de Cuba (1976a). *Constitución de la República de Cuba. Tesis y resolución* La Habana: Departamento de Orientación Revolucionaria.
———. (1976b). *Tesis y resoluciones. Primer Congreso*. La Habana: Editora Política.
———. (1980). *Un quinquenio de desarrollo socioeconómico 1976-1980*. La Habana: Editora Política.
———. (1981). *Lineamientos económicos y sociales para el quinquenio 1981-1985*. La Habana: Editora Política.
———. (1986). *Lineamientos económicos y sociales para el quinquenio 1986-1990*. La Habana: Editora Política.
———. (1997). Resolución Económica al V congreso del Partido Comunista de Cuba. 8 de Octubre de 1997. http://www.pcc.cu/congresos_asamblea/v_congreso/ resolucion.pdf.
Pastor Jr., M. and A. Zimbalist (1996). "Cuba and Cuban Studies: Crossing Boundaries During a 'Special Period', *Latin American Research*, Vol. 31. No. 3.
———. (1997). "Has Cuba Turned the Corner? Macroeconomic Stabilization and Reform in Contemporary Cuba," *Cuban Studies*, Vol. 27. Pittsburgh and London: Pittsburgh University Press.
Pearson, R. (1998). "The Political Economy of Social Reproduction: The Case of Cuba in the 1990s," *New Political Economy* 3, No. 2: 241-59.
Peña Castellanos, Lázaro (2006). "Globalización y desarrollo local: Una vision desde la actualidad de la academia cubana," 17-44 pp. in Ana Guzón (2006). *Desarrollo local en Cuba*. La Habana: Editorial Academia.
Pérez, Victoria (2000). "Ajuste económico e impactos sociales. Los retos de la educación y la salud pública en Cuba" en Cuba Investigación Económica (La Habana) Año 6, N° 1.
Pérez Jr., Luis A. (1988 [2006]). *Cuba: Between Reform and Revolution*. New York: Oxford University Press.
———. (1999). *On Becoming Cuban: Identity, Nationality and Culture*. New York: Harper Collins.
Pérez Cruz, Felipe de Jesus (2001). *La alfabetización en Cuba: Lectura histórica para pensar el presente*. La Habana: Editorial de Ciencias Sociales. Pérez Rojas, N. and

O. Echevarria (1998). "Participación y producción agraria en Cuba: Las UBPC," *TEMAS*, No. 11, July-September, pp. 69-75, Havana.
Pérez-Lopez, J.F. (1983). "Review: Two Decades of Cuban Socialism: The Economic Context." *Latin American Research Review* 18, No. 3: 227-42.
———. (1995). *Cuba's Second Economy: From Behind the Scenes to Center Stage*. New Brunswick: Transaction Publishers.
———. (2002). "The Cuban Economy in an Unending Special Period," Proceedings of the Twelfth Annual Meeting of the Association for the Study of the Cuban Economy: *Cuba in Transition*.
Pérez-Lopez, J., and S. Díaz-Briquets (2005). "Remittances to Cuba: A Survey of Methods and Estimates,." Proceedings of the Fifteenth Annual Meeting of the Association for the Study of the Cuban Economy: *Cuba in Transition*.
Pérez-Sarduy, Pedro and Jean Stubbs (eds.) (2000). *Afro-Cuban Voices: On Race and Identity in Contemporary Cuba*. Miami: University Press of Florida.
Pérez-Stable, Marifeli. (1993). *The Cuban Revolution: Origins, Course, and Legacy*. New York: Oxford University Press.
———. (1999). "Caught in a Contradiction. Cuban Socialism between Mobilization and Normalization," *Comparative Politics*: 63-82.
Perez Villanueva, Omar Everleny (1991-92). "La integración. Condición para la supervivencia," *Revista Cuba Económica*, Año 2 No. 3, Octubre-Marzo, pp.441-461.
———. (1998a). "La inversión extranjera en Cuba. Peculiaridades," Centro de Estudios de la Economía Cubana, Havana (mimeo).
———. (1998b). "Cuba's Economic Reforms: An Overview," in Jorge F. Pérez López and Matías Travieso-Diaz (eds.), *Perspectives on Cuban Economic Reforms*. Arizona State University Center for Latin American Studies, Tempe.
———. (2006). "La inversión extranjera directa en el desarrollo económico. La experiencia cubana," in Omar Pérez Villanueva (ed.) *Reflexiones sobre la economía cubana, Ciencias Sociales*, La Habana.
———. (2007). *Reflexiones sobre economía cubana*. La Habana: Ciencias Sociales.
Peters, P. (1998). "Cuba's Small Business Experiment: Two Steps Forward, One Step Back," *Cuba Briefing Paper Series*, March, Georgetown University.
Petras, James (1981). *Class, State and Power in the Third World*. London: Zed.
Petras, J. and R. Eastman-Abaya (2007). Cuba: Continuing Revolution and Contemporary Contradictions," *Dissident Voice* [Rebelión], August 13. Available at http://www.rrojasdatabank.info/petrasjuly07.pdf
Petras, James and Morris H. Morley (1992). "Cuban Socialism: Rectification and the New Model of Accumulation," in Sandor Halebsky and John M Kirk, et al., eds., *Cuba in Transition: Crisis and Transformation*. Boulder, CO: Westview Press.
———. (1992). *Latin America in the Time of Cholera: Electoral Politics, Market Economics and Permanent Crisis*. London: Routledge.
Petras, James and Henry Veltmeyer (2001). *Globalization Unmasked: Imperialism in the 21st Century*. London: Zed.
Pino-Santos, Oscar (1975). *El asalto a Cuba por la oligarquía financiera yanqui*. La Habana, Editorial Orbe.
Pollitt, Brian (1977). "Some Problems of Enumerating the Peasantry in Cuba," *Journal of Peasant Studies* 5, No. 2, January.
Portuondo, José A. (1980). *Itinerario estético de la Revolución*. Havana: Editorial Letres Cubanas.
PNUD (1997). *Desarrollo Humano en Cuba 1996*. La Habana.
———. (2000). *Investigación sobre desarrollo humano y equidad en Cuba 1999*. La Habana.
———. (2000). "Caracterización Y Prioridades Del Municipio De La Habana Vieja: Lineas Directrices, Para La Tercera Faze Del Programa De Desarrollo Humano Local." L.H.V Asamblea Municipal Poder Popular, PDHL de Cuba, Oficina del Historiador. Havana: Programa de Desarrollo Humano Local.

———. (2005). *Objetivos de Desarollo del Milenio: Segunda Informe de Cuba.*
———. (2010). *Informe regional sobre desarrollo humano para America Latina y el Caribe 2010.* New York: UN.
Proveyer, Clotilde (2002). "Las políticas sociales en la esfera educacional: la experiencia cubana" en Burgos, Nilsa (ed.) Política social y trabajo social, San Juan de Puerto Rico: Universidad de Puerto Rico.
Puerto Sanz, Luis Miguel (2008). *Economia para el desarrollo.* Madrid: Catarata
Quintana Mendoza, Didio (1992). "Vías de acceso de la población al consumo total de bienes y servicios," *Informe de Investigación.* La Habana: Instituto Nacional de Investigaciones Económicas,
———. (1995). "La seguridad social y la distribución de los ingresos en Cuba. Un enfoque para la situación actual. Cuba Investigación Económica," Año 1, No. 4, Epoca II, Diciembre, INIE.
———. (1995a). "Mercado Agropecuario: Apertura o Limitación?" Investicación Económica, INIE, No. 4, December, pp. 21±54, Havana.
———. (1995b). "La seguridad social y la distribución de los ingresos en Cuba. Un enfoque para la situación actual," *Investigación Económica*, INIE, No. 4, (December): pp. 55-69 [Havana].
———. (1996). "Ingresos de la población por territorios en los 90," *Cuba Investigación Económica*, Año 2, No. 2, Epoca II, Abril-Junio/96, INIE.
———. (1997). "El sector informal urbano en Cuba: Algunos elementos para su caracterización," *Investigación Económica*, INIE No. 3, April-June, No. 3.
Quirk, Robert (1993). *Fidel Castro: The Full Story of His Rise to Power, His Regime, His Allies, and His Adversaries.* New York: W.W.Norton.
Ramos, Maribel (2001). "Pobreza: definiciones internacionales y alternativas metodológicas," *Cuba Investigación Económica* [La Habana] Año 7, Nº 3.
Randall, Margaret (1981). *Women in Cuba: Twenty Years Later.* New York: Smyrna.
Ranis, G. and S. Kosack. (2004). *Growth and Human Development in Cuba's Transition.* Miami: Institute for Cuban and Cuban-American Studies, University of Miami.
Ridenour, Ron. (2007). *Cuba: Beyond the Crossroads.* London: Socialist Resistance.
Ritter, A.R.M. (1974). *The Economic Development of Revolutionary Cuba: Strategy and Performance.* New York: Praeger.
———. (1985). "The Bodies of People's Power and the Community Party: The Nature of Cuban Democracy," in S. Halebsky and J. Kirk, eds., *Twenty-five Years of Revolution.* New York: Praeger.
———. (1995). "The Dual Currency Bifurcation of Cuba's Economy in the 1990s: Causes, Consequences and Cures," *Cepal Review*, No. 57, December.
———. (1998). "Entrepreneurship, Microenterprise, and Public Policy in Cuba: Promotion, Containment, or Asphyxiation?" *Journal of Interamerican Studies and World Affairs* 40, No. 2: 63-94.
———. (1998). "Cuba's Economic Reform Process, 1998: Paralysis and Stagnation?, Paper presented at the symposium 'Reintegration into World Society: Cuba in International Perspective," 27-28 September, New York.
———. (2006). "Cuba's Economic Reorientation." Pp. 3-25 in *Cuba: In Transition? Pathways to Renewal, Long-Term Development, and Global Reintegration*, ed. M.A. Font, 3-25. New York: Bildner Center for Western Hemisphere Studies, City University of New York.
———. (2010). "Has Cuba's Catastrophic Decline in Real Wage Levels Been Reversed?, Published online at: http://thecubaneconomy.com. Posted June 22.
Rodríguez, Carlos Rafael (2006). "Sobre la contribución del Che al desarrollo de la economia cubanaa," pp. 319-346 in Guevara (2006). *El Gran Debate sobre la economia en Cuba.*
Rodriguéz, José Luis (1963). "Cuatro años de reforma agraria," *Cuba Socialista*, No. 5.
———. (1990). *Estrategia del desarrollo económico en Cuba*, La Habana: Editorial de Ciencias Sociales.

——. (2002). "Globalización y equidad. Breve análisis crítico," en *Cuba Socialista*, N° 25 [La Habana].
Rodríguez, José Luis and George Carriazo (1983). *La erradicación de la pobreza en Cuba*. La Habana: Ciencias Sociales.
Rodríguez, José Luis et al. (1985) *Cuba: revolución y economía 1959-1960*. La Habana: Ciencias Sociales.
Rodríguez, Lázaro (2006). "Modelos de salud en Cuba. Habla un protagonista," *Temas*, N° 47.
Rodríguez, Pablo et al. (2004). "¿Pobreza, marginalidad o exclusión?: un estudio sobre el barrio Alturas del Mirador," *Informe preliminar de investigación*, Centro de Antropología, La Habana.
Roemer, M. (1976). *Cuban Health Services and Resources*. Washington: Pan American Health Organization and the World Health Organization.
Roman, Peter (1995). "Worker's Parliament in Cuba," *Latin American Perspectives* 22, 87 (Fall).
——. (2003). *People's Power: Cuba's Experience with Representative Government*. Rowman and Littlefield Publishers.
Romero Gómez, Antonio F. (1998). "Cuba: transformaciones económicas y reinserci internacional en la década del noventa," *Análisis de Coyuntura*, Año 2, N° 2 [La Habana].
——. (2001). "Crisis, Economic Restructuring and International Reinsertion," pp. 61-70 in Brundenius, Claes and John Weeks (eds.).
Rosendahl, Mona. (1992). "The March of History. Revolution as Development in Cuba," in G. Dahl and A. Rabo (eds), *Kam-ap or Take-off. Local Nations of Development*. Stockholm: Stockholm Studies in Social Anthropology.
——. (1997a). *Inside the Revolution. Everyday Life in Socialist Cuba*. Ithaca: Cornell University Press.
——. (1997b). "The Ever-changing Revolution," in M. Rosendahl (ed.) *The Current Situation in Cuba: Challenges and Alternatives*. Stockholm: Institute of Latin American Studies.
——. (2001). "Household Economy and Morality during the Special Period," pp. 86-101 in Brundenius, Claes and John Weeks (eds.).
Rushton, Mark and Henry Veltmeyer (2008). "Cuba as a Socialist Model of Human Development: Policy Dynamic and Changing Condiditions," Paper presented at a panel on Kerla and Cuba, *CASID–Canadian Association for the Study of International Development*, Vancouver, June 6.
¡Salud! (2006). Documentary. Produced by Connie Field and Gail Reed. [Video]
Saney, Isaac (2003). *Cuba: A Revolution in Motion*. Halifax: Fernwood Publishing; London: Zed Books.
——. (2006). "African Stalingrad: The Cuban Revolution, internationalism, and the end of apartheid." *Latin American Perspectives* 35 (5): 81–117.
——. (2009a). "Looking Towards the Future Through Global Cooperation: Cuba's Internationalism," powerpoint presentation, Symposium of Latin American Transformations, Saint Mary's University, Halifax.
——. (2009b). "Homeland of Humanity: Internationalism within the Cuban Revolution," *Latin American perspectives*, Issue 164, Vol. 36 No. 1, January, pp. 111-123
Santos, Pino (1960). *El imperialismo norteamericano en Cuba*. Havana: Editorial Lex.
Sautié Mederos, Félix (2007). *Socialismo y reconciliación en Cuba: Una mirada desde adentro*.
Save the Children (2010). State of the World's Mothers 2010: Women on the Front Lines of Heath Care, May. Accessed at: http://www.savethechildren.org/atf/cf/ {9def2ebe-10ae-432c-9bd0-df91d2eba74a}/SOWM-2010-Women-on-the-Front-Lines-of-Health-Care.pdf

Schuyler, George (2000). "Venezuela and Cuba in the Age of Globalization: Healthcare and Development," Working Paper No. 00.10.4. Halifax: International Development Studies, Saint Mary's University.
Serviat, Pedro (1986). El problema negro en Cuba y su solución definitiva. Editora Politica.
Silverman, Bertram (1973a). "Economic Organization and Social Conscience: Some Dilemmas of Cuban Socialism," in *Cuba: The Logic of the Revolution*, ed. David Barkin and Nita Manitzas. Andover, Mass: Warner Modular Publications.
——. (ed.) (1973b). *Man and Socialism in Cuba: The Great Debate*. New York: Atheneum.
Smith, L M., and A. Padula (1996). *Sex and Revolution: Women in Socialist Cuba*. New York: Oxford University Press.
Spalding, Hobart (2003). "People's Power in Cuba," *Monthly Review* (February).
Stubbs, Jean (1989). *Cuba: The Test of Time*. London: Latin American Bureau.
Suarez Salazar, Luis (1991). *Cuba: Isolation or Reinsertion in a Changed World*. Havana: Editorial José Martí.
Suárez Hernández, Georgina (1992). "Political Leadership in Cuba," in Centro de Estudios Sobre America, ed., *The Cuban Revolution into the 1990s*. Boulder CO: Westview Press,
Susman, Paul (1998). "Cuban Socialism in Crisis: A Neoliberal Solution?" In Thomas Klak (ed.) *Globalization and Neoliberalism: The Caribbean Context*. London: Routledge.
Sweezy, Paul M. (1990). "Cuba: A Left U.S. View," *Monthly Review* 42, 4 (September).
Sweig, Julia and Kai Bird (eds.) (1997). *Denial of Food and Medicine: The Impact of the U.S. Embargo on Health and Nutrition in Cuba*. Washington: American Association for World Health.
Taylor, Henry Louis Jr. (2009). *Inside El Barrio: A Bottom-Up View of Neighbourhood Life in Castro's Cuba*. Sterling, VA: Kumarian Press.
Tharamangalam, Joseph (2008). "Human Development as Transformative Practice: Lessons from Kerala and Cuba," *Paper to be presented at the annual HDCA Conference*, New Delhi, September 11-14.
Thomas, Hugh (1971). *Cuba: Or, The Pursuit of Freedom*. London: Eyre & Spottiswoode.
Togores, Viviana (1999). "Cuba: efectos sociales de la crisis y el ajuste económico de los 90," La Habana, Centro de Estudios de la Economía Cubana, Informe de Investigación.
——. (2004). "Ingresos monetarios de la población, cambios en la distribución y efectos sobre el nivel de vida" en 15 Años del Centro de Estudios de la Economía Cubana. La Habana: Feliz Varela.
Togores, Viviana and Anicia García (2004). "Consumption, Markets and Market Duality in Cuba," pp.245-96 in Jorgé Domínguez, et al., *The Cuban Economy at the Start of the 21st Century*. Cambridge, Mass: Harvard University Press.
Toro-Morn, M.I., A.R. Roschelle, and E. Facio (2002). "Gender, Work, and Family in Cuba: The Challenges of the Special Period." *Journal of Developing Societies* 18, No. 2-3: 32-58.
Torres, Julia (1993). "Pobreza. Un enfoque para Cuba", La Habana, Instituto Nacional de Investigaciones Económicas, Informe de Investigación.
Tovar, Carlos Mendez (1997). *Democracy in Cuba?* Havana: Editorial José Martí.
Tulchin, Joseph S. and Romero, Bernice (eds) (1995). *The Consolidation of Democracy in Latin America*. Boulder CO: Lynne Rienner.
Turnbull, Charles (2000). "Economic Reforms and Social Contradictions in Cuba." *Cuba in Transition* 10 (August).
UNDP—United Nations Development Programme (1996). *Investigación sobre el desarollo humano en Cuba 1996*. Havana: UNDP.

Uriarte, Meren (2002). *Cuba, Social Policy at the Crossroads: Maintaining Priorities, Transforming Practice*. Boston: Oxfam America.
———. (2008). "Rediscovering *Lo Local*: The Potential and the Limits of Local Development," pp.90-115 in Alexander Gray and Antoní Kapcia (2008). *The Changing Dynamic of Cuban Civil* Society. University Press of Florida.
Valdés Paz, Juan (1994). "La transición socialista: continuidad y cambio" en Valdés Paz, Juan et al. *La transición socialista en Cuba. Estudio sociopolítico*. La Habana: Ciencias Sociales.
———. (2000). "El sistema político cubano de los años noventa: continuidad y cambio" en Monereo, Manuel et al. (coord.), *Cuba construyendo future*. Madrid: El Viejo Topo.
———. (2003). "Cuba en el Período Especial: de la igualdad a la equidad", Seminario Cambios en la sociedad cubana desde los 90 hasta el momento actual, FLACSO, Santo Domingo.
Valdés, Juan Gabriel (1995). "Changing Paradigms in Latin America: From Dependency to Nneoliberalism in the Iinternational Ccontext," pp. 127-38 in Joseph S. Tulchin with Bernice Romero (eds) *The Consolidation of Democracy in Latin America*. Boulder CO: Lynne Rienner.
Vazquez, A. (2007). Desarrollo local, una estrategia para tiempos de crisis. http://www.dete-alc.org/-%20archivos/biblio/104.pdf.
Vellinga, Menno (2001). "Continuity and Change in the Cuban Revolution," *European Review of Latin American and Caribbean Studies* 71, October: 139-43.
Veltmeyer, Henry (2006). *Human Development at Issue: Framing a Comparative Analysis of Kerala and Cuba*. Paper presented at the first workshop of the Kerala-Cuba Project in Trivandrum, December 13-15.
———. (2007). "The UNDP in Cuba: Towards a Model of Sustainable Human Development," Paper Presented at the 2nd workshop of the Kerala-Cuba Project, Saskatoon.
Vidal Alejandro, Pavel (2007). "La dualidad monetaria en Cuba," *Boletín trimestral del CEEC*, La Habana.
Whiteford, L. and L. Branch. (2008). *Primary Health Care in Cuba*. New York: Rowman & Littlefield Publishers Inc.
Wilkerson, Loree (1965). *Fidel Castro's Political Programs from Reformism to Marxism-Leninism*. Gainesville, Forida.
WHO–World Health Organization (2007). *Core Health Indicators for the Americas*. The WHOSIS DATABASE. Geneva: WHO.
Xalma, Cristina (2002). "La dolarización cubana como instrumento de intervención económica. Eficacia y sostenibilidad de una alternativa," tesis doctoral, Universidad de Barcelona, septiembre.
Yepe, Manuel E. (2008). "Cuba Reforms its Food Production Process,"
Zabala, María del Carmen (1996). "Familia y pobreza en Cuba", Tesis de Maestría, FLACSO, La Habana.
———. (1999). "Does a Certain Dimension of Poverty Exist in Cuba?" in José Bell Lara et al. Cuba in the 1990s. Habana: Instituto Cubano Del Libro.
———. (1999). "Alternativas de estrategias comunitarias para la atención a la pobreza," en *Caminos*, (La Habana) N° 15-16.
———. (2002). "Situación de la pobreza en el Caribe: actualidad y perspectivas. Cuba en el contexto caribeño,", Seminario Internacional Estrategias de Reducción de la Pobreza en el Caribe: los Actores Externos y su Impacto, CLACSO-CROP, La Habana, mimeo.
———. (2003). "Los estudios cualitativos de la pobreza en Cuba," ponencia presentada al Taller XX Aniversario del Centro de Investigaciones Psicológicas y Sociológicas, La Habana.

———. (2007). "Is There Poverty in Cuba? Analysis from the Family Perspective," Paper presented at Workshop on the Human Development Experience of Kerala and Cuba, Havana, December 4.

Zeitlin, Maurice (1970). *Revolutionary Politics and the Cuban Working Class.* New York: Harper Torchbooks.

Zimbalist, Andrew (1985). "Revolutionary Cuba: Economic Growth with Equity," *Monthly Review*, November.

Zimbalist, A. and C. Brundenius (1989). *The Cuban Economy. Measurement and Analysis of Socialist Performance.* Baltimore and London: The Johns Hopkins University Press.

———. (1989). "Crecimiento con equidad en una perspectiva comparada," *Cuadernos de Nuestra América*. Nº 1 [La Habana].

Zimbalist, A. and Susan Eckstein (1987) "Patterns of Cuban Development: The First Twenty-Five Years," in Andrew Zimbalist (ed.) *Cuba's Socialist Economy: Toward the 1990s.* Boulder, CO: Lynne Reinner.

INDEX

Africa 28, 61, 176, 202, 244–5, 247–51, 294, 295
agrarian reform 62, 76, 80–1, 83, 142, 185–7, 191, 201, 267, 269, 308
agriculture 49, 77, 79–81, 82, 86, 93, 98, 100, 106, 111, 177–8, 181, 185–6, 195, 259, 286, 288, 291, 292, 309
ALBA, *see* Alianza Bolivariana para los Pueblos de Nuestra América
Alianza Bolivariana para los Pueblos de Nuestra América 246, 295
Angola 247–251

Babeuf, Gracchus 22
Bay of Pigs 80, 215
Bolivia 36, 38, 48, 53–4, 58, 92, 221, 242, 275, 294
Bretton Woods 15, 27, 36, 43, 45, 322

campesinos 145, 148–9, 201
Castro, Fidel 42, 57, 58, 75, 92–3, 95, 97, 99–100, 102, 107, 108, 109, 111–2, 127, 129–130, 140, 142–3, 145, 151, 173, 184–5, 195, 200, 202–3, 205, 214–6, 218, 224, 226, 227, 229, 232, 237, 240, 244, 246, 248–9, 251, 256, 258, 259–60, 269, 273, 279, 282, 286–7, 290, 293, 300–1, 303, 307, 312–8
Castro, Raúl 50, 58, 156, 232, 249, 282, 286, 288, 290–2, 299, 301–3, 305, 307–311
CDR, *see* Comité para la Defensa de la Revolución
Central de Trabajadores de Cuba 96, 97, 104, 110–11, 156, 197, 229, 280–1
Chávez, Hugo 9, 44, 222, 246, 283
civil society 3, 8, 14, 37–42, 46–49, 69, 220, 222, 227–232
class 14, 24, 37, 38, 45, 59, 73, 88, 93, 94, 96, 99, 131, 133, 136, 140, 141, 158, 172, 174, 175, 181, 194, 203, 204, 206, 217, 237
  capitalist 21, 25, 27, 34–5, 65, 192, 267, 324
  -less 21, 102, 121, 126, 127–8, 134–5, 202
compromise 8, 64
consciousness 126, 129, 138
division 59, 73, 99, 131, 161, 175–6, 192, 207, 218, 237–241, 304–5, 328
formation 93, 102, 161, 294
income 263–266, 293
landowning 17
middle 77–9, 149, 155, 174, 180, 183, 289
occupational 160, 193, 262
relations 30, 241, 327
ruling 18–19, 22, 65, 75, 77, 155, 176, 223, 233, 301, 324–5, 328
struggle 9, 15, 24, 35, 62, 128, 218, 220
working 9, 21, 46, 48, 73, 78, 84, 122, 126, 129, 132, 137, 183, 185–6, 192, 219, 282, 315–16
Comité para la Defensa de la Revolución 94, 163, 197, 225–231, 279, 281
crisis 43, 48, 57, 62, 93, 102, 108, 112–13, 121, 149, 155–6, 161, 165, 167, 178, 191, 222, 250–251, 256–258, 296, 297, 299, 303, 320, 322, 331
debt 36–8, 172, 188
demographic 290
fiscal 5, 36–8
food 307–9
housing 185
production 5, 15, 16, 36–8, 47, 255, 258–259, 260, 264, 266, 269–273, 274
propensity towards 25
social 178
socialist production 44, 114, 307, 323
systemic 293
CTC, *see* Central de Trabajadores de Cuba
culture 13, 16, 32–3, 44, 88, 91, 139, 141, 147, 148–9, 157–8, 175, 190, 195, 198, 200–202, 209, 217, 225, 239–242, 252, 272, 273–5, 280, 290, 313–317, 323, 330

democracy 8, 9, 17–22, 34, 37–40, 54, 62, 72, 96, 107, 115, 123, 137, 140,

185, 218–221, 222–25, 228–230, 230–232, 234–5, 238–242, 243, 245, 257, 260, 270–273, 280, 329
depression 35, 178, 283, 285, 316
  Great 5, 25–7

economic model 6, 58, 64, 69, 82, 89, 99, 103, 169, 255, 323, 326
Engels, Frederic 20, 22, 25, 121, 126, 128, 130–7
Enlightenment 4, 15–17, 216, 229

farmers 17, 60, 78, 81, 84, 86, 93, 96, 98, 101–2, 104, 108, 180, 186–7, 193, 195, 206, 229, 258, 270, 282, 285, 288, 303, 308–9, 327–8
food 26, 29, 81, 91, 93, 98, 104, 114, 151, 153, 157–8, 161, 166, 182, 190, 205, 256, 259, 264, 268, 270, 281, 282, 283, 286, 288, 290–291, 298, 302, 307–9, 310–13, 328
  security 107, 284, 287
Fourier, Charles 21–2
freedom
  definition of 3, 13, 15, 17–21, 24, 43, 159, 173, 242
  development as 9, 29–32, 66, 121–122, 159, 228, 233, 322, 327, 328–30
  economic 6, 40, 45, 47, 64–65, 102, 112, 123, 212–3, 226, 239, 323–4
  and equality 4–5, 15, 16, 17, 23, 65, 72, 119–120, 124–126, 139, 205, 216, 218, 251–2, 321–4, 327, 330–331
  and equity 8
  forces of 36, 38
  individual 129, 131, 139–40, 173, 213, 226
  of labour 122
  political 35, 152, 213, 221–5, 270–3, 295, 313–4
  of thought 151, 234–235
  and socialism 71–72, 87, 91, 110, 115, 120, 125–7, 141, 192, 205, 209–235
  struggle for 73, 128–30, 136–8, 216

gender 160
  and development 151
  empowerment 152
  exclusion 153
  inequality 33, 152, 153, 172, 174, 196–200, 201, 202

parity 152
policy 198, 203
relations 198
and solidarity 238, 241
Gini 57, 154, 159, 190, 266, 304
globalization 1, 6–8, 28–9, 39, 42, 45, 46, 47, 57–8, 70, 148, 172, 233, 241, 255–276, 281–2, 292, 296, 297, 315, 321, 323, 331–2
Guevara, Ernesto 'Che', 22, 61, 82, 84, 87–99, 110, 112, 119–120, 122, 125–127, 129, 134–139, 141–6, 148, 200, 209, 218, 238, 248, 278, 314, 319

ul Haq, Mahbub 21, 29, 31, 295
Havana Declaration 214
HDI, *see* Human Development Index
Hegel, G.W.F., 17, 24
Human Development Index 5, 71, 151, 159, 165, 199, 211, 213, 217, 275, 295–6, 331
humanism 2, 44, 75, 88, 120–1, 123–27, 129, 136, 171–207, 209–235, 237–252, 323, 327

ILO, *see* International Labour Office
IMF, *see* International Monetary Fund
India 13, 297
industry 20, 21, 74, 77, 92, 93, 151, 163, 177–8, 181, 185, 201, 229, 256, 257, 259, 287, 320,
inequality 7, 41, 57, 67, 69, 71, 90, 92, 103, 109, 141, 149, 154–6, 171–90, 203, 242–3, 260, 262–6, 270, 293, 304, 326
  gender 33, 151, 152, 153, 172, 174, 196–200, 201, 202
International Monetary Fund 28, 150, 237, 261, 286
International Labour Office 69
internationalism 119, 130, 240, 244, 247–251, 294, 295, 318

July 26th Movement 62

Kerala, ix 13, 14, 28, 75, 141, 143, 169, 326

labour 19, 23, 48, 68, 76, 93, 101, 102, 112, 121, 127, 129, 131–3, 135–6, 151, 161, 181, 184, 190, 194–6, 205, 242, 259
  absenteeism 97

agricultural 97–8, 149, 268, 288, 308–9
alienated 23, 125
-capital relation 25–6, 34–6, 78, 91, 96, 123, 160, 192,267
child 20
conditions 20–1, 77, 137
discipline 97
division of 58, 110, 240–1
factory 20
freedom 65, 122, 128, 130, 139, 324
market 6, 30, 49, 78, 107, 172, 188–9, 198, 206, 257, 262, 328
movements 6, 38, 85
productivity 90, 105, 109, 146, 289
regulation 38, 73, 91, 197, 266, 302–4, 305
surplus 79, 177–8
union 96, 104, 155, 197
voluntary 89, 96–7, 106–7, 111
wage 25, 46, 51, 72–3, 128
women 198–200
Lenin, Vladimir 59, 63, 83–85, 137, 219
Liberalism 4–5, 15, 18, 21, 43, 56, 75, 139, 174, 218–9, 221, 233, 234, 251, 293, 313, 322, 328
neo-, 2, 5, 7, 8, 37, 40, 42, 47–50, 54, 106, 186, 213, 238, 261, 275
social 16, 51, 174, 209, 321
libreta 94, 114, 161–2, 262, 305

Mandela, Nelson 248–9
market 3, 15, 24, 27, 32, 33–7, 46, 48, 60, 67–9, 71, 73–5, 77, 79, 80, 86, 90, 97, 103–4, 112, 114, 131, 134, 136, 152, 156, 168–169, 177, 178, 183, 193, 239, 256, 282, 287, 295, 308, 326–7, 328
black 93, 98, 101, 108, 234, 259, 268, 270, 290, 293, 304
domestic 84, 94, 105, 259, 294, 311
farmers', 93, 101–2, 107–8, 258, 261, 270, 285, 288
free 2, 4–7, 16, 25, 38, 43, 45, 47, 50, 64, 70, 72, 101–2, 108, 109, 122, 127, 140, 155, 209, 238, 260, 268, 284, 286, 291, 321–3
housing 101, 109, 212
labour 6, 30, 49, 78, 107, 172, 188–9, 198, 206, 243, 257, 262, 328
regulation 35, 40, 47, 83, 100, 106, 177, 191, 195, 257–261, 269, 275, 283, 292, 317

socialist 61, 81, 89, 110, 126–128, 309
Marx, Karl 5, 15, 22–5, 146, 150
crypto-marxists 75–6
and equality 211
and freedom 66, 210, 324–5
and Lenin 63, 219
marxist theory 9, 37, 46, 59–61, 71, 80–4, 89–90, 96, 119–21, 122–3, 124–39, 193–4, 203, 219, 224, 315
and revolutionary change 17, 41
and social consciousness 100
on the state 34
transition to socialism 20
and utopian socialism 98, 194, 321
Morales, Evo 242

nationalization 77, 186, 189, 191, 206, 271, 328
neoliberalism,
New Deal 25–7
New Man 88–91, 110, 125, 138–9, 143, 146, 148, 194, 252, 314, 330
NGOs, *see* non-governmental organisations
non-governmental organisations 7, 38–42, 313

Operation Miracle 246–7
Owen, Robert 21–2

participation 29, 33, 38–42, 47–9, 52–6, 58, 61, 82, 84, 87, 92, 110, 144–5, 149, 152, 163, 173, 181, 185, 196, 199, 203, 216, 219–223, 228–235, 259–260, 269, 273–6, 281, 292, 295, 310, 313, 329–332
Partido Comunista de Cuba 62–3, 97, 228, 235, 259
PCC, *see* Partido Comunista de Cuba
peasants 63, 73, 76, 78, 84–5, 121, 141, 147, 179, 181, 182, 185, 193, 197, 220
pensions 98, 109, 113, 132, 153, 194, 195, 284, 299, 305–7
poverty 1, 6–8, 15, 20, 28–9, 33, 39, 41, 48, 49, 51–2, 54, 56–8, 67–71, 98–9, 135, 152–62, 172, 175–6, 179–184, 187, 190, 194, 204, 215, 217, 233, 238,239, 242, 244, 247, 264–5, 269, 286, 296
privatization 2, 40, 47, 50, 258
proletariat 24, 46

property 13, 18–19, 22–4, 34, 59–65, 72, 76, 86, 107, 127–32, 141, 157, 171, 175, 176, 190, 193, 206, 209, 237, 238, 267–8, 293, 309, 316, 324, 327

ration card, see libreta
rectification 62, 100, 102, 106–114, 255–6, 259, 285, 318
reform,
   agrarian 76, 80–1, 142, 185–7, 191, 201, 267–9, 288
   of capitalism 2–3, 9, 13, 16, 20, 22, 27–8, 31, 45–66, 72, 175, 190, 213, 323
   educational 318
   institutional 30, 32, 71–2, 175, 184, 251, 330
   land 35, 206, 327
   neoliberal 36, 155
   policy 192, 199, 275, 310
   political 218, 228, 321
   and poverty 172, 176
   of Raúl Castro 156, 299–310, 311
   social 15, 22, 43, 67, 75–6, 143, 218, 238, 321–2, 323
   socialist 25–6, 100, 106, 184, 257–62, 267, 270, 273, 279, 315, 317
   in the Soviet Union 99, 103, 195
   state-led 30, 68–9, 295–7, 322
   structural 8, 35–6, 38–40, 68, 187, 194, 275, 277, 292, 297, 323
   urban 185, 201
   wage 104, 189
Revolution,
   -ary consciousness 2, 61, 87, 119–207, 209, 240, 242, 249, 278, 280, 319, 325, 327, 332
   French 19–21, 238, 252, 330
   Industrial 9, 18–21, 34, 219
Roosevelt, Theodore 26–7
Russia 18, 22, 32, 43, 60, 80, 82, 83, 84–5, 89, 121, 135, 137, 206, 252, 282, 284, 295, 322, 328, 330–331

Saint-Simon, Henri 21–2
Sen, Amartya 3, 5, 29, 42, 127, 209, 217, 274
solidarity 1, 15, 16–17, 23, 33, 43–4, 72–3, 89, 115, 119–20, 138, 141, 144, 149, 152, 157–8, 173, 175, 205, 208, 216–17, 219, 226, 237–52, 279–280, 285, 290, 294, 295, 311, 313, 315, 319, 321–3, 327, 330–331

Soviet
   model 13, 60–1, 64, 82–6 88, 99, 323
   Union 1, 13, 26, 41, 57, 60, 78, 80, 81, 83, 85, 86, 99, 103,250, 255, 257, 260–261, 272, 303
"Special Period", 16, 50, 62, 99, 106, 112–13, 148–50, 155–6, 160–1, 165, 183, 199, 202, 204, 251, 255, 257–8, 262, 269, 274, 277–9, 282, 287, 289, 291–2, 295, 297–8, 303, 307, 315–17, 320
Stalin, Joseph 60, 79, 81, 83–4, 85, 221

UNDP (United Nations Development Programme), 2–7, 9, 13–15, 29–33, 38–41, 46–9, 52–4, 56, 65, 70–1, 105, 114, 123, 127, 151, 152, 154, 159–160, 164–5, 167, 172–5, 190, 199, 205, 210–14, 217, 222–3, 242, 247, 251, 274–6, 295–7, 323–4, 327, 330–331
United Nations (UN), 2, 27, 35, 151, 244
Utopia 9, 18–23, 98, 100, 126, 194, 219, 321

Venezuela 9, 44, 53, 119, 125, 213, 217, 221–2, 244, 246, 283, 294–5, 312

wage
   -labour 25, 46, 72, 73
   living-, 25, 122–3, 192
   -reform 104, 189,
women,
   empowerment 29, 33, 64, 220, 229, 323
   health 157, 163, 165, 196–7
   in labour force 20, 54, 144, 181, 196, 198–200
   and poverty 19, 305
   rights 197, 199–200, 203
workers 23–4, 57, 60, 63, 65, 70, 74, 78–9, 89, 91–3, 96–8, 104–5, 109–11, 121–3, 128–32, 138, 141, 146, 149, 155–6, 160, 179, 181, 185–6, 190, 194–6, 200–1, 204, 213, 220–3, 231, 244–5, 258–262, 267–70, 273, 276, 279–281, 284, 285–93, 299, 302, 305–6, 316–17, 319, 324, 331
World Bank 1, 29–33, 38, 40, 41, 47–9, 51–2, 54–55, 69–71, 140, 150, 176, 179, 296

youth 144–6, 148, 153, 197, 203, 220, 227, 316

www.ingramcontent.com/pod-product-compliance
Lightning Source LLC
Chambersburg PA
CBHW071146070526
44584CB00019B/2682